D0872170

Friends
of the
Danville Library

This item is a gift
from the

Friends of the Danville Library

NAKED

WITHDRAWN

NAKED

A CULTURAL HISTORY OF AMERICAN NUDISM

Brian Hoffman

NEW YORK UNIVERSITY PRESS
New York and London

NEW YORK UNIVERSITY PRESS
New York and London
www.nyupress.org

© 2015 by New York University
All rights reserved

References to Internet websites (URLs) were accurate at the time of writing.Neither the author nor New York University Press is responsible for URLs thatmay have expired or changed since the manuscript was prepared.

Library of Congress Cataloging-in-Publication Data
Hoffman, Brian.
Naked : a cultural history of American nudism / Brian Hoffman.
pages cm   Includes bibliographical references and index.
ISBN 978-0-8147-9053-3 (cl : alk. paper)
1. Nudism—United States—History. 2. Nudism—Social aspects—United States. I. Title.
GV450.H64   2015
613'.194--dc23   2014044418

New York University Press books are printed on acid-free paper,and their binding materials are chosen for strength and durability.We strive to use environmentally responsible suppliers and materialsto the greatest extent possible in publishing our books.

Manufactured in the United States of America

10 9 8 7 6 5 4 3 2 1

Also available as an ebook

For Uncle Danny

CONTENTS

ACKNOWLEDGMENTS

When I told colleagues, friends, and family that I was working on a book titled *Naked: A Cultural History of American Nudism*, I was frequently met with awkward stares, smirks, and sweaty handshakes followed by the question, why? To counter the assumption that I was a committed nudist looking to justify a cause, I developed an articulate explanation for the motivations behind my project. I asserted that everyone has a naked body, and just as no one can escape one's gender, sexuality, race, ethnicity, class status, or age, we all at some point have to undress. The long and rich history of nudism represented a way to analyze a social and cultural experience normally hidden from history. And like other social categories that have received a great deal of historical analysis, American conceptions of nakedness have changed over time, were informed by a constantly shifting social, cultural, and political landscape, and were shaped by the complex subjectivities that define identity. Why wouldn't someone write a history of nudism in the United States?

I was fortunate to be part of a history department at the University of Illinois at Urbana-Champaign that did not hesitate to support unorthodox projects and was equipped with a faculty possessing the necessary insights and specialized knowledge to develop them fully. Leslie J. Reagan proved to be the ideal adviser. She challenged me to pursue the questions and themes critical to writing a social and cultural history of American nudism, all the while stressing the importance of rigorous research and analysis. Tamara Chaplin, Elizabeth Pleck, and David Roediger offered an array of suggestions and advice that strengthened my analysis, pushed the project in new directions, and ultimately, made me a better scholar. I also benefited enormously from the seminars, conversations, and critiques of Mark Leff, Craig Koslofsky, Jim Barrett, Rayvon Fouche, Sharra Vostral, Paula Treichler, and Antionette Burton. It is hard to imagine completing this project without these people and without this history program.

The graduate community at the University of Illinois fostered both intellectual debate and collegial amusement. I enjoyed (and benefited from) sparring with a graduate cohort dominated by labor historians who preferred the analysis of the working experience over an examination of what they considered silly men and women who chose to cavort naked. Will Cooley, Mike Rosenow, Thilo Schimmel, Tom Mackaman, Dave Hageman, Bryan Nicholson, and Jason Kozlowski offered valuable critiques that ultimately grounded my cultural analysis in social history. The IPRH medicine/science reading group—which brought together Mathew Gambino, Kristen Ehrenberger, Michelle Kleehammer, Rosewell Quinn, and Amanda Brian—provided a supportive forum to interrogate the way in which nudism deals with conceptions of health, healing, and alternative medicine. Brian Ingrassia, Kwame Holmes, Danielle Kinsey, Karen Rodriguez, Karen Phoenix, and Jamie Warren also deserve thanks for reading drafts, for making astute comments and suggestions, and for their unwavering support over the years.

My journey through the ups and downs of a very difficult job market brought me to unexpected places and, in the process, helped me grow as a scholar, a teacher, and a professional. A postdoctoral fellowship at the University of California–San Francisco in the Department of Anthropology, History, and Social Medicine gave me the enormous privilege to focus on revising my manuscript, to publish articles and book chapters, to present at numerous conferences, and to teach at the graduate level. The advice, mentorship, and support of Dorothy Porter, Elizabeth Watkins, Brian Dolan, and Ian Whitmarsh have also been incredibly valuable as I navigated the early stages of a career in academia. My experience working with Jethro Hernández Berrones on a fascinating preliminary exam that explored the history of alternative medicine through a transnational perspective also contributed tremendously to my work. As a visiting assistant professor in the Department of American Studies at Wesleyan University, I took advantage of a dynamic interdisciplinary curriculum and a welcoming student body to develop courses such as "The Politics of Obscenity," "Healers, Quacks, and Mystics," and "The Sex of Things." The support of Patricia Hill, Indira Karamcheti, and Ann Wightman gave me hope that maybe one day this would all work out. I am also especially grateful to Maxwell Bevilacqua, the Shapiro Center and Russell House Arts Fellow, for thoroughly copyediting the manuscript and preparing it for publication.

A number of talented colleagues have also been instrumental in bringing this project to fruition. I was extremely fortunate to be found by Leigh Ann Wheeler, who enthusiastically shared her own work and research on nudism and its relationship with the American Civil Liberties Union. We then joined with Peggy Shaffer and Andrea Friedman to put together the first (to my knowledge) panel on American nudism at the 2011 annual meeting of the Organization of American Historians. I am also thankful to have met Whitney Strub, who provided an excellent model of how to successfully accomplish unorthodox and innovative research. Finally, I am grateful to all those who joined me at an assortment of conferences to present work that dialogued so well with the history of nudism.

Naked: A Cultural History of American Nudism would not have been possible without the assistance and support of the nudist community. The professionally preserved and maintained holdings of the American Nudist Research Library, located on the grounds of the Cypress Cove Nudist Resort in Kissimmee, Florida, gave me a rare window into nudism's past struggles and triumphs, its leaders, and its clubs. Helen Fisher deserves special praise for overseeing the collections and for her generous and skilled support of scholarly research. Robert Proctor's assistance in scanning countless images was also critical to illustrating the colorful history of American nudism. The support of Courtney N. Bischoff (aka Curt Bish), who not only granted me permission to use the many images from the *Nudist* and *Sunshine and Health* but also shared with me his insights and observations from his own involvement in nudism, were invaluable as well.

I am also indebted to the many librarians and archivists who never batted an eyelash as they helped me locate materials that were often unconventional and even a bit quirky. The New York State Archives was an early supporter of my project. As the recipient of the Larry J. Hackman Research Residency Award in 2006, I had the opportunity to receive excellent guidance from Jim Folts about conducting historical legal research. The Michigan State Law Library, the Library of Congress, the National Archives and Records Administration, and the Federal Bureau of Investigation Records provided other crucial legal documents, court decisions, and correspondence. The unique, eccentric, and extensive collections held at the Kinsey Institute for Research in Sex, Gender, and Reproduction, Cornell University's Human Sexuality Collection, Yale's Manuscripts and Archives, and the Bancroft Library provided an array of materials documenting important perspectives on nudism in the twentieth century.

I am grateful to my family for exposing me to a wide variety of life experiences and ideas, all of which, directly and indirectly, contributed to the themes developed in this book. I was fortunate to grow up in a clothing-optional household/community in the Mount Washington neighborhood of Los Angeles, California. Weekends were often spent gallivanting around the backyard sans clothing, block parties featured nude forays into Peter and Pam's pool, and the family photo album recorded all these memories for posterity. It was the realization—as I grew older—that most people did not share the same childhood memories that sparked my interest in the cultural attitudes and anxieties that define nakedness in the United States.

In addition to always providing love and support, my father, a lawyer, and my mother, a nurse, led numerous family discussions that helped prepare me to embark on a project that dealt heavily in legal research and issues of health. No less important were Uncle Jack and Danny, who will always be with me. I am also very grateful to my father-in-law, who introduced me to the Korean Spa and offered to wash my back. Finally, I am forever grateful to Byunghwa and Danny for always inspiring me with their unconditional love and support.

INTRODUCTION

Going Naked

On December 5, 1929, over spareribs with mustard and sauerkraut, three German immigrants met at New York City's Café Micholob to discuss the possibility of bringing nudism to the United States. It was then that Kurt Barthal, now known as the founder of America's oldest nudist group, launched the American League for Physical Culture.[1] The three dinner companions had enjoyed participating in the popular German nudist movement known as *Nacktkultur* and yearned for a similar organization in the United States. Yet exposing the body to the sun, light, and air to correct the ills of modern society and to receive physical, mental, and moral benefits had few precedents in the United States. In the nineteenth and early twentieth centuries, isolated attempts to set up clothing-optional communities by free-love advocates, anarchists, and sex radicals withered as a result of public hostility as well as internal disagreements over ideology and practice.[2] Barthal also acknowledged that the subject was "downright undiscussable amongst decent folks," and he feared that Americans might "shoot and quarter them right in the beginning."[3] Yet the three immigrants proceeded to set up the first nudist organization in the United States and, in the process, sparked an ongoing debate that revealed the multiple, shifting, and contradictory ways Americans have understood the naked body.

Barthal and his two fellow countrymen practiced nudism as an expression of their *Volkisch* German identity. Nudism grew out of a much broader *Lebensreform*, or "life reform," movement in Germany at the end of the nineteenth century. In response to rapid industrialization and urbanization, many Germans desired a return to the "genuine forces of life" and turned to vegetarianism, antialcoholism, nature healing, and land reform to regenerate the nation.[4] As part of the *Lebensreform*, going naked in a natural setting represented a return to Germany's authentic

1

preindustrial past and symbolized a rejection of urban life as immoral and materialistic. Nudists also harnessed the power of the sun to treat diseases such as tuberculosis, and through active movement, exercise, and calisthenics, rather than leisurely sunbathing, they attempted to strengthen the body. By the 1920s, the practice of nudism spread beyond small, eclectic *Lebensreform* sects to a much broader German audience. Numerous groups catered to the middle classes with a nationalist ideology that presented nudism as a way to regenerate the *Volk* and to guard against immorality. Worker nudist groups, such as the Proletarian Lifestyle Reform and Free Physical Culture, a part of the labor movement's People's Health Association (Verband Volksgesundheit), emerged after the First World War and presented the act of going naked as a way of liberating the proletarian body. Kurt Barthal, along with the many other German immigrants who came to the United States prior to the rise of National Socialism, drew on their experiences with the nationalist and proletarian forms of nudism rather than a Nazi variation that emphasized racial purity above all else. For Barthal and his two dinner companions, nudism was as intrinsic to their national identity as the "spareribs with mustard and sauerkraut" they ordered at the Café Micholob.

American nudists, like their German counterparts, championed the natural healing powers of the sun, light, and air. In the early 1930s, many Americans first learned about nudism through tourists and reporters who wrote several popular books about their experiences with *Nacktkultur*. Francis and Mason Merrill's *Among the Nudists* (1931) and their follow-up study, *Nudism Comes to America* (1932), went through several editions and inspired many health enthusiasts, sex reformers, and immigrants to organize and join nudist groups across the United States.[5] Meeting at gymnasiums and at private countryside retreats, small groups of men and women removed their clothes and participated in exercises that included tossing medicine balls, vigorous calisthenics, and swimming. Nudists believed that the experience of going naked was essential to maintaining physical and mental health. For many, the removal of clothing served an important hygienic purpose since it freed the excretory functions of the skin from sweating garments that clung to the body and restricted free-flowing movement. Exposing the body to the air also guarded against several diseases and encouraged muscle and bone growth by maximizing the production of vitamin D. In addition, several early advocates wanted to reform what they considered a psychologically unhealthy conception of the body as shameful and erotic. American nudists contended that being naked with the opposite sex satisfied the "natural" curiosity to see and know about the body, promoted a "wholesome" way of thinking, and ultimately strengthened the relations between men and women.[6]

The social and cultural assumptions that defined the naked body as shameful and immoral in the United States played a significant role in shaping the development of alternative medicine and made it possible for nudism to define itself as therapeutic rather than erotic. In the nineteenth and twentieth centuries, the importance placed on preserving modesty and propriety drew female patients away from the male-dominated medical profession and toward alternative therapies that embraced female practitioners and less invasive procedures. Alternative healers often recruited women as practitioners because they made female patients more comfortable in seeking treatments that required intimate access to the body. Female midwives declaimed the rise of scientifically trained male midwives, in part because they threatened to undermine the long-practiced tradition that required all men to be absent during childbirth to preserve the mother's modesty and propriety. Hydropaths, who urged both male and female patients to immerse themselves in various cold-water baths and to wrap themselves in wet sheets, needed female practitioners to administer treatments to avoid upsetting the moral sensibilities of their mostly middle-class patients.[7] In the twentieth century, the discomfort that women felt subjecting themselves to breast and gynecological exams administered mostly by male physicians resulted in delayed diagnoses—a major public health concern that contributed to the popularity of alternative cancer healers who offered treatments without invasive exams or radical surgical procedures such as the mastectomy or hysterectomy.[8]

The nudist movement, in defining itself as therapeutic, built on previous alternative therapies that employed gendered approaches to discreetly examine, diagnose, and treat the naked body. Nudists, however, sought to redefine the naked body as healthy and rejected the notion of the body as a source of shame. Unlike previous alternative healers who avoided the illicit connotations that came from exposing the body to a physician of the opposite sex, nudists encouraged men and women to disrobe together to overcome feelings of shame and immorality that prevented them from gaining the physical and mental benefits of going naked.

Although nudism did not define American identity the way it did for Germans, its emergence in the 1930s reflected the growing tolerance of sexual expression in the United States. During the first decades of the twentieth century, many Americans began to reject the strict moral absolutism of the nineteenth century and embraced what John D'Emilio and Estelle Freedman termed "sexual liberalism." This new set of beliefs "detached sexual activity from the instrumental goal of procreation, affirmed heterosexual pleasure as a value in itself, defined sexual satisfaction as a critical component of personal happiness and successful marriage, and weakened the connections between sexual expression and marriage by providing youth with room for some experimentation."[9] Whereas nineteenth-century society treated all forms of sexuality with suspicion and hostility, the first decades of the twentieth century saw American society and culture embrace heterosexual pleasure and desire.

In small towns and large cities across the United States, for example, young men and women, who attended an expanded public education system and enjoyed the privacy and mobility afforded by cars, participated in a dating culture that was no longer restricted by parental supervision or the moral authority of community and religious leaders.[10] Other working men and women moved away from their family homes to find work and greater sexual independence in cities that offered a number of "cheap amusements."[11] At the same time, bohemians, feminists, and sex radicals began to campaign for legal access to birth control and called for a companionate form of marriage based on romantic love and sexual satisfaction rather than procreation and economic status. By the 1920s, a growing consumer culture expanded sexual liberalism beyond the young, the working classes, or bohemian communities. Popular films, newspapers, magazines, and books, once censored by powerful vice societies such as the New York Society for the Suppression of Vice (NYSSV), began to use sex and erotic expression to attract audiences and readers from all segments of American society.[12] In many ways, the rise of sexual liberalism created the ideal circumstances for nudism's emergence and development in the United States.

Yet the growing social, cultural, and legal tolerance of heterosexual pleasure in modern American society depended on the exclusion of threatening, violent, or deviant forms of sex. This era of sexual liberalism promoted and enforced heteronormative boundaries that restricted sexual expression to adult, white, middle-class, heterosexual couples within the nuclear family. Once reviled materials such as birth control pamphlets, literature containing sexual themes, and titillating men's magazines gained reprieve in the early 1930s with court rulings that protected material with literary or scholarly merit. The state and federal court system, however, continued to use repressive nineteenth-century laws or subjective community standards to suppress depictions of homosexuality, films dealing with interracial sex, and burlesque shows that catered to male audiences.[13] Long-standing laws banning interracial marriage made sexual contact between the races illicit and influenced many civil rights groups such as the National Association for the Advancement of Colored People (NAACP) to adhere to the politics of respectability rather than to make marriage, and interracial sex, part of its struggle for racial equality.[14] Beginning in the 1930s, the media frequently sensationalized violent sexual crimes against young children, encouraged widespread fear of the "male sexual psychopath," and pressured state legislatures to pass reactionary legislation that often targeted homosexuals.[15] In addition, the U.S. government, which previously prosecuted homosexual behavior through obscure campaigns against perversion, developed a social policy in the postwar period that privileged heterosexual relationships and explicitly denied homosexuals rights and social benefits.[16] The rise of sexual liberalism in the United States did make erotic expression acceptable. However, it was tightly restricted by the parameters of heterosexuality, practiced by white Americans, and contained within the nuclear family.

The place of nudism within the boundaries of sexual liberalism was tenuous and required constant negotiation. The therapeutic principles of the nudist movement challenged American assumptions that tied the body to shame, eroticism, and immorality and clashed with local police, politicians, and community leaders who raided the movement's camps and gymnasiums, seized its magazines and films, and accused nudists of immoral acts. The nudist movement, however, made it difficult for law enforcement, judges, and juries to distinguish so-called deviant sexualities and materials from examples of morally acceptable heterosexual behavior and display. Nudism appealed to white, middle-class families in search of health, recreation, and an alternative sexual ethic as well as to men and women of all sexualities who saw nudism as a way to view pornography, to make sexual contacts, or to engage in intergenerational sex. In addition, despite attempts by camp owners and members to promote a white-only movement, nudist leaders called for the racial integration of camps, frequently romanticized the naked nonwhite body as natural and healthy, and argued that obscenity laws that only permitted the display of naked "primitive" bodies discriminated against white nudist representations.

Respectable and illicit, therapeutic and erotic, nudism both conformed to and violated the heteronormative boundaries of sexual liberalism. The assumption that acceptable heterosexual forms of erotic behavior and display could easily be distinguished from marginal, deviant, or unacceptable forms of sexuality anchored sexual liberalism. Nudism, however, demonstrated that these distinctions remained deeply ambiguous, often overlapped, frequently shifted over time, and were very subjective. By encouraging men and women to go naked together as a form of physical and mental healing, nudism confronted an ideology of shame and distanced itself from public anxieties about same-sex desire. At the same time, the presence of naked men and women invited comparisons to burlesque shows and an underworld of commercial sexuality. Similarly, the need to advertise the therapeutic benefits of nudism through attractive and healthy male and female bodies helped recruit new members and generate interest in the movement even as it provided a source of pornography for both heterosexual and homosexual readers. The celebration of the nudist family as a symbol of innocence and purity countered many of the public's fears and accusations of unrestrained eroticism. Yet it also created a haven for intergenerational sex as nudists as well as local authorities, judges, and juries clung to the assumption that the heteronormative domestic environment effectively constrained sexual deviance. By revealing contradictions and instabilities in sexual liberalism, the nudist movement ultimately undermined it and helped bring about the dramatic changes in sexuality that occurred in the 1960s and 1970s and the explosion in eroticism that has increasingly defined the modern American consumer economy.

The rise of sexual liberalism in the twentieth century left many major religious faiths in the United States unable to articulate a clear sexual ethic in the first decades of the twentieth century, even influencing some liberal Protestant groups to look to American nudism for a modern conception of sex and the body.[17] After decades of struggle, sex radicals, birth control proponents, and free speech advocates successfully challenged the moral authority of nineteenth-century institutions such as the New York Society for the Suppression of Vice (NYSSV) and the Women's Christian Temperance Union (WCTU). Many liberal Protestants who desired a modern sexual ethic that allowed women access to sexual knowledge and birth control turned to nudism, which offered a religious leadership that critiqued repressive religious organizations, provided a nudist reading of sacred doctrines, and articulated a positive spiritual interpretation of the naked body. In books, magazines, films, and statements to the press, nudist leaders sought to make social nudity more palatable to the American public by advancing the idea that nudism, in satisfying "the natural curiosity" to see the naked body, curtailed promiscuity, premarital sex, sexual perversion, and prostitution. In contrast to censorship efforts or suggestive clothing designed to heighten erotic desire, visiting a nudist camp, scanning the many pictures in its magazines and books, or watching one of its promotional films eliminated the desire to consume indecent literature, to attend risqué burlesque performances, or to frequent a prostitute. Although religious leaders frequently attacked nudism as a sign of society's increasingly lax morality, the movement appealed to individuals and families in search of an alternative moral ethic.

Even as a religious nudist leadership officially argued that going naked with other men, women, and children eliminated erotic desire, the movement embraced the politics of sexual liberation. Nudism welcomed the support of the many liberal activists, birth control advocates, free lovers, political radicals, and civil libertarians who gathered in New York City's Greenwich Village to discuss, debate, and challenge the conventions that dictated daily life as well as the boundaries restricting free speech and sexual expression. The bohemian communities that flourished in Greenwich Village in the 1910s and 1920s experimented with alternative living arrangements such as open marriage and free love that promised erotic pleasures, honesty, individual autonomy, and gender equality. Nudism also intrigued the Greenwich Village community as another way to challenge conventional life and to free the naked body of shame, inhibition, and artificiality. The sociologist and economist Maurice Parmelee, whose *Nudism in Modern Life: The New Gymnosophy* (1931) helped introduced nudism to the United States, developed many of his radical critiques of capitalism, marriage, sexual regulation, and organized religion at the clubs, cafés, and settlement houses he frequented in Greenwich Village. Parmelee envisioned a nudist movement that encouraged sexual experimentation, embraced eroticism, and advocated for radical social, economic, and political change. In addition, Jan Gay, a lesbian journalist who assisted several sex researchers studying homosexuality in the 1930s, also spoke to the prominent gay and lesbian communities in Greenwich Village in her book *On Going Naked* (1932). The willingness to incorporate advocates of sexual freedom, political radicals, and sex researchers, despite the risks they posed to the nudist movement's respectability, signaled that many nudists identified with the cause of sexual liberation.

The bohemian communities of Greenwich Village also played an influential role in shaping nudism's legal defense over the course of the twentieth century. Many of the artists, writers, intellectuals, and birth control advocates residing in Greenwich Village frequently violated local, state, and federal obscenity laws and turned to the American Civil Liberties Union (ACLU) for legal assistance. The ACLU had originally formed in response to the Red Scare of 1919 in order to oppose antiunion government policies and to defend the civil liberties of political radicals. With its headquarters located in the heart of the Lower East Side neighborhood, several members of the ACLU, including cofounders Roger Baldwin and Crystal Eastman, frequently experimented with open marriage, nude sunbathing, and free love. In the 1920s and early 1930s, these experiences influenced ACLU attorneys to join with anticensorship activists, who had long sought to improve access to birth control and sexual education, to fight resurgent efforts to censor public discussions of sexuality and to resist a strong "public reaction against the nudity and racy language that was common in films."[18] As part of an expanded defense of sexual expression and knowledge, the ACLU defended nudists as early as 1934 when the New York State legislature passed an antinudity ordinance, prohibiting all nudist activities. In 1940, it also helped Maurice Parmelee overturn the seizure of *Nudism in Modern Life* by the U.S. Customs Service and in the early 1950s initiated the decade-long legal battle that culminated in the 1958 Supreme Court decision that stopped the U.S. Postal Service from seizing nudist magazines from the mail. The illicit and respectable characteristics of nudist activities, magazines, and films made nudism an ideal vehicle for anticensorship advocates to extend their battle for freedom of expression in the United States.

The perceived eroticism of the naked body remained a constant threat to the therapeutic and religious character of nudism, which was promoted by American nudist leaders. Many Americans associated the public exposure of the body, especially in urban areas, with commercial forms of sexuality and leisure that threatened to undermine the boundaries of sexual liberalism. In Germany, *Nacktkultur* maintained a network of urban gymnasiums, often operated by socialist groups, that served a large working-class membership. Before Hitler's ascendency and the banning of all socialist activity in 1933, the membership of the Zentralkommission fur Arbeitersport und Korperplflege (Central Commission for Workers' Sport and Hygiene), which included subsections that participated in nudist activities, had grown to 1,456,162.[19] In the United States, however, many social critics and moral reformers asserted that nudism's therapeutic ideals and principles masked the movement's effort to profit from the commercial appeal of the naked body. Local police, community leaders, politicians, and judges conflated nudist gatherings where men and women came together to exercise in a gymnasium or to sunbath at a park with a rapidly expanding sexual urban underworld where burlesque shows entertained large, rowdy crowds of men. There they believed prostitutes used their scantily clad bodies to entice customers; seedy bookstores, theaters, and newsstands brandished nudity for profit; and naked men met in bathhouses to engage in homosexual acts.[20] The growth of commercial leisure and sexuality in American cities during the first part of the twentieth century made nudist activities and meetings a threat to heteronormativity and sexual liberalism.

The nudist movement's link to commercial sexuality and radical sexual politics faded in the wide-open spaces of the American countryside. Quite in contrast to current assumptions that link sexual expression with the city, the sparsely populated regions just outside major metropolitan areas provided hospitable spaces for men and women to go naked. American nudists, like their German counterparts, contended that city life weakened the individual physically and morally, and they encouraged men and women to return to nature at rural camps where they could expose their bodies to the sun, light, and air. In the early twentieth century, many intellectuals, health reformers, and physical culture promoters also worried that Americans' increasing disconnection with their natural environment would weaken the nation. These anxieties fueled efforts to promote a closer relationship with nature that included going naked in the wilderness.[21] Kenneth Webb, one of the main promoters of organized camping in the United States, for example, considered nudity the "fifth freedom" in an Eden-like setting that would also be free of fear, want, hunger, and religious persecution.[22] In addition, in small towns throughout the United States, the habit of taking a swim in the local lake or river sans clothing remained so common that the practice occurred across racial lines and doubled as a site for homosexual experimentation.[23] In the 1930s, a network of rural nudist camps that built on the idealized relationship between nature and nudity emerged. Nudist camps such as Lake O' Woods in Valparaiso, Indiana (fifty-five miles southeast of Chicago), Sky Farm in Mays Landing, New Jersey (located fifteen miles away from Atlantic City), and Elysia in Riverside, California (about forty miles outside Los Angeles) allowed urban residents to escape the noise, pollution, and stresses of the city and removed barriers that separated the individual from nature. Large camps offered rolling hills, open fields, expansive lakes, lush vegetation, and towering trees, which allowed nudists to take full advantage of all outdoor activities and all their associated benefits. Far away from prying neighbors and local police, nudists could enjoy hiking, athletic competitions, swimming, rowing, and of course, sunbathing.[24]

The rustic nudist camps of the 1930s transformed in the postwar period into well-equipped resorts that catered to families. Prior to the Second World War, nudist parks resembled their German counterparts with Spartan grounds where groups participated in rigorous exercises and reconnected with nature. After decades of economic depression and war, however, American families began to pursue leisure and recreation with a renewed vigor. With over half of American families owning a car by 1948, more workers compensated with paid vacations than ever before, and an expanding interstate highway system, travel became easier, more affordable, and anonymous.[25] While many families packed in the car to experience the nation's natural beauty, camping at national parks, or concluding their trip at a popular amusement park such as Disneyland, which had recently opened,[26] others could just as easily veer off the beaten path to enjoy a relaxing, therapeutic, and fun-filled day of nude sunbathing, swimming, volleyball, and waterskiing. Vacation spots such as Coney Island and Provincetown had long been places where visitors could experience "new sorts of pleasures" and "experiment with new, often less restricted, rules of conduct and behavior."[27] In many instances, the tourist experience often implicitly or explicitly accepted the uncovering of the body, the public expression of sexuality, and even casual eroticism.[28] While certainly eccentric, nudist resorts served the function of relaxing otherwise-entrenched social conventions, as was a contemporary trend in vacationing culture.

Despite nudism's therapeutic ideals and network of rural camps, censors targeted nudist materials as another example of pernicious, commercial sexuality and forced the courts to disentangle the illicit from the respectable. The books, magazines, and films of nudism served the needs of individuals interested in participating in nudist activities while also providing a source of erotica for a variety of sexualities. Individual nudist groups began to publish monthly magazines to promote a fledgling network of camps, to provide information on upcoming activities and events, and to recruit new members through an ongoing discussion of nudist principles and ideals. Magazines such as the *Nudist*, which began its thirty-year run in May 1933, featured large, glossy pages and numerous photos alongside lengthy articles on a variety of nudist topics. Displayed at newsstands and sent through the mail, the *Nudist* sold thousands of issues each month and played a significant role in financially supporting national nudist organizations such as the International Nudist Council (later renamed the American Sunbathing Association). The editors and leaders of the nudist movement wanted the many pictures in their magazines to show the benefits of going naked at a nudist camp; but the display of the naked body also allowed for multiple readings. An image of a naked muscular man presented readers with a symbol of strength and athleticism or a source of titillation for both women and men. The display of full-frontal female nudes of all body types exhibited nudism's commitment to showing the body without shame while also providing glimpses of genitalia rarely displayed in other forms of commercial pornography. The many images of children in the magazine communicated the natural joy of going naked and gave individuals seeking out intergenerational sex a venue to gaze at prepubescent youth.

Filmmakers tested the legal and moral boundaries of decency by bringing the therapeutic ideals and principles of nudism to theaters around the country. In the early 1930s, filmmakers released several nudist films that closely resembled the format, content, and style of exploitation films that addressed health and the practice of medicine early in the twentieth century.[29] Prior to the 1931 Hays Production Code, health reformers frequently used films to address controversial and sensitive topics such as abortion, birth control, and euthanasia and used the "allure of popular entertainment to attract audiences . . . for their own educational, recruitment, and fundraising purposes."[30] When the studios began to enforce the code in 1934 to avoid government regulation, they specifically targeted medical films that exhibited bodies or focused on "repellent subjects" and significantly limited what could be seen in most movie theaters.[31] The code, however, did not regulate independent theaters and art houses, which continued to screen controversial films that projected enough merit and respectability to avoid the ire of local censorship boards and authorities. Because nudist films had the merit of a social movement, they made it difficult for censors to deny filmmakers licenses to exhibit the movies. Although publicity and curiosity drew in large male audiences, the films generally featured tame plots that revolved around the health benefits of nudism, providing only brief glimpses of the naked body. The legal battles over nudist films, like those that involved the movement's books and magazines, forced the courts to decide on what did and did not constitute indecency.

The nudist movement's struggle to conform to the boundaries of sexual liberalism revealed the eroticism that the family was suppose to, but perhaps was unable to, control. With its books, magazines, and films promoting the therapeutic and recreational character of the movement but also serving as sources of pornography, nudism attracted a variety of individuals and sexualities. Many nudists often found it difficult to distinguish members interested in health and familial recreation from those who wanted to ogle at the naked men, women, and children wandering nudist parks without clothes. Deciding who posed a threat and why proved to be a continual source of struggle within the movement. Without a wife or family to confirm heterosexuality or moral integrity, single men elicited fears of homosexuality, posed a threat as potential voyeurs, and represented individuals who might pursue intergenerational sex. Many visitors at nudist parks also echoed fears of the hypersexual black male body when they asserted that admitting people of color into nudist parks posed a threat to white female nudists and invited accusations of inappropriate sexual behavior.[32] Nudists' continuing struggle to limit threats to the movement's respectability revealed how anxieties about gender, race, sex, and age defined nakedness in the United States.

The respectable character of nudism clashed with the many young men and women coming of age in the late 1960s who saw public nudity as a way to advocate for the politics of sexual liberation. The nudist movement's legal victories in the late 1950s undermined the heteronormative boundaries of sexual liberalism and helped bring about a revolution in sexual attitudes and values. A new market of racy nudist magazines flooded newsstands, independent art theaters enticed audiences with uncensored nudist films, and more and more young men and women began throwing off their clothes at concerts, on beaches, and in protest marches. The men and women of the counterculture that emerged in the late 1960s saw public nudity as a way to challenge what they considered to be the hypocritical values and social customs of mainstream society. According to sociologist Sam Brinkley, they wanted to "loosen [themselves] from the strictures of tradition, overcome the fear of social sanction and opprobrium, and recover the immediacy, the sensuality, and the experience of a truly shared moment."[33] Yet an aging nudist membership preferred its private, secluded, rustic clubs and clung to rules restricting sexual behavior, and club owners maintained exclusionary policies based on race and gender. A more inclusive approach to nudism that emerged primarily on sandy beaches and in urban parks and that accepted single men, homosexuals, and people of color, as well as feminists, political dissidents, and a variety of eccentric personalities, ultimately remade nudism into a movement of sexual liberation.

Naked: A Cultural History of American Nudism analyzes a social movement as well as the larger cultural phenomenon of public nudity in the United States. Many leaders, editors, club owners, activists, regional affiliates, organizational strategies, and legal battles have shaped the development of organized nudism since it officially began in 1931. Rather than attempt to chronicle every internal struggle, leadership change, or shift in organizational policy, this book focuses on the events, people, and trials that reveal the hidden and often overlooked customs, values, and assumptions that shaped and defined American society and culture over the course of the twentieth century. It highlights particular discussions, debates, and conflicts within the movement that reflect the way gender, ethnicity, race, and sexuality informed the way Americans understood the naked body. It selects particular gymnasiums, camps, clubs, resorts, and beaches that best represent the hundreds of others that have come and gone over the years and that demonstrate the way physical spaces and landscapes can both restrict and liberate sex, sexual expression, and sexual identity. It chronicles the legal battles that not only determined how nudism could be practiced and represented but also influenced what could be seen, experienced, and consumed in the United States.

Naked begins in the first years of the Great Depression by analyzing the hostile reception nudism received from antiobscenity activists, whose intent was to reverse the advances of sexual liberalism. Chapter 1 examines how local police, doctors, and community leaders in Chicago and New York campaigned against nudist activities held in urban gymnasiums, at beaches, and at public parks to reestablish a clear boundary that defined the illicit from the respectable. Chapter 2 explores a growing network of rural camps constructed around the therapeutic ideals of a religious leadership. Though nudists still chafed against instances of moral outrage in rural America, this chapter argues that the innocent settings and wide-open spaces surrounding the metropolis tempered the eroticism of going naked. The American countryside helped define the therapeutic, nature-oriented, and moral principles of nudism and gave the movement the respectability necessary to develop and prosper in the United States.

The next three chapters explore the shifting boundaries of sexual expression in the United States during and after the Second World War. Chapter 3 examines how nudists' attempts to display the nude body in books and magazines provoked a repressive sexual politics that represented nudism as politically subversive and ultimately led to renewed censorship efforts by postal officials. Chapter 4 analyzes the role that race and gender played in positioning the postwar nudist resort within the exclusionary domestic ideals of early Cold War culture. By strictly managing or excluding naked bodies that evoked uncontrolled eroticism, such as the single man or the nonwhite body, nudists enforced a rigid form of corporeal heterosexuality based on family, marriage, middle-class status, and race. Chapter 5 outlines the legal strategy that freed nudist magazines and films from censorship to show that white, middle-class family values played a critical role in defeating postwar antipornography campaigns. It also documents how the movement's legal victories ultimately contributed to the commercialization of sex occurring in the last decades of the twentieth century.

Chapter 6 examines how the fall of sexual liberalism transformed the American nudist movement in the last decades of the twentieth century. It analyzes the emergence of a more activist approach to nudism that embraced the values of sexual liberation and incorporated feminist antipornography advocates. The struggles to sustain these alliances reflected the divisive sexual politics of the 1980s and influenced nudists to refocus their efforts on promoting nude recreation.

This cultural history of American nudism reveals how a marginal social movement that started in a small New York café can help us understand many of the major themes and conflicts that have shaped modern American life.

INDECENT EXPOSURE

The Battle for Nudism in the American Metropolis

The first men and women to go naked in New York City for the purposes of improving their health grabbed headlines when police raided the Heart of New York Gymnasium on the night of December 8, 1931. However, no sooner had the *New York Times* announced the official arrival of nudism in the United States with the ominous headline "24 Seized in Raid on Nudist Cult Here"[1] than it reported the dismissal of all the charges against the naked men and women.[2] The article explained that Judge Jonah Goldstein did not necessarily agree with "nudity in a gymnasium," but he recognized, "What is all right on the beach today would have meant arrest three years ago."[3] The introduction of American nudism to the United States in the first years of the Great Depression seemed to reflect emerging conceptions of sexuality and nudity, as much as the lifestyle clashed with persistent attempts to impose a repressive sexual ethic.

For a brief moment, American nudism seemed poised to expand the shifting boundaries of modern sexual liberalism. In the 1920s, the appearance of the one-piece bathing suit on beaches, at swimming pools, and in beauty pageants dramatically changed which parts of the body could be exposed in public.[4] It remained unclear, however, if this line could be pushed further by bringing naked men, women, and children together to exercise in locked gymnasiums. Although the favorable Goldstein ruling suggested that nudism might establish itself in cities across the nation, many neighbors, police officers, judges, and politicians saw the fledgling movement as the final threat to remaining standards of decency, modesty, and morality. They fought to remove nudist bodies from city beaches, parks, and gymnasiums to ensure the continued coverage of genitalia, breasts, and buttocks in American public space.

The nudist groups that began forming across the country encountered contrasting approaches to regulating sex and sexual expression. The emergence of sexual liberalism and the growing tolerance of heterosexual pleasure and leisure in the twentieth century did not immediately spell the demise of voluntary moral reform organizations that continued to advocate the moral absolutism of the nineteenth century. Well into the twentieth century, women's clubs, moral purity organizations, and religious organizations implemented grassroots campaigns to influence local politicians to act against vice, pornography, and the distribution of birth control information. In Chicago, women's groups and local politicians reacted with scorn to a proposal to build a nudist enclosure on Rogers Park Beach and waged a campaign against the immigrant groups that supported the nude-sunbathing enclosure. In New York City, however, the demise of elite Protestant vice societies such as the New York Society for the Suppression of Vice (NYSSV) in the first decades of the twentieth century led to the formation of a state-centered legal system that regulated sex and sexual display according to the values of the average person. Subjective and shifting, this approach to obscenity left the indecency or decency of nudism open to debate. Authorities found it difficult to convict nudists who never exhibited any "lewd" activities at their meetings other than naked men and women engaging in quotidian exercise routines. Rather than attempting to influence local politicians to stamp out nudist gatherings, antiobscenity activists in New York introduced state legislation that defined nudism as a commercial activity and a threat to public decency. In both Chicago and New York City, ethnic tensions, hostile political organizations, and the identification of the urban environment with commercial sexual activity and sex spectacle impeded the development of nudism in urban environments.[5]

The effort to crack down on public sexuality during the Depression alarmed anticensorship groups, which saw the campaign against nudism as part of a larger effort to suppress the discussion of sex and sexual expression. An anticensorship coalition, which included the ACLU, birth control advocates, and free speech activists, contended that the attack on nudism represented a serious threat to every individual's right to privacy. Under the proposed New York State antinudist legislation, the presence of naked bodies transformed spaces that authorities otherwise considered private—such as a locked gymnasium or an enclosed beach—into public venues that potentially served illicit commercial purposes and required state regulation. Making nudism illegal, according to anticensorship advocates, gave state authorities the power to peer into almost any space that might contain naked bodies. By framing the proscription of nudism as a threat to personal privacy, nudist supporters spoke to the values of the average person and made nudism relevant to the wider public. The battle over the legality of nudism played a crucial role in determining the place that sex, sexual display, and public nakedness would occupy in modern American society and culture.

Rogers Park

A proposal to establish a place for nude sunbathing in the Rogers Park neighborhood of Chicago revealed a willingness to experiment with therapeutic forms of nakedness as well as the existence of a vocal opposition rooted in the moral, ethnic, and class politics of the city. On March 10, 1932, Dr. Arne L. Suominen, a "distinguished American Naprapath" and "designated spokesman for a large group of citizens interested in sunbathing," solicited the Forty-Ninth Ward alderman to introduce a resolution to the city council to build an enclosure for sunbathing. Suominen, who toured Germany's clinics, colleges, and sanitariums in search of drugless physicians practicing hydrotherapy, heliotherapy, pythotherapy, and other diet systems, returned to the United States convinced of the "benefit of the sun rays, which build up the body."[6] He endeavored to create a venue where the many immigrant groups in Chicago could sunbathe without the hindrance of clothing.[7] One 1923 survey of seven thousand Chicago patients suggested that Suominen's proposal might very well find substantial support in the nation's second-largest city. It revealed that almost 86 percent of Chicago's residents had at some point "dabbled" in irregular medicine.[8] Suominen drew support from ethnic organizations ranging from the "Y.M.C.A. and Y.W.C.A." to "Danish-American, Swedish-American, Finnish-American, Scandinavian, German, and other clubs," as well as the promoter of physical culture Bernarr Macfadden. He asserted that "20,000 sunbathers" would frequent the enclosure on Rogers Park Beach and predicted that after its completion the number would "increase to 200,000."[9]

The popularity of Bernarr Macfadden's physical-culture publishing empire in the first decades of the twentieth century suggested that Americans might be willing to explore how nude sunbathing could improve one's personal health and well-being. After transforming himself from a slender, weak youth to a muscular gymnastics teacher and amateur wrestler, Macfadden promoted the preventative health philosophy of physical culture in magazines and books and at various sanatoriums. For people to achieve strength and physical fitness, Macfadden offered the same advice that nineteenth-century health reformers such as Sylvester Graham and Andrus Alcott promoted in their books and pamphlets: an unstimulating diet, exercise, sunshine and fresh air, cleanliness, and no medicine. Unlike previous health reformers, however, Macfadden saw sexual virility as a sign of overall health and fitness, and he fought to expand the public discussion of sex. He displayed the benefits of his physical-culture program by posing nude while flexing his muscles in his magazines and books. He also celebrated the female bosom and published a series of photographs of bare-breasted women exercising in his book *The Power and Beauty of Superb Womanhood* (1901).[10] While Macfadden frequently clashed with postal officials and the police, his magazines proved popular and financially successful. Suominen hoped that the success that Macfadden enjoyed in the first decades of the twentieth century would carry over to his proposal to create a place for nude sunbathing in Chicago.

Furthermore, many urban public facilities in the first decades of the twentieth century welcomed naked or scantily clad bodies to ensure proper hygiene and health. Suominen saw his sunbathing enclosure on Rogers Park Beach as an extension of Chicago's network of municipal public baths. Since the late nineteenth century, the city's many women's clubs and settlement-house reformers urged city officials and leaders to construct public baths throughout the city. They worried that the lack of bathing facilities for the city's growing immigrant population posed a major public health risk and threatened to undermine the poor's moral character, which they closely associated with cleanliness. Only the most privileged residents of the city enjoyed the benefits of indoor plumbing. The vast majority of the city's residents lived in cramped, poorly built tenements and often used buckets of water or wet rags to bathe. They rarely ever fully undressed and washed the entire body. By promoting good hygiene through regular bathing at municipal baths, many middle-class female reformers hoped to institute the domestic roles of the mother and homemaker and to make the city a clean, healthful, attractive, and moral place to live. In addition, female reformers such as Julie R. Lowe and Gertrude Gail Wellington, both of whom graduated from homeopathic colleges, saw municipal public baths as a space to apply natural healing methods.[11] Water-cure centers, homeopathic colleges, and numerous other healing systems had long embraced women as practitioners, even though most regular medical schools denied admission to female students. In many ways, the effort at the beginning of the twentieth century to encourage immigrants to visit public baths where they undressed and washed their bodies to avoid disease and promote their moral and physical health shared the same goals and characteristics that defined the sunbathing enclosure in Rogers Park.

Suominen also believed that the popularity of public baths among Chicago's immigrant communities would carry over to his sunbathing enclosure. In 1894, city officials constructed the first public bath in Chicago using land donated by Jane Addams's Hull House. Located on the city's west side, it provided the mostly Italian-immigrant neighborhood with a small facility that consisted of dressing rooms, a small waiting area, and nearly thirty showers. Unlike New York City's municipal baths, Chicago's facilities lacked swimming pools or Turkish baths and only provided brief time allotments for bathing. In 1910, despite the lack of amenities and opportunities for recreation, city residents took 1,070,565 baths in Chicago's fifteen bathhouses located in the city's ethnic and working-class neighborhoods. The popularity of Chicago's network of municipal baths, along with the participation of reformers who supported alternative healing, gave Suominen good reason to believe that two hundred thousand sunbathers would frequent his enclosure on Rogers Park Beach.[12]

The sunbathing proposal also drew strength from the popularity of swimming pools in the 1920s and 1930s. Attendance at public baths began to decline as cities passed laws and building ordinances that required new tenement apartments to include private toilets and bathtubs.[13] At the same time, city officials began to support the construction of municipal swimming pools, often converting outdated public bathing facilities, in order to promote public cleanliness as well as recreation. The tremendous popularity of swimming pools resulted first from a period of economic prosperity that increased the demand for recreation and subsequently as a form of relief from the hard times of the Depression. These often-massive venues, accompanied by sandy beaches, grassy lawns, and broad concrete decks, catered to a wide range of people hoping to sunbathe and socialize with their friends, family, and members of the opposite sex. Although pool officials sought to encourage family activities, according to the historian Jeff Wiltse, they quickly saw the "downsizing of swimsuits" and the creation of a place where males and females came to view "one another mostly unclothed."[14] With swimmers and spectators "visually consuming" their bodies, Wiltse argues that the venue of the swimming pool contributed to making the "public objectification of female and male bodies" acceptable and helped define public decency as the exhibition of an "attractive appearance rather than protecting one's modesty."[15] The proposal to create a place where men and women could sunbathe in the nude as a health measure did not seem as far-fetched given the popularity of swimming pools as places where both the middle and working classes came to display and consume the body in addition to enjoying a swim.

Suominen proposed that his sunbathing enclosure follow the same rules and precautions practiced in municipal public baths. European nudist camps encouraged men and women to participate in nudist activities in each other's company in order to satisfy the individual's curiosity about the body. Suominen, however, understood that he needed to take precautions against the "sniflish ladies and gentlemen who have sniffed at the carryings on of nudist cults in Germany and elsewhere in Europe."[16] In the United States, the municipal public baths served as a useful model: they encouraged attendees to disrobe in order to improve their physical and mental health, and they avoided accusations of moral impropriety by strictly separating men from women. The popularity of municipal baths and the support Suominen hoped to receive from middle-class female reformers who previously called for public baths influenced him to propose that his sunbathing enclosure have "separate spaces for men and women." He also included plans to construct walls that would "obstruct any view of the interior from nearby buildings or other vantage points."[17] Suominen hoped that compromising nudist ideals that encouraged men and women to go naked together would make his sunbathing enclosure as acceptable as the one-piece bathing suit, the municipal public bath, or the swimming pools of the 1930s.

Suominen's proposal for a nude-sunbathing enclosure on Rogers Park Beach collided with a local system of censorship shaped by the many moral purity organizations active in Chicago. Censorship in Chicago received support from a broad coalition of conservative women's groups and progressive reformers including the Women's Christian Temperance Union (WCTU), the Juvenile Protection Association (JPA), the City Club, the Chicago's Woman's Club, Hull House, Chicago Commons and the Northwestern University Settlement, the Vice Commission, and the Committee of Fifteen.[18] Since the late nineteenth century, groups such as the WCTU, the Young Woman's Christian Association (YWCA), and numerous other conservative women's clubs sought to protect so-called vulnerable members of society—namely, young women and children—from the sexual dangers of the urban environment.

Through grassroots campaigns and movements, these organizations pushed local police and politicians to take action against prostitution, burlesque shows, and questionable films. In 1907, for example, the city enacted a censorship ordinance that gave the police chief the power to cut or prohibit any film prior to its first screening. When the police chief ignored the law, the Juvenile Protective Association conducted a survey of nickel theaters that aroused civic reformers who demanded enforcement and, beginning in 1909, made police officials eliminate scenes of murder, robbery, and abduction.[19] The close relationship between the coalition of moral purity organizations, women's clubs, and civic groups and local police and politicians defined Chicago's system of censorship in the first decades of the twentieth century.

Just as WCTU club women campaigned against a variety of social vices in the Chicago area, they played a key role in opposing the establishment of the nudist enclosure on Rogers Park Beach.[20] The WCTU established its national headquarters only a few miles north of Rogers Park in the suburb of Evanston, where it directed its broad moral reform agenda at the national and local levels. The *Chicago Tribune* labeled the residents who opposed the sunbathing enclosure the "conservative Roger Parkers," in part because they employed the methods of the nearby WCTU. The Rogers Park Woman's Club president, Mrs. Earl G. Whittaker, declared, "It's absurd to think that the club women of this district would sanction such a thing," since, according to her, the Roger Park residents were "much too conservative for such a plan."[21] To preserve the moral character of the neighborhood, these women employed the "petition drives and political lobbying" strategies that the historian Alison Parker argues allowed the WCTU to "pass stricter censorship laws at the federal and state levels."[22] They immediately began organizing "several councils of war," in which they drafted a resolution in protest against the sunbathing proposal.[23] The group also distributed fifty thousand circulars decrying nudism and submitted letters of protest to Mayor Anton Cermak and Alderman George A. Williston of the Forty-Ninth Ward.[24] If Suominen's proposal for a nude-sunbathing enclosure was to be successful, he needed to overcome Chicago's local system of censorship.

The support that the sunbathing enclosure received from several immigrant groups also upset members of the Rogers Park community. In the first decades of the twentieth century, Rogers Park transformed from a middle-class, suburban community with large houses on sizable lots into an urban, multiethnic neighborhood. After the Northwestern Elevated Railroad Company opened its Howard station in 1908, the neighborhood's population grew dramatically, from 7,000 in 1910 to 26,857 in 1920, and then doubled again over the course of the next decade.[25] Multiunit buildings quickly replaced single-family homes and attracted German, Irish, Russian, Welsh, and Swedish immigrants. By 1930, 15 percent of the residents of Rogers Park were first-generation American born, and another 34 percent were second generation. The growing German-immigrant community in Rogers Park made it an ideal location for Suominen to establish his nude-sunbathing enclosure. Yet in the Rogers Park Hotel, led by James White, the secretary of the Forty-Ninth Ward Republican Civic League and an alderman candidate in the upcoming local primary, residents expressed concern that Suominen's sunbathers resembled the *Nacktkultur* groups gaining popularity in Germany and declared that they desperately wanted to "halt this sunbathing movement before it starts."[26] The residents remained convinced that permitting individuals to "indulge themselves in moronic exhibitions" transcended the "limits of morality and seriously endanger[ed] the standards of decency" that they had "cherished in this part of Chicago."[27] They feared that the enclosure would attract "undesirables" who would "destroy the wholesome residential atmosphere that . . . surrounded [their] homes and hold this splendid community up to scorn and ridicule by clean people of the city." This would, of course, lower property values as well.[28] Unwilling to tolerate an influx of socially undesirable immigrants practicing nudism, White dismissively suggested that the sunbathers build their "nudist cult stockade on the banks of the drainage canal, where the sun is just as hot and the opposition is cooler."[29]

Suominen's nude-sunbathing enclosure quickly succumbed to the protests of Chicago's many voluntary moral reform organizations and the city's local system of censorship. The socially conservative residents of Rogers Park used letters and their political influence to persuade the mayor of Chicago, Anton Cermak, to oppose Suominen's proposal, even though he depended heavily on the political support of immigrant groups across the city.[30] Mayor Cermak, reacting to the "protests of the residents of Rogers Park," asked Alderman John Wilson, chairman of the council committee on playgrounds, to "pigeonhole" the proposal for the beach enclosure.[31] After receiving "letters of the most insulting kind," he remarked, "[The] whole thing makes me sick."[32] Cermak went so far as to repeat the nativist rhetoric of the Rogers Park residents by bluntly asserting, "Nude sunbathing is not done in this country and the city never intended that it should be started in Chicago."[33] Unwilling to challenge the power and influence of the WCTU and the Rogers Park community, Mayor Cermak suppressed the proposal for a nudist stockade on Lake Michigan.

The mayor's public response to the Rogers Park protests did not immediately end interest in nudism in Chicago. Cermak originally anticipated support for the enclosure and thought he would introduce the measure to "ascertain if people had any objections."[34] Although not "advocating nude sunbathing," Cermak acknowledged his private support for Suominen's sunbathing proposal and accepted responsibility for the ensuing controversy. Confessing that he regularly took "sunbaths," Cermak made sure to point out that he did not think it was "necessary to be nude to get the healthful ultra-violet rays."[35] After the controversy dissipated, however, Cermak maintained his interest in nudist parks. In the summer, the mayor and his staff made a trip to Germany to publicize Chicago, to encourage financial investment in the city, and to promote the Chicago World's Fair. As Cermak tried to counter the image of a crime-ridden Chicago, his advisers took the time to visit two nudist camps.[36] The county commissioner Charles H. Weber and Mathias (Paddy) Bauler, a Democratic ward committeeman, visited a "city operated" park and a nudist camp "run by communists."[37] Stunned that the city managed the park "just like Lincoln Park in Chicago," the two advisers recalled being taken to an observation gallery where they witnessed children "running around bare" with their "fat mammas and papas."[38] At the communist-run park, they witnessed five hundred men, women, and children "running around without any clothes."[39] Mayor Cermak's interest in the sunbathing enclosure and his staff's visits to German nudist parks demonstrated the continued ethnic support for nudism in Chicago and a willingness to experiment with the therapeutic possibilities of exposing the body to the fresh air.

A year after Suominen's first attempt, he tried again to establish another space for nudism and quickly encountered resistance from local politicians and moral reformers in the heart of Chicago. Reintroduced by the *Chicago Tribune* as a "nature cure specialist" and the "friend of . . . Mayor Cermak," Suominen submitted a petition signed by ten thousand persons requesting an enclosure for nude sunbathing in Lincoln Park.[40] The new proposal called for nine-foot-high walls lined with sheet metal, shutting off views from the high-rise building next to the park.[41] Invoking the influence of the WCTU, the president of the park board remarked that he had already received several "protests from north side residents." As Suominen did with his Rogers Park sunbathing proposal, he sought to mute potential accusations of indecency that might emerge from men and women undressing in the same space. He introduced a regimen that scheduled men to "bask in the sun for a period" and then, at a different time, allowed female sunbathers to enter the facility. Rejecting "mixed nudism," he understood the need for caution since "such experiments" needed to be practiced only by the "most highest-minded persons without inhibitions."[42] Suominen hoped that his petition, along with his plans to strictly separate men and women, would be enough to convince the Chicago city council to allow a sunbathing area in Lincoln Park.

By then, however, political circumstances had changed. Mayor Cermak was assassinated on March 6, 1933, and without strong support from the mayor's office, Lincoln Park commissioners did not take the proposal seriously.[43] While making a tour of the park to evaluate possible sites for the stockade, the commissioners "waxed hilarious over the proposal."[44] One official stated that he opposed it on "esthetic grounds," especially "now that everybody is drinking 3.2 beer [sic]."[45] Officially, the commission cited the excessive costs of the high-quality lumber required to construct the walls of the enclosure.[46] Designed with towering walls to prevent "an epidemic of peeping Toms," the enclosure's cost and its limited appeal to "members of a small cult" led city officials to the conclusion that it did not constitute an appropriate use of funds or park space.[47] Although nudism received a great deal of support from immigrant groups that embraced alternative forms of healing, the grassroots campaigns of Chicago's many voluntary moral reform organizations stifled any discussion of the merits of nudist activities and influenced municipal politicians to reject proposals for a sunbathing enclosure on Rogers Park Beach.

"24 Seized in Raid on Nudist Cult Here"

The various attempts to go naked in New York City gymnasiums tested the boundaries of an emerging state-centered approach to regulating obscenity and sexual expression. In the first decades of the twentieth century, the vice societies and women's voluntary organizations that had campaigned for strict censorship laws and repressive legislation came under attack from working-class groups, middle-class moderns, civil libertarians, and members of the entertainment industry. Men and women began to demand and fight for access to birth control information while also affirming "self-expression and pleasure seeking as individual and social goods." By the 1930s, according to historian Andrea Friedman, a new system of obscenity regulation emerged that established a democratic structure to determine the decency of sexual representations. New Yorkers rejected the voluntary moral purity organization in favor of a "state-centered system of criminal prosecution" that judged questionable materials and activities according to the standards of the average person and guaranteed the right to trial by jury.[48] In contrast to Chicago's local system of censorship, the democratic processes that defined New York's modern regime of obscenity regulation afforded nudists and their supporters the opportunity to dispute accusations of immorality, to present their therapeutic principles, and to assert their right to privacy. It also required antiobscenity activists to introduce legislation that linked nudist activities to commercial sexuality in order to expand the state's power to regulate naked bodies in nearly any space or venue.

Judge Goldstein intended to uphold New York's emerging democratic regime of obscenity regulation when he dismissed the public indecency charges against the men and women who went naked in the "Heart of New York Gymnasium" on the night of December 8, 1931. In the first decades of the twentieth century, many Americans gradually began to accept fashion trends that displayed parts of the body that had previously remained hidden under heavy skirts and restrictive bodices.[49] The 1907 introduction of the one-piece bathing suit by Annette Kellerman, revealing, for the first time, women's legs, shoulders, and arms, immediately provoked reprisal, debate, and enormous public interest.[50] The police arrested Kellerman for indecent exposure when she wore her bathing suit on a promotional campaign in Massachusetts. In the coming years, however, the suit gradually gained acceptance across the country. The growing leisure time enjoyed by the affluent led couples and families to seaside resorts, where they found the lighter material of the one-piece swimsuit far more appropriate for actual swimming than the bulky full-length bathing suits of the nineteenth century. By the 1930s, clothing companies began to use nudism to convey the feeling of nakedness when promoting the one-piece bathing suit. One 1934 advertisement in the *New York Times* for "Bathing Suits of Stocking Silk" boasted that the suit was "so light that you will find yourself glancing down occasionally to reassure yourself that you have not absent-mindedly gone nudist."[51] The clothing advertisement used nudism to refer to the growing popularity of less restrictive and more revealing styles of female fashion in the 1920s and 1930s while also using humor to communicate the importance of covering the body.

Nudists differentiated themselves from these questionable commercial exploitations of the body by shunning audiences and requiring men to be as naked as women during exercise routines. Nudism did not alarm advertisers or Judge Goldstein, if it stood apart from the increasingly popular and morally dubious spectacle of the swimsuit competition. Commercial entrepreneurs in Atlantic City, New Jersey, sought to profit from the more revealing fashion trends when they began the Miss

America Beauty Pageant in the early 1920s. The end-of-summer event relied on the bathing-suit competition, which celebrated the scantily clad adolescent female body, to attract large male audiences.[52] The unwillingness of the beauty pageant's promoters to mute the underlying eroticism of parading young, partially nude women in front of a crowd of ogling men eventually forced the popular end-of-summer event to close in 1928.[53] The absence of men who were present for the primary purpose of viewing the naked female body made it difficult for Judge Goldstein to condemn nudist activities that seemed to extend current fashion trends more than they resembled the commercial spectacle of the bathing-suit competition.

Nudists also built on the popularity of previous physical-training programs that offered health through strenuous activity and specially designed machines and apparatuses. Many of the first nudist meetings occurred in gymnasiums, where health reformers had urged urban dwellers to exercise underused muscles in order to ward off disease, to relax the nervous system, and to strengthen moral behavior.[54] In response to Progressive Era fears that the rapid pace of urbanization caused physical and moral degeneration, educators encouraged men and women to frequent gymnasiums, where they participated in callisthenic routines, used specially designed exercise equipment, or did gymnastics. By the turn of the century, hundreds of gymnasiums affiliated with schools, universities, athletic clubs, hospitals, and various other institutions offered individuals the opportunity to exercise the whole year.[55] Building on this tradition, nudists gathered at gymnasiums, where they tossed the medicine ball, engaged in rigorous callisthenic routines, and participated in exacting swimming exercises. In contrast to previous gymnastic training systems, such as Muscular Christianity, which attempted to correct aberrant sexual behavior through physical fitness, nudists contended that wearing clothes hindered movement and was patently unhygienic in collecting perspiration while exercising. Nudist activities appeared to be an eccentric extension of previous popular physical-training systems.

Even after the Great Depression, the market for displaying the body in swimsuits, onstage, and in books continued to grow. The Miss America Pageant reemerged and drew large audiences in 1935, and burlesque theaters took advantage of falling rent prices to move into Times Square.

Although the Depression had made it difficult for many publishers to stay in business, nudists found a large audience for illustrated texts such as Jan Gay's *On Going Naked* (1932), Maurice Parmelee's *Nudism in Modern Life* (1931), Frances and Mason Merrill's *Among the Nudists* (1931), and the Merrills' subsequent volume *Nudism Comes to America* (1932).[56] While nudist publications still had to contend with censors, the financial crisis of the Great Depression influenced many businesses to embrace the exposure of the body as one of the few remaining profitable ventures still available.

Concurrent with the increasing acceptance of feminine sexual display emerged an effort to regulate public sexuality—especially the display of the body. A day before the Miss America Pageant crowned its first winner in 1921, the local police attempted to arrest a female beachgoer for refusing to wear stockings with her one-piece bathing suit.[57] In New York City, police periodically targeted venues that housed or displayed naked bodies for violating public decency statutes. Burlesques, many of which sought to increase their flagging sales by introducing suggestive striptease acts that teased audiences with dancers brandishing suggestive tights or briefly flashing audiences, often attracted the attention of police in addition to their audiences.[58] Further, Progressive Era bathhouses, many of which functioned as sites for gay men to engage in sexual encounters, occasionally experienced raids from police or vice societies hoping to catch naked men in compromising positions.[59]

When the police received an anonymous complaint that twenty-four men and women had assembled naked in the "Heart of New York City Gymnasium" on Seventh Avenue, they reacted with the seriousness and swiftness as if someone had reported a particularly suggestive burlesque performance or the location of a bathhouse that catered to a homosexual clientéle.[60] To investigate the locked gymnasium, the four policemen climbed up to the roof of an adjacent building and then down a ladder onto the gymnasium's roof, where they peered into the building's skylight. After seeing the seventeen men and seven women entirely nude and engaged in physical exercises, the police then proceeded to "break in the door" and arrested them on "charges of nudity."[61] The police considered the meeting a public indecency that warranted the dramatic raid, despite the nudists' precautions of privacy and seclusion.

In contrast to Chicago's local censorship system, in which voluntary moral reform organizations pressured the police and politicians to act, New York's reliance on the courts as well as the legislature to regulate obscenity provided a forum to evaluate and debate the place of the naked body in urban spaces. Rather than condemn the presence of the naked body as illicit and a symbol of the low morals of immigrants, the New York legal system recognized places and circumstances that allowed for the display of the naked body in public urban spaces. George Chauncey has pointed out that the police who raided bathhouses made sure that they arrested "only the men against whom they had specific evidence of homosexual activity," so as not to further erode public confidence and to avoid the scandal of arresting men for merely bathing in the nude.[62] Burlesque, with its mixture of erotic display and ribald humor, negotiated the boundary between the illicit and the benign, as the courts hesitated to shut down a commercial institution that continued to be profitable in the early years of the Great Depression.[63] Evaluating the decency of several naked men and women exercising in a gymnasium, Judge Goldstein asked the arresting police officer if he observed "anything else going on outside of the setting up of exercises" and if the officers saw anything of an "indecent character by any of the defendants."[64] One police officer simply responded to the judge's question with the statement, "Not outside the nude, no, sir."[65] According to the judge, the officers merely described an exercise class in a normal gymnasium that just happened to be occupied by naked, health-conscious men and women.

The absence of "indecent" behavior represented a critical distinction according to the state laws of New York in 1931. Section 1140a of the penal law stated, "A person who willfully and lewdly exposes his person or the private parts thereof in any public place, is guilty of a misdemeanor."[66] The nudists may have willfully exposed their bodies, but Judge Goldstein did not accept that their naked condition alone constituted a lewd exposure. The prosecution had not offered any evidence that the men and women in the gymnasium exposed their bodies to audiences for a fee, nor did they show that those in attendance engaged in any sexual acts that might be considered inappropriate. Recognizing this omission, the judge wanted to avoid the "whole question of nudity" and "whether it is right or not." While he believed that keeping one's "trunks put on in the gymnasium . . . would serve much better to keep [one's] mind on the gymnastics," he maintained, "I am merely deciding this case on the law as I read it."[67] Since the police officers testified that they had "no sex desires aroused by reason of anything they saw," he granted the defendants' motion to dismiss the charges.[68] This early favorable decision demonstrated the limits of the law and revealed a willingness to differentiate between lewd and decent forms of nakedness.

The effort to prosecute the seventeen men and women arrested for going naked in a New York City gymnasium also tested the legal definitions of public and private space in an urban setting. The prosecution struggled to convince Judge Goldstein that an "actual outraging of public decency occurred."[69] First, the judge noted that the men and women in attendance participated in the evening's activities without voicing any objections.[70] Second, he observed that no non-nudists had attended the event.[71] Nudists did not invite an audience, as the Miss America Pageant did. The men and women in attendance consented to be naked in each other's presence to better their physical and mental health. On that basis, the judge concluded that nudism constituted a private act and should not be considered a public indecency.

The nudist movement's early legal success translated into several favorable reports from the media. A 1933 *Literary Digest* article declared in one of its headlines that nudism constituted an "Educational and Social Force" in the United States.[72] Describing the movement as "one of the observable phenomena rising on the American scene, and occupying a paragraph in the daily record," the article echoed Judge Goldstein's recognition that conceptions of the body were changing rapidly when it observed that "near-nudism is being practiced on practically every beach in the country."[73] The national magazine included a picture of a Victorian woman wearing a bulky bathing suit that covered her shoulders, head, upper arms, legs, and ankles and included the caption "No Nudism in 1890" to illustrate the dramatic changes in dress styles that had occurred in the preceding few decades.[74] The article introduced nudism as an unusual yet harmless reflection of rapidly changing attitudes toward sexuality, the display of the body, and styles of dress. The dramatic emergence of organized nudism in the United States in the 1930s benefited from the popularity of more expressive approaches to sexuality and nudity.

Keystone

NO NUDISM IN 1890

A 1933 *Literary Digest* article titled "Nudism as Educational and Social Force" emphasized the dramatic changes in bathing attire by displaying a woman wearing a Victorian Era bathing suit with the caption "No Nudism in 1890."

The positive reports and depictions of nudism that emerged after Judge Goldstein's early municipal court ruling, however, failed to protect other nudists from arrest and prosecution. On April 3, 1934, two undercover officers, a female and a male, paid one dollar to enter a gymnasium on Broadway Avenue.[75] After seeing several men and women naked, taking a tour of the facilities, and observing the group's exercise routine, the two officers led a raid on the group and arrested Fred Topel, the owner of the gymnasium; Vincent Burke, the director of the Olympian League; and Frank Maniscalco, the exercise instructor.

As the Depression worsened, the economic struggles of men and women strained gender norms and caused city officials to target public expressions of sexuality, such as nudist activities. Throughout the

1930s, men struggled to find jobs, corporations employed women to take advantage of the lower pay scales, and the divorce rate reached unprecedented levels. In this context, the alternative sexualities of gay men represented an intolerable threat that required new laws prohibiting the gathering of homosexuals in restaurants and bars and the banning of homoerotic representations.[76] In New York City, the movement of burlesques theaters into Times Square, combined with the perception that these performances catered to unemployed men, further exacerbated sexual anxieties stemming from the Depression. The lack of a female audience, the unrestrained responses of men to strippers and sexual humor, and the inappropriate gestures made toward women on the streets outside burlesque houses all combined to shift attention to disciplining male sexuality.[77] The gender crisis occurring during the Depression also produced new concerns about sex crime, best exemplified by the sensational arrest and trial of the child murderer and pedophile Alfred Fish in 1934.[78] In response to this apparent decline in public morality, the recently elected Mayor Fiorello LaGuardia promised to clean up New York City and "protect its morals."[79]

In *New York v. Burke*, the prosecutor painted nudists as devious and degenerate threats to the general public, portrayed their activities as a commercial enterprise, and rejected any possibility that nudism might offer therapeutic benefits unrelated to illicit sexuality. He charged Topel, Burke, and Maniscalco with "lewdly exposing their persons," "maintaining a public nuisance," "permitting the use of a Building or portion thereof for a public nuisance," and "Openly Outraging Public Decency."[80] He also accused the defendants of "contriving and wickedly intending" to "debauch and corrupt the morals of persons and to create in their minds inordinate and lustful desires" for their own "lucre and gain."[81]

The prosecutor ignored Goldstein's earlier ruling that nudist activities should be considered private and set out to show that even behind closed doors, the interaction of naked men and women represented a threat to public morality. Vincent Burke wanted to encourage strong attendance to the opening event of "'Nudism Forward' month" in order to demonstrate the strength of nudism in light of the "opposition to the nudist movement." He thought the early spring meeting would provide an "excellent opportunity for those who have not practiced nudism" and suggested that members bring their friends.[82] After stumbling on an open invitation to this meeting, the police decided to investigate its activities. According to the prosecution, no members inquired about the two officers' "relationship," they made no attempt to ask "why these two people, total strangers," wanted to attend the meeting, nor did Burke ask for any references or attempt to gauge the reasons for their interest in nudism.[83] This lack of caution proved that the "meeting was open to all."[84] The prosecution asserted that the gymnasium opened its doors to the "young as well as the old, to the inexperienced as well as the experienced, to the weaker members of society as well as the strong, to those pruriently curious as well as those, who by chance, might be sincerely interested in the movement."[85] Since anyone could easily enter the gymnasium, it constituted a "public place," despite the "fact that the door was closed and locked."[86]

The prosecution also felt that the exercises undertaken at the gym constituted lewd acts. The male and female officers remained too "bashful" to disrobe and participate in the meeting's activities despite the persistent urging of several members in attendance. This did not stop them from staying and observing the exercise routine of the Olympian League.[87] Sitting in chairs, officers Barr and Brady voyeuristically watched as Maniscalco directed the more than a dozen naked men and women to stretch and exercise their bodies. The officers recalled how the instructor asked the participants to "cross their legs over and to raise on their shoulder blades," to "kick their legs back and forth in a sort of scissor stroke," to open and close their legs while they "lay on their backs," and to "stoop over and to touch the tips of their fingers to the toes of their feet."[88] Although on cross-examination, one officer admitted he had not seen any exercises that would be "improper if they had their clothes on,"[89] the prosecution believed that to the normal "bystander," this "exhibition was lewd."[90] The police officer's description of naked men and women crossing and kicking their legs in scissor-like motions while bending over with their breasts exposed recalled the same movements of a performer on a burlesque or cabaret stage. The officers' repeated focus on the motion of the legs rather than exercises that emphasized the upper extremities also revealed their shock at seeing the exercising nudists' genitalia, which even burlesque performers hesitated to display onstage. The prosecution asserted that the potential non-nudist audience would find it sexually arousing and pleaded with the court to recognize the danger that nudist exercise routines posed in a densely populated urban area.

In addition, the prosecution argued that the profit obtained from these gatherings added to the unwholesomeness of the event. Topel testified that he charged Burke five dollars for each Tuesday evening and seven dollars for every Thursday evening that the nudists used his facilities.[91] Burke explained that the monthly dues for the club amounted to four dollars a month for individuals and married couples. He added that members who "cannot afford to pay four dollars at one time" had the option to pay weekly.[92] Twenty members attended the April 3 meeting and paid one dollar to exercise. Nevertheless, the prosecutor thought the Olympian League's profits of fifteen dollars at the height of the Great Depression was "respectable."[93] In 1931, the Minsky chain of New York burlesque houses charged a similar rate of seventy-five cents to one dollar and fifty cents for tickets to a single show.[94] Comparing the costs of nudist meetings and burlesque theaters gained further credence since the latter had prospered during the Depression by appealing to middle-class patrons with increasingly provocative shows that relied heavily on salacious performances culminating in the undressing of female performers. Yet, unlike burlesque audiences that purchased tickets to see a show, nudists paid an admittance fee to participate in exercise routines. Despite this difference, the prosecutor dismissed Burke's claim that the evening's profits contributed to the group's efforts to build a nudist club outside the city's limits.

On June 11, 1934, the Court of Special Sessions, presided over by three judges, convicted Topel, Burke, and Maniscalco on all counts. In contrast to Judge Goldstein's ruling, the three judges saw nudist activities as public, commercial, and lewd. The prosecution emphasized the public accessibility and profits of nudist gatherings in order to argue that nudism represented a clear case of commercial sexual display that resembled the stock burlesque performances that also prospered in the early years of the Great Depression. The majority of judges on the Court of Special Sessions, eager for a way to establish a precedent that could be used to prosecute public sexual display, responded favorably to this conflation and used their sentencing power to show that they would not stand for "that kind of conduct."[95] One judge felt that the defendants should have been fined five hundred dollars or sentenced to thirty days in jail, even though none of the defendants could afford the imposed fine of fifty dollars, in order to demonstrate that efforts to go naked would be "punished."[96] Rather than defining nudism as a harmless sign of the times, the Court of Special Sessions deemed nudist activities a danger to society that needed to be expunged from the city.

The law, however, had not changed to match the rapidly shifting attitudes toward nudism, nudity, and sexual display. One judge dissented based on his interpretation of the law and a continuing recognition that nakedness was not inherently indecent. As in the Goldstein ruling, New York's Section 1140a required that exposure of the body be both willful and lewd to be considered a crime. While no one could deny that the Olympian League participants willfully disrobed, the lewdness of their activities lacked the same certainty. The trial failed to offer any testimony that documented lewd acts, such as sexual contact between men and women, homosexual activity, or salacious performance. Patrolman Barr admitted that the exercises he witnessed resembled those at any other gymnasium. As a result, Justice Frederic Kernochan did not feel that the "law at present" was "sufficiently broad enough to render a conviction on this evidence."[97] The contradictory connotations of the naked body as both healthy and erotic made the nudist activities difficult to prosecute under indecency laws that required explicitly lewd conduct. The dissenting judge went on to assert that gender also played a defining role in establishing the illicit character of the meeting. Just as Suominen assumed that separating men from women would make his sunbathing enclosure equivalent to public municipal baths, the judge reasoned that the event would have gone unnoticed if the group had "one day for men and one for women."[98] According to Judge Kernochan, "Should the Legislature see fit to stop [nudism]," it needed to expand the law to equate all forms of nudity with indecency.[99]

Even though the case threatened to undermine the professionalism that the ACLU sought to build in its formative years and did not involve the defense of political radicals, a number of influential members of the organization felt compelled to appeal the unfavorable ruling from the Court of Special Sessions. According to the historian Leigh Ann Wheeler, select ACLU leaders developed an interest in cases involving the birth control movement, sexual display, and freedom of expression due to their participation in the unconventional bohemian, artistic, and often politically radical communities that surrounded the ACLU's central offices in New York City's Greenwich Village. Figures such as Roger Nash Baldwin, Crystal Eastman, Elmer Rice, and Dorothy Kenyon "partook of the sexual experimentation for which Villagers became famous." In particular, Baldwin, who helped found the ACLU with Eastman, frequently enjoyed going naked while summering at Martha's Vineyard and on weekend trips to his New Jersey farm, Dell Brook. Like nudists, he hoped that going naked casually and naturally with his children would prevent the development of "a false sense of prudery about the body."[100] As part of the ACLU's larger commitment to expanding sexual freedom and expression, Lee Hazen represented Vincent Burke free of charge and approached the pending appeals trial as a "test case."[101] Building on Judge Kernochan's dissent, he appealed the *Burke* verdict to the New York State Supreme Court, citing the lack of willful and lewd exposure required under New York's Section 1140a.

The success of Hazen's appeal depended on the New York courts continuing to take into account the changing social mores of the average person. He pointed out that clothing at beaches had changed considerably over the preceding twenty years; he noted that the New York Supreme Court had just allowed the distribution of James Joyce's controversial *Ulysses* and observed that many individuals appreciated the nude in well-respected art galleries across the city.[102] As a reflection of these changes and developments, Hazen portrayed nudism as a "genuine effort to overcome what [nudists] regard as the physical and psychic handicaps attendant upon the maintenance of a rigid and unwholesome body taboo."[103] With nudists' activities carried out without "ribaldry, licentiousness, obscenity or immorality," he argued that many nudists believed their lifestyle actually led to the "eradication of sex aberrations and eroticism" by eliminating the "disturbing provocations of the partially clad body."[104] In addition, Hazen denied that the Olympian League meeting represented an open and public act. He asserted that his clients performed their acts in the "privacy of a gymnasium."[105] Consequently, "nobody was shocked; nobody's sense of propriety was invaded; nobody's sensibilities were offended."[106] The nudists, he asserted, practiced their "clean and moral pursuit" without violating public space.[107]

On December 24, 1934, the Supreme Court of New York ruled in favor of Burke, Topel, and Maniscalco.[108] The majority of the judges found that Judge Kernochan's original dissent was "based upon a solid foundation."[109] By agreeing with Kernochan's interpretation of the law, the higher court merely confirmed that the New York State statutes did not apply to the peculiarities of nudist activities, though the judges did not find that Kernochan endorsed nudism. The judges acknowledged that the phrasing of the 1140a penal statute that required "lewd" behavior excluded nudists who did not demonstrate any explicit sexual acts other than being naked. The appellate judges felt that changes needed to be made to state policies and statutes in order to resolve the legal questions that emerged around nudist activities.

The McCall Antinudism Bill

Under New York's state-centered censorship regime, antiobscenity activists who objected to the *Burke* decision needed to influence the state legislature to put an end to nudist activities in New York. Three days after the court's decision, Al Smith, the former governor of New York, 1928 Democratic presidential candidate, and well-known Catholic, wrote a letter calling Governor Herbert Lehman's attention to the court's reversal. Speaking for the Catholic Legion of Decency, Smith expressed shock that "anybody could operate a swimming pool in New York where men and women could swim in the one room without clothing."[110] He saw the public tolerance of naked male and female bodies in a gymnasium as an endorsement of sexual contact between the sexes and a complete affront to standards of decency held by the Catholic Church. Smith evoked the safety of children in order to protest the *Burke* ruling, similar to the way antiobscenity activists had used the perceived vulnerability of the child to justify the censorship of birth control information and pornography and the removal of any material relating to sexual knowledge from the postal system. He asserted that it was "senseless" to even "talk about the effect of anything like [nudism] on young people."[111] Offended by the idea of nudism, Smith knew how to navigate the political process and influence New York's state-centered obscenity regime.

The emergence of the Catholic Church as a source of moral authority in American society and reform movements proved politically useful for Smith, whose career had been limited by his Catholic background. For most of his time in politics, Smith drew his support from urban ethnic communities that identified with his Catholicism and anti-Prohibition stance.[112] Smith's inability to appeal to rural Protestant voters in the South, due in large part to his Catholic beliefs, limited his national political ambitions. He failed to win the Democratic presidential nomination in 1924, and after gaining the nomination in 1928, Calvin Coolidge soundly defeated him, despite Smith's support from Franklin and Eleanor Roosevelt. After the election of Roosevelt as president in 1932, Smith had little influence in national politics.

The decline of Protestant antivice societies in the first decades of the twentieth century allowed Smith to use the nudist issue to position himself as a leader of a new democratic antiobscenity coalition while broadening his appeal with voters. The transition to an obscenity regime defined by democratic processes and judged according to the standards of the average person required that antiobscenity proponents build new coalitions that claimed to represent public opinion rather than the interests of elite moral reformers. Stepping into this void, Smith joined forces with an increasingly influential coalition that allied Catholics and Jews striving for respectability and a place in mainstream society with Protestant ministers hoping to continue to regulate public morals.[113] Smith's effort to ban nudism from the state of New York reflected the transition from moral progressive reforms that targeted immigrants to a renewed Catholic-led effort to curb the growing toleration of sexuality and sexual display in magazines, films, and theaters.

Smith pursued his new moral agenda as head of the Catholic Legion of Decency (CLD).[114] The group wielded a great deal of influence in the state and the nation, in part because it enlisted the services of several influential figures. The former mayor of New York City John P. O'Brien and the Reverend Edward Moore, who represented Cardinal Patrick Joseph Hayes on the CLD, became strong allies.[115] Originally organized to "aid in the drive against objectionable films," the CLD, referring to nudism, felt it could not ignore the "latest challenge to the enforcement of decency in reality."[116] After a meeting in Smith's office in the Empire State Building, the CLD dramatically declared that it could not "overlook indecency in substance while condemning it in the shadows."[117] The CLD set out to ban nudism from the state of New York.

The CLD wanted to bar nudism by defining any exposure of the body—whether by a child, among only men or only women, carried out in a private gymnasium, or on a stage—a danger to public morals. The group felt particularly disturbed that the courts found the present penal law inadequate to prevent the "public mingling of naked men and women." The CLD intended to ask the legislature to amend Section 1140a to stop "indecency such as may be practiced under the guise of nudism."[118] In a bill sent to the president of the state senate and the speaker of the assembly, the CLD sought to remove the provision in the statute requiring "lewd" behavior to successfully prosecute a charge of indecency. Instead, it purposed to make it a misdemeanor to be naked in "any place, in the presence of two or more persons of the opposite sex."[119] Aware that one of the defendants in the *Burke* case only rented the venue to the group, the CLD also wanted to make it a crime for any person who "aids or abets any such act, or procures another so to expose his person."[120] It suggested that any owner, manager, lessee, director, promoter, or agent who in "any way hires, leases or permits property 'to be used for any such purposes'" should be prosecuted under this new amendment.[121]

Nudists found it "startling[ly] inconsistent" that the former governor would come out strongly against nudist activities, as many considered Smith a "leader of toleration."[122] Smith had defined his political career by opposing Prohibition and asserting that individuals could not be made moral through legislation. Nudists felt unfairly targeted as a source of indecency since there had been no evidence of sexual performance or indiscretion introduced at the *Burke* trial. In fact, the CLD's unusual deviation from the regulation of indecent films to campaign against nudism caused many nudists to suspect that the group might be "setting itself up as a blue nosed guardian of public morals." However, Edward Moore denied an expanded role for the CLD. Instead he restated the group's original intent to pursue indecent films and maintained that nudism represented a "direct affront" that could not be ignored.[123]

The democratic system of obscenity regulation in New York allowed nudists and their supporters to voice their opposition to the antinudist bill that was sponsored by state senator John T. McCall. The attempt to pass legislation that banned any display of the body disturbed defenders of civil liberties, who had fought for decades to permit the discussion of sex and sexual expression. Not willing to lose these hard-won victories, civil libertarians, including birth control advocates, religious humanists, and anticensorship groups, came to the defense of nudists. At the public hearing for the antinudism bill, the senate and assembly committees sat before a well-attended committee room where opponents "denounced the bill as 'freakish' and 'dangerous' in its implications."[124] Mary Ryskind, who represented the National Council of Freedom from Censorship and spoke out in defense of nudists, argued that politicians such as Smith threatened to undermine New York's system of obscenity regulation. Asserting that the "best judges of obscenity are courts and juries rather than official, politically appointed censors," Ryskind commended the New York court system for fairly evaluating the activities of nudists while also challenging the legitimacy of the bill and Smith's authority. Charles Francis Potter, founder of the First Humanist Society of New York, which included Julian Huxley, John Dewey, Albert Einstein, and Thomas Mann on its board, stated that the bill represented an "infringement on human freedom" and classified the measure in the "same class of freak legislation as anti-evolution bills."[125] He felt the bill would make it "illegal to be natural" and "assumes that a person cannot be moral if he is naked."[126] Another group of non-nudist religious leaders released a statement voicing their support for the "honest and sincere people" who consider nakedness "healthy and natural."[127]

Opponents also presented the antinudist bill as a violation of personal privacy, in order to persuade the legislature, as well as the public, that its passage would adversely impact all the residents of New York and not just the members of a group who enjoyed going naked in gymnasiums. In New York's democratic system of obscenity regulation, both antiobscenity and anticensorship proponents sought to make their arguments on behalf of the average person. While only a small minority practiced or endorsed nudism, the antinudist bill's opponents believed that many New Yorkers would find it troubling that the bill would "pave the way for dangerous invasion[s] of the home by the state."[128] In addition to banning the practice of nudism in "private parks and sanitariums far removed from the public view, where no outsider could possibly be offended," Ryskind argued that the bill constituted an "encroachment on personal freedom and personal privacy which is not in the public interest." In a letter signed by the birth control advocate Mary Ware Dennett, Roger Baldwin (director of the ACLU), and Wilton Barrett (director of the National Board of Review of Motion Pictures), the bill was characterized as a "serious violation of personal privacy."[129] The same coalition that had its roots in Greenwich Village and had fought against the restrictions imposed on birth control and sexual knowledge asserted that the vague and broad antinudist bill had the potential to "punish two brothers and a sister for swimming together without bathing suits," to make it illegal for a mother to bathe her children in her own home or for art classes to use nude models for instruction. Framing opposition to the antinudist bill using the issue of privacy allowed allies of the nudist movement to emphasize the absurdity of the legislation and to claim that they represented the interests of the wider public.

Very few committee members at the hearing took the bill seriously. State senator Elmer Quinn, who presided over the session and stated his distaste of "morbid curiosity-seekers," had to threaten to clear the room after "laughter rose over at some of the opposition oratory."[130] After the meeting concluded, the committee indicated that it would "sound the death-knell of the measure" since its "provisions were too broad."[131] The bill appeared dead from its inception, with no supporters at the meeting, several vocal opponents, and far-reaching legal implications. The New York State legislature apparently did not agree with the Catholic Legion of Decency that going naked represented an immediate public threat that should be outlawed from the state.

The former governor of New York still had a great deal of political clout in Albany. The following month, the bill "unexpectedly came back to life" when Smith amended his proposal to "prevent its application within the home or in any other private place."[132] The effort to frame the antinudist bill as a threat to all New Yorkers' right to privacy proved effective and forced Smith to alter the wording of the bill to win the votes of concerned legislators. Under these new provisions, the Senate and Assembly Codes Committee recommended a favorable vote on the measure. For many legislators, the critical role Smith played in ensuring the bill's survival made it suspect, and opponents argued that the longtime politician did not represent the values of the average person. Assemblyman Oswald Heck of Schenectady, who led the attack on the legislation, asserted that everyone in Albany knew that "there is only one man behind this bill and he is former Governor Smith."[133] As a result, many representatives questioned the motivations behind the influential political figure's commitment to the bill. Assemblyman Jacob Livingston, a Brooklyn Democrat, found a "blue nosed" Smith odd since he had long stated that lawmakers "could not legislate morals into people."[134] Assemblyman Heck went on to speculate that the once "liberal and tolerant" Smith "must have been mingling with some puritan ideas" in his "late years."[135] Pointing out that Tennessee became known as the Monkey State after it passed its infamous antievolution law, Heck lamented "what New York will be called" if Smith's antinudist bill became law.[136] The mixed responses to the antinudist bill, which depended on Smith's political influence for survival, reflected a system of obscenity regulation that judged questionable behavior and materials according to the standards of the average person.

Smith, nevertheless, rallied support for the bill by convincing Democratic assemblymen that the average person associated nudism with commercial sexuality. Many Democrats who supported Smith also supported his bill. Assemblyman Daniel McNamara, a Democrat from Brooklyn, worried that the "present law was insufficient to deal with the practice of nudism."[137] Meanwhile, Mr. Killigrew, the Democratic floor leader, declared the bill an "important piece of legislation."[138] Much of their opposition to nudism rested on misrepresented facts. Killigrew felt that action needed to be taken against nudist camps since he had been "told that some of them admit visitors for $1 to watch inmates perform."[139] He then stated, "If that is true it means that the nudists are not sincere."[140] The assemblyman equated nudist activities with the growing number of burlesque houses that charged a similar entrance fee and often displayed the naked female body for large audiences of men. The legislators ignored the fact that in the *Burke* case, the police officers, who gained entry to the nudist gathering after paying a one-dollar entrance fee, posed as interested nudists and refused several requests by members to disrobe and participate. Legislators assumed that the police officers joined an audience that watched nudist activities rather than acknowledging that all men and women normally attended nudist meetings naked. The additional claims by Smith that the interaction of naked men and women endangered the nation's youth further persuaded the senate to pass the bill 35 to 10,[141] and the assembly "snowed under" the antinudist bill 120 to 11.[142] Nudists now appeared in danger of being banned from the state of New York.

Nudists relied on anticensorship activists to urge Governor Lehman to veto Smith's antinudism bill. The cartoonist Will Johnstone in the *New York World-Telegram*, a liberal New York City newspaper formed in 1931, ridiculed the state legislature with six ridiculous scenarios that might arise under the new law.[143] He mocked moralists who desperately clung to clothes with sketches of a rich man and woman on their way to the opera overly dressed to the point of immobility and with his drawings of animals and statues cloaked with clothes. He also directly defended nudists by drawing them draped in cellophane or writing "taxpayer" across a barrel used to cover a nudist running away from an overly aggressive police officer.

Nudists argued that the bill's support rested with one individual's political ambitions rather than the values of the average person or the majority of New York citizens. Nudist supporters thought that the limited support behind the bill, which they attributed mainly to Smith's political efforts and the Catholic Church's influence, demonstrated that the majority did not share the legislature's assumption that public nudity endangered public morals. One letter to Governor Lehman accused Smith of pursuing the antinudism bill in order to "get his name in the front page" because he "wants to run for President."[144] The letter writer believed that the legislature had no interest in the bill except that the Catholic Church wanted the measure passed. He advised the governor to veto the bill since Smith had no chance of defeating FDR in the next presidential election. Referring to Smith's political career, he asserted, "Once your [sic] out, there is no comeback."[145] A nudist went a step further by attacking Smith's Catholic background, as many southern Protestants had done in past national elections, by pandering to widespread fears that the Vatican planned to infiltrate the nation's government. He asserted that the bill had no chance of passing until the "long arm of the Catholic Church reached out from Rome."[146] The former governor, he speculated, "told the Democrats in the legislature that the anti-nudist bill must be passed in order to save his political face."[147]

Governor Lehman ignored the many calls to veto the bill when he also equated nudist activities with the commercial exploitation of sexuality. Lehman feared the "professional exploitation of nudism for profit," especially after the appeals court ruled in favor of Burke, Topel, and

Maniscalco.[148] On May 1, 1935, he signed the bill into law.[149] The governor explained, "Irrespective of the merits of the sincere practice of nudism," there could be no "justification for some of the so-called nudist gymnasiums or colonies where the general public is admitted on the payment of an admission fee."[150] He maintained that the "failure to enact such a statute at this point would lead to widespread use of exhibitionism for financial gain which our present laws would be ineffective to prevent."[151] Governor Lehman found the arguments made by a few "sincere" nudists unpersuasive in a censorship system that relied on democratic processes and the values of the average person. Rather, he believed that the average New Yorker associated the naked body with commercial sexuality and that permitting nudist activities in New York City posed a serious threat to the remaining boundaries of public decency.

Conclusion

The 1935 passage of the McCall antinudism bill in New York linked nudist activities to the lewd exposure of the body. Nudism no longer referred to naked men and women gathering in a gymnasium for callisthenic exercises. At the 1939 World's Fair held in New York City, Robert Nevins, Samuel J. Friedman, and Harry R. Dash attempted to publicize the Cuban Village by setting up a "Miss Nude of 1939" contest. The men did not have any relationship with the nudist activities that had been banned from the state a few years earlier, but they wanted to use the spectacle of parading two women with their "breasts exposed" to bring in large audiences, just as the Miss America Pageant and burlesques houses had done throughout the Depression. With the antinudism bill in place, however, Sheriff Maurice Fitzgerald did not hesitate to arrest Marge Berk of the Frozen Alive Show and Dolores of the Cuban Village when he "raided" the event. After charging the two women with indecent exposure, a police officer conflated their attempt to exploit female sexual display with nudism—just as the governor had equated nudist meetings with burlesque performances. The officer bragged, "The Nude of the Nudists did not go on as scheduled."[152] The next day, the *New York Times* echoed the officer's equation of nudism with commercial eroticism when it announced the creation of a special investigative commission by New York City's Mayor Fiorello LaGuardia with the headline

"Mayor Puts Curb on Nudist Bakers."[153] The police, the press, and the mayor now used "nudism" to refer to the erotic display of the female body for a paying male audience.

This had not always been the case. Nudism came to the United States at a moment when public attitudes toward sexuality, nudity, and display were shifting away from repression and exhibited an unprecedented willingness to experiment with exposure of the body. The first nudists arrested in New York City saw the charges against them dismissed because the judge recognized the dramatic changes occurring in public attitudes. The movement also received substantial support from immigrants, especially from Germany, who wanted to re-create the *Nacktkultur* they had enjoyed in their homeland. Nevertheless, equating nudism with commercial sex, concerned citizens, progressive reformers, and politicians saw the open interaction of men and women as a direct threat to remaining standards of decency that required their immediate efforts to permanently remove nudists from city beaches, parks, and gymnasiums. Unwelcome in Chicago and New York City, the thousands of American men and women who enjoyed nudism set out in search of a space free of the assumptions and prejudices that made nakedness a crime.

OUT IN THE OPEN

Rural Life, Respectability, and the Nudist Park

After attending a showing of *This Nude World* at the Castle Theater in Chicago, Alois Knapp and his wife, Lorena, decided to convert their two-hundred-acre farm located in Roselawn, Indiana, into a nudist camp. Although they had never dreamed that they would go into the "naked-ness business," the idyllic scenes that they had seen on screen—of nude men and women frolicking naked in Germany, France, and the United States—profoundly affected the couple, who had privately enjoyed "sun-baths for over ten years."[1] Witnessing the unfriendly reception that nudist proposals received in Rogers Park, the couple thought that Lorena's fam-ily farm, located fifty-five miles south of Chicago and surrounded by thick woods, could avoid controversy by providing privacy and thereby creating the perfect weekend escape for men, women, and children to enjoy nature, sunbathing, and fresh air in the nude. They did not worry about the local community since Lorena had spent "practically all of her life among the people of Roselawn."[2] Instead, the middle-aged couple gave "Zoro Nature Park," founded on July 16, 1933, a distinctly mom-and-pop character. In little more than a month, the small group grew to over fifty members. By October, Alois and Lorena limited the membership to two hundred in order to preserve the "community spirit among them."[3]

The history of nudism's emergence in the United States reveals that the sparsely populated rural areas of the United States proved more hospi-table to the fledgling movement than did the major cities. Until recently, migration into the cities in the twentieth century influenced historians of sexuality to focus primarily on the urban landscape. Scholars have ex-amined the many ways urban life expanded or restricted the expression of human sexuality in the United States.[4] This analysis has created a rich and complex narrative and unearthed numerous sources that have given voice and agency to working-class men and women, African Americans, and the gay and lesbian community. Yet it has often overlooked the rural communities surrounding the American metropolis. In *Men Like That*, John Howard addressed this omission by detailing the everyday practice of homosexuality in small towns across rural Mississippi. Analyzing private residences, local swimming holes, truck stops, and diners, he noted how "notions of propriety and transgression . . . shift with the site."[5] As Howard observes, "some sites enabled homosex; others hindered it."[6] Nudists discovered that urban spaces, and the repressive movements and authorities there, accentuated the eroticism of the naked body, while rural locations allowed for multiple and contradictory conceptions of nakedness that could be molded and constructed around nudist ideals. Though nudists still chafed against instances of moral outrage in rural America, the movement defined the wide-open spaces surrounding the metropolis as innocent in order to temper the eroticism of going naked. The American countryside provided the ideal setting for the healthy, nature-oriented, and moral principles of nudism and gave the movement the respectability necessary to develop and prosper in the United States.

Emerging around small towns scattered across the country, many nudist camps gained a fragile hold on respectability by embracing an idealized rural conception of nudity linked closely with nature, health, and recreation. Amid rapid urbanization and the rise of a consumer-oriented economy dominated by giant corporations and white-collar work, many intellectuals, physical-culture promoters, and urban reformers thought that Americans' increasing disconnection with their natural environment threatened to weaken the nation. These anxieties fueled efforts during the Progressive Era to preserve the natural environment through a national park system,[7] to support youth organizations such as the Boy Scouts and Camp Fire Girls,[8] and to encourage the public's fascination with cultural primitivism, as evidenced by the popularity of Edgar Rice Burroughs's *Tarzan of the Apes* books and the curiosity generated by the discovery of Ishi, the "last wild Indian."[9] The rural nudist camp both allowed urban residents to escape the noise, pollution, and stresses of the city and removed the barriers that separated the individual from nature.

The problems that plagued nudists' efforts in Chicago and New York also reemerged in rural Indiana and Michigan. Going naked at a local lake or stream on a hot day remained part of everyday rural life, but the isolation and secrecy of some nudist camps bred suspicion and put the group's moral character in doubt. The interaction of nude men and women in large numbers particularly upset gendered notions of modesty and sexuality. As a result, the same debates over the boundaries of sexual liberalism triggered by nudist activities in the city exploded in small rural towns.

The nudist movement's tenuous claims to respectability depended on blurring the erotic and the therapeutic. Nudists responded to a hostile public and an unfriendly court system by unifying scattered groups across the country into a national organization that worked to reframe nudism in accordance with American moral and ethical values. In addition to stressing the therapeutic value of going naked, nudist leaders such as the Reverend Ilsley Boone and the Reverend Henry Huntington attempted to communicate a moral understanding of nakedness that might make social nudity more palatable to American society. Yet a reticent nudist leadership also embraced the participation and contributions of committed political radicals, sex researchers, and civil libertarians, many of whom participated in the bohemian communities of New York City's Greenwich Village. Maurice Parmelee's *Nudism in Modern Life: The New Gymnosophy* (1931) and Jan Gay's *On Going Naked* (1932) helped introduce nudism to the United States while also critiquing the modern capitalist economy, promoting sexual freedom, and appealing to emerging gay and lesbian communities. The therapeutic, familial, and rural character of nudism sheltered a number of liberal-minded activists who approved of the erotic possibilities of social nudity and advocated for radical change. The coexistence of the erotic and the therapeutic put nudists' claims to respectability at risk. However, it also allowed the movement to build on the natural settings of its camps, to grow its membership, and to sustain a place in American society and culture.

Zoro Nature Park

In 1933, Alois and Lorena Knapp's family farm seemed to provide the perfect setting for Zoro Nature Park, but to make the nudist camp respectable, the couple still needed to manage its grounds, to shape its membership, and to cultivate its relationship with the surrounding community. A lawyer and a writer, respectively, by occupation, Alois and Lorena lacked both extensive experience organizing a nudist camp and financial resources to invest in the project. And still, with only Jan Gay's *On Going Naked* and Francis and Mason Merrill's *Among the Nudists* to guide them, Alois and Lorena set out to establish and operate one of the first active nudist camps in the United States. Even without comprehensive resources or organizing experience, the camp benefited from the unique geographical features of the Midwest and soon stood out as an example for nudists around the country to follow and emulate. Alois and Lorena Knapp projected respectability in managing a rustic setting where members enjoyed the sun, fresh air, and physical activity without disrupting the moral sensibilities of the local community.

In the decades prior to the founding of Zoro Nature Park, the removal of clothing in the wilderness had come to symbolize an idealized and nostalgic relationship with nature. In 1912, Joseph Knowles grabbed headlines in the Boston area when he went naked into the woods to prove that he could survive for two months without relying on any element of civilization.[10] As urbanization took hold on the United States, the obscure woodsman obtained celebrity status across the nation. In 1919, the Boy Scouts of America re-created Knowles's experience in the woods in the first of a series of five books titled *Boy Scouts in the Wilderness*. The two main characters of the novel prove their worth to the scouting movement when they go naked into the wilderness to live off the land for an entire month.[11] Kenneth Webb, one of the main promoters of organized camping in the United States, considered nudity the "fifth freedom" in an Eden-like setting that would grant freedom from fear, want, hunger, and religious persecution.[12] Independent of Progressive Era reforms, in rural small towns throughout the United States, the habit of taking a swim in the local lake or river sans clothing remained so common that the practice occurred across racial lines and doubled as a site for homosexual experimentation.[13] The idea of bringing urban dwellers to Zoro Nature Park may have been unusual, but it was neither unprecedented nor out of line with the rural values of America's small towns.

Far away from Greenwich Village, burlesque theaters, and dance halls, America's rural heartland provided many physical advantages for those who were interested in starting a small nudist colony. The Northeast region saw open spaces disappear and land prices rise. The Midwest, on the other hand, still had plenty of available flat, open, and affordable land near major cities such as Chicago, Columbus, and Detroit. Expecting to spend between $3,000 and $12,000 for fifty or more acres, nudists valued the surrounding areas of middle-sized cities, where the "open country [lay] much closer to the heart of the city and large farm acreages [were] much more readily found."[14] The success of these distant camps depended on the growing availability of the car and the development of an expanding network of roads to transport interested members to far-off locations where they could wander freely without having to worry about neighbors making unflattering insinuations. Using their cars, many families and individuals by the 1930s began visiting national parks, enjoying weekend sojourns into the country, and participating in the affordable practice of "auto-camping."[15] Located close to Chicago, where nudism had recently been suppressed, and just off the interstate highway, Zoro Nature Park was positioned for success.

For Alois and Lorena to link their nudist activities to a desexualized and idealized conception of rural nudity, they needed to create a bucolic environment that lent itself to recreation, relaxation, and health. The woods that circled their farm had the makings of a place where men and women could sunbathe in privacy, participate in athletic activities, and take a break under tall trees that offered reprieve from the sun. Alois, cognizant of the current financial crisis, felt strongly that the natural setting of Zoro Nature Park would provide men and women with the "relaxation and repose" necessary during this "time of stress and strain."[16] The rustic grounds of Zoro Nature Park, which were soon developed into baseball fields, volleyball courts, and "woodsy walks, trails, and bridle paths," satisfied many of the ideal requirements of a nudist camp. Nudists preferred a "sandy loam" that remained "soft and resilient" to the feet, "ample" play fields "well laid out in open meadows," and the proportion between cleared and forested land to be "one to three or one to four."[17] The grounds of nudist camps not only provided a site where members could participate in group recreation but also minimized suspicions concerning sexual activity.

The construction of a swimming pool, a mess hall, and dormitory buildings over the years at Zoro Nature Park further cultivated the recreational character of the grounds and set the bar for nudist camps around the country. The boom in the construction of swimming pools in the 1920s and 1930s[18] and a membership skilled in a wide range of occupations contributed to the development of the camp's built environment. Lacking ample funds, Alois and Lorena relied on the "cooperation of [their] members" to begin the building process "without going into debt."[19] For this reason, the camp recruited members who were willing to "plan and work" and who felt bound to "promote and to protect, to beautify and to love, their nature home which they [could] not help loving."[20] Alois and Lorena claimed that almost "every trade [was] represented among [the] membership," including a minister whom they placed "in charge of [the] playground," a plumber who took "care of [the] sanitation needs," and a carpenter who did the building.[21] Not wanting the camp to "become a commercial project," however, the owners set yearly dues at the affordable rate of ten dollars to pay for the grounds' "taxes and to put in the most essential improvements."[22]

The Lake O' Woods club, also in rural Indiana, followed a similar path of development to Alois and Lorena Knapp's Zoro Nature Park. It began with only a few members who sought out the perfect location to go naked. After an extensive search, they located the vast and secluded grounds near Valparaiso, Indiana, and in 1933 signed a lease in considerable "excess of [their] club income" in the hope that the expansive grounds would attract future members.[23] The property, however, required a "number of safeguards and improvements," and the founding members often had to rely on their own personal funds to maintain the lease agreement.[24] With far fewer members than Zoro Nature Park, the improvements made to the Lake O' Woods grounds created a great deal of debt for the founding members. By 1935, the club had accumulated a $2,500 balance and had not even attracted enough members to cover its operating expenses. On the verge of collapse, the club decided to follow the Knapps' decision to reduce its membership rates to attract more interest. Originally charging a twenty-five-dollar entrance fee and five-dollar monthly dues, the club reduced its rates to ten dollars for admission and three-dollar monthly dues. Soon after this adjustment, membership began to grow.[25] With the club capable of paying down its debt, it now began exploring the possibility of purchasing the grounds.

Rural Indiana was a haven for nudist clubs such as Zoro Nature Park and Lake O' Woods because of the state's laws regarding nudism. The passage of antinudist legislation in New York, as well as the hostile reception that nudism received in Chicago, taught nudist groups to search for states where the laws did not legislate against organized social nudity. In addition to Indiana, nudists identified favorable laws in Arizona, California, Florida, Idaho, Montana, New Jersey, Ohio, Oregon, South Dakota, and Utah. Nudists did not object to indecency statutes that contained specific language intended to regulate behaviors unrelated to the practice of nudism. Several states' indecency laws, for example, required "other persons to be offended or annoyed thereby" for individuals who exposed their genitalia to be guilty of a misdemeanor.[26] Nudists argued that the men and women participating in nudist activities in a camp or at gymnasium could not be convicted of a misdemeanor under this statute because they did so willingly and the participants did not find it offensive or annoying. In addition, nudists approved of Florida's indecency statutes, which strictly forbade the exposure of the body to the opposite sex but included an exception that made nudist camps explicitly legal. The Florida law concluded that this section should not be "construed to prohibit the exposure of such organs or the person in any place provided or set apart for that purpose."[27] Other states only required that nudists keep their activities private and away from the public eye. The Maryland Health Society, for example, became one of the first clubs to be incorporated by a state, with the Maryland state attorney general promising no interference from authorities as long as the organization did not have any "public demonstration," denied admission to "outsiders," and restricted its operations to its "members and their immediate families."[28] The Lake O' Woods club also received a state charter as a nonprofit corporation in Indiana since the state used English common law to define exposure as indecent only if "practiced in a public place."[29] As long as nudist colonies such as Lake O' Woods and Zoro Nature Park carefully constructed their grounds to avoid opening themselves to public view and actively managed their memberships, the risk that a state legislature might change the law to prosecute nudist activities remained low.[30]

Alois and Lorena Knapp actively promoted the respectability of their camp by closely monitoring the selection of new members. To ensure that no undesirable characters infiltrated the group, Alois personally interviewed every application for membership to the camp. In this interview, he asked a "good many questions" to the applicant about his or her "family life, social attachments, religious preferences, and similar matters."[31] To gain access to the camp, applicants needed to prove the sincerity of their interest in nudism by demonstrating their moral character either as a responsible parent, as an active member of a church, or through their occupation. After observing this individual for a day, Alois either invited him or her to become a member or denied the applicant further invitations and did not allow the individual to return. Alois's efforts to ensure that all members demonstrated the necessary maturity and high moral character to be nudists played a critical role in protecting Zoro Nature Park's respectability.

Regulating photography at nudist clubs represented another essential task for club owners hoping to attract new members and to avoid controversy. Frequent camera use at camps, especially by new members, suggested that the photographer might have illicit intentions in visiting the camp. One member who enjoyed photography as a hobby noted the "ever present attitude of suspicion" directed toward a "new member with a camera."[32] Many nudists feared that untrustworthy members might use photos from a nudist camp as personal pornography or even publish them in a disreputable magazine. In addition, many other visitors saw the camera as a threat to the anonymity promised by the distant location of a rural nudist camp. The dissemination of photos taken without a member's permission and then displayed in a newsletter or magazine might ruin careers, relationships, and/or social standing. To protect members' privacy and to guard against the risk that photos might be abused as erotic material, many camps issued "very strict rules governing the use of cameras" or appointed an "official photographer."[33] At Zoro Nature Park, for example, Alois forbade photography that did not have the consent of all individuals in the photo.[34]

Alois and Lorena felt that the camp's long-term success also depended on maintaining a strong relationship with the surrounding local community of Roselawn, Indiana. Even though the local residents knew that nudism was being practiced at the camp, they did not oppose the group since it attracted customers to local businesses.[35] Rather than assuming local hostility and trying to hide, Zoro Nature Park integrated itself into the Roselawn community and avoided the raids and moral outrage that exploded in Chicago and New York City.

Other rural nudist camps also made a conscious effort to reach out to surrounding communities. Hobart Glassey, founder of Elysia, a nudist park located nearly forty miles outside Los Angeles near Lake Elsinore in the Cleveland National Forest and surrounded by "conservative farmers from Iowa," recommended that camp owners establish strong relationships with the community and local authorities.[36] Glassey made it a point to announce the opening of his camp to the local newspapers. He established an open dialogue with a hostile attorney general, and he made financial contributions to local organizations.[37] He also aggressively sought to shape the public's opinion of nudism and won invitations to speak at the Lions Club in Elsinore and Riverside, the Los Angeles Elks, and the San Bernardino Twenty Thirty Club. Glassey eventually came to consider the "townspeople . . . uniformly well disposed and cordial" and felt that he had made the "position of Elysia secure in the community."[38] The operators of Zoro Nature Park, Lake O' Woods, and Elysia all understood that an open and friendly relationship with the local community would add to the security of their camps' future.

The Sun Sports League

The Sun Sports League in Allegan, Michigan, in contrast to these camps, failed to create friendly ties with the community; and within a year the camp was raided by local police. Fred Ring, a Kalamazoo dance instructor, and his wife, Ophelia, thought they had found the perfect location for their nudist camp. Located two miles away from the nearest highway and surrounded by thick woods, the members of the Sun Sports League never expected any problems with the local authorities. Nevertheless, on Labor Day, September 4, 1933, Mary Angier, the sixty-year-old owner of an adjacent lot, led the town sheriff, Fred Miller, two deputies disguised as fishermen, and the town prosecutor over a steep hill to raid twenty unsuspecting naked men, women, and children. The sheriff then arrested Fred and Ophelia and nineteen additional members on charges of indecent exposure. Although isolated in the rural backcountry of Michigan, Fred Ring's camp, unlike Zoro Nature Park, Lake O' Woods, and Elysia, failed to ingratiate itself with local residents and struggled to mold to its environment. This left the Sun Sports League vulnerable to suggestive newspaper coverage and accusations of sexual impropriety from local authorities.

The Ring family and the members of the Sun Sports League searched for an isolated camp location that would avoid conflict and controversy;

they had no intention of offending their neighbors. Most of the camp's membership made the long trip to Michigan specifically to avoid the risks that came with going naked in dense urban spaces. Edward Murray, a Chicago man who visited the camp to help his "high blood pressure," stated that he did not know of any places in Chicago where he could "take off clothes."[39] He added that his neighbor "would object" if he disrobed in his backyard. In order to "test [nudism] out," he and his wife traveled to the camp, where he paid fifty cents for the "privilege of taking sun baths, nothing else."[40] Several other members arrested at the club also resided in Chicago. Of the nineteen people who gave their names and addresses the day of the raid, eleven listed Chicago residences, while four others, the Ring family, gave Kalamazoo, Michigan, as their place of residence.[41]

The failed attempts of Arne Suominen to establish an enclosure for nude sunbathing in Chicago forced nudists there to look to the countryside to continue practicing nudism. The moral outrage that greeted attempts to establish nudism in Rogers Park and in the New York State legislature, however, also emerged in the small town of Allegan, Michigan. Mary Angier had recently moved from Chicago, where she had done a "great deal of welfare work." She was an active reformer, and her husband worried that she would try to "run the town" when they retired to Allegan.[42] Sure enough, "much disturbed by the noise" and "afraid of fire," she began "wondering what was going on up there."[43] But she made it clear that she did not really care about fire, noise, or even trespassing. She simply did not "consider people who strip themselves naked in a community like that as the right kind of people."[44] For the retired welfare worker, it was the "idea" of them living in "absolute nudity" that did not "appear . . . to be the right thing."[45]

The partial visibility of the grounds to outsiders made the Sun Sports League vulnerable. Ring knew that Mary Angier's proximity to his property and the views through the surrounding vegetation put him at risk. He offered to buy her land and compensate her for building a dock on her property, and he began planting evergreens along the bank of the creek to block potential views into the camp.[46] Ring was unable to follow through with these attempts, and Mary, along with the prosecuting attorney and the town sheriff, stood on the branch of a fallen tree to look over at the adjacent lot, where they saw the camps' residents in the nude.[47] At the ensuing trial, Mary and the sheriff testified that they could see naked men and women along a sandy dirt road leading into the camp grounds and around a small creek at the edge of her property.[48] The sanctuary that Fred and Ophelia Ring had envisioned for their nudist activities had been jeopardized.

Scandal stories, inspired by incidents such as the raid of the Sun Sports League, provided national and local newspapers with the opportunity to publicly comment on otherwise hidden or taboo behaviors.[49] The trial of Fred Ring featured prominently in the *Chicago Tribune* and several Michigan daily newspapers and even in the more distant *Washington Post*, which ran the headline "Court Battle in Nudist Camp Case Promised." The *Los Angeles Times* ran a front-page article with the header "Nudist Colony Heads into Court."[50] Newspaper coverage of sex scandals, Lisa Duggan has argued, create moments for "public voyeurism and intervention" because they represent "violations of . . . respectable normalcy." She asserts that these incidents allowed newspapers to establish and reinforce public expectations of normal behavior through "moral lessons" while also providing audiences with the "subversive pleasure" of seeing that "life was not always what it seemed beneath the patina of bourgeois respectability."[51] Through the exhibition of the Ring trial, the national press presented the wearing of clothes as expected, decent, and, if violated, worthy of intervention. The reporting of the Ring trial came replete with numerous naked pictures of the defendants, key witnesses, and the grounds of the Sun Sports League. The spectacle both reinforced the appropriateness of wearing clothes and fed the public's appetite for sexual scandal.

The images that brought the Ring trial to life gave newspaper readers permission to stand in judgment of the unsavory secrets of the seemingly wholesome Ring family while also looking at suggestive photos and following its pornographic details. The *Chicago Tribune* recognized that readers might feel uncomfortable with the subject matter of the trial, and to allay these anxieties, the daily paper included images that would sanction readers' interest in the scandal. In recording the opening day of the trial, the *Chicago Tribune* juxtaposed a picture of the young Ring family next to a scene that included a "throng of spectators, most of them men with gray or thinning hair" and "fewer than a dozen women, most of them bespectacled and elderly." To further comfort readers, the caption below the latter image read, "Eager crowd listens to the testimony in Michigan Nudist Trial." The *Tribune* also included a close-up portrait of a spectacled, tight-lipped, gray-haired Mary Angier displaying her respectability and middle-class status with a fur coat and beret. The photo of a moral reformer alongside a courtroom audience of elderly local residents, who "nudged each other gently" and "sat forward" with their "hands cupped behind ears," allowed audiences to borrow the moral authority of an aging generation of antiobscenity activists who stood in opposition to the increasing acceptance of sexual display while still consuming the trial's scintillating details.[52] Ironically, efforts to regulate obscenity—from Anthony Comstock's battles with Victoria Woodall to the trial of Mary Ware Dennett in 1928 (and in the many confrontations with Margaret Sanger)—often resulted in the greater publicizing of sex via a scandal-driven media.[53] The photo of Fred Ring wearing a suit and embraced lovingly by his smiling teenage daughter and wife in a "high necked sports dress and brown felt hat" titillated readers' interest further by suggesting that hidden beneath the image of the respectable American family lay sordid secrets requiring public intervention.[54]

The pictures displaying the grounds of the Sun Sports League provided a stark contrast with everyday life and enabled readers to enjoy the "sensual pleasures" that came with escaping accepted social norms. To satisfy the curiosity of readers, many of whom were likely unaware of the growing network of rural nudist clubs, the *Chicago Tribune* recreated the setting of the raid through a series of pictures of the Sun Sports League. The newspaper highlighted nudism's radical departure from modern urban life by contrasting an image of distant nudists wandering naked with a picture of the jury fully clothed and immersed in the camp's dense vegetation. Other images left it to the readers' imagination to determine what infidelities might have occurred on the rustic grounds. One photo of a small shack used for changing suggested that the camp provided just enough privacy for members to engage in possible sexual trysts. In another photo, the newspaper encouraged the reader to imagine the naked bodies of nudists showering under makeshift bathing facilities that consisted of elevated barrels filled with water. Although the *Chicago Tribune* stopped short of featuring close-up images of naked bodies, it relied heavily on suggestion to illustrate the prosecution's arguments that nudist camps functioned as a site for illicit sexual behavior.

The Ring trial created another battleground in the long-running debate over the boundaries of decency and indecency in the United States. After dismissing the charges against the other nineteen members arrested at the camp, the state prosecutors used Section 335 of the Michigan Penal Code to charge Fred and Ophelia Ring with "lewd and lascivious cohabitation, gross lewdness, and indecent exposure."[55] Unlike New York's antinudist legislation, the Michigan statute did not require the exposure of the body to be lewd, and it failed to specify if those who were present at the time of the exposure needed to claim distress or outrage. It stated that "any man or woman, married or unmarried, who shall be guilty of open and gross lewdness and lascivious behavior or shall designedly make any open or indecent or obscene exposure of his or her person, or of the person of another, shall be guilty of a misdemeanor." The subjective terms of the law—"open," "indecent," and "designedly"—left it unclear what constituted illegal behavior and failed to differentiate public from private.[56] In fact, the vagueness of Section 335 of the Michigan Penal Code made it potentially illegal for a husband and wife to undress in front of each other or their children in the privacy of their own home.

As in the debates over the antinudist legislation in New York, the arguments of the defense and the prosecution at the Ring trial focused on the issue of privacy. The attorneys representing Fred Ring maintained that he and his wife practiced nakedness for their mental and physical health far away from the public eye and on their own private property.[57] The issue of privacy allowed Ring to present the raid on his camp as a threat to the rights of all Michigan residents—not just those practicing nudism. In the city, police raided abortion clinics and gay bathhouses and bars to humiliate and intimidate clients, patients, and patrons who frequented these spaces.[58] Feminists, joined by the ACLU, often framed their attempts to win legal protection for birth control and abortion in terms of a family's, a patient's, or a doctor's right to privacy.[59] This shifted courts' focus away from a single woman's morality to a discussion of what any individual should have the right to do or see. Although this legal approach did not yield tangible results until the Supreme Court's 1965 ruling in *Griswold v. Connecticut*, Ring's attorney, Carl Hoffman, attempted to suppress the sheriff's testimony because the sheriff's actions abrogated Ring's Fourth Amendment rights, the privileges of private property, not to mention the defendant's dignity. Allowing the sheriff's testimony, Hoffman argued, permitted an officer, "whatever [his] motives may be," to "force his way into a home, into the private bedroom of a man and there, if he sees men and women naked," to arrest and then convict them on the basis of this wrongfully obtained evidence. Hoffman felt the state had no right to convict Ring for exposing himself "on his own property, to those to whom his conduct is not offensive, [and] for no ill purpose."[60]

In support of a defense built on the right to privacy, Hoffman pleaded with the court to allow the jury to visit the camp as evidence of its isolated locale, far away from public view. The judge asserted, however, that the camp's location was irrelevant, seeing as it only mattered that Ring exposed himself to other men, women, and children.[61] Hoffman replied that the jury had to understand the "circumstances, the place, the purposes" to determine the intent behind the exposure. He asserted that "whether it was a camp, a hospital, or a public square . . . the purpose for which [a space] was made" determined the decency or indecency of public exposure.[62] For Ring, spaces open to individuals to visit and see— such as the town square—constituted a public space where naked bodies should not be exposed or displayed. Other sites that served a specific purpose, especially a health-related one, and did not invite observation, such as a physician's office in a hospital *or* a nudist camp, should be classified as private. Hoffman argued that allowing the jury to see the seclusion of the camp, specifically its distance from the adjacent road and the density of the vegetation, might help them decide if the nudist camp constituted a public or private space. The judge reluctantly gave in to Hoffman's arguments and allowed the jury to visit the infamous camp site.

The rest of Fred Ring's defense depended on showing that the lifestyle and activities of the Sun Sports League served the "purpose of improving the health" of members, treating disease, and "improving their mental condition, their morality."[63] To these ends, the defense began by calling Dr. John R. C. Carter, a practicing physician since 1902, who had made a "special study of the effect of sunlight and air on the human body and on the mind." Carter was also the official epidemiologist for the Michigan Department of Health, and over the preceding ten years, had traveled throughout the United States, Canada, Europe, and even

North Africa to further his research.[64] The judge, however, quickly ruled that the testimony should not be allowed since the expert did not visit the Sun Sports League and could only speak in general regarding the effect of the "sun's rays on health."[65] The judge explained that he would only allow the "medical testimony" if it addressed the "beneficial effect of a man being naked in the presence of women."[66] The court then added that even if the sun did benefit individual members' health, that still would not "excuse the promiscuous exposure of the nude, naked person to members of the opposite sex."[67] The court assumed that the interaction of naked male and female bodies necessarily entailed sexual activity. According to the judge, the immodesty of bringing naked men and women together overshadowed any health benefits claimed by the defendants at trial and negated their right to privacy.

The arguments made against Fred Ring by the prosecution reflected an unwillingness to accept the emergence of sexual liberalism and an approach to moral regulation that depended less on suppression and more on education and access to sexual knowledge. Ring testified that the Sun Sports League guarded against illicit desires and behaviors by allowing children to view naked bodies. He believed that young women had a "great desire to know just what the male sex looked like" and that denying this curiosity created a greater interest in sex.[68] Ring also assumed the inherent innocence and purity of the family, and he used his own daughters, a seventeen-year-old and a young child, as an example of the moral benefits of sexual liberalism. Ignoring the possibility of intergenerational sex, Ring asserted that his young children "didn't care anything" about the opposite sex after they had the "opportunity to see [men] whenever they wanted."[69] The sheriff and the prosecutor, however, clung to a nineteenth-century approach to moral regulation that depended on suppression to protect the household from immorality. The sheriff considered Ring's acceptance of his daughter's sexual curiosity a radical departure from "anything about morals as [he] understood them."[70] Despite the admission of almost all the witnesses that they did not see "any acts of immorality," the prosecution's rejection of the values of sexual liberalism led to accusations of illicit behavior and sexual impropriety.[71]

The sheriff's testimony proved controversial and dramatic, as he had originally chosen not to include a disputed incident in his first appearance on the stand. Sheriff Miller reluctantly testified that in the moments before he raided the camp, he had witnessed the illicit actions of a male and female nudist "half-way down the bank."[72] The sheriff recalled that he saw a woman walk down from the top of a bank, where a man "came out of the bushes" about a third of the way down and then "took his hand and felt of her private parts."[73] The couple then "turned out and went over in the bushes."[74] The reason for this original omission remained unclear. The *Chicago Tribune*'s detailed description of the sheriff's testimony suggested his unease in recalling the events of the raid on such a public stage. In chronicling his "embarrassed recital," the newspaper noted his "glumly" demeanor and the way his body "halted here and shifted uneasily, . . . eyes on the floor."[75] However, the newspaper's description of the prosecutor's appearance—"a youngish man whose pink cheeks, possibly heightened in color by the necessity of urging the reluctant sheriff on," and whose "dry nasal voice took on a rasping quality" during the trial—suggested that the young state attorney may have been overzealous in such a highly publicized case.[76] Perhaps, enjoying the media attention, the young prosecutor pressured the sheriff to elaborate on his testimony to ensure a dramatic victory. With Fred Ring watching the testimony with an "expression of hurt astonishment," Hoffman immediately began to challenge what he sardonically labeled the prosecution's "ace in the whole."[77] On cross-examination, the sheriff admitted that he hesitated in "bringing that up" because he did not want to discuss sex so publicly and explained that he decided to testify about the incident only after the prosecutor told him that he "ought to tell it, explain it" to the court.[78] Although it remained uncertain if the incident actually transpired the day of the raid, it proved that the visibility of the grounds made the camp vulnerable to accusations of sexual impropriety.

The prosecution used the Ring trial to reject the values of sexual liberalism. The prosecutor found it particularly disturbing that Ring "exposed himself naked" in the "presence of his wife and daughters and other men, women, and children assembled" at the camp.[79] He found little credence in the belief that access to sexual knowledge and experience might lessen illicit desires and behaviors. He also remained skeptical that the innocence and purity of the family insulated the camp from indecency. Since Ring exposed himself "not only in camp but on adjoining land," the prosecutor concluded his case by declaring "organized nakedness" to be about the "exploitation of sex."[80] The visibility of the camp to non-nudists allowed the prosecution to equate the activities of the Sun Sports League with the burlesque shows that reformers campaigned against in New York City and Chicago. A stand against nudism went beyond regulating questionable theatrical performances, though. As for nudist opponents in the city, it represented the last line of defense for appropriate behavior between the sexes. Implying that the lack of clothing at a nudist camp led to random acts of sexual intercourse, the prosecutor declared the open social interaction of men and women in the nude to be a "reversion to the animal state." He then expressed concern that Ring "advertised for members to join in this dangerous fad" and asserted that the movement represented a "menace to society, and especially to the peaceable and law abiding people of Allegan County."[81] Any association with nature, health, and morality that Fred and Ophelia Ring hoped to benefit from was lost when they upset traditional notions of modesty by visibly bringing naked men and women together in the same space.

The prosecution's effort to present nudism as another indecent sexual perversion proved far more persuasive than Fred Ring's defense of an individual's right to privacy. On November 18, 1933, Judge Fred T. Miles sentenced Ring to sixty days in the county jail and fined him $300 plus court costs of $53.79. When the judge issued his sentence, he defended the town of Allegan, Michigan, by chastising Ring for entering a "quiet, decent, and law abiding community" where he undoubtedly "shock[ed] everybody's sense of decency." By imposing this strict sentence, he hoped to produce a public reaction that would prevent a person, "be he ever so degenerate," from attempting to follow Ring's example.[82] On June 20, 1934, after all of Fred Ring's appeals had run their course, Ophelia, in a separate legal proceeding independent of her husband's trial, pleaded guilty to indecent exposure and received two years probation.[83]

The International Nudist Conference

After unfavorable trials and legislation in New York City, Chicago, and Allegan, Michigan, nudists realized the need for a national organization that could give voice to the movement's ideals and activities, positively shape American conceptions of nudism, and provide legal protection for its network of camps. Until the spring of 1933, nudists lacked such an organization. Although Kurt Barthal, a German immigrant who had practiced *Nacktkultur* in Europe, founded the American League for Physical Culture in 1929, most nudist activities continued to depend mostly on the efforts of isolated individuals, couples, and groups. This left nudists vulnerable to raids, sensational press coverage, and antiobscenity activists who wanted to use nudism to fight the rapidly expanding tolerance of sexual expression. Further limiting the effectiveness of Barthal's American League for Physical Culture was its status as a "foreign born importation."[84] Hoping that the group would "become American," Barthal selected the Reverend Ilsley Boone as vice president in 1931.[85] Boone appeared to be the perfect choice to reshape nudism's image to reflect American moral and cultural values. He had graduated from Brown University as an ordained Baptist minister, was a married man with children, and was "an accomplished orator."[86] Over the next decade, Rev. Boone crafted nudist principles and ideals around the values of health, morality, and psychological well-being in an effort to bring much-needed respectability to the still-obscure social movement.

In 1933, Boone broke away from Barthal's organization to found the International Nudist Council (INC) in order to address the problems impeding nudism's development in the United States. Aware of the uncoordinated efforts of nudists across the country, Boone wanted the INC to provide a forum that "place[d] the experience of each group at the disposal of all."[87] To do this, Boone established an inclusive organizational structure that accepted active "groups" and allowed "cooperative" memberships for individuals who lived in areas that lacked an active local association.[88] The INC also sought to counter the scandals involving nudism by actively influencing the "formation of an informed and understanding public opinion" on the physical and mental benefits of going naked.[89] Finally, the INC pledged to provide aid to resolve the "legal or legislative problems" that might arise with local authorities and the courts.[90]

The INC set out to accomplish these goals, in large part, through the monthly publication and distribution of the *Nudist*, which began its publication in May 1933. Boone designed the *Nudist* as a resource for organizational news, as a forum for members to communicate with one another across the United States, and as a medium through which the movement might shape the public's impression of nudism. A variety of articles, editorials, and letters to the editor advertised the movement's growing network of rural camps and instructed readers about nudist ideals and principles. The large, glossy pages that displayed numerous photos of naked men, women, and children enjoying the sun, light, and air at camps scattered around the country also appealed to a wider audience that consumed the magazine as a form of pornography. The distribution of the magazine through the mail and on the newsstands in many cities allowed the publication to profit from readers who wanted to view naked bodies as erotica. The *Nudist* achieved success as a source for sexual arousal while also publicizing nudism's goal of creating a "healthy mind in a healthy body."[91]

The strong emphasis on health in nudism caused many journalists to dismiss the movement as another cult or fad. "Doctors Call Nudism Loony," a *Chicago Tribune* headline declared, "Warn Cultists to Don Bathing Suits to Resist Sun, Citing the Neanderthaler's Hairy Hide." The reference to cavemen and the declaration that the movement was "loony" portrayed nudism as reminiscent of animal behavior and therefore irrational. In the featured Sunday-magazine article, a prominent doctor advised health enthusiasts to "get enough sun but not too much" since "one extreme can be just as bad as another."[92] Addressing the "psychological influence of going nude," he suggested readers "follow tradition and common sense, and stick to clothing" until society reached a "higher plane of morality."[93] Gretta Palmer, in the *Commentator*, equated nudists with "addicts of Yogi breathing exercises [who] almost inevitably let their beards grow," "anti-vivisection groups [that] overlap with opponents of vaccination," the "Live Food fan, who eats turnips raw," and the "practicing numerologist." She mockingly lamented that "no American . . . can join one cult and call it a day."[94] Similarly, Anthony Turano, in the *American Mercury*, labeled nudists as "escapist[s]" and dismissed their "new faith" as "neurotic psychology."[95] To prosper in the United States, nudism would have to overcome intensely critical scrutiny in the popular press.

Skeptical journalists and critical medical professionals interpreted the health claims of nudism as another one of the many drugless healing systems emerging in the early twentieth century. Natural healing approaches such as naturopathy resonated with a public that was unsatisfied with the harsh and ineffective medicines prescribed by poorly trained doctors. They also appealed to a public that was anxious about the ill effects of an increasingly urban society and the growth of white-collar professions that separated middle-class men and women from the natural environment. Naturopaths believed that all diseases originated from within the body and that nature, rather than drugs, needed to be harnessed to restore health. According to James Whorton, this amounted to a "therapeutic universalism" that included "a virtual infinity of healing agents" such as diet, exercise programs, massage, sunbathing, and herbal treatments.[96] The methods of naturopathy overlapped with the goals of nudism. At Yungborn, a naturopathic health resort located in New Jersey's Ramapo Mountains, guests went for long hikes in the mountains and then separated into sex-segregated groups, disrobed, took a swim in a lake, and finished by sunbathing in the nude. By the early 1930s, almost a dozen naturopathic schools awarded degrees, numerous health resorts operated across the country, and journals espousing the group's natural healing principles proliferated on magazine stands. Bernarr Macfadden, the popular health reformer who pushed the boundaries of acceptable display in his physical-fitness and bodybuilding magazines and books, frequently promoted the naturopathic message as well. Physicians, however, considered naturopathy a "medical cess-pool" that was nothing more than a "cult [with] no basic idea but to be rather a nature-cure hodgepodge."[97] Even though naturopathy proved popular with the public and endorsed nudity as a therapeutic experience, it also threatened to further marginalize nudism as another cult.

Nudists felt that the scientific methods and clinical practice of physicians and medicine would give credibility to the movement.[98] The emerging field of heliotherapy, in the first decades of the twentieth century especially, validated the natural healing approaches of American nudism. In Europe and the United States, heliotherapists designed therapeutic strategies that dictated how patients exposed their body to the sun to cure diseases such as tuberculosis as well as skin lesions and rashes. In many ways, heliotherapy applied scientific and clinical approaches to customs and traditions that had long used the sun and fresh air as a natural disinfectant. Throughout the nineteenth century, according to the historian Nancy Tomes, doctors and public health reformers encouraged families to build homes in sunny spots and to air out the dirty laundry to eliminate diseases and frequently advised patients to visit warm, sunny locales to recuperate from illnesses such as tuberculosis that many physicians attributed to darkness, poor ventilation, and damp spaces.[99] In the twentieth century, the acceptance of swimming pools paralleled a surge in the popularity of suntanning in the mid-1920s. Previously, tanned skin had been associated with field labor, but with the growing popularity of outdoor recreation, it began to communicate youth, health, and beauty, while pale, white skin signaled factory labor. The well-established association of the sun and fresh air with health represented a boon to heliotherapy and allowed nudism to build on its success.

By the 1920s, Dr. Augustus Rollier had established his "air cure" clinic in the Swiss Alps, which drew the attention of the wider medical community to the benefits of heliotherapy. There, Rollier broke the body down into zones and designed an exact therapeutic procedure that directed his patients to expose their entire bodies to the sun and fresh air. Each zone, beginning with the feet, would be exposed to the sun on the first day for three short intervals of five minutes. The next day, the doctor exposed the legs using the same short five-minute intervals, while the patient's feet remained uncovered for three ten-minute periods. By the fifth day, when the doctor unveiled the thorax, the whole body lay exposed to the sun. After the fifteenth day of treatment, the entire body could remain uncovered for a period of three or four hours. In 1928, a *New York Times* article praised Rollier's clinic as the "mecca for those suffering from tuberculosis of the skin, bones and joints" and mentioned that many physicians believed that it was "destined to become one of the landmarks of modern medicine."[100]

American nudists made an effort to embrace the clinical methods and precautions of heliotherapy. Far removed from the physician's office or the grounds of a sanitarium, nudists still considered Rollier an "apostle of a new therapy."[101] They felt that his willingness to use surgery "whenever necessary," the presence of "orthopedic apparatus of the most modern type" in his clinic, his reliance on "diet, massage, and appropriate medication," and his "fractional method" proved that he was "not a faddist."[102] They also agreed that therapeutic nudity "must be used intelligently and with discretion."[103] Articles in the *Nudist* warned sunbathers to avoid the midday sun since its heat rays "enervate, destroy our body cells, promote fever, and therefore are devitalizing."[104] They added that "excessive sun tanning may be the means of seriously injuring the skin."[105] Nudists promoted a moderate approach to nude sunbathing by suggesting that neophytes disrobe for half an hour to start and then increase the time of exposure to an hour as they built up their tolerance. They also felt "alternating day by day" between the chest and back would leave the sunbather "invigorated, feeling fine, and strong."[106] The absence of a trained physician did not stop nudists from implementing regimented approaches to sunbathing that were designed to limit injuries while increasing the therapeutic benefits of going naked.

The messages of health, professionalism, and recreation that began to define nudism reached film audiences through the 1933 release of *Elysia*. One of nudism's earliest movies, its format, content, and style resembled early exploitation films that used the narrative of health and medicine to offer audiences the spectacle of sex or nudity.[107] The genre of exploitation films, according to the film historian Eric Schaefer, developed from "two of the hallmarks of progressivism—exposé and education."[108] Small, struggling film studios that were looking to make quick profits exploited the early efforts of Progressive Era reformers to inform audiences about the dangers of social evils such as venereal disease or prostitution through the exhibition of detailed and graphic exposés. *Elysia*, named after the nudist park founded by Hobart Glassey just outside Los Angeles, chronicled a fictional reporter's efforts to investigate the headline-grabbing nudist phenomenon. After briefly visiting a bookstore and inquiring about the movement, the reporter is referred to a "Dr. King" for more information. Imparting respectability and paternal authority, the elderly physician, who wears a formal suit and sits in an ornate and spacious office, introduces nudism through the ancient Greek figures of Herodotus and Hippocrates. He continues his introduction to nudism by showing an anthropological-documentary-style collection of film clips exhibiting the "fine physical attributes" of the exotic naked bodies of "dark Africa." Nudism provided an ideal premise for an exploitation film.[109]

Elysia made a case for American nudism through its capacity as a legitimate health measure and as an answer to the racial weaknesses of modern Depression Era society. In the 1920s, Margaret Mead's *Coming of Age in Samoa* (1928), along with the release of Robert Flaherty's early ethnographic films *Nanook of the North* (1922) and *Moana* (1926), greatly increased the public's interest in fieldwork-based ethnography. After the stock market crash of 1929, it also gave rise to a genre of exotic exploitation films that offered "images of a way of life unconstrained by pressures of the modern consumer economy."[110] Documentary-style films set in the jungle or other exotic locales offered scenes of plenty, a sexual utopia with beautiful, half-naked women available for the taking. Further, the display of the abject black primitive reinforced the self-esteem of white workers. Similarly, in *Elysia*, the character of Dr. King promised audiences that the "exposure of the body to the sun was absolutely necessary to recuperate and build up the flesh" and critical to the "success of the civilized race."[111] To show the benefits of heliotherapy and nudism, he exhibited several short travelogues with naked nonwhite men, women, and children dancing, swimming, and working in the fields. The film echoed previous nudist books and magazines that explained how the practice of nudism strengthened the race since the removal of clothing exposed the weak and diseased while also empowering men and women to select mates with strong and healthy bodies.

American nudism repeated the eugenic rhetoric popular in the United States since the beginning of the twentieth century. The rise of National Socialism in Germany in 1933 gave voice to racists within the nudist movement, such as Richard Ungewitter, Heinrich Pudor, and Hans Suren, who had long participated in nationalist strains of nudism but now experienced greater prominence under an ideology of National Socialism; for them, nudity was another way to promote Aryan racial purity. In the United States, most nudists sought to distance the movement from its German origins and the unpopular Nazi ideology. Many, however, still subscribed to eugenic racial ideology. Just as the psychologist G. Stanley Hall had once sought to reverse the effects of overcivilization by urging white, middle-class children to behave like savages, so too did the actor playing Dr. King in *Elysia* when he argued that men and women should adopt "strictly natural measures" that gave primitive bodies the "muscular character of a thoroughbred race horse or perhaps a jungle animal."[112] Offering white men physical strength, virility, and triumph over a failed consumer society, the film relied on the same eugenic tropes that Gail Bederman argues defined white, middle-class manhood in the first part of the twentieth century.[113] Dr. King promised mostly white, male audiences that abandoning the "unhealthy garments" worn "for the sake of . . . custom or convention" would build the necessary strength to "outdo the savage at any sort of game, pastime, sport or fight the savage might purpose."[114] Through the presentation of exotic peoples as racial inferiors but also as superior physical specimens, the film used the fears of overcivilization and race suicide to make a case for the therapeutic values of American nudism.

The reliance on medical authority persisted throughout the film with the continuing screen presence of Dr. King. Leaving the physician's office, the film exhibits the camp's physical distance from the city and social convention through a prolonged transition to the grounds of Elysia. The reporter, along with the audience, is transported by Dr. King's secretary, via a long, twisting ride in a convertible, through the San Bernardino Mountains. The next day, the doctor graciously joins the skeptical reporter and disrobes, giving his guest the courage to also go without clothes. He then gives the reporter and the audience a tour of the facilities, all the while providing therapeutic justifications for going naked with other men and women in a natural setting. In one instance, the doctor again employs the image of the "exotic other" to rationalize nudism when he asserts that the "American Indian never caught colds until the white man put clothes on him."[115] *Elysia* introduced American nudism not only as a health movement but also as an answer to the racial weaknesses of modern Depression Era society.

Despite the film's pretensions, *Elysia* failed to satisfactorily address the erotic and immoral associations attached to the exposure of the naked body in public spaces and to the opposite sex. Heliotherapists, not unlike their predecessors and other practicing physicians, labored to convince patients that nudity had a therapeutic purpose. Rollier expressed disappointment about social understandings of nudity. He acknowledged the "considerable prejudice against the reduction of clothing," even in the case of small children, whom many people did not consider "'decent' unless they [were to] wear more clothes." Furthermore, Rollier contended that the "habit of living naked in the open air not only does not provoke any sensuality, but suppresses the very *raison d'être* of the unhealthy curiosity which often troubles the mind of the child."[116] Other physicians specializing in heliotherapy expressed frustration with "ingrained ideas of modesty and dress," in reference to the difficulty they had in get-

ting patients to unclothe and appreciate "air baths."[117] Articles on heliotherapy suggested that physicians use "considerable tact" to convince
patients that the "unconventional procedure" of the "full exposure of
the body to air baths" could yield health benefits.[118] Not even the setting
of the doctor's office and the authority of clinical medicine could fully
answer the moral anxieties aroused by the public exposure of the naked
body to the opposite sex.

The perceived immorality of bringing naked men and women together proved to be one of the main obstacles to nudism's future success.
Representing a resurgent effort within the Catholic Church to assert itself against the moral failings of a consumer society, Pope Pius XI, on
March 5, 1935, "severely condemned" nudism. In an address to Lenten
preachers, he asserted that the "cult of nudity . . . should be singled out
amidst the pagan tendencies of our modern time."[119] The rise of organized nudism in Europe, especially in Germany, influenced the pope
to see the movement as part of a larger "mania" occurring in society
that made people want to "see everything and enjoy everything to the
full[est]."[120] Referring to the "cult of nudity" as a "horrible word and
horribly blasphemy [sic]," the pope thought that nudism only concerned
itself with the "quest after pleasure and . . . amusement" and "exhibited
an immodesty that often exceeds that of ancient pagan life."[121] The growing tolerance of sexual expression in modern society motivated moral
leaders such as Pope Pius XI to publicly oppose nudism in order to reestablish a boundary that demarcated the illicit from the respectable.

The Reverend Ilsley Boone seized on the pope's well-publicized comments to make a case for the spiritual and moral foundations of American nudism. He answered the pope's harangue against the international
movement by boldly asserting in the New York Times that "His Holiness"
had been "misinformed" about the "Character of American Nudism."
Boone cited the "members of the Protestant clergy and Catholic laymen
of unquestioned integrity" who participated in American nudism and
maintained that, "from its inception," the movement had been of a "uniformly high moral order."[122] The centrality of religion in nudism dated
back to its founding in Europe. Richard Ungewitter, one of the founders
of Nacktkultur in Germany in 1905, was a Lutheran minister, and the
Reverend C. E. Norwood, a Congregational Church pastor, wrote the
"best handbook on nudism in England."[123] In the United States, Rev.

Boone and Rev. Henry Strong Huntington, a Unitarian minister, played a critical role in shaping nudism in the United States.[124] Rev. Huntington served as the first president of the INC from 1933 to 1934, and in 1934, Rev. Boone assumed the position he was to hold for decades as the organization's executive secretary. Rev. Boone declared that the presence of devout leaders in Germany, England, and the United States proved that nudism "cannot be very radically out of harmony with a Christian life nor contrary to the Scriptures."[125]

The many religious leaders in the movement gave nudism a distinctly spiritual character. Between 1930 and 1940, numerous articles and even more letters, editorials, and commentaries appeared in the *Nudist* discussing the relationship between nudism and religion.[126] Nudist leaders hoped to support Christian values by developing the moral character of participants through their naked lifestyle. Although the scriptures defined the body as the source of carnal desires, the disciple Paul also referred to it as the "temple of God." Christian spiritual texts encouraged the "solicitous care" of the body and had taught worshipers that they had "no right to abuse [their] body or health."[127] Boone presented nudism as a resource for devout Christians to take care of their bodies in a spiritually sound manner. While there was no "'converting power' in nudism," the social practice, according to Boone, would "change the moral character of a man" and provide a "powerful reinforcement to the inner Christian life."[128] He asserted that when the "sincerely minded nudists . . . experienced the truth of the all-cleanness of the human body in social nudism they know a freedom and mental liberation never before experienced."[129] For the Christian, Boone believed this feeling of revelation represented an "unquestionable confirmation of the rightness of nudism and its consonance with Christian idealism in the personal life."[130] Boone declared that the "Christian view of the body is in perfect harmony with the nudist conception of the body."[131]

By incorporating religious and moral values into nudist principles and ideals, nudists also repositioned themselves in the ongoing battle to define the boundaries around sexual liberalism. Nudists asserted that physical attraction decreased by permitting men and women to see each other naked in a nonerotic setting rather than accentuating sexualized parts of the body as the bathing suit or burlesque show did. Rev. Huntington defined nudism as the "breaking of the taboo on the sight of the body."[132] Another congregational minister believed that nudist practices "hold the key to the solution of obscene plays, pictures, language and literature" because through nudism these "things cease to interest; they fall flat."[133] This did not mean, however, that nudists intended to "destroy sex interest."[134] They wanted to restore the "natural function of procreation stripped of obscene and salacious elements."[135] Many nudists maintained that the interaction of naked male and female bodies of all age groups would make sex *morally* healthy.

The effort to explain and present nudism through Christianity resonated with individuals searching for an alternative sexual ethic. Francis and Mason Merrill's *Nudism Comes to America* surveyed over two hundred nudists and found devotees mostly from "liberal" Protestant sects, such as Unitarians, Congregationalists, Episcopalians, and "modernist Presbyterians."[136] The pope's public hostility to nudism likely made many Catholics wary of the movement. Nevertheless, the authors felt that the "religious attitudes" of nudists were especially "significant" since "nakedness, sex, and the bible have for so long been made religious concerns." In their survey, they found "three or four good Catholics" and "a half a dozen who put themselves down as belonging to the Jewish religion." But they recorded an overwhelming presence of Protestant denominations that were "represented both by Church members in good standing and nominal Protestants who are not greatly concerned with religious duties."[137] While the range of Protestant denominations varied, the authors did not document any members of the "more exotic religious cults." Rather, they declared, "our nudists are nothing out of the ordinary way of godliness."[138]

Several prominent social reformers who fought to expand the boundaries restricting freedom of expression and access to sexual knowledge also turned to Christian values and morality to win support for their cause. Margaret Sanger, in addition to couching her arguments in socialism, feminism, eugenics, and medical science, appealed to Protestant perfectionism by arguing that once men and women abandoned an unclean conception of sex, healthy marriages and families would produce "a race that is morally and spiritually free."[139] Sanger blamed Christians for creating immorality by denying women access to sexual knowledge and birth control. She especially resented Roman Catholic organizations that fervently resisted making birth control available to women.

Yet the growing popularity of companionate marriage, the success of the suffragist movement, and new consumption patterns helped Sanger successfully court Protestant groups that accepted the role that birth control and sexual knowledge played in promoting healthier, stable, and moral families.[140] Hoping to make progress in the struggle to expand the boundaries of sexual expression, American nudists followed birth control advocates such as Sanger who built broad coalitions to win support for the open distribution of birth control.

Like many American psychologists who subscribed to the writings of Sigmund Freud, the religious leaders of nudism hoped to promote a healthy psychological state of mind by alleviating sexual repression. Rev. Huntington especially wanted to address the sexual repression of men and women who grew up in "Christian homes" and learned to "fight so-called evil thoughts" and "resist such temptations."[141] Since many Christians learned to "conquer the flesh with the sword of the spirit," he lamented Christianity's concealment of the body. As an alternative, Huntington claimed that the nudist lifestyle "produces quite remarkable psychological and social results and may have decided effects upon the character."[142] Covering the body, he argued, perverted the normal human interest in sex and produced sexual degeneracy.[143]

The efforts of American nudists to produce a healthier mind by bringing naked men and women together drew the attention of prominent academic psychologists. Howard C. Warren, the head of the Department of Psychology at Princeton University in 1903 and president of the American Psychological Association in 1913, took a strong interest in the nudist movement. As the editor of the *Psychological Review*, Warren not only recognized the emerging movement but endorsed nudism in an article that presented his experiences as a participant-observer in a German nudist camp. Warren's "Nudism and the Body Taboo" corroborated nudists' claims that their practice minimized eroticism.[144] Although he admitted to an initial shock, he commented on how quickly he became comfortable in a social environment of naked men and women. He did not witness any "petting or flirting, no trace of ribaldry, no presumptuous behavior," and certainly "nothing to suggest that social nudism induced the virile reflex." In fact, he went so far as to declare that "*social nudism does not in any way foster eroticism.*" Instead, it promoted a "saner sex outlook and more natural relations between men and women, even during the years of early sexual maturity."[145] From his findings, he drew two conclusions of "considerable psychological importance." He determined that the body taboo cannot be considered a "fundamental human trait" since it can be "broken without detrimental results." Second, he did not accept that social nudism constituted indecency but rather argued that a "widespread and persistent social convention had made it so."[146] Endorsed by psychologists opposed to sexual repression, nudism framed its principles and ideals as morally, mentally, and physically beneficial to its members.

Alongside a leadership that built a national nudist organization around respectable therapeutic principles and religious ideals emerged another group of early nudist promoters who saw social nudity as part of a radical critique of modern life and as an opportunity to advocate for sexual freedom. In *Nudism in Modern Life: The New Gymnosophy*, Maurice Parmelee introduced a vision of nudism that grew out of his critiques of the capitalist system, his interest in eugenics, and his calls for sex reform. The radical, bohemian intellectual community that flourished in New York City's Lower East Side shaped Parmelee's worldview and writings. While working at a University Settlement House from 1904 to 1906, Parmelee associated with Eugene Debs, Emma Goldman, Upton Sinclair, and Jack London and joined radical and liberal organizations such as the Collectivist Society and the Sunrise Club. He also frequented the Liberal Club, a favorite Greenwich Village locale where left-wing bohemian intellectuals, artists, and civil libertarians frequently gathered and debated the major issues of the day. These early associations and experiences shaped his career as an influential sociologist and later as a government bureaucrat. After graduating from Yale in 1904 and receiving his Ph.D. from Columbia University in 1909, Parmelee published numerous books on world politics, anthropology, criminology, and economic theory and held professorial chairs at the University of Kansas, the University of Missouri, the University of Minnesota, and the College of the City of New York before leaving academia during the First World War to serve as a government economist. Over the course of his academic career, Parmelee had developed a reputation as a socialist and a atheist and, he believed that this ultimately led to him being "shunted out of [academia] mainly by the fact that many of [his] ideas

A 1931 portrait of Maurice Parmelee (1882–1969), a prominent sociologist and the author of *Nudism in Modern Life* (1931). (Courtesy of Maurice Parmelee Papers, Manuscripts and Archives, Yale University Library, New Haven, Connecticut)

which [he] expressed in [his] writing were not acceptable to the powers that be in the American Academic World."[147]

Parmelee based his belief that sexual repression caused far more problems than it solved on his own experiences growing up in a socially conservative, religious family. The son of missionary parents, Parmelee spent his early childhood in Turkey, and when he returned to the United States at the age of thirteen, he grew up in "small communities under rigid puritanical discipline" and did not have an "opportunity for sex expression until past adolescence."[148] Parmelee resented his devout upbringing, and in contrast to Rev. Boone and Rev. Huntington, he rejected the "superstition of Hebraic-Christian religion that sex is unclean" and unapologetically discussed sex relations, birth control, and sex education.[149] He hoped that his writings would "promote the sex freedom which is essential for the emergence of integral man and woman possessing a rich and well rounded personality."[150]

Parmelee's liberationist approach to sex drew on eugenic arguments as well as the works of progressive sexologists. Social reformers such as Sanger frequently used the rhetoric of eugenics to make a case for birth control because it limited the number of children born into poverty, making future families healthier, lowered crime rates, and helped produce an overall stronger race. Nudism, according to Parmelee, also served a eugenic purpose by aiding the process of "sexual selection" since "deformities and malformations are all too apparent in a state of nudity." Rather than focus on a "small portion" of the body such as the face or genitalia, men and women would "make their choice, so far as physical traits determine choice, according to the beauty of the body as a whole." This led to a happy marriage and ensured "fit parents for the more beautiful mankind of the future."[151] In addition, for over thirty years, Parmelee corresponded with Havelock Ellis about sex customs, personal morality, and moral reform. The well-respected sex researcher wrote the foreword to *Nudism in Modern Life*, in which he praised Parmelee's contributions to sociology and promised readers that the nudist treatise offered valuable insights about the "general direction in which our civilization is to-day moving."[152] Parmelee's 1918 book *Personality and Conduct* relied on Ellis's scientific approach to sex research to critique a "sexual double standard" that encouraged male promiscuity while requiring female chastity. He also explained the need for frank sex education to guard against venereal disease and unwanted pregnancy, justified the legalization of prostitution as a public health and safety measure, and called for a contractual form of marriage that incorporated open relationships and made it easier to file for divorce. Parmelee's most provocative proposal involved an institution called an "amatorium" that would "facilitate the rapprochement of prospective sex partners and mates" by providing a site where young adults could visit and experiment with sex with one another rather than visiting a prostitute or entering marriage without any sexual experience.[153] Through the science of eugenics and modern sexology, Parmelee presented a radical critique of repressive sexual mores.

In *Personality and Conduct*, Parmelee expressed ambivalence toward homosexuality. On the one hand, he felt that it was "wholly indefensible to penalize homosexuality," and he considered homosexuals "useful members of society." Yet he also referred to gay men and women as "unfortunate persons" and asserted that "normal hetero-sexual relation is doubtless the most desirable."[154] Despite Parmelee's ambivalent attitude toward homosexuality and the therapeutic and familial character of nudism that was promoted by a religious leadership, Jan Gay, a lesbian journalist, children's book author, and sex researcher, also played an important role in introducing nudism to the United States. Gay's *On Going Naked* (1932) provided another early account of nudism in Europe and suggested that the nudist movement appealed to and accepted gay men and women.

Gay's active and open participation in New York City's emerging gay and lesbian community shaped her writings about her nudist experiences in America and Europe. Gay assisted a number of scientific studies on homosexuality that were being conducted by physicians, sex researchers, and social scientists in response to the perceived growth of the homosexual population in New York City in the early 1930s. Gay had worked as a journalist since 1922 and had attracted the attention of sex researchers by interviewing a number of European and American lesbians. According to the historian Jennifer Terry, Gay hoped that "scientific explanations of sex variance would engender greater tolerance toward lesbians and homosexual men."[155] Gay, who lived openly with her partner, Zhenya Gay, and had worked with Magnus Hirschfeld at his Institut für Sexualwissenschaft in Berlin, helped gain the confidence of gay men and women participating in a study overseen by the privately funded Committee for the Study of Sex Variants (CSSV). In *On Going Naked*, Gay followed the lead of Rev. Boone and Rev. Huntington by denying that eroticism played a significant role in nudism. She asserted that "few things are so conducive to chastity as the observation of a great many unattractive human bodies."[156] Nevertheless, she communicated her sexual orientation to readers when she described a trip to the countryside, where she sunbathed nude with Zhenya and two homosexual men. The text made it clear that Zhenya and Jan were lovers, as were the men, John and Hall. After they swam in a cold stream, Gay recalled, "Zhenya toweled me vigorously, while Hall gave John a rubdown." Then "John and Hall chose the sloping bank for their siesta, while Zhenya and I each curled up on a shallow step of the dam."[157] While many readers likely remained oblivious to the same-sex intimacy imparted by Gay in *On Going Naked*, the text implicitly welcomed gay men and lesbians to nudism. Advertised in the *New York Times* and sold in the *Nudist* alongside other early nudist treatises, Gay's *On Going Naked* helped introduce nudism to the United States as well as to early gay and lesbian communities.

In contrast to Gay, Parmelee looked to nudism to encourage healthy eroticism. While Parmelee conceded that nudism likely "decreases sexual stimulation through the visual senses," he contended that it might be "more than compensated by its heightening through the tactile sense." Parmelee saw sex as more than a reproductive process. He asserted that the strong emotions produced by eroticism or sexual stimulation were just as important as visual stimulation or physical pleasure. He believed that the concealment of the body "accentuates lust by intensifying curiosity" and prevents the "play function of sex," which he defined as the emotional component of sexual relationships.[158] The nudist camp proved to be an ideal environment to promote the "play function of sex" since "psychic impotence and phobias" caused by the "ignorance of sexual facts" disappeared in a setting where men and women interacted without clothes, shame, or inhibitions. Unhampered by a constant desire to see the body, men and women could focus on "training in the art of love."[159] Nudism, according to Parmelee, had the capacity to redefine eroticism as a necessary component of a healthy relationship.

Parmelee took issue with nudist leaders who tried to "demonstrate that nudism has nothing to do with sex." Parmelee envisioned nudism as a "movement of dissent [that] asserts the rights of individuals and of minority groups to regulate their own conduct and morals as they see fit as long as they do not interfere with the rights and welfare of others." In his unpublished autobiography, written in the early 1960s, he regretted that a "good deal of Puritanism is displayed by some of the nudists," and he opposed the effort to "chain the movement, so to speak, to marriage as a legal and sacramental institution and to the family which is to result from this institution." Yet the nudist leadership's aversion to sexual expression did not necessarily mean that all nudists rejected the erotic potential of the movement. Parmelee explained that the effort to frame nudism as therapeutic or familial came about as a "precautionary reaction against the fear of suppression by conventional, moral, and legal restrictions" and were "incidental accompaniments of the movement at its present stage of development."[160] Parmelee maintained that the image of respectability promoted by nudist leaders concealed a membership that embraced the eroticism of nudism.

Parmelee's close relationship with Rev. Huntington and Rev. Boone also suggested that nudism's image of respectability may have been more of a façade than a reality. Parmelee and Rev. Huntington both graduated from Yale University and continued to correspond with each other for over sixty years. In one letter, Rev. Huntington expressed that he had "more in common with [Parmelee's] points of view about life in general than almost any other member of [their] class." Even though the two old classmates clashed over religion—with Parmelee asserting that Jesus was "mainly a mythical character" and Huntington proclaiming that he was "quite an enthusiast" when it "comes to Jesus"—nudism, and presumably Parmelee's perspective on sexual freedom, served as common ground.[161] Huntington endorsed Parmelee's early role in promoting nudism when he asserted that it was "too bad that [Parmelee's] book on nudism [was] not clearly recognized as the first in English on the topic." In the 1950s, Rev. Boone also stood behind the book, selling it in the *Nudist*, and he claimed to have sold fifty thousand copies of *Nudism in Modern Life*.[162] Although many early nudist leaders projected an image of respectability by stressing the movement's therapeutic, religious, and familial character, they also felt comfortable associating with Parmelee and marketing his far more radical vision of American nudism.

To grow and prosper in the United States, American nudism negotiated the fluid boundaries of sexual liberalism by architecting an appearance of respectable normalcy even as many of its early advocates supported sexual experimentation, radical politics, and homosexuality. The increasing acceptance of heterosexual pleasure in popular culture, in the courts, and in bohemian communities such as Greenwich Village made nudism especially appealing to individuals interested in advancing the cause of sexual freedom in the early 1930s. Yet the perception that nudism constituted another form of commercial sexuality, encouraged promiscuity, or served as a haven for gay men and women required that nudist leaders take steps to situate nudism within the heterosexual boundaries of sexual liberalism. The rural settings of its camps, the focus on the physical and mental benefits of going naked, and the presence of a religious leadership gave nudism the familial and therapeutic character critical to maintaining its tenuous claims to respectability.

The Fifth Annual International Nudist Conference

In the summer of 1936, the fifth annual International Nudist Conference, held on the "spacious and beautiful" grounds of the Lake O' Woods nudist camp in Valparaiso, Indiana, celebrated the rural growth and prosperity of nudism in the United States.[163] The convention drew almost a hundred nudists from twelve states representing forty of the eighty-five active nudist colonies in the United States.[164] Occupying tents, auto trailers, and summer cabins during the two-day event, conference participants enjoyed a program that intended to expand the influence of nudism. Attendees explored four major themes: the "relation of nudism to education, publicity and the nudist movement, the development of the national nudist community and the place of nudism in a changing social order."[165] By the fifth annual International Nudist Conference, the nudist movement had emerged as a stable and growing organization in the United States that had plenty of reasons to look forward to a bright future.

The images documenting the celebratory conference reflected the rural character of American nudism, hinted at the potential eroticism of its representations, and revealed the constraints in which nudism still operated in the United States. One image that headlined the *Nudist*'s coverage of the fifth annual International Nudist Convention demonstrated the movement's perilous balancing of the illicit and the respectable. It shows a young woman whose genitalia was airbrushed and who stands in front of dense vegetation, a hidden path, and a sign announcing the location of the Lake O' Woods camp. The image enticed a mostly male readership to the article through the figure of a young and attractive, though censored, woman smiling welcomingly. Other images illustrating the article echoed the bucolic environment of the camp by displaying the "cleared woods, rolling hills and dales, and a matchless lake,"[166] fully equipped with "piers, diving boards, and rafts."[167] In contrast to the images that had appeared in the *Chicago Tribune* during the

Lake-o-the-Woods Club

The Characteristic Hospitality of Nudists was well exemplified

Although frequently censored, nudist imagery emphasized the rural character of the movement while exhibiting young and attractive women who likely still appealed to male readers. (*Nudist*, November 1936, 7; courtesy of the Sunshine and Health Publishing Company)

Ring trial, which displayed male and female nudists awkwardly walking among dense vegetation, one of the images in the *Nudist* showed a solitary athletic man preparing to dive into a pristine lake surrounded by bountiful vegetation. Emphasizing strength and, with the image of a canoe in the bottom right-hand corner, recreation, the photo focused attention away from the eroticism of the naked body and instead used a wide-angled perspective to recall a pastoral ideal of nakedness linked with the tradition of skinny-dipping. It made it easy to envision children playing along the shore, families paddling a canoe around the lake, or young boys and girls innocently going out for an afternoon swim.

The nation's newspapers saw the conference as an opportunity to reexamine the development of nudism in the United States. Three

Lake-o-the-Woods Club
The diving platform was popular in early morning

Many nudist images used a wide-angled perspective to recall a pastoral ideal of nakedness associated with the tradition of skinny-dipping. (*Nudist*, November 1936, 9; courtesy of the Sunshine and Health Publishing Company)

years after the Ring trial, sensational newspaper headlines and text disappeared. The *Chicago Tribune*, the *New York Times*, the *Los Angeles Times*, the *Washington Post*, and the *Hartford Courant* approached the conference as a perfunctory event and curtly announced its location, the number of attendees, and the election of new officers.[168] Closer to the events, the *Chicago Tribune* treated the conference as front-page material while avoiding sexual overtones. One author began his exposé by revealing that he or she intended to write an "introductory short cut into the actuality of the everyday practice of nudism as witnessed at the Lake O' Woods camp."[169] Posing as a visitor who had not decided to disrobe, the writer witnessed the "ordinary routine of a nudist colony" and wrote that "camp life" resembled that of "any summer resort."[170] The writer observed a bridge game, swimming, a man and a woman strolling through a clearing with their two young children, members lounging in deck chairs under a big oak tree, and even a "typical family argument."[171]

Outside of the city, nudists appeared nonthreatening, family oriented, and normal.

The members who frequented the Lake O' Woods club displayed respectability and represented the increasingly American character of the movement. The *Chicago Tribune* reporter explained that nudists admitted members only after a "visit to their homes and with an eye to cultural background."[172] Primarily they hoped to avoid admitting "morons" who wanted to "look at [their] wives and daughters."[173] For this reason, they often excluded "elderly bachelors" and had expelled one man, a "Harvard Professor," who occasionally came back from town "unpleasantly drunk."[174] Although the Rogers Park community opposed the nudist stockade in their neighborhood because they thought the presence of foreigners and the immorality of public nakedness would reduce their property values, the reporter found "several well known Chicagoans" who attended the conference, including a concert pianist, a Chicago radio executive, an authority whose name was "well known to readers of two national weekly magazines," an "Oak Park writer; a Highland Park school teacher, and a Chicago railroad executive."[175]

Nudists closed the celebratory conference by promising to bring their "tenets . . . before the American Public."[176] Undaunted by their expulsion from Chicago, New York City, and Michigan, nudists remained steadfast in their ideals and principles and their commitment to expanding a growing network of rural nudist clubs. Confident that the therapeutic, spiritual, and psychological benefits of going naked would bring the movement and its rural camps respectability and stability, delegates at the fifth annual International Nudist Conference took steps to ensure that the movement's message would not succumb to censors, hostile local officials, or unscrupulous pornographers. The Findings Committee recommended that the organization and its flagship magazine change its name to avoid associations with "morbid and burlesque types of nakedness." Several leaders bemoaned the fact that many "burlesque theater managers, night club troupes, disorderly road houses, and exposition side shows" used the terms "nudist" and "nudism" to "further their own business enterprise in the field of commercialized pornography."[177] To promote the movement's emphasis on health and recreation instead, nudists adopted a new moniker, the American Sunbathing Association (ASA), to represent the national organization and renamed the *Nudist, Sunshine and Health*. The conference delegates then secured financial support for their flagship publication and made plans to wage a campaign in Michigan to amend the law in the state that resulted in Fred Ring's conviction. Al Flynn, the operator of Sunshine Park in Mays Landing, New Jersey, concluded the conference by declaring, "Let us go out and sell nudism to outside groups and carry it to the four corners of the earth."[178]

BETWEEN THE COVERS

Nudist Magazines and Censorship in Midcentury America

-ᘒ

To prosper in the United States, the nudist movement needed to overcome long-standing obscenity statutes that limited nudists' ability to produce and distribute their publications. In addition to facing opposition from hostile neighbors in Rogers Park, being outlawed by the New York State legislature, and suffering legal setbacks in the Ring trial in Allegan, Michigan, the nudist movement chafed against federal laws designed to impede the distribution and importation of scandalous materials. In 1933, the U.S. Customs Service seized Maurice Parmelee's *Nudism in Modern Life* when the John Lane Company shipped twelve copies of its British edition to the United States. Since the late nineteenth century, the Customs Service had played a central role in preventing birth control information, publications dealing with sexual themes, and potentially illicit images from entering the United States from Europe.[1] The twenty-three illustrations that accompanied the early nudist treatise's discussion of the philosophy, principles, and practicality of nudism made it vulnerable to seizure by U.S. customs agents. Yet the respectability that nudism attracted by emphasizing the physical, mental, and moral benefits of going naked put the movement in a position to challenge these obscenity statutes. The legal and financial success of nudism leading up to and during the Second World War empowered the movement to resist the censorship of its publications while also provoking state authorities to target its leaders as subversives and ultimately to suppress its flagship magazine, *Sunshine and Health.*

The political response to the emergence of nudism in the 1930s and early 1940s revealed a sexual politics that used individuals' private behavior to undermine their public authority. Pushed out of the headlines by the events of the Second World War, Representative Martin Dies (Republican, Texas), the head of the House on Un-American Activities Committee (HUAC), burst back onto the political stage by using Maurice Parmelee's appointment to the Board of Economic Warfare to launch a broader attack against the New Deal policies of the Roosevelt administration. Dies's campaign against nudism grabbed headlines, generated public support, and secured funding for his controversial committee because the supposed sexual perversion of nudism offered clear penalties and a palpable resolution. The prosecution of homosexual acts by the state, in contrast, remained hidden behind obscure statutes directed at limiting poverty through immigration restrictions—Depression Era social policies that only supported adult men with dependents or contemporary laws that prohibited public sexual acts by military personnel. In the decades leading up to the Second World War, according to the historian Margot Canaday, bureaucratic agencies and politicians avoided directly prosecuting homosexual acts or behavior since the government "lacked not only an adequate regulatory apparatus but also conceptual mastery over what it desired to regulate." In contrast to the secretive and ambiguous prosecution of homosexual behavior, Congressman Dies excoriated Parmelee as a nudist and a communist by drawing on the same sensational tactics he had used against union leaders and suspected radicals in the 1930s. Despite the defense of New Deal liberals, including Vice President Henry Wallace, the persecution of prominent nudists in the early years of the Second World War exposed the movement's ties with political radicalism and alternative sexualities.[2]

Regardless of Dies's attacks, Parmelee's vision of nudism as a place for eroticism and sexual expression as well as health benefits gained prominence in the pages of *Sunshine and Health* during the Second World War. The total war effort threatened to end organized nudism in the United States. Camps languished or closed completely as the rationing of tires and gas made it difficult for guests to visit. Additionally, the national organization lost several key figures and camp owners to military service and wartime employment. The sales of *Sunshine and Health*, however, grew as soldiers wrote to the magazine praising its pictures, while other readers scanned classified advertisements looking for companions or offering "physique photos." Rather than object to the new interest in the flagship nudist magazine on moral grounds, Rev. Ilsley Boone saw an opportunity to sell more magazines and support his struggling movement. Boone, the longtime managing editor of *Sun-*

shine and Health, frequently placed financial concerns and interests over principle and ideology. According to Rev. Henry Huntington, one of his first conversations with Boone involved "how to get away from the consequences of bankruptcy."[3] Already selling Parmelee's controversial book as well as Jan Gay's *On Going Naked*, Boone introduced suggestive representations into the magazine, adopted a playful format, and featured articles with erotic content that appealed to men and women of all sexualities. During the war, the eroticism that Parmelee wanted to be at the forefront of nudism assumed a more prominent place alongside the movement's therapeutic and familial character. The popularity of *Sunshine and Health* among men and women of a variety of sexualities put the respectability of the movement under suspicion and led to renewed efforts to censor the publication in the postwar era.

"It Cannot Be Assumed That Nudity Is Obscene Per Se"

Parmelee decided to write a book on nudism after visiting several German nudist camps while serving in Berlin as a special assistant to the Department of State. Assigned to evaluate Germany's economic situation at the end of the First World War, Parmelee seized the opportunity to learn more about *Nacktkultur* and to expand on his academic interest in sex reform. Parmelee objected to the writings of Richard Ungewitter, who promoted *Nacktkultur* as a way to "exalt German nationalism and racialism," but he eventually located several "liberal minded" nudist groups in which he regularly participated in nudist activities with "great profit and pleasure."[4] Parmelee thought the experience of going naked was a "remarkable opportunity to study a very significant movement from a psychological and sociological viewpoint," and encouraged by Havelock Ellis, he began writing the book when he returned to New York City in the winter of 1923.[5]

After Parmelee completed what he originally titled *The New Gymnosophy* in 1924, he struggled to find a publisher unafraid of challenging book censors.[6] He submitted the completed manuscript to "several of the more progressive publishers of New York City" only to be turned away and as a result was forced to put the project on hold for several years. In 1927, after editing out a large section of material that dealt with the more "technical and less easily understood phases of the subject,"

Parmelee secured a small publisher willing to distribute his book if he contributed to the project.[7] The federal district attorney for the Southern District of New York, however, immediately threatened prosecution. The publisher then distanced himself from the book, and Parmelee assumed full legal and financial responsibility and began distributing it "under the counter" at one of the most prominent booksellers in New York City.[8] He also consulted with the ACLU. Its general counsel advised him to send copies to the U.S. Customs Service in order to initiate proceedings requiring the collector of customs to show cause for its official action and to create an opportunity for the ACLU to officially object through the courts. Yet, in a 1927 letter, the Customs Service did not find that the book "offends Section 305 of the Tariff Act" and, therefore, stated that "there should be no objection to its admission so far as any question of obscenity."[9] In 1931, following the lead of several British and European publishers, Alfred Knopf agreed to publish Parmelee's book under the title *Nudism in Modern Life*. A new, more "liberal minded" district attorney made no objections, and the book gained a widespread readership. When the Customs Service seized twelve copies of *Nudism in Modern Life* mailed by the John Lane Company, Parmelee again enlisted the help of the ACLU to resist censorship of the book.

Alfred Wheat, the judge who presided over the *Parmelee* case in the U.S. District Court for the District of Columbia, upheld the Hicklin test when he disregarded the content of *Nudism in Modern Life* and focused on the erotic potential of the images in the book. According to the 1868 Hicklin test, the courts need only establish the potential of material to "deprave and corrupt those whose minds are open to such immoral influences, and into whose hands a publication of this sort may fall" in order to deem it obscene.[10] Beginning in 1873, Anthony Comstock and his New York Society for the Suppression of Vice (NYSSV) used this broad definition of obscenity to suppress pornography, medical treatises, and reproductions of art because they all might influence morally weak individuals who found these materials stimulating or morally corrupting.[11] Judge Wheat sought to protect individuals from having their morals corrupted by an extended discussion of nudity when he asked the court marshal to determine "whether any women were in the court room" and then "ordered to remove them" to honor their virtue.[12] This gesture had little practical effect since no women were present at the sparsely attended opening proceeding. Rather, it revealed the judge's belief that women were vulnerable members of society and needed to be protected from the discussion of nudity and obscenity. Following the Hicklin test to the last letter of the law, Judge Wheat only concerned himself with the "photographic illustrations which appear at various places in the book" and the impact these nude photos might have on the public. Since the photos had "no relevancy to the written text at the place in which each of said photographic illustration is set in the book," he felt no reason to take the text into consideration.[13] To protect the vulnerable members of society, such as women, the judge ignored arguments from nudists, sociologists, and health enthusiasts who defended the legitimacy of the text's content.

Measuring two and a quarter by three and a quarter inches, most of the twenty-three illustrations did not alarm the court. They featured large groups, displayed nude figures from a distance, and obscured the genitalia. One such image that displayed a nudist wrestling match avoided the homoeroticism of exhibiting two interlocked naked men by focusing the image on the many spectators watching the event. It showed numerous naked figures surrounding the wrestlers with their backs to the camera or sitting with their genitalia hidden. Although all the people in the image lack clothing, the distance of the camera along with the positioning of the figures makes it difficult to distinguish men from women. The wide angle of the photo, which captures trees in the background, brush in the bottom right corner, and the horizon of the sandy hill where the main action takes place also sought to link the scene to nature. Images such as this one made it difficult for the court to argue that even the most depraved or vulnerable reader would be aroused or titillated by *Nudism in Modern Life*.

Three or four other pictures, however, of "full front views of nude female figures" and two images in which "nude male and female figures appear together" drew the court's objections.[14] Including men and women in the same picture, in the judge's view, suggested intimacy between the sexes and hinted at potential sexual contact. One image, titled "In the Meadow," produced this effect by showing two women exchanging a flower while a man crouches to place a crown on the head of one of them. This scene invited multiple and contradictory interpretations. On the one hand, it showed the camaraderie between nudists and nature

A Wrestling Match

Most of the illustrations in Maurice Parmelee's *Nudism in Modern Life* featured large groups, displayed nude figures from a distance, or obscured the genitalia. (Parmelee, *Nudism in Modern Life* [New York: Knopf, 1931], 136)

while recalling the classical nude form that, according to the art historian Kenneth Clark, sought to represent an "organic and geometric basis of beauty."[15] The symbolism of women touching a flower while staring lovingly into each other's eyes likely also communicated lesbianism. When read alongside Jan Gay's *On Going Naked* and its descriptions of gay men and lesbians going naked in the American countryside, the image communicated homoeroticism. The presence of the man in the background preparing to "crown" one of the women added to the photo's illicit character by raising the possibility of group sex. Another image, titled "The Javelin-Thrower," displayed a woman holding a javelin and unabashedly displaying her breasts and her pubic hair. The full-frontal nudity shown in the image recalled the athleticism of Greek or Roman marble statues. However, as a photograph in a book, it constituted an object of erotica that could be consumed privately.[16] On the basis of these select representations, Judge Wheat ruled that the book constituted obscenity.

The ACLU, along with a number of prominent writers and academics, recognized the significance of Judge Wheat's unfavorable de-

IN THE MEADOW

According to Judge Wheat, images that featured men and women suggested intimacy between the sexes and hinted at potential sexual contact. (Parmelee, *Nudism in Modern Life* [New York: Knopf, 1931], 43)

THE JAVELIN-THROWER

The full-frontal nudity shown in "The Javelin-Thrower" recalled the athleticism of Greek or Roman marble statues, but as a photograph in a book, Judge Wheat considered it an example of erotica. (Parmelee, *Nudism in Modern Life* [New York: Knopf, 1931], 22) cision for the future of nudism and for freedom of expression. H. G. Wells wrote that he considered the book a "perfectly decent work" and quipped that the "U.S.A. seems to be afflicted just now for a mania for suppressing everything except cruelty and raucous vulgarity." Sinclair Lewis recognized Parmelee as a "sociologist of the highest international standing" and asserted that to "interfere with its publication, would be abominable." Havelock Ellis maintained, "No person with any reasoning power at all, indeed, could fail to see that this is a book of highly moral character . . . without a single offensive word in it from beginning to end." Meanwhile, H. L. Mencken, the famous literary critic and editor, promised to do whatever he could to help Parmelee's book.[17] The ACLU again took an interest in this case as part of its effort to broaden its focus beyond forms of government censorship that targeted union activity and radical political organizations. Morris Ernst, who according to the historian Leigh Ann Wheeler had a "resume rich with experience defending birth control and attacking censorship," led this transition by successfully defending Mary Ware Dennett against the U.S. Post Office in 1928, challenging the U.S. Customs Service's 1929 ban on Marie Stopes's *Contraception*, and, in 1933, defeating the prohibition of James Joyce's *Ulysses*.[18] Fighting against government censorship yet again, Ernst assisted in the appeal of Parmelee's case to the U.S. Court of Appeals of the District of Columbia.

Due in large part to Ernst's earlier victories against censorship, the justices on the U.S. Court of Appeals disregarded the Hicklin test and evaluated *Nudism in Modern Life* in its entirety; since Hicklin had been "repudiated," the justices turned to community standards to resolve the question of obscenity.[19] This proved difficult, however, because nudism had only recently emerged in the United States, and the justices felt that testimony from experts only revealed the "profound ignorance of psychology and sociology." They also felt uncomfortable classifying its photos as clear examples of art, medicine, or erotica. Without precedent to guide them or qualified experts, the justices had to "compensate . . . by noticing, judicially, evidence which is available to [them]" and, as a result, relied heavily on the "book itself" to guide them in their decision. Taking the recent *Ulysses* verdict into consideration, the judges used a standard that considered the book as a "whole, in its effect, not upon any particular class, but upon all those whom it [was] likely to reach."[20]

Since the courts protected materials exhibiting literary or scholarly merit, Ernst argued that Parmelee's book examined nudism as a "serious movement" with "many supporters in the United States."[21] The respectability that nudism embodied by conforming to the heteronormative boundaries of sexual liberalism through its principles of health, heterosexuality, and family orientation and its focus on nature played a central role in swaying the court. Ernst contended that nudism had been "widely endorsed" in the United States because of its hygienic, educational, psychological, sociological, and aesthetic merits. He noted that heliotherapy maintained that the "exposure of the body to sun rays has an important health value" that might be hindered by even "scanty" clothing.[22] The assumption implicit within sexual liberalism that the family precluded illicit sexual behavior allowed Ernst to invoke the expert opinion of Dr. Howard Warren, who echoed Fred Ring by making the claim that nudism eliminated sex curiosity among children while also curing "psychological maladjustment" resulting from the concealment of the body.[23] Ernst also distinguished nudism from "back to nature" movements by asserting that the movement encouraged a love for nature and was based on the principles of "true democracy."[24] Parmelee's attorneys contended that *Nudism in Modern Life* did not constitute pornography, that current social mores justified the frankness of the pictures, and that the whole work must be judged according to its effect on the average man.[25]

The Court of Appeals equated nudism with a type of medical therapy, accepted its scholarly character, and recognized its legitimacy. The justices believed that works of sociology in which the "erotic matter is not introduced to promote lust and does not furnish the dominant note of the publication" should receive the "same immunity" as works of physiology, medicine, and the social sciences.[26] In contrast to Judge Wheat's immediate condemnation of the images in *Nudism in Modern Life*, the appellate judges recognized "such evident truthfulness in its depiction of certain types of humanity" and that the book "is so little erotic in its result" that they ruled that the work did "not fall within the forbidden class."[27] Echoing the arguments made by Ernst in the written opinion, the judges referred to works of art that displayed full-frontal naked female and male bodies and referenced the *Encyclopedia Britannica* as a source in which images containing nude men and women regularly appeared without protest. Finding similar scholastic merit in *Nudism in*

Modern Life, the judges found the work in question to be an "honest, sincere, scientific and educational study and exposition of a sociological phenomenon" written by a "well qualified writer in the field of sociology."[28] The respectability of Parmelee and the therapeutic principles of American nudism influenced the court to see *Nudism in Modern Life* as an academic treatise rather than a source of illicit material.

The acknowledgment that nudity had a place in American society by the Court of Appeals, the second-highest court in the country, impacted obscenity law beyond granting legal protection to nudist books. The justices declared, "it cannot be assumed that nudity is obscene *per se* and under all circumstances."[29] In defending this statement, the court acknowledged the subjective experience of nakedness. The justices quoted Havelock Ellis's *Psychology of Sex*, in which he asserted that clothing, rather than complete nudity, causes eroticism, and referenced extensively William Graham Sumner's anthropological work *Folkways* in order to compare the different taboos toward nudity from around the world. By 1940, the justices believed that "no reasonable person at the present time" would object to medical treatises that displayed the nude figure. Although the justices did not necessarily endorse nudism, they maintained that "normal, intelligent persons" would recognize that a need exists for the scientific study, exposition, and picturization" of nudist ideas.[30] They felt that "civilization has advanced far enough, at last, to permit the picturization of the human body for scientific and educational purposes."[31] The *Parmelee* decision established that any work with scholarly or academic merit could legally display the naked body.

The significance of the appellate ruling did not escape the national media. Newspapers covered the decision as another example of changing obscenity laws that no longer could be used to ban literary and artistic works that conveyed sexual themes. The *New York Times* pointed out the obvious in its headline "Nudity in Art Upheld as Proper by Court," and the *Washington Post* placed the decision in the context of the landmark *Ulysses* decision.[32] Yet the decision also raised concerns. On February 25, 1942, the *Washington Times-Herald* published an article by Frank Waldrop that brought attention to Parmelee's other books and suggested that "some gentleman in Congress might take a peek into these and find out the shadow of coming events, as foreseen by a public servant of Mr. Parmelee's temper."[33] Waldrop had a reputation for being a "sort of journalistic spokesman" for Congressman Martin Dies, the chairman of the House of Representatives Committee on Un-American Activities.[34]

"Brash Mr. Dies"

On March 30, 1942, a month after Frank Waldrop's column, the *Chicago Tribune* ran the front-page headline "Dies Hits 35 U.S. Officials as Reds."[35] Dies declared that Parmelee was "outstanding among these officials" because he had written *Nudism in Modern Life*.[36] In a letter to Vice President Henry Wallace, Dies condemned Parmelee's recent appointment as the chief economic adviser to the Board of Economic Warfare along with his three-hundred-page nudist treatise as "an attack upon the moral structure of our society."[37]

Despite Parmelee's reputation within American academia as a radical, he worked as a government bureaucrat for a number of years prior to his appointment to the Board of Economic Warfare. Even though he had become "*persona non grata* in the academic world mainly because the suspicion had arisen that [he] was a severe critic of the capitalist system," Parmelee took advantage of the fact that "no one concerned with [his] early appointments in the government service had any acquaintance with [his] writings."[38] In 1918, Parmelee accepted a position on the War Trade Board, which oversaw the domestic and foreign commerce of the United States. He then participated in the administration of the Allied blockade by monitoring the surplus rations provided to the nations bordering Germany. This work caught the attention of the Department of State, which hired him in 1920 as a special assistant responsible for assessing the postwar economic situation in western and central Europe. When the United States entered the Second World War, Parmelee's experience as a government bureaucrat during the First World War made him a logical choice to serve as the chief economic adviser on the Board of Economic Warfare.

The legal controversy surrounding *Nudism in Modern Life*, however, drew the attention of government officials to Parmelee's unconventional views and radical critiques. In 1938, when Judge Wheat ruled against *Nudism in Modern Life*, Parmelee was working for the Department of Agriculture. Not long after the decision had been announced in the press, Parmelee received a warning from the head of his division that the "Department of Agriculture would tolerate no socialist in its service." Four months later, he was terminated due to "reorganization." It then became very difficult for Parmelee to maintain government employment. He received an appointment in the Treasury Department in the Division of Monetary Research, only to be terminated a few months later. Another temporary position in the Department of the Interior ended in early 1941. After ten months of unemployment, he joined the Board of Economic Warfare. Although Parmelee's experience with the War Trade Board during the First World War made him "peculiarly suitable" for the position, the U.S. Court of Appeals decision made him particularly vulnerable to political attack and persecution.[39]

The rapidly shifting political climate of the Second World War called for new tactics and methods from conservative politicians. The growth of union activity, government programs, and the Communist Party during the Depression years had led to an upsurge in anticommunist hysteria from the political Right in the United States. Beginning in 1938, HUAC held sensational public hearings where congressmen accused union leaders, New Deal agencies, and a multitude of other organizations of being under communist influence.[40] The beginning of the Second World War shifted public attention and support away from fears of foreign radicalism. Americans stood united behind the war effort. Citizens not only dramatically mobilized to support the troops but rallied behind the leadership of the Roosevelt administration. The United States even allied itself with the Soviet Union. For Martin Dies, these new alliances threatened to undermine his campaign to find and root out radical subversive forces in the United States. To justify appropriating more funds to his controversial committee, he needed sensational headlines to rally the public behind his anticommunist agenda. Employing individuals' private behavior to undermine their public authority, Dies's persecution of Parmelee proved to be the perfect spectacle to recapture the public's attention and to justify the continued financial support of his recently overshadowed HUAC.

The nonthreatening character of nudism in the public eye made it an ideal platform to use people's intimate sexual behavior to undermine their public authority. Nudism did not carry the same gravity as homosexuality. After the end of Prohibition, states such as New York passed a series of laws designed to exclude homosexuals from previously underground bars and cabarets and censored theaters that featured gender-impersonation performances. In addition, in the 1934 Motion Picture Production Code, Hollywood studios banned any references to homosexuals or "sex perversion" in films. In contrast, the media presented the nudist movement as more of an oddity than a threat to the strained gender norms of Depression Era American society. Throughout the 1930s, newspapers across the country regularly printed stories covering nudist raids, trials, and conventions. Since nudism could be discussed freely, Dies did not hesitate to condemn Parmelee's work on the nudist movement. He asserted that Parmelee "advocates the widespread practice of nudism in this country," including in the home, in the office, and in the factory. He courted more controversy when he quoted Parmelee's speculation that sex differences would abate in a nudist society to the point that the "convent and monastery, harem and military barrack, clubs and schools exclusively for each sex will disappear, and the sexes will live a more normal and happier life together."[41]

With nudism providing the necessary headlines, Dies employed the same tactics he had used to persecute alleged communist subversives in the late 1930s. In the first HUAC hearings in 1938, congressmen linked witnesses to communism by accusing them of engaging in lawful activities with suspected subversive organizations. They then dramatically concluded that this participation showed the witnesses' commitment to the communist cause. Dies employed this same tactic when he revealed that Parmelee's name had appeared on the list of members of the American League for Peace and Democracy. To associate Parmelee with European radicalism, Dies also made it a point to depict the sociologist as a foreign national. Parmelee, the son of missionaries from Vermont, had been born in Constantinople and had traveled extensively in Europe, the Soviet Union, India, and China. Twisting this information, Dies failed to mention that Parmelee's parents were born in the United States and, instead, implied that he had "spent several years in Nudist camps in Europe."[42]

Parmelee's many academic works also provided an opportunity for Dies to offer the public additional incriminating evidence. After receiving a Ph.D. at Columbia University in 1909, Parmelee quickly became a prominent figure in the emerging field of sociology. *The Principles of Anthropology and Sociology in Their Relations to Criminal Procedure* (1908), *Inebriety in Boston* (1909), *Poverty and Social Progress* (1916), and *Criminology* (1918) all established Parmelee as an expert in the field of sociological criminology. His other works, titled *Farewell to Poverty* (1935), *Bolshevism, Fascism, and the Liberal Democratic State* (1934), and of course, *Nudism in Modern Life* (1933), caught the attention of Dies.[43]

Dies contended that "any one of thousands of passages could be cited from these volumes to show the communist viewpoint of the author."[44] Dies then singled out a passage in which Parmelee explained that "customary nudity is impossible under the existing undemocratic social, economic and political organization." To further link communism and nudism, Dies referenced another passage in *Nudism in Modern Life*, which stated, "While gymnosophists [nudists] are not necessarily socialists or communists, these colonies furnish excellent opportunities for experiments along communistic lines."[45] Dies used Parmelee's radicalism to characterize all nudists as a threat to social convention, sex differences, and the existing political and economic system.

In calling for Parmelee's resignation, the congressman from Texas challenged the entire Roosevelt administration in the first months of the Second World War. Dies questioned how Parmelee received his appointment under Vice President Wallace.[46] The congressman wondered how someone who "advocates such a crackpot and immoral plan," who clearly had a "warped and unhealthy mind," could receive such an important appointment. Dies, referring to Parmelee's prominent role in successfully appealing the Customs Service's seizure of *Nudism in Modern Life*, asserted, "It cannot be said . . . that the government did not have notice of Mr. Parmelee's background."[47] Dies attacked Parmelee's credentials further when he questioned why Wallace did not fill this important post with someone whose "outlook in life is wholesomely American and not embellished with crackpot ideas of nudism, technocracy, communism, or any other brand of revolution."[48]

Extending beyond the halls of Congress, the effort to use Parmelee and the nudist movement to attack New Deal policies and the Roosevelt administration made its way into popular culture. The *Chicago Daily Tribune*, which voiced the conservative ideology of its editor, Colonel Robert McCormick, joined Dies's cause by mocking potential postwar nudist colonies. McCormick, who resented the increase of federal

Editorial cartoons in the *Chicago Tribune* used Martin Dies's attack on Maurice Parmelee to link the secretive and illicit activities of the nudist camp with New Deal policies. ("An Appropriate Haven," *Chicago Daily Tribune*, March 31, 1942, 10)

power under the Roosevelt administration and opposed the United States' entry into the Second World War, was a more-than-willing ally to Congressman Dies. An editorial cartoon titled "An Appropriate Haven" used nudism to critique the New Deal coalition. Under a sign that reads, "post-war economy Nudist Camp," a smiling, skinny, bespectacled, pointy-mustached Maurice Parmelee stands with a sash that reads, "Nude Dealer," while he bellows, "Welcome Comrade!" The cartoon then mocks the size and waste of the federal government by picturing a fat, sloppy tax collector who holds a long list that reads, "Waste, Bungling, and Boon-Doggling." Just outside the colony stands a short, meek taxpayer who has lost his shirt and possibly will lose his pants next.[49] The title of the cartoon combined with the high fence in the image to compare New Deal policies to the secretive, illicit, and shameful activities of the nudist camp.

In a letter that appeared in the nation's newspapers alongside articles announcing Dies's accusations, Vice President Wallace attacked the representative from Texas as a threat to public morale.[50] Challenging Dies's patriotism in "these days of crisis and tension," Wallace asserted that the congressman's actions "might as well come from Goebbels himself."[51] Wallace saw the congressman as a "greater danger to . . . national safety than thousands of Axis soldiers within [America's] borders."[52] Because Wallace believed that most Americans considered nudism either harmless or insignificant, he denounced Dies's tactics as a threat to national unity and the war effort.

Wallace's defense of Parmelee implied that nudism remained so marginal that it posed little threat to American morality. The small number of people practicing nudism in the United States allowed the vice president to argue that Dies's tactics would be "overlooked as the product of a witchcraft mind" or "would make him the laughing stock of the country."[53] Wallace asserted that Dies's "intense itch for publicity" was the main source of the current controversy, since "not one person in 100,000 in this country is interested in nudism."[54] While he had "never heard of the gentleman [Parmelee] until last Saturday morning," he promised that the Federal Bureau of Investigation would investigate the matter and stated that the accused would be dismissed if Dies's accusations turned out to be true.[55] Wallace nevertheless called for a "public apology to the men whose reputations Mr. Dies has smeared without giving them a chance to be heard."[56] The vice president then defended Parmelee's reputation by pointing out that Alfred Knopf, "one of the established publishing houses in this country," published *Nudism in Modern Life* and by noting Parmelee's standing as a sociologist whose "textbooks have been long known and used in the colleges and universities of this country."[57] For Wallace, the Texas congressman's actions represented a "malicious distortion of facts" meant to "inflame the public mind."[58]

Many liberal members of Congress followed Wallace's lead by treating nudism as harmless or insignificant, by focusing on Dies's impact on morale, and by suggesting that the congressman desperately sought publicity. James O'Connor, representative from Montana, who had previously supported HUAC, found it disturbing that Dies would attack the Board of Economic Warfare when he should be rooting out the "numerous agents and sympathizers" of Germany and Japan.[59] O'Connor then introduced an editorial printed in the typically conservative *Washington Post* under the heading "Brash Mr. Dies" to reject the self-serving motives of Dies.[60] The editorial described Wallace's "tongue lashing of Martin Dies" as a "thoroughly workmanlike job" that the "brash congressman from Texas had . . . coming to him."[61] Questioning why Dies "chose this moment to assail these persons," the editorial speculated that the congressman sought out "headlines" that would help him "overcome the reluctance of the Appropriations Committee to approve funds for the continuation of the Dies Committee."[62]

The *Nation* objected to Dies's new tactic, which "combines politics with sex," and denounced the "Texan's unsavory methods."[63] The liberal magazine presented the same argument as Wallace and his supporters, but it did not avoid the sex angle. Dies's turn to sex through his persecution of Parmelee revealed the struggling congressman's desperate efforts to regain headlines with subject matter that captured the public's attention through titillation. The magazine found that Dies's tactics and methods also relied on deliberate inaccuracies. It noted that Parmelee happened to be born in Constantinople only because his parents left their home state of Vermont as Congregationalist missionaries to Turkey. It then pointed out that Dies neglected to mention that the lower court's unfavorable verdict was reversed by the Court of Appeals, "which paid tribute to Parmelee as a writer."[64] The weekly periodical then defended Parmelee's long career as a government bureaucrat. Dies ignored the fact that Parmelee left academia for government service in 1918. Beginning with the First World War, Parmelee worked for the War Trade Board administering the Allied blockade in London and later served as special assistant to Secretary of State Charles Evans Hughes.[65] Far from the image of a roving foreign radical presented by Dies, the *Nation* presented Parmelee as a long-serving government bureaucrat with a distinguished record of service. The *Nation* saw this incident as another attempt by Dies to "hound progressives out of the government" and called on its readers to "fight now against the grant of an appropriation to him by Congress, and to defend the Board of Economic Warfare."[66]

Nudists saw Congressman Dies as another example of modern American Puritanism. Referring to Parmelee as a "gentleman and a scholar," the editors of *Sunshine and Health* maintained that there was "nothing subversive or revolutionary" in *Nudism in Modern Life*.[67] Nudists saw Dies as "prejudiced, and ignorant in matters of everyday cleanmindedness and healthful living."[68] They felt, like Wallace and the *Nation*, that Dies represented a "cheap politician . . . trying to promote his own self aggrandizement by way of the social, business or political injury of another."[69] They believed that Dies had overestimated the popular prejudice against nudism and contended that most politicians, like the general public, were "either sympathetic or at the worst indifferent" toward nudism.[70] Nudists presented the incident as an anomaly and took pleasure in Wallace's rebuke of Dies and in the fact that attacks against nudism were "now so infrequent."[71]

Despite the opposition of Wallace, the New Deal community, and nudists, Dies's tactics produced the desired results. Dies caught the public's attention and won political support for his larger campaign against New Deal liberalism.[72] His staff received "hundreds of telegrams and letters praising the committee for its courage in fighting 'crackpotism' and subversive elements in the government structure."[73] The *Washington Post* mockingly reported that Dies's uncovering of a nudist on the Board of Economic Warfare "touched off the first Congressional debate on nudism in the history of American Legislation."[74] Other congressmen repeated Dies's sexual politics to attack the Roosevelt administration. One Democratic representative from Georgia "wav[ed] copies of Parmelee's *Nudism in Modern Life*" as he exclaimed that the illustrations in the book were "filthy and dirty."[75] The congressman added that he regarded the vice president as "one of the cleanest, finest men" he had ever known, even though he regretted Wallace's "rather bitter attack" on his "colleague from Texas [Dies]."[76] Another Democratic representative from Illinois, however, took the attack against Wallace a step further when he declared that "only crackpots would select crackpots to help plan our war program or our post war program."[77]

The public took an interest in Dies's latest cause as much for its potential eroticism as its political drama. Yet Dies's turn to sexual politics did not necessarily win him legitimacy. Many congressmen took notice of the controversy more because of their curiosity to see nude photos than their serious concern for the moral integrity of the American government. The *Washington Post* reported that the book circulated widely among representatives, who "avidly scanned" its illustrations.[78] While most of the pictures of "pot-bellied men and women cavorting in a manner to cause raucous laughter" proved "disappointing to most of the art seekers," an image of a "young girl throwing a javelin," which had previously alarmed Judge Wheat, caught the attention of several congressmen, who thought it was "worthy of a place in a high class saloon."[79] (See figure at the bottom of page 93.)

With congressional concession of the book's illicit character, Dies successfully forced Parmelee's resignation from the Board of Economic Warfare on April 19, 1942. This development proved devastating for Parmelee, who desperately appealed to Vice President Wallace and Milo Perkins, the executive director of the Board of Economic Warfare, to keep his job. He also contacted several newspapers and magazines to tell his side of the story. Although Parmelee went on to work as the chief economist of the U.S. Railroad Retirement Board in Chicago (and again came under Dies's scrutiny), he continued to feel betrayed by "so-called liberals as Henry Wallace."[80] Three days after Parmelee's dismissal, Congress debated the appropriation of funds to sustain the Dies committee. Unlike previous years, the funding for the House Committee on Un-American Activities did not receive automatic approval from Congress. The Committee on Accounts "received hundreds of letters from all over the United States and also resolutions adopted from various organizations requesting the committee deny any appropriation whatsoever to the Dies Committee."[81]

Many liberal congressmen no longer supported Dies. Congressman O'Connor, who had previously favored HUAC, now objected to the unethical tactics of Dies. He specifically took issue with how Dies gave "information to the press and to the public without first giving it to the Department of Justice or to the Vice President of the United States."[82] Other congressmen suggested that Dies's actions did not justify the committee's extravagant expense since he actually undermined the war effort by persecuting government agencies.[83] Since the committee's inception on June 9, 1938, Congress appropriated $385,000 for it, "the largest appropriation that any committee of the House has ever had."[84] With the House now voting to grant another $110,000 to sustain the committee through January 3, 1943, many congressmen did not see the need for an agency that chose to focus on progressive subversives rather than fascist agents.[85]

Dies successfully gained publicity, public support, and congressional allies for his conservative politics by conducting a voyeuristic attack on the nudist movement. Dies's fear that his political enemies would use the war to discontinue HUAC drove his campaign against Parmelee. This strategy proved victorious when Congress chose to reward Dies's controversial tactics. Conflating nudism, communism, and the New Deal, the conservative *Chicago Daily Tribune* reported that the House voted by a wide margin, despite the "vehement objections of left wing congressmen," to appropriate $110,000 to the Dies committee.[86] By presenting nudists as radical subversives and members of a peculiar and marginal group, Dies's self-serving tactics undermined the health-oriented philosophy and religious values that American nudism had established as its public face during the 1930s. The Parmelee incident both represented a step backward for American nudism and signaled to future senators that private behavior could be used to undermine public authority.

"It Is Good to Be an American; It's Grand to Be a Nudist"

Nudism answered Martin Dies's persecution of Maurice Parmelee by adopting a patriotic tone through a sustained commitment to the war effort. The loss of leadership and resources during the Second World War threatened to end organized nudism in the United States. Unwilling to fade away in the face of these challenges, nudists maintained their organization by dedicating themselves to the nation and by appealing to the American soldier.

From individual camp owners to national leaders, the Second World War devastated the core leadership that had emerged over the course of the previous decade. The "absorption of camp owners into the defense program whether in one of the service branches or in industry" had cut the "group leadership virtually to zero."[87] The national organization, also, as a whole, suffered during the war. The previous year, the president of the American Sunbathing Association, Carl Easton Williams, left the organization for national defense work with an "important and confidential . . . West Coast shipbuilding concern."[88] To make matters worse, the personnel at national headquarters was "invaded" when one of their "most valued workers" entered the army, and two others remained in the draft and planned to enter either the army or defense work.[89] Without leaders to maintain a still-developing network of camps and a national organization to unify the groups scattered across the country, nudism risked falling into obscurity during the Second World War.

The impact of the war on leisure activities also pushed many nudist camps to close. The "necessary rationing of tires and gas" limited travel and vacationing opportunities across the country and reduced "regular attendance to a minimum" at many camps.[90] Scattered over greater distances and requiring long car trips, the camps on the West Coast experienced declining attendance and membership.[91] In Oregon, one nudist group, known as the "Hesperians," "felt compelled to close—perhaps permanently."[92] In Washington State, "The Beavers" continued to operate but with "sharply curtailed activity."[93] In California, "the De Anza Trail" had been taken over by the "local rent control authority."[94] Nudist leaders called for members to provide additional sources of revenue to support these clubs. In Stockholm, New Jersey, "Rock Lodge," one of the largest and best-equipped camps in the country, faced the possibility that it would be forced to close "unless drastic measures [were] taken."[95] The owners of the camp, Dr. Herman Soshinski and his wife, Katja, who stood out "among the pioneers of American nudism," needed to raise $3,000 to keep the camp open.[96] In *Sunshine and Health*, the editors pleaded with readers to send in gifts ranging from $5 to $100. The editors felt that "failure in this endeavor would be about as severe a blow as could possibly come to [the] Association at this time."[97] According to them, "every affiliated group would feel the adverse effect" of the closure of Rock Lodge.[98]

The American Sunbathing Association (ASA), hoping to preserve its national network of clubs, recommended dormancy for struggling camps that might be in a better position to take advantage of potential postwar interest in nudism. Nudist leaders suggested that camps maintain a "framework organization" that continued their listings and publicity in *Sunshine and Health* while also holding the "membership interest" using "'round Robin' letters" circulated among the members.[99] They also thought group consciousness could be sustained through "visitation and occasional meetings at members' homes."[100] By maintaining a "skeleton existence throughout our global struggle," nudist clubs would be "all set for the up-surge of interest in nudism which is most certainly sure to follow the war."[101]

War rationing also threatened to adversely impact *Sunshine and Health*. Paul Hadley, one of the main contributors of photographs to the magazine, reported that the war "threatens to do away with amateur photography, and even threatens professional photography to a great extent."[102] The war had made film and metals scarce and limited the availability of cameras, lights, lamp bulbs, and other photographic apparatus. Hadley feared that photographic studios might be closed for the duration of the war and would limit the "photographic illustrations of [the] movement . . . to pictures made in the past months."[103] By October 1943, Hadley's fears were realized. In the "Publisher's Desk" section of *Sunshine and Health*, the editors reported that limitations placed on "roll films designed for amateur use" had made it virtually impossible to acquire film.[104] The shortage of paper also threatened to alter the appearance of the flagship nudist magazine. The editors of *Sunshine and Health* downgraded to a lesser-quality paper and planned a reduction in the weight of paper to reduce the total tonnage of the magazine.[105] They also anticipated reducing the page size used in the magazine and eliminating large photos.[106] Like other magazines in the United States, the nudists' official publication—the lifeline of their organization—faced major alterations.

The difficult circumstances brought about by the Second World War did not deter the nudist movement from contributing to the war effort in a variety of ways. Several clubs, individual members, the national headquarters, and the magazine purchased war bonds.[107] Recurring advertisements in *Sunshine and Health* encouraged readers to buy several thousand-dollar war bonds and updated the amount of funds contributed toward their purchase.[108] The editors of *Sunshine and Health* also suggested that nudists send "our boys in service" postcards, letters, and occasionally gift packages.[109] The recording secretary of the national organization even sent an "omnibus newsletter from her town" to nudist

Daughter: "I'm going to write to the President about this. How can we save on clothes by keeping clothes on?"

During the Second World War, nudists sustained the national organization against political attacks and low club morale by embracing patriotism and by appealing to the American soldier. One illustration used humor to suggest that the movement's promotion of public nudity would prevent the deterioration of old clothes and would aid rationing efforts. (*Sunshine and Health*, February 1943, 16; courtesy of the Sunshine and Health Publishing Company)

soldiers.[110] The editors believed these efforts would "maintain a high level of morale among the fellows in uniform."[111] Nudists also joked that their abandonment of clothes would prevent the deterioration of old clothes and aid-rationing efforts. Using a pun, a satirical cartoon featured a naked man and woman reading a newspaper that announced a "wool shortage" on one page and displayed the headline "Nudism Banned" on the other page to question the logic behind antinudist hostility when the movement had so much to offer the war effort.[112]

Nudists also suggested that the adoption of nude sunbathing would create a healthier army. Asserting that a "sick man is always a liability and never an asset" and lamenting the "number of rejections in our fighting forces by reason of physical defects," nudists boasted that "not a single nudist has been found wanting."[113] Although it was extremely unlikely that Americans would take up nude sunbathing to prepare for military service, the navy actually experimented with the idea of exposing soldiers to the sun to promote their health and prepare them for deployment in the South Pacific. The *Journal of the American Medical Association* reported that the Army Medical Department's *Bulletin* described an "experiment in graduated sun bathing" that occurred on a troopship sailing to the South Pacific.[114] Reenacting Rollier's regimen in "parades" around the ship, soldiers, while always wearing a helmet, exposed the front and back of the body and limbs for "ten minutes on the first three days, for twenty minutes on the next three days, and then for half an hour daily for a week."[115] Tanned men then could sunbathe independently, and after three weeks the "parades were discontinued" and the men were not allowed to "wear more than shorts all day, and helmets were no longer compulsory."[116] The "senior medical officer of the troopship" reported "satisfactory results." He found "(1) improvement in general health, (2) diminution of . . . skin disorders, (3) low incidence of sun burn and of heat stroke, (4) relief of heavy strain on laundry facilities, and (5) accelerated acclimatization on arrival in a tropical country."[117] Meanwhile, the commanding officer of the troops observed upon landing in India that his "men were sufficiently inured to the sun to take the field at once" and concluded that the "results of this valuable experiment admit of no argument."[118] Nudists took pride in the fact that sunbathing aided troops fighting in the tropics and reprinted the *Journal of the American Medical Association* article in *Sunshine and Health.*

The contributions of American nudism and *Sunshine and Health* to the war effort garnered a favorable response from soldiers. Although many of the soldiers feigned interest in the organization to obtain copies of the magazine, more than one soldier reading *Sunshine and Health* likely also developed an appreciation for its articles on the moral and physical benefits of going naked. The editors boasted that most of the soldiers' letters sent to the flagship nudist publication expressed their "convictions that the basic principles of nudism are sound and have their unqualified approval."[119] One "draftee in the army" became an ardent devotee to nudism after he read an article in *Sunshine and Health*. After experiencing an unhealthy childhood and "other senseless habits" in early adulthood, the soldier declared that his "life's ambition [was] to be able to live the nudist life and be a worker for the movement."[120] Another soldier attributed his good health to regularly "playing baseball, football, and many other games in the nude."[121] He believed that regularly exposing his body to the outdoors "fortified [his] body against disease" and helped him through his "tough training."[122] Still another soldier professed nudism to be "one of the most worthwhile organizations for health there is."[123] Letter after letter complimented the health benefits of nudism, offered money to become a member of the organization, requested information about clubs in the area where the soldier was stationed, and promised to support the movement when the war ended.

In fact, the Second World War provided an opportunity for nudists to express their patriotism. Alois Knapp, who was elected the president of the American Sunbathing Association in 1943, used his "President's Message" to state the nudist position on the war: "We believe our country is right; we believe in democracy."[124] Since nudists considered their lifestyle to be the "utmost in freedom and democracy," they found it unproblematic to support America's battle against fascism.[125] Although the movement certainly struggled to establish itself in the United States, Knapp maintained that nudists remained "intensely patriotic."[126] They believed that their "way of life is inherently guaranteed under a democracy," while it would be "merely tolerated under some other form of government."[127] Knapp, an Austrian immigrant, concluded his "President's Message" by declaring, "It is good to be an American; its grand to be a nudist; it's glorious to be alive and free!"[128]

"A False Front for Unleashed Passion"

Nudism's commitment to sexual frankness attracted the attention of lonely troops stationed far away from the moral restraints of their homes and emboldened the nudist movement to display more erotic content in its publications. In the April 1942 issue of *Sunshine and Health*, the editors claimed, "not since the beginning of the American nudist movement have we witnessed the measure of interest in our program which is manifest today."[129] The editors boasted that they received "letters by the thousand from our armed forces scattered throughout the world" and within the past year had added "over a thousand soldiers and sailors" to their mailing list. The editors went on to speculate that "ten times that number" purchased the magazine in "canteens and newsstands."[130] The internal U.S. migration of young men and women into port cities for wartime jobs also exposed *Sunshine and Health* to an audience that had disposable income and most likely would not have come in contact with the magazine in their hometowns. The editors welcomed the new "enthusiasm" displayed by the "thousands of [people] in no wise connected with the services."[131]

Despite many years of promoting the therapeutic and moral benefits of nudism, the changing content and style of *Sunshine and Health* indicated that Rev. Boone sought to profit from the erotic desires and sexual fantasies of heterosexual soldiers. To capture the attention of soldiers who might be perusing the magazine for its pictures, the editors of *Sunshine and Health* highlighted a new "Letters from Men Far Afield" section with the silhouette of a naked woman leaning against a globe and standing in front of a large image of the letter V. The silhouette made little effort to mute the eroticism of the female body. It took the shape of a reclining woman with hair back, nipples erect, and arms open and awaiting the embrace of a lover. The editors then made it plain who they believed would be reading the letters, with titles above individual entries such as "With Our Armed Forces," "With the British Empire Forces," and "From a Brother in Khaki."[132] Far from objecting to the prurient gaze of the soldier, Boone transformed the style of *Sunshine and Health* to increase its circulation among soldiers and war workers.

Although the nudist magazine incorporated a more alluring style, Boone hesitated to introduce more graphic pictures that would upset censors. To limit the potential eroticism of the naked bodies in the magazine, the editors used deliberate posing and group pictures and retouched pubic hair and genitalia. The magazine offered a guide to readers who wanted to submit pictures to the publication. The "most preferred" photos diverted attention from the eroticism of the body through movements that captured "work or play activities, whether indoors or outdoors." Hoping to encourage the submission of pictures showing families, the editors also solicited images of "groups . . . from three to six persons." More risqué images that displayed "two or more persons" needed to show activities such as volleyball, swimming, or hiking and to "tell a story" to ensure that the photo depicted nudist principles rather than titillating the reader.[133] Pictures featuring "larger groups, couples, and singles" were undesirable since they might resemble pinups, evoke homosexuality, or imply group sex. A typical snapshot to remember family and friends, in which naked men and women stood "in a row in front of the camera," represented the "worst possible picture," according to the editors, because the naked body itself became the principal focus of the image.[134] Relying on movement, recreational activities, and familial groups, the images in *Sunshine and Health* presented a desexualized aesthetic.

The decision to exclude genitalia from *Sunshine and Health* restrained the potentially illicit character of the magazine, but it also betrayed the movement's commitment to sexual frankness. Since the magazine's inception in 1933, the editors followed the criteria laid out by John Sumner and the NYSSV and self-censored the pubic hair and genitalia of men, women, and occasionally children. Nudists resented the "mutilated pictures" that regularly appeared in *Sunshine and Health*.[135] The editors preferred to avoid airbrushing or scratching out the pubic area of men and women. This not only looked grotesque but, in direct opposition to the nudist cause, communicated shame and scorn for the natural body. Rather than appearing as hypocrites, they relied heavily on posed images that hid the pubic area but still appeared natural. In requesting pictures from readers, the magazine discouraged images that seemed to "call undue attention" to the pubic area, such as "full front views."[136] Instead, they asked photographers to send in pictures using "front quarter views and semi-side views" in order to "produce a 100 percent nudist picture [against] which no adverse criticism [could] be brought."[137] Numerous letters to the editor called for the publication to stop the practice, leaders within the movement felt that it disgraced the natural body,[138] and nudist photographers decried the omissions as inartistic.[139] Boone also objected to the assumption that the open display of genitalia constituted lewdness or prurience. Yet the managing editor of *Sunshine and Health* knew "he could not do otherwise at present."[140]

The aesthetic of nakedness constituted another major factor in the depiction, promotion, and eroticism of American nudism. On the one hand, the movement wanted to present nudism as it was practiced at nudist camps across the country; on the other hand, the magazine also aspired to promote the benefits of the health-oriented nudist lifestyle. These often-conflicting interests resulted in a debate within the magazine over whether to include less aesthetically pleasing images alongside the many svelte, young, well-proportioned bodies that simultaneously advertised the therapeutic benefits of going naked and appealed to the non-nudist reader looking for erotica. One photographer recognized, "we are trying to sell social sunbathing to our fellow citizens," and felt that the pictures should "present it honestly but attractively."[141] Although he maintained that "individuals showing the results of years of unhealthy living in the form of unsightly abdominal protuberance, scrawny limbs, or others having the misfortune to need trusses or leg irons" should be "welcomed and liked for their personalities" when met in camp, he maintained that including them in the magazine would "give a wrong impression to those who have not experienced the wonderful spirit and goodwill and wholesomeness that pervades [the] camps."[142] The aversion to exhibiting trusses and leg irons particularly conformed to public expectations that the disabled be hidden from public view. The Roosevelt administration went to great lengths to conceal the president's disability at public appearances and in the media in order to assure the electorate of his health, strength, and competency to lead.[143] Similarly, the photographer speculated that non-nudists would respond to such images by saying, "Do I have to look at that kind of thing if I go to your camp?"[144] Many nudists thought that the display of healthy, young, and athletic naked bodies in *Sunshine and Health* testified to the physical benefits of nudism and encouraged membership growth.

The inclusion of the aesthetically pleasing body alongside more quotidian examples of nakedness helped blur the lines separating the pornographic from acceptable visual representations. By incorporating the attractive and unattractive, the magazine tried to balance its goals of presenting the health benefits of the nudist lifestyle, comforting apprehensive potential converts, and avoiding the ire of censors. In a "defense of the potbellies," one nudist agreed that "no one will seriously contend that these [images] intrinsically are beautiful."[145] Yet he went on to observe that non-nudists most likely do not resemble "Apollo or Aphrodite" and maintained that an interested outsider might be "impressed with the fact that the nudists do not look like perverts, roués or idiots."[146] The non-nudist might be convinced to join the movement by seeing men or women who did not fear to show their less attractive body types. Although he hoped to "preserve them their quota of space in the magazine," the author of the article also reminded readers that nudists "by definition love nature and everything that is beautiful."[147] He called for pictures of "beautiful women and strong men even though such pictures may obviously be posed."[148] He felt that these pictures when combined with "truly nudist pictures" such as the "potbellies" would not "impair [*Sunshine and Health*'s] function in the non-nudist field."[149]

The effort to distinguish nudist representations from more erotic images did not stop *Sunshine and Health* from circulating widely among the troops serving in the Second World War. The editors of the magazine took pride in the fact that "thousands of boys in the services receive [the] magazines regularly."[150] Several men who wrote to the magazine to inquire about subscriptions or even to offer their endorsement confirmed the frequency with which soldiers shared and exchanged issues of the magazine with one another. One navy seaman admitted that the magazine "came into [his] hands quite by accident" when he was on a "ship in Pearl Harbor"; an initially skeptical soldier reported being won over to nudism after he "accidentally found" an issue, while another soldier "ran across it in the barracks," and still another soldier got his "hands on it" after the magazine had "made the rounds" in his sleeping quarters.[151] Letters that commented on the widespread sharing of *Sunshine and Health* revealed the magazine's popularity and open acceptance within the U.S. military.

The restrained eroticism of *Sunshine and Health* made the magazine attractive to military officials, who enforced a policy that gave troops the freedom to pursue their sexual desires as long as they did so with discretion. The editors of the magazine reported that "several commanding officers" endorsed the publication's "shipment to their commands abroad" and "certified that nudist publications were in the interests of the morale of the forces."[152] Generals and commanding officers valued virile soldiers and recognized that their troops needed to have an opportunity to satisfy their sexual desires while stationed far away from home. Yet they also worried that venereal disease posed a serious threat that needed to be avoided at all costs, and they assumed that reports of sexual indiscretions by soldiers would likely erode support for the war at home. These anxieties shaped military policies that publicly denied soldiers' sexual activities even as commanding officers distributed condoms to men going on leave or, in some cases, played a role in setting up places of prostitution in an occupied territory or country. Domestically, the military hoped to satiate soldiers' sexual appetites with respectable female companions rather than prostitutes, who in previous conflicts were blamed for spreading venereal disease.[153] The military relied heavily on "patriotutes," or women who provided entertainment, companionship, and even sexual favors to uplift the spirits of the troops.[154] Displaying more graphic images than most pinups but under the guise of a health movement, *Sunshine and Health* directed troops' attention away from prostitutes while still maintaining the appearance of respectability.

The nonthreatening, even humorous, character of American nudism found a place in *Yank*, a weekly magazine published by the U.S. military and written for and by soldiers during the Second World War. The military designed *Yank* to entertain and uplift the soldiers' spirits. Priced at five cents, the widely read magazine represented a particularly good value for soldiers seeking humorous cartoons, reports about the home front, and sexual content. Each issue included a suggestive pinup of an attractive, often well-known celebrity such as Ingrid Bergman, Lucille Ball, Rita Hayworth, and Marilyn Monroe (one of the first published images of Monroe). In one issue, next to a pinup of the actress Gloria De Haven in a bathing suit, *Yank* ran a "People on the Home Front" feature on American nudism.[155] The tongue-in-cheek column featured an interview with Alois Knapp and introduced the principles of the nudist movement while hinting at the erotic pleasures to be had in its publications. As Knapp explained the contributions that nudism could make to the war effort, improving health, promoting social equality, and minimizing voyeurism, the article described a picture displayed on the wall above his desk of a "brunette who has all the right trajectories" and "is peeled right down to the buff," which the writer found to be "delightful buff." The article also announced that *Sunshine and Health* included many similar "pictures which [did] not have titles" and "[spoke] for themselves."[156] *Yank*'s short profile on the nudist movement used humor to discreetly inform soldiers not already familiar with nudist publications that the magazine exhibited images far more graphic than the pinups officially sanctioned by the U.S. military.

The editors of *Sunshine and Health* began to experiment with more erotic content as more and more Americans felt comfortable with the erotic desires of the troops. The massive mobilization of troops into a sex-segregated environment provoked public fears of homoeroticism, because the "boys are deserted there with other boys," and interracial sex, since the troops might also "be surrounded and seduced by women of other nationalities, races, or class backgrounds."[157] To restore the illusion of "normative middle-class American heterosexuality," Despina Kakoudaki argues that the public embraced the pinup and insisted that "male soldiers need to be surrounded by photographs of sexy young women."[158] The shift toward greater tolerance for heterosexual desire and expression resembled nudist arguments that healthy sexual relationships depended on satisfying the "natural curiosity" to see and experience the naked body. While it also gave nudists greater liberty to use images and content that exhibited more than just sexually frank depictions of the body, the transformation of *Sunshine and Health* during the war weakened the movement's arguments that nudist materials contrasted markedly with commercial publications that profited from sex and sexual display.

The letters printed in *Sunshine and Health* acknowledged and accepted the troops' erotic interest in the publication. A soldier, who had been a botanist at the University of Illinois, wrote to the magazine reporting that "one of the fellows had brought it in thinking it was another of the 'strip-tease' publications which are so common here."[159] Expressing gratitude for the magazine, a member of the Army Air Force complained, "We get so lonesome at times that it is miserable," and added, "We can't find much comfort in the USO clubs," since he did not care for the "very cold business" of "paid hospitality."[160] Another soldier, who had found the magazine floating around the barracks, admitted that his "first reactions were quite the same as those of the other fellows."[161] He thought, "It was a pleasure to have in my possession such a priceless gem!" After "scanning it from cover to cover," however, he began thinking about nudism as a "sensible world movement rather than a false front for unleashed passion, which is the impression most people . . . seem to have of it."[162]

Some soldiers used the publication for more than just pictures. Some used the publication to advance their social lives after they returned from the battlefront. They took advantage of the "Nude Culture" section to advertise their desire to meet other nudists. One "ex-air-gunner" provided information about his marital status, physical appearance, and interests in a letter he sent to the magazine.[163] An "American of Polish decent" and a "widower by death" stated that he was "36 years of age," stood "5 feet 5 inches tall," had "brown hair and eyes," and weighed "150 pounds."[164] The recipient of a "fair education," he listed his interests: "outdoor sports, amusements, enjoy good health and interested in art, nudism."[165] He concluded his letter by soliciting "others, both men and women regardless of age, who are interested in similar ideas."[166] Listing his physical traits, interests, and marital history while soliciting communication without a reference to attending a nudist camp or function, his letter read more like a dating advertisement.

Sunshine and Health also celebrated the sexual virility and promiscuity of American soldiers on the battlefield. In an article titled "The Adventures of Hughie," the reader relived "D-day and H-Hour" as the "Headquarters representative at the front" recounted his "experiences and feelings during an Amphibian landing against the Japs."[167] Referring to Hughie as "our hero" and detailing every explosion, the article highlighted the soldier's bravery in the field. The Japanese's prompt retreat into the jungle prevented the story's hero from engaging in combat but did not stop him from boasting that he "would like to shoot a Jap for each of [his] girlfriends." The deliberate reference to multiple "girlfriends" hinted at Hughie's sexual prowess and celebrated his heterosexuality by acclaiming his promiscuity. The article, then, employed explicitly hyperheterosexual language that resembled the foreign-policy rhetoric of the Cold War, which relied on metaphors of penetration to articulate masculinized nationalism.[168] Hughie bragged that if given the opportunity to meet a Japanese soldier, he would "shoot him in the Rising Sun, jab his trench knife into his Grand Chrysanthemum, and then kick him in the swastika. The wicked villans!"[169] The assertion that the protagonist would forcibly castrate or sodomize Japanese soldiers with his knife or gun demonstrated the character's passionate hatred for a queered or feminized enemy while again evidencing his hyperheterosexuality.

The nudist movement's commitment to showing both male and female naked bodies appealed to men and women who began to explore their homosexual desires during the Second World War. The mass migration of people to cities such as San Francisco, Los Angeles, and New York City freed young men and women from the moral restraints of their families and small towns and created an environment where they acted on feelings they had previously been forced to deny or keep secret. Prior to the war, little homoerotic content appeared in *Sunshine and Health*. Many articles in the magazine maintained that satisfying the natural curiosity to see the naked body guarded against "perversions" such as homosexuality that came about, according to nudists, because of repressive religious organizations and misguided government censorship policies. Nevertheless, many gay men and women turned to *Sunshine and Health* during the war as a safe way to view images of the naked body. The classified advertisements in the back of the magazine also offered a space and a vocabulary to safely contact other gay men and women. Rather than discourage this interest, the editors began to include images, articles, and advertisements that appealed directly and indirectly to a gay male audience.[170] The support of a gay readership furthered the nudist goal to frankly display the naked body of both sexes and pushed the nudist movement to challenge the heteronormative boundaries of modern sexual liberalism.

Many of the images of naked men in *Sunshine and Health* resembled the highly stylized representations used in male physique magazines that also gained popularity with a gay male audience during and after the Second World War. At the turn of the twentieth century, the physical-culture movement began publishing magazines that encouraged male readers to participate in sports and to develop a muscular body as a symbol of masculinity during a period in which white-collar work threatened to weaken middle-class bodies. However, according to the historian David K. Johnson, as more gay readers purchased physical-culture magazines and placed classified advertisements requesting "physical culture studies," a group of gay-owned magazines emerged that used the trope of ancient Greece and bodybuilding to "legitimize male admiration for the bodies of other men."[171] In the

Many of the images of naked men in *Sunshine and Health* resembled the highly stylized representations used in male physique magazines that also gained popularity with a gay male audience during and after the Second World War. (*Sunshine and Health*, March 1947, inside cover; courtesy of the Sunshine and Health Publishing Company)

early 1940s, Bruce Bellas, who later became known as Bruce of Los Angeles, began one of the earliest beefcake mail-order businesses using his photos of strong, muscled, nearly nude bodybuilders at competitions, at beaches, in his backyard, or in his studio.[172] The snapshots often showed models outfitted as cowboys, Indians, or Greek gymnasts and reached gay audiences through the mail and on newsstands in the form of small, pocket-sized magazines. In *Sunshine and Health*, similar images of strong, handsome men flexing in a studio and posing to highlight the muscles in their back, chest, arms, or legs likely attracted gay readers who may not have been comfortable purchasing a physique magazine that increasingly served as a symbol of homosexual identity. Scattered in between images of men of all ages and body shapes participating in recreational activities, spending time with children, or working on a labor-intensive project stood the occasional picture that bore a striking resemblance to the representations featured in gay owned and operated physique magazines. By continuing to include images of strong flexing men, the editors revealed that they hoped to reach the same gay readership that purchased physique magazines as erotica.

The anxieties and fears that homosexuals served secretly in the U.S. military redefined the many images of naked men in *Sunshine and Health* as potentially homoerotic. During the Second World War, many psychologists and military officials believed that male nudity portended homosexual behavior. According to Allan Bérubé's *Coming Out under Fire*, one technique that psychologists employed to uncover latent homosexuality was to force soldiers to expose themselves to examiners.[173] The degree that the "naked selectee" felt discomfort or self-conscious about his exposed body represented "'slight signs' that might suggest homosexual tendencies."[174] The suggestion that the selectee should be made to remain naked through the interview further indicated that many psychologists believed that "physical nakedness could reveal the 'naked truth' about the hidden aspects of a man's personality."[175] The idea that the naked male body somehow unmasked homosexual tendencies may have had little merit, but it did demonstrate that many military officials and personnel associated male nudity with homosexuality. First Lieutenant Norman H. Noel, who served in the South Pacific, where he not only observed the naked bodies of indigenous peoples but also found that "nudity became an everyday occurrence," worried, "fellows might think I was queer to encourage [nudism]."[176] In a sex-segregated environment, where military officials attempted to expose homosexuals and soldiers worried about appearing "queer" because they went naked, the images in *Sunshine and Health* of strong, svelte, and handsome young men fostered the anxiety of communicating homoeroticism as much as its many images of attractive naked women catered to heterosexual desires.

Other content in *Sunshine and Health* revealed that the magazine in fact did appeal to men of all sexualities. In an exposé titled "A Nude

Night in Normandy," the magazine featured the romantic story of two male soldiers determined to sleep naked in a bunker that was being heavily bombed by Nazi forces. Alone and setting up camp for the night, the two men planned to "take off all [their] clothes, sleep in the nude above ground, and be really comfortable for a change."[177] With strong homoerotic tones, the article then described how the two soldiers "crawled luxuriously down between the blankets, snuggled up against each other, and prepared for a really heavenly night."[178] The article alluded almost explicitly to a sexual encounter between the two men only to have bombs interrupt the scene. Determined nonetheless, the two soldiers vowed that they "would sleep without clothes this one night even if it did have to be below ground, and regardless of the fact that the Nazis had apparently determined to make it an unpleasant night for [them]."[179] Hidden behind covers of attractive, large-breasted, naked women but placed alongside images of naked men, articles such as "A Nude Night in Normandy" drew the interests of a homosexual audience.

Sunshine and Health also provided a space for homosexual readers to contact and communicate with one another. In the back of each issue appeared numerous classified advertisements offering private and confidential developing of uncensored "art photos." Martin Meeker has found that gay men who feared arrest under the Comstock laws often exchanged nude images using such terms as "physique photos" or "athletic model photos."[180] One advertisement for a "graduate masseur" named Leo Lehman suggests that *Sunshine and Health* ads also used coded language such as "bodybuilding" and "Swedish Massage" to signal a desire for either photos or sexual contact or both. The advertisement, which began appearing in the July 1942 issue of *Sunshine and Health* and ran continuously for the next five years, also listed an address that located Lehman near a part of Los Angeles known by police as a "gay pick-up grounds."[181]

The image of the homoerotic, naked male body even represented the nudist movement in the pages of *Yank* magazine. A large photo of a middle-aged, naked Alois Knapp stood next to the profile of the nudism feature in *Yank*. The photo stood in stark contrast to the many images *Yank* used to excite the heterosexual male soldier. It conveyed a distinctly homoerotic quality with its exhibition of Knapp's fit and tan body and his warm, friendly face turning toward the camera and through the

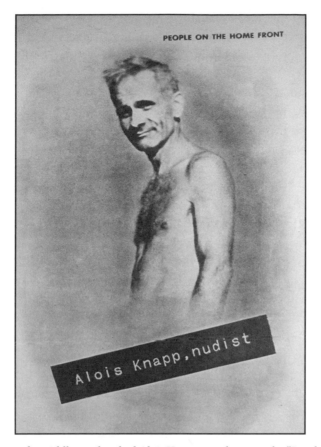

PEOPLE ON THE HOME FRONT

Alois Knapp, nudist

This photo of a middle-aged, naked Alois Knapp stood next to the "People on the Home Front" feature on American nudism in the June 22, 1945, issue of *Yank* and conveyed a distinctly homoerotic quality with its exhibition of Knapp's fit and tan body and his warm, friendly face turning toward the camera and through the playful effort of the editors to obscure his penis with a phallic black label. ("Alois Knapp, Nudist," *Yank*, June 22, 1945, 7)

playful effort of the editors to obscure his penis with a phallic black label that read, "Alois Knapp, nudist."[182] The blocking out of the penis represented a common trope in postwar beefcake images. According to Richard Meyer, decorative objects served to "both obstruct and insist upon the sexual display of the male body."[183] The choice to represent American nudism with an image of Alois Knapp that brought attention to his penis through a large, black, rectangular image more than likely reflected an effort to label the movement as queer. Private Debs Myers, the author of the article, completed his coded communication of nudism's homoeroticism by concluding the article with the example of a *Sunshine and Health* classified advertisement from an officer deployed at sea who wanted "to meet a companion who also enjoys sunshine and health."[184] Myers, perhaps invoking the campaigns waged by the U.S military during the war to crack down on the homosexual community in San Francisco, made a point to note that the ad listed a "San Francisco post office box."[185] He then sarcastically ended his piece by writing a skeptical "Un-huh" as a final remark on the sexual orientation of the author of the classified advertisement.[186] The article on nudism in *Yank* showed that for many in the military, nudism represented a queer movement.

The popularity of *Sunshine and Health* during the war emboldened nudists to challenge the boundaries of acceptable representation further by gradually including full-frontal nudity. In the magazine's first ten years, 1933 to 1943, very few images of genitalia appeared in the nudist publication. In the next seven years, almost 370 images that included genitalia graced the pages of the magazine.[187] Initially, the publishers sneaked a glimpse of pubic hair into the magazine amid the many pictures that avoided or airbrushed the region. It then began using uncensored images of men and women taken from a distance, gradually including pictures of women standing and facing the camera completely uncensored and, by the end of the war, violating the taboo against showing close-up images of the male penis.

Although these images exhibited genitalia, they still followed many of the previous conventions of nudist photography that attempted to mute eroticism. They relied on implied movement and activity and natural backgrounds and made sure that the subject of the photo did not directly interact with the camera. One image capturing a couple walking naked on a path surrounded by dense vegetation and seemingly unaware of the photographer emphasized the act of hiking while exhibiting the full naked body. In other images, *Sunshine and Health* guarded against implying sexual contact by isolating single men or women in representations that exhibited genitalia. Here men and women looked away from or past the camera with relaxed stances that displayed the genitalia but did not accentuate or draw further attention to the area. The images re-

The editors of *Sunshine and Health* often sneaked a glimpse of pubic hair into the magazine amid the many pictures that avoided or airbrushed the region (*Sunshine and Health*, August 1945, 15; courtesy of the Sunshine and Health Publishing Company)

Other images presented full-frontal nudity from a distance. (*Sunshine and Health*, January 1945, 17; courtesy of the Sunshine and Health Publishing Company)

NUDISM IS AN ELEMENTAL PART OF ANY BROAD PROGRAM OF MENTAL HEALTH

After the war, close-up full-frontal female nudity became increasingly common in *Sunshine and Health*. (*Sunshine and Health*, June 1946, inside cover; courtesy of the Sunshine and Health Publishing Company)

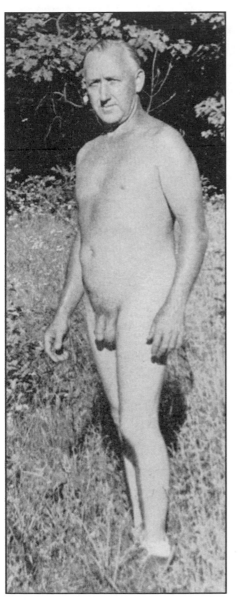

Even close-up full-frontal male nudity began appearing on the pages of *Sunshine and Health* in the postwar period. (*Sunshine and Health*, January 1947, 12; courtesy of the Sunshine and Health Publishing Company)

flected the movement's longtime goal to shamelessly exhibit the naked body while also satisfying the desire for more explicit erotica.

The same period that brought pubic hair to the pages of *Sunshine and Health* also witnessed the increasingly provocative imagery of the publication. While most of the covers in the decade prior to the war attempted to portray nudist life, many of the covers during and after the war served the same function as pinups. These issues featured full-breasted women exclusively, did not recall the natural setting of the nudist camp, and lacked the sense of realism that the magazine had long tried to convey in its pictures. The publishers officially announced this shift when they proposed using a "wide variety of treatments in respect to front covers" in order to determine what would be most popular.[188] The article prepared readers to see covers using "full color, duotones, combination of line cut and half tone, crayon reproduction, water colors and oil paintings."[189] The March 1947 cover, for example, featured a colored sketch of a full-breasted, smiling woman with windblown hair from the chest up. Officially, the editors explained that this shift would provide readers with the opportunity to "freely express their own judgment as to what appeals to them as most effective in the public presentation of our principle and practices."[190] Nevertheless, the increased emphasis on artificiality, the focus on full female breasts, and the exaggerated windblown hair of the March 1947 issue suggested that the magazine attempted to appeal to consumers who had no intention of visiting a nudist camp.

Conclusion

The exhibition of pubic hair for the first time and the use of pinup-style covers during the Second World War transformed *Sunshine and Health*. The increased sales of the flagship magazine and its acceptance within the ranks of the U.S. military gave its editors the confidence and security to stop self-censoring and posing its images restrictively. The movement, however, also provoked an almost immediate response from censors. Nudist covers that directly appealed to male readers attracted not only soldiers but the attention of postal agents. The U.S. Post Office refused to deliver the March 1947 issue of *Sunshine and Health* in New York City, Chicago, Philadelphia, Ohio, and many other locations across the country.

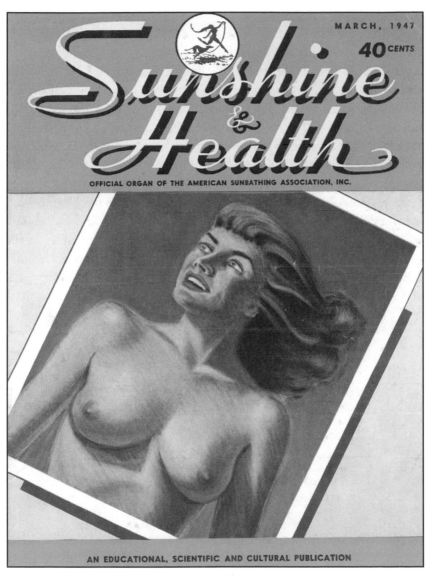

MARCH, 1947

40 CENTS

Sunshine & Health

OFFICIAL ORGAN OF THE AMERICAN SUNBATHING ASSOCIATION, INC.

AN EDUCATIONAL, SCIENTIFIC AND CULTURAL PUBLICATION

While most of the covers in the decade prior to the war attempted to portray nudist life, many of the covers during and after the war served the same function as pinups. (*Sunshine and Health*, March 1947, cover; courtesy of the Sunshine and Health Publishing Company)

Facing "complete financial ruin" but no longer willing to submit to the guidelines that constrained the magazine during its first decade in circulation, the editors of *Sunshine and Health* chose not to back down from a historic struggle to define the decent and indecent.[191] Instead of airbrushing their images or using subtle posing to avoid the display of genitalia, the editors dramatically confronted the Post Office by blocking out all the private parts of men, women, and children from the magazine. Placing small white pieces of paper over the breasts, genitalia, and even the buttocks, the editors mocked what they perceived to be the ridiculous policies of the Post Office. The editors considered the looming court battle in the federal courts "by far the most important, the most significant, and the most costly that [will have been] undertaken."[192] Neither the Post Office nor the nudist movement was willing to compromise anymore. The legal battle that ensued over the next decade offered a unique moment to determine where the lines of sexual expression should be drawn in American society.

NAKED IN SUBURBIA

Family Values and the Rise of the Nudist Resort

The August 1946 issue of *Sunshine and Health* printed a letter from a soldier who recently returned from serving overseas. Having discovered nudism in Europe, the soldier expressed enthusiasm for the lifestyle and an interest in the movement from a "health angle."[1] At first glance, the letter confirmed the beginning of a long-anticipated and unprecedented period of growth and prosperity for American nudism, spurred on by interested veterans and a pent-up desire for leisure. As a self-admitted "single man," however, the letter writer complained that several groups did not welcome him into their clubs.[2] Club managers informed him that they maintained "strictly a family group"; another emphasized that the club was "absolutely a family group," while others had suddenly "fizzed out" or reported that they would "never think of taking in younger members." The letter writer, citing his trouble-free experiences in European nudist clubs, did not understand the need to "ostracize the single man" in the United States.[3] Many club managers refused to accept single men because they raised concerns about voyeurism, infidelity, and homosexuality and ultimately threatened nudism's tenuous place within the heteronormative boundaries of sexual liberalism.

The use of eroticism to sell the therapeutic principles of the nudist movement during the Second World War attracted single men to nudist camps. The large number of bachelors attempting to enter the movement after the war highlighted the eroticism that many camps had attempted to mute through rustic locations and a commitment to health and recreation. Admitting members without girlfriends and wives invited accusations of voyeurism, raised the possibility of sexual transgressions, and simultaneously threatened to define camps as homosexual spaces. Although nudism profited from the interest it generated through the sensual images and content displayed in its flagship

131

magazine, the movement's continued prosperity in the postwar period depended on maintaining its precarious position within the boundaries of sexual liberalism by promoting the family-oriented character of the nudist camp.

The popularity of domestic tourism presented a particularly good opportunity for nudists to advance their cause in the postwar era. Vacationing spots often relaxed otherwise-entrenched social conventions. Resorts, historians have shown, had long been a place where visitors could experience "new sorts of pleasures" and "experiment with new, often less restricted, rules of conduct and behavior."[4] The tourist experience often implicitly or explicitly accepted the uncovering of the body, the public expression of sexuality, and even casual eroticism.[5] Ellen Furlough has described how the postwar French Club Mediterranean resort derived much of its allure from the potential pleasures that guests could explore in a climate that "relaxed the rules regarding sexuality."[6] Karen Dubinsky has shown that at Niagara Falls, the "honeymoon capital of the world," "sex tourism" flourished during otherwise sexually repressive historical periods. Niagara Falls, especially in the postwar period, relied on strict heterosexuality and the institution of marriage to prosper as a site where young couples "learned what was expected from them in entering public sexual culture."[7] Within the boundaries of marriage and the vacationing experience, many Americans experimented with public sexuality.

American nudists presented their resorts as familial, heterosexual, and respectable like Niagara Falls and hoped to prosper from the postwar tourist boom. By strictly managing or excluding individuals with naked bodies that suggested uncontrolled eroticism, nudist camps projected respectability by excluding the single man and the nonwhite body. American nudists protected themselves from legal troubles by conforming to homophobic, racist, and domestic heterosexual ideals. With a tenuous respectability earned through enforcing a rigid form of heterosexuality based on family, marriage, middle-class status, and whiteness, nudists subverted the proscription against public sexuality. The promotion of images of naked married men, women, and children on scenic grounds, sunbathing next to expansive lakes, and enjoying games of volleyball allowed the movement to successfully defend its expanding network of resorts against police raids.

An analysis of the postwar nudist resort demonstrates that early Cold War culture incorporated alternative sexual practices into its rhetoric of domesticity, conformity, and consensus. In 1958, the State Supreme Court of Michigan overturned the long-standing legal precedent established by the Ring trial that had prohibited nudist activities since the early 1930s. The decision resulted from a decade of rapid growth in nudist camps, fueled by respectable, middle-class, white families that accepted nudism as a legitimate vacationing experience defined more by family recreation than explicit eroticism. By the mid-1950s, 124 nudist parks were operating in all but ten states.[8]

"The Single Man Problem"

The naked bodies of single men represented a threat to all nudists regardless of their gender or age. The editors of *Sunshine and Health* explained that the "unlimited admission" of single men into a camp might "overbalance the membership of any group," driving away families and defeating the very purpose of social nudism.[9] The editorial reported that many nudists believed that the "motives of all single men who apply for nudist membership cannot not be accurately known at the outset."[10] Fearing heterosexual predators as well as latent homosexuals, camp members worried that a few "scalawags of the worst sort" might ruin the movement.[11] The insecurities of jealous husbands, in particular, led to fears that several "wolves on the prowl" would take advantage of their wives or children.[12]

Child molestation represented the greatest threat to the movement's respectability. At camp, few barriers existed to prevent members, whether single or married, from taking advantage of the club to abuse the naked bodies of nudist children. Fathers could just as easily be accused of molestation as single men.[13] Yet the growing numbers of single men brought the issue of child molestation at nudist clubs to the forefront. At the Cobblestone Suntanners in Yelm, Washington, on January 2, 1957, the local police charged Otis Paulsell, a two-time divorcé and father of four children, with "carnal knowledge and having a 14-year old girl pose in the nude for him." Since July 1951, Paulsell had regularly attended the club with his children; he had actively served on several committees and had always conducted himself in the "highest caliber and no one ha[d] ever doubted his integrity."[14] The discovery of five photos of his children, one of which may have exhibited an image of the "worst" kind,[15] caused Fred Barnett, president of the Cobblestone Suntanners to take action to "protect the club."[16] Barnett contacted Norval Packwood, then president of the ASA, who immediately enlisted the help of attorneys, held special meetings with club members about the arrest, and completely cut any ties the club had with Paulsell.[17]

While Paulsell had appeared to be a model nudist, his past and the circumstances surrounding his arrest seemed to confirm the hidden dangers of admitting single or divorced men to camp. Paulsell had been convicted of rape in 1938 and was released on probation after only two years because of a technicality. Known as a "camera bug" at camp, Paulsell explained that he took the questionable photo after he suspected his daughter of having sexual relations with her boyfriend one night and then pushed open her bedroom door and snapped a picture in the dark. According to Barnett, he had only retained the picture to "shame the kids into decency."[18]

The assumption within sexual liberalism that the family served as a barrier to sexual dangers allowed nudist leaders to avoid controversy and cover up incidents involving children. Despite claims that nudism had a flawless record when it came to protecting children at its camps, Packwood acknowledged after the Paulsell incident that "such happenings" were a "most unfortunate and an ever present danger" and that there seemed to be "little of anything" that could be done "to prevent them, other than for all clubs to take every possible precaution."[19] Yet few incidents of pedophilia or accusations of underage pornography at nudist camps came to light in the nation's newspapers or in the courts in the postwar period. Since the public clung to the assumption that the family guarded against illicit forms of sexuality and since the subject of child molestation remained a difficult topic to address publicly, nudist leaders easily maneuvered to hide potentially damaging incidents involving children. Packwood advised Barnett to handle the Paulsell matter with "extreme care" since it could be a "very messy thing" that might "put a bit of tarnish" on the nudist movement's record "in connection with juvenile sex delinquency."[20] Hiding behind the innocent conception of the family within sexual liberalism, nudist groups began to enact policies that would protect the movement from other potential scandals that might result from the interaction of naked men and children.

The need to guard against male sexuality resulted in a number of different policies. Officially, the ASA advised clubs to admit only single men who demonstrated good character.[21] Each individual nudist club, however, reserved the right to make its own policy regarding single men. Some clubs limited their membership to married couples exclusively; others made no restrictions based on marital status. Still others used a strict quota system to ensure balanced sex ratios.[22] Clubs that received a great deal of interest from bachelors, who, they felt, jeopardized the familial status of the camp, often chose to completely deny single men membership and implored these men to bring women. Some went so far as to award prizes to men who brought women.[23] These groups justified their policies by claiming that men who hid their nudist lifestyle from their wives or girlfriends risked undermining these relationships.[24] Moreover, most clubs did not accept married men whose wives refused to participate in nudism. One article declared, "if she will not become a nudist, he had no business being one himself."[25] Clubs with a more stable and balanced membership often sought out a compromise by limiting how many times a single man could visit the club,[26] by charging him higher rates,[27] or by trying to maintain a gender ratio of five men to three women.[28] Regardless of official membership policies, single men often felt excluded by married couples or family-oriented groups. One single man, who later deserted the movement, complained that he had been "'frozen out' of every camp he had attended over a three year period."[29] The exclusionary policies of nudist clubs threatened to limit the growth of the movement in the postwar period.

The restrictive policies toward single men at nudist camps also limited the number of homosexual men who participated in nudism. The fledgling gay rights organizations that emerged in the postwar period, nevertheless, took a positive view of nudism. Rudolf Geinreich, one of the founders of the Mattachine Society, an early gay rights organization formed in New York City in the 1950s, identified himself as a homosexual and a nudist. Geinreich believed that the "taboos against homosexuality and nudity encouraged shame, self-loathing, and the social control of personal behavior."[30] In 1959, *One*, a publication that the Mattachine

Society used to communicate with other gay rights organizations and to reach out to a broad homosexual audience, featured an article titled "The Homosexual Nudist" written by Kermit Josephs.[31] The article echoed Geinreich's understanding of nudism by asserting that the "mental attitude of the nudist and of the homosexual . . . is in many ways so similar that the homosexual is perfectly at home." Josephs explained that the "attitude of respect and admiration for the body is common to the nudist and the homosexual."[32] The many articles, photos, and classified ads that appeared in *Sunshine and Health* that appealed to a gay readership during the Second World War created a positive impression of nudism within the gay community emerging during the postwar period.

Yet the article asked, "Why then is homosexual representation in nudist clubs so small?"[33] Josephs, referring to his own experiences, maintained that nudist clubs did not make it a policy to exclude homosexual applicants. He remarked, "overtly homosexual applicants might possibly be eliminated at the first personal interview with officials of the clubs; but to my knowledge, this has not been the case."[34] Rather than homophobia, Josephs identified the exclusion of the "single man" as the primary reason behind the lack of homosexual men participating in American nudism. He described how any "unmarried men, singly or in pairs, even if superior in intelligence, well educated, or of good appearance, responsible in the business and professional world, . . . find the doors of nudist organizations closed to them."[35] Nudist clubs enforced this policy, according to him, in response to the disproportionate number of male applicants. He reasoned that it only required the greater participation of women to make nudism available to male homosexuals. Josephs declared that women would be "doing a service for the male homosexual" by joining the nudist movement, where "a happy way of life awaits him."[36]

While some single men accepted their exclusion, others vehemently objected to being treated as pariahs. One of the "much frowned upon single men" wrote that he found it "gratifying" that a group admitted him into camp, and he hoped that other groups would not "become too dogmatic" regarding the single man problem.[37] N. L. Hansen, a twenty-six-year-old single man, also continued to offer his "support, moral and otherwise and hope for the best."[38] Other unmarried nudists resented the rhetoric printed in *Sunshine and Health*. W. L Vannort, a single man who held an officer position in a nudist club in Oregon, described the material as "hopeless trash."[39] He thought that the fear of a gender imbalance dooming nudism originated from people who "imagine too much."[40] He particularly resented the discriminatory policies imposed on single men. Responding to clubs that required men to bring a female companion, he retorted, "don't ask the single outsider to do your missionary work for you."[41] Acknowledging that he was "swinging with both fists," he implored nudists, "Let the Single man have his place in the sun."[42]

Single men of "good character" represented a valuable asset to an emerging and developing movement. Some nudists recognized that bachelors were "more willing to pitch in and work" and often carried their "share of the financial load even when their fees [were] somewhat higher." It was also hypothesized that they would most likely bring their future wives and families to camp in the future.[43] These nudists argued that excluding all single men from the movement "*en masse* would be to deprive nudism of an excellent source of recruits."[44] In addition, exclusionary policies ignored the need for "new blood" in the form of "youthful individuals who will catch the spark and carry it on."[45] One letter to the editor worried that the "prejudiced public" looked on the "elder generation" of nudist leadership as "old fogies" and "sexy crackpots."[46] According to him, "every single youth being denied admission and membership to various groups is just one more nail in the coffin of that particular group."[47] Young singles, many who might be returning from war, not only would contribute to the construction and maturation of nudist clubs but also would lead nudism through its next phase of development in the United States.

With the issue threatening to stall the growth of the movement, many nudists wrote to the editor of *Sunshine and Health* in defense of single men. Vilma Bartlix of Portland, Oregon, believed there was "really no singles problem" since she had personally witnessed both naked single men and women interacting without any lingering looks, sexual indiscretions, or unwanted advances.[48] Rudolph Johnson of Yelm, Washington, encouraged readers to remember that "humans are humans be they single, married or just paired off for the purpose of attending meetings," in the hope that they might adopt a more tolerant perspective toward singles.[49] Other letter writers thought that the movement should have more confidence in its ideals. They believed that even if the single man came to camp with a "tongue-in-check attitude," the ideals of nudism would change his perspective. Any others "who prove undesirable" would quickly be weeded out.[50] Many nudists who advocated for the admission of singles did not embrace the free expression of public sexuality. Rather, they framed their defense by pointing out the absence of sexual indiscretions by singles and the role of nudist ideals in reshaping unacceptable erotic behaviors and by relying on expulsion as a last resort. They assumed that the appearance of a rigid form of heterosexuality centered on marriage and family life needed to prevail in order for nudism to continue its growth as a recreational activity. Like members who advocated for the expulsion of single men, defenders of single men understood the need to prevent the nudist camp from being seen as a place to pursue sexual relationships with other men, women, or even children.

Yet many single men found it very difficult to convince women to visit a nudist camp. For married men who developed an interest in nudism, the process of telling their wives could be daunting and risky. Clifford Kennedy, a man who turned to nude sunbathing to cure a "bad pair of lungs," found it extremely difficult to convince his wife that the practice would be beneficial for the entire family. His wife considered him "despicable, indecent, indelicate, offensive, obscene, immodest, vulgar, and [an] incurable moron" and sought a divorce.[51] Another single man "found it almost impossible" to "meet a nudist minded, decent, healthy girl."[52] Although the letters he read in the "Readers Forum" made "it sound easy," he reported losing "several very good girls" after he talked with them about nudism.[53] Gender ideals that expected modesty from young women, wives, and homemakers made the idea of exposing one's naked body to unfamiliar men highly erotic, taboo, and dangerous. While women with unconventional backgrounds and upbringings might have been willing to visit a park, the vast majority of women, subscribing to common gendered notions of modesty, represented a major obstacle for many single men hoping to join a local nudist camp.

Seeking to resolve the single man problem while continuing to encourage the movement's growth, the October 1947 issue of *Sunshine and Health*, featuring Rose Holroyd, who served as the recording secretary of the ASA, wrote that nudists could not "expect to have a movement

HOW CAN HE BEST TELL HER ABOUT NUDISM?

HERE'S a young man who's really got a problem on his hands! He wants to know how he can most effectively spread the doctrine of nudism. How can he best get across the facts that he has learned about living in the sun?

Who is he—and who is she? He is any young, intelligent, up-and-coming fellow whose mind has been opened to the manifold benefits and fun of the nudists' way of life. And she is any young, well-adjusted girl with the innate modesty, good looks and quick mentality that characterize the modern American girl. They live anywhere. They work at anything. They're active, ambitious, dependable—they're young America on the way up!

We want them in the nudist movement! We want them to enjoy nudism, to work for nudism to build nudism for the youngsters they'll some day bring into the world. For upon such young people the sound growth of nudism depends. If we can enlist the active interest of the many thousands of such young men and women, our troubles with local prudery and official bigotries will evaporate in their own stupidity.

How can we best enlist their support and interest? SUNSHINE & HEALTH sees the answer to that question as YOUR BUSINESS! Throughout this year we will devote much space in this magazine to YOUR ANSWERS to that question. Therefore, we invite you —one and all—to send us your best thoughts on this most important question.

Malcolm Ganteaume

SEND US YOUR ANSWER — IN A LETTER, AN ARTICLE OR A STORY

Advertisements in *Sunshine and Health* sought to address imbalanced gender ratios by offering men advice on how best to invite a woman to a nudist camp. (*Sunshine and Health*, January 1949, 6; courtesy of the Sunshine and Health Publishing Company)

large enough to give it the strength it so badly needs" if they continued to "make rules of exclusion."[54] She suggested that members "divert some of this energy" from excluding single men to conduct a campaign to "get single women in the movement."[55] The editors of *Sunshine and Health* heeded this call with an advertisement titled "How Can He Best Tell Her about Nudism?" Alongside a picture of a pontificating man flanked by one dressed and one undressed woman over his shoulders and a question mark over his head, the magazine called on readers to submit their opinions and suggestions.[56] Describing the man in the picture as "any young, intelligent, up and coming fellow" and the woman as "any young, well-adjusted girl with the innate modesty, good looks, and quick mentality that characterize the modern American girl," the advertisement declared, "We want them in the nudist movement!"[57]

To appeal to more women, the editors of *Sunshine and Health* again changed the appearance and content of the long-running nudist publication. The editors began running several columns in *Sunshine and*

Health that were written by women and for women and established a distinctly female focus and tone by addressing the anxieties, concerns, and interests of women. Evelyn Rawlings's "Women's Page" dismissed the "man's ideas or the man's viewpoint about nudism" and declared, "we girls should stand up and have a chance to speak for ourselves" rather than being "dissected and examined like some fly under a microscope by a bunch of men."[58] In subsequent columns, she related her battles to overcome her own conservative religious upbringing, offered practical suggestions that would enhance the female nudist experience, and pointed out the therapeutic benefits of a nudist lifestyle from a woman's perspective.

Other female nudists critiqued the gender ideals of American society and suggested that gendered social roles shaped the imbalanced interest in nudism. According to Evelyn Zimmerman, men were "naturally more unconventional than women and find it easier to do the things they like" even if they went against social norms. Women, on the other hand, had "always been more sharply criticized for [their] departure from the conventional patterns" and placed more importance on what their "friends would sanction," making them "more cautious."[59] Zimmerman then went on to describe how women suffered from a "deeply ingrained . . . shame complex." Due to "generations of emphasis on modesty and the gentle art of being a female decoration," she theorized that the attributes of the ideal wife became "demureness, modesty, innocence."[60] In addition, women fought their inhibitions. They often used the excuse that their "figure [was] not just right, too thin, too fat, an operation scar or some other alibi," to avoid attending a nudist camp.[61] To resolve the single man problem, American nudism had to overcome gender ideals that defined nakedness as an intimate and erotic experience and made many women uncomfortable exposing their bodies regardless of the environment or setting.

Although *Sunshine and Health* transformed itself into a more female-oriented magazine, nudists did not try to challenge the restrictive gender ideals that they believed led to the imbalanced sex ratios at their resorts. The movement wanted to reach out to women who conveyed middle-class respectability to ensure that nudist resorts communicated family, recreation, and health rather than illicit behavior. As a result, nudists framed their appeal to women by evoking the very characteristics that made women reluctant to display their naked bodies. They invoked the attributes and responsibilities of the ideal wife to convince women to give the nudist lifestyle a try. One article, titled "Why We Women Went to Camp," described the ideal nudist woman as a wife whose "principle duty is to keep her husband happy."[62] The wife is the one who will "smile the brightest when she is weariest, who attends a movie with a splitting headache, who entertains after a busy day." But most of all, the ideal wife should go to a "nudist camp for the first time . . . all because he asks it of her." Women, according to Mary Columbus, the author of the article, had no interest or desire to go to nudist camps. She remembered the "trepidation in her heart" the first time she attended a camp.[63] She only went along with her husband's unusual interest to "keep 'him' happy."[64] Other articles echoed this sentiment when they encouraged women to "give your husband a break, try their nudist ideas."[65]

The genre of the short story also sought to reassure skeptical wives in the pages of *Sunshine and Health*. These stories regularly featured an extremely reluctant wife or female companion who had to overcome her anxieties and fears about nudism, either willingly or through the chicanery of her husband, friend, or boyfriend.[66] Acknowledging that many women remained uncomfortable with, skeptical of, and even scared of visiting a camp, nudists used the articles and images in *Sunshine and Health* to show everyday, middle-class homemakers that they could uphold their role as a respectable and dutiful wife even when they agreed to visit a resort with their husband.

Other articles went beyond the topic of nudism to appeal to women readers. Engaging the female experience, regular columns took up the topics of pregnancy, childbirth, parenting, cooking, shopping, and exercise. Although the authors tried to relate these topics to nudism by explaining the way that sun and exercise benefited the pregnant mother[67] or by discussing how early exposure to the opposite sex's naked body would help a child's mental development,[68] articles also specifically focused on exclusively feminine topics such as "Your Obstetrician May Be Too Impersonal."[69] Other columns sought to make the homemaker's daily routine a little easier or more enjoyable. Margaret A. B. Pulis's "Eat Healthy and Like It" listed recipes that "reduce[d] the homemaker's work" and saved the family money. Recipes such as "home made biscuit mix," "Cinnamon Buns," "Steak and Peppers," and

"Party Chicken" helped the housewife feed her children, please her husband, and entertain her friends and neighbors.[70] "Marge's Mail Mart" offered women advice on shopping and provided women the option of purchasing domestic products such as flexiclogs, pot holders, knife holders, bathroom-tissue holders, matching his and her watches, and a marriage medal through the magazine.[71] Still other columns offered advice on exercise routines that aesthetically improved parts of the female anatomy. Dick Falcon's "Trim & Firm Those Hips and Thighs" came replete with nude pictures of athletic young women performing specific exercises, alongside detailed instructions from the trained fitness instructor on the various methods that led to an attractive, shapely, and healthy body.[72] Although the attractive and shapely women that almost exclusively graced the covers of *Sunshine and Health* continued to appeal to individuals seeking naked images of men and women, many of the magazine's pages began to read like a women's magazine.

A controversy surrounding Rev. Ilsley Boone's control over the ASA's finances also created the opportunity for several new female leaders to take a greater role in the nudist movement. Women such as Zelda Suplee, who operated Zoro Nature Park with her husband, Alois Knapp, since the early 1930s, had long contributed to the operation of nudist clubs and helped the movement maintain its "mom and pop" character.[73] Yet, prior to the postwar period, no women occupied official leadership positions in the ASA. Yet whisperings and accusations that Rev. Boone improperly managed the organization's finances to his benefit eventually led to his downfall and the emergence of several prominent female nudist leaders. The postwar influx of new members led to the formation of several regional organizations with their own independent leadership networks. Many of these new voices began to question Boone's "despotic tendencies, manipulations of organizational funds, and monopolistic control of its affairs through an intricate system of dummy corporations." To reestablish stability and to communicate the importance of family to new members, several middle-aged women, such as Margaret A. B. Pulis, emerged to fill the leadership void left by Boone.[74] These women brought respectability to the movement at a time when the influx of single men threatened the stability of camps.

Pulis, Rev. Boone's daughter, represented the ideal figure to assume leadership in the nudist movement. With three children and two grandchildren and as an active member of her local Parent Teacher Association (PTA), Pulis displayed the moral authority of a mother and grandmother. With volunteering representing one of the defining duties of the 1950s homemaker, Pulis encouraged nudist women to participate in their local communities as representatives of the movement. She suggested that members join local community organizations such as the "state mental Hygiene Associations, the Boy Scouts, the Parent Teacher Association, the YMCA and YWCA, Red cross, Chambers of Commerce, 4h Clubs, church organizations, etc."[75] Here, women might not only contribute to "building a broader and wider understanding of nudism in the minds of the general public" but would also demonstrate that "nudists are nice people, willing workers, valued members of the community."[76] Pulis held up her experiences in her New Jersey community as a successful model to follow. During the war, she worked as the secretary of the Civilian Defense Council and was later appointed chair of Community War Services. After the war, she twice served as president of a high school PTA and later acted as the county social hygiene chair in the PTA. In addition, she boasted of being the secretary of her local political club and continued to be a member of her nearby Woman's Club. Asserting "[I do not] know of a single instance where I have lost a friend because of my acceptance of nudism," Pulis called on other nudists, especially women, to act as representatives of the movement in their communities.[77]

The effort to reduce the disproportionate attendance of single men in nudist clubs by bringing more women into the movement resulted in increasingly balanced sex ratios. In 1956, Frederick Geib surveyed over seventy adult members of a northeastern nudist camp and found a ratio of thirty-seven males to twenty-nine females at the camp.[78] Geib's data confirmed that the "restrictions the movement places on unmarried persons" accounted for the lack of younger members and the familial makeup of the camp's membership.[79] Far more likely to be single when young and also lacking the discretionary income to join a camp, the average member waited until he or she approached middle age to begin participating in a local club.[80] The vast majority of members fell between the ages of thirty-five and forty-five with the youngest being twenty-three and the oldest being seventy-seven. This resulted in a mean age of 40.7 years—significantly higher than the average age of most Americans, which, according to the 1950 census, was 31.9 years.[81] In addition, 81 percent of the adult membership reported being married, 9 percent reported single status, and the other 10 percent represented widows, the divorced, or the separated. Although the incident involving Otis Paulsell and his children at the Cobblestone Suntanners Club showed that the problem of child molestation persisted regardless of the marital status of the men at a camp, the number of children who attended nudist clubs did not decline in the postwar period. Of the 91 percent of the nudists in Geib's survey who were married or had been married, 77 percent had children and brought them to camp.[82] According to Geib's data, the organization's unfriendly stance toward single men and its promotion of families resulted in an overwhelmingly middle-aged, family-oriented membership.

National Negro Sunbathing Association

The fear of the single man and his uncontrolled eroticism was not the only threat to the American nudist resort. The continued migration of African Americans from the South to work in war industries heightened fears of racial mixing around the country.[83] As a result, many presumably white nudists remained "fearful" that the interaction of naked white and nonwhite bodies would negatively impact the image of the movement and "considered any discussion of this question as untimely."[84] One man, fearful of what he assumed to be hypersexual African Americans, wrote to the editor claiming that only a person with a "sinister object in mind" would want to bring other races into nudist camps.[85] Urging members to "keep the nudist camps free from scandals," he suggested that "separate camps for Negro and separate camps for white can hurt no one."[86] The discrimination and prejudice that structured American society, specifically with stereotypes of the hypersexual racial other and the rampant fears of racial mixing, shaped a nudist policy of racial exclusion.

Even though few African Americans frequented camps, white nudists conformed to a society still divided along lines of race. One camp in Jamal, California, explained its policy of exclusion with the statement, "Double prejudice is a long row to hoe."[87] As a "naturally suspect group," nudists felt that they had to "bend over backwards" to comply with the "rules and morals of a community."[88] While they might not necessarily want to discriminate and exclude nonwhite people, many nudists believed that the "presence of Negroes would jeopardize the very existence of their camps because of pressure from prejudiced neighbors."[89]

The effort to exclude the nonwhite body conflicted with the way American nudism idealized and romanticized the racial other in its ideology and principles. Since the 1930s, nudists had held up the indigenous body as an example of health and uncorrupted morality. In the context of the Second World War, when American soldiers came in greater contact with nonwhite peoples around the world, this trope did not abate.[90] One 1944 article declared, "The original American Indian wasn't subject to colds. The same applies to the Eskimo and other primitive races. The South Sea Islanders were the most healthful people of earth until the missionaries put Mother Hubbards on them and doomed them to extinction."[91] Pointing out that the white man, bundled up in suits and several layers of garments, had brought the "common cold, pneumonia, tuberculosis, and kindred ailments," the writer suggested that the reader take a "few lessons from our more primitive brothers."[92] He commended the "Indian, the African native, the Polynesian" for only wearing clothing when "necessity demanded" since this allowed the skin to gather strength and resilience.[93] To eliminate ill health in modern Western society, the writer asserted that we only had to "prove ourselves as smart as the unlettered savages."[94] As a part of the distant natural world and landscape or a forgotten historical trope, the bodies of the racial other posed little threat to American society or nudism.[95]

This romantic view of nonwhite peoples, however, established a foundation for some nudists to call for the integration of camps. Having long sympathized with the "negro, who probably suffers more greatly from undue clothing than does the dominant race," one writer reminded readers that nudists should "not look for the emergence of a race of white nudists alone."[96] The fight against fascism during the Second World War also pushed nudists to address the role of race in their movement. Alois Knapp, in his June 1943 "President's Message," recognized that the "sons of all mothers the world over are now fighting aggression in the far-flung corners of the globe." He noted that the "blood of many of them mingles into one pool, oozing out of the body of the white man, Negro, Indian, yellow man, [and] brown man."[97] On the basis of these observations, he then went on to assert that nudists could not "seriously criticize the anti-social philosophy" of their enemies until they themselves "get the all human viewpoint."[98] Stating that American nudism never made any test of politics, religion, or philosophy, he called on nudists to have the "courage" to add "race and color" to the rubric.[99] Inspired by the African American community's Double Victory campaign, many nudists felt the need to open their movement to African Americans.[100]

The abstract debate over racial integration in *Sunshine and Health* became reality when Lewis Harding White, the secretary of the Western Conference, visited an African American husband and wife at a nudist camp near Los Angeles.[101] He asserted that he was "proud to meet" them and recalled their good sense, sanity, and balance when discussing nudism. The couple impressed White so much that he called for any African Americans interested in nudism to write to him personally for more information. He specifically asked them to include an account of themselves, including their background, whether they had practiced nudism, and if they spent any time in the army. E. J. Samuels, the African American man whom White met in Los Angeles, went on to write several columns in *Sunshine and Health* addressing the racial integration of nudism. Samuels reasoned, "You were born without clothes. You were born without racial hatred. You were taught to wear clothes. Likewise, you were taught racial prejudice."[102] Now that nudists had become "unconventional enough" to remove their clothing, he thought it would be "just as easy to remove racial prejudices."[103] Rejecting assumptions that his ideas were too idealistic, he recounted his pleasant experiences visiting White's home club. "Unmistakably Negroes," he and his wife went "swimming, played volleyball, took long hikes, lolled in the sun" just like any other nudist. Recalling the experience, he stated that he and his wife "never had so much fun in all [their] lives." Welcomed as a frequent dinner guests, visiting other guests in their trailers, and making true and fast friendships, he enjoyed the atmosphere of "friendship and brotherly love." This initial experience influenced him to join the club, although he hoped to form a club of his own that would "open [its] doors to all nudists, regardless of race, color, creed, or national origin."[104] Samuels positioned his and his wife's first experience at a nudist camp as a successful example of racial integration.

In a long, well-illustrated 1951 article by Herbert Nipson titled "Nudism and Negroes," *Ebony* also used Samuels and his wife, the "first Negro delegates ever to attend a nudist convention in America," as an example of racial progress.[105] Using pseudonyms, the article recalled the feelings and experiences of the Samuelses' first visit to a nudist camp. Throughout their first day, they experienced "absolute racial equality" dining, playing, swimming, hiking, and sleeping in the same rooms with the white nudists.[106] The *Ebony* article then related the struggles of nudists as an extreme minority to the experience of African Americans in the United States. Nipson explained that the lifestyle had been "outlawed in many parts of the country, . . . groups have been hounded by the police, snickered at by the general public, shadowed by peeping toms, . . . and even felt the lash of . . . the Ku Klux Klan which has stamped anything 'so different' from the accepted norm as evil and un-American."[107]

Despite the best efforts of the Samuels to advocate for integration and *Ebony*'s presentation of nudism as a symbol of racial progress, many white members of nudist clubs remained opposed to interacting with nonwhite nudists, and others worried that the interaction of naked white and nonwhite bodies might provoke unwanted attention. The ASA responded to calls for integration with a policy of segregation. Based primarily in the Northeast, upper Midwest, and West, the ASA proposed the development of independent "groups of nudists of the colored race" at a moment when unprecedented numbers of African Americans relocated to urban centers of these regions in order to take advantage of wartime job opportunities. Recognizing the increasing fears of racial mixing within the movement and in society as a whole, the national organization felt it would make for "greater sociability and congeniality on the part of any distinctively social or racial group if it were to support and develop its nudist tendencies within its own group."[108] Nudist leaders proposed that future "Negro nudists" form their own organization, under the title of the National Negro Sunbathing Association, with its own elected officials, headquarters, and magazine.[109] *Sunshine and Health* would help the development of this proposed organization by running a separate column devoted to "negro activities," listing the new groups forming, and providing information about the formation of the organization.[110] Hoping to deflect accusations of racism, the ASA explained that this policy of segregation was designed "purely" to encourage "the happier development of the local social unit or group."[111]

In a column published in *Sunshine and Health*, Samuels explained his opposition to segregated nudist camps. He felt that segregation would simply not work economically because a future group of African American nudists would not be able to support their own network of clubs financially, let alone their own magazine.[112] He proposed that all nudists should belong to the same organization and that local clubs or groups be left free to choose who may or may not be admitted to their club. He then asserted that the word "Negro" should be used for "identification purposes and not discrimination."[113] Further, Samuels thought all clubs should have the right to vote in white or black members regardless of the racial traits of their membership. However, the persistently unfriendly racial climate of the country influenced Samuels to recognize the need for nudist organizations to remain "careful in selection."[114] He understood that the "standard for the Negro has always been the worst Negro."[115] If "one bad Negro is discovered—that is the end of the Negroes in that camp," and the "entire race is penalized for the misconduct of one."[116] Although Samuels rejected an official policy of segregation, he also recognized the risk involved in admitting African Americans into nudist camps and reluctantly endorsed high membership standards.

Many nudists also considered the ASA's segregation proposal racist. In a letter to the editor of *Sunshine and Health*, Dr. and Mrs. L. S. Bambauer felt "surprised and disappointed" that the ASA would support a policy of segregation.[117] Believing that this policy could only be the "offspring of race prejudice," the couple felt the need to "register a strong protest against any such move."[118] They thought nudism stood for the "principle of the inner worth of every man and woman, regardless of religion, social position, or accidental color of one's skin."[119] Echoing the argument that other nudists had made in defense of single men, the Bambauers asserted that a policy of segregation "would do great harm to the whole nudist movement" by further "dividing" the group at a time when nudism needed all the support it could get.[120] They hoped that, rather than create an entirely separate organization, the national association would "encourage [African Americans] into [nudists'] fellowship, not out of it."[121] However, these calls for racial unity fell on deaf ears. For many individual clubs, the need to suppress any potential hint of racial mixing was far more important than incorporating any future contributions that nonwhite nudists might make to the movement.

"A Nudist Mecca"

To overcome the challenges posed by the sexual anxieties and racial fears of postwar society, the American nudist movement transformed its fledgling network of isolated rustic camps into well-equipped resorts ready to cater to young, middle-class, white families in search of leisure and recreation. American nudism benefited directly from the increasing availability of leisure in the 1950s. With over half of American families owning a car by 1948, more workers earning paid vacations than ever before, and an expanding interstate highway system, travel became easier, more affordable, and potentially anonymous.[122] While many families packed in the car to experience the nation's natural scenic beauty by visiting patriotic landmarks, camping at national parks, or concluding their trip at a popular amusement park such as the recently opened Disneyland,[123] others could just as easily veer off the beaten path to escape the stresses of modern life with a relaxing, therapeutic, and fun-filled day of nude sunbathing, swimming, and volleyball.

Nudism fit seamlessly into an already well-established culture of camping. Late-nineteenth-century reformers, concerned about the rise of industrial capitalism and the expansion of the corporate workplace, organized a summer-camp movement to help children and their parents escape squalid urban environments and the monotony of office work.[124] The locations, activities, and climate of these summer camps shared the back-to-nature idealism of the postwar nudist resort. Located outside urban centers near major highways and with campers enjoying outdoor exercises, hiking, swimming, and rowing, nudist camps were essentially summer camps without clothes.[125] Even this difference seemed to fade away at times. In addition to children occasionally choosing to skinny-dip at the local lake, Kenneth Webb, one of the main promoters of organized camping in the United States, suggested as part of his back-to-nature philosophy that campers embrace nudity at campsites.[126] Nudists nestled into an already well-established tradition of camping with similar activities and values.

Participation in nudism and regular attendance at a nudist club required both time for leisure and disposable income. Nudists often reported high levels of education that resulted in desirable occupations. While the 1950 census found that Americans had, on average, 9.3 years of education, the average nudist reported 13.4 years of education.[127] Nudists also earned higher incomes. In 1950, the average family earned $2,992.[128] In comparison, 47 percent of the members at one nudist camp reported incomes between $3,000 and $4,999, and 48.5 percent earned incomes between $5,000 and $9,999.[129] Another 3 percent took home less than $3,000, and 1.5 percent made more than $10,000.[130] Reflecting a growing reliance on women's wages to support the high standard of living enjoyed by many postwar families, 24 percent of the members at one nudist camp also reported that their wife contributed to household earnings.[131] Further reflecting the white-collar character of nudism, the most common profession at the camp fell in the category of clerk (27.1 percent), while unskilled labor constituted the least prevalent occupation at 2.2 percent. Skilled workers and farmers (25.0 percent); proprietors, managers, and officials (20 percent); semiskilled workers (14.5 percent); and professional persons (10.4 percent) constituted the other occupations at the camp.[132] On the basis of these higher-than-average education levels and incomes and more distinguished occupations, American nudism was defined by a demographic with the means to pursue leisure and travel.

The dramatic growth of nudist resorts in the postwar period made it easy for middle-class families to frequent the nudist club of their choosing. The 84 clubs that *Sunshine and Health* listed as active in 1936 had grown to 124 by 1954.[133] Taking into account the high failure rate of early nudist clubs makes the 124 clubs listed in 1954 an even more dramatic figure. Only 10 percent of the clubs from 1936 appeared on that same list in 1954. Norval Packwood, then president of the ASA, explained that the organization had reduced its "turn-over" rate to 4 percent and improved its rate of increase to 25 percent after the Second World War.[134] With many camps suffering dramatic membership losses due to gas rationing and the war effort in the 1940s, the dramatic postwar growth of American nudist clubs signaled a significant shift toward more accepting attitudes toward nudism and a willingness to participate in nudist activities.

An estimated ASA membership of twenty thousand practicing nudists around the country supported a dispersed network of clubs.[135] The biggest increase in nudist resorts by region occurred in the West.[136] This trend likely reflected the expansion of the national highway system, a more temperate year-round climate, the availability of land, and a mythology that idealized individuality and freedom. Including the mountain and Pacific states, the West accounted for 37.8 percent of American nudist resorts in 1954—up from 20.5 percent of the total number of clubs in 1936.[137] The Northeast and North Central regions, however, both showed a significant decline in clubs. Reflecting the impact of hostile legislation that banned the lifestyle in Michigan and New York and the unfriendly reception nudism received from Chicago residents, the movement's early strongholds in the Midwest and Northeast declined dramatically from a zenith of 48.7 percent of nudist resorts in 1936 to only 39.6 percent in 1954. The membership of the South's nudist clubs during this same period stayed steady, with approximately 20 percent of the total number of nudist clubs, despite a warmer climate.[138] While clubs were more plentiful in the West than in the Northeast, the Midwest, or the South, Americans from almost any part of the country would not have found it difficult to travel by car to a nearby nudist club.

In the early years of American nudism, managers selected campsites on the basis of their seclusion, availability, and price. After the war, these rustic and austere spaces were transformed into well-equipped scenic resorts ready to cater to prosperous middle-class families. Rather than stressing the need for isolation, numerous articles in *Sunshine and Health* advised prospective camp managers to identify grounds with large lakes, flowing streams, and bountiful vegetation if they wished to establish a successful club that would attract members and visitors.[139] Sunshine Park in Mays Landing, New Jersey, stood out as the preeminent example of the new nudist resort. Located just fourteen miles outside Atlantic City, the national headquarters of the ASA contained a large lake and beautiful sprawling grounds spreading out over one hundred acres.[140] In the postwar years, the construction of a new office building, dining hall, and kitchen and many other improvements to the already impressive grounds established Sunshine Park as "a nudist mecca."[141] Constructing an atmosphere that revolved around family, domesticity, and traditional gender ideals, nudists created a space for their camps within the postwar vacationing experience.

Sunshine Park's redesigned entrance symbolized the beginning of a new era for American nudism. In the summer of 1946, the camp manager dismantled the "old natural-log entrance" and replaced it with a "new semi-elliptical concrete wall" that had two openings on either side for cars to freely enter and exit.[142] The imposing new entrance functioned to deter unwanted onlookers just as the old log entrance had, but its permanent concrete structure also communicated a sense of stability and permanence that gave visitors confidence in the resort and the movement's place in American society. In a photograph used to advertise the new improvements to Sunshine Park, the redesigned gate also exhibited the heterosexual character of the park. Featuring a middle-aged naked man and woman standing on opposite sides of the structure to welcome guests, the image displayed the gate's size and signaled that the camp preferred established heterosexual couples over single men or women. Exhibiting stability and domesticity, nudists felt "proud of the austere dignity" that the new entrance bestowed on Sunshine Park.[143]

Additionally, the camp manager understood that the privacy and anonymity afforded by the automobile allowed more Americans to frequent the parks than ever before. To encourage this trend, he designed the entry at Sunshine Park to instill a "feeling of exhilaration" for motorists. Driving past "ornamental wrought-iron gates" and through a long "roadway shaded by tall majestic pine trees," visitors entered a private sanctuary far away from their stressful lives and, most importantly for nudists, far from restrictive social conventions.[144]

Sunshine Park's sprawling grounds, highlighted by the "Great Egg Harbor River," did not disappoint tourists in search of nature. The "unusual body of water" located at the center of the grounds constituted a unique ecological resource. With the river displaying a "strong color of tea" and containing "remedial elements derived from the cedar forest through which it flows," the camp boasted of its natural therapeutic qualities to visitors and guests.[145] Nudists claimed that the river soothed muscles and relieved any itching and irritation from rashes, bug bites, and sunburns. With a permanent dock installed on its banks, the river also lent itself to a variety of recreational activities. Completely enclosed

The spacious entrance is one's initial introduction to the spirit of gracious hospitality that characterizes Sunshine Park.

The construction of a permanent concrete gate in front of Sunshine Park in Mays Landing, New Jersey, communicated a sense of stability and permanence that gave visitors confidence in the resort and the movement's place in American society. (Dana, "Sunshine Park: A Nudist Mecca," *Sunshine and Health*, June 1954, 14; courtesy of the Sunshine and Health Publishing Company)

by the dense vegetation that surrounded the river, members could use the dock to freely sunbathe, dive, or swim in the nude. More adventuresome guests could also partake in canoeing, rowing, waterskiing, or even power boating.[146]

Assuming a standard gender division of labor that assigned women the responsibility for child care, a 1957 promotional piece presented the sandy beach of Sunshine Park's river as the perfect play area to keep "junior out of Mother's way for hours."[147] With a "bucket and shovel," children could create "sandy castles for Daddy to admire, and holes in the beach in which he may sprain an ankle."[148] Therapeutic and recreational, the nature-oriented grounds of Sunshine Park provided the setting for an idyllic, nature-filled family vacation without undermining the gender ideals and expectations that grounded the postwar ideology of domesticity.

For nudist parks not equipped with a natural body of water like Sunshine Park's, the swimming pool represented an absolute necessity. Like many postwar motels and hotels that used glittering pools to entice traveling families to stay a night or two, nudist resorts made sure to design swimming pools that would impress visitors and make them want to return.[149] The ideal pool at a nudist park would be surrounded by a "beautifully patterned concrete sunning space, handsome tables and chairs, umbrellas and possibly trees."[150] In the absence of trees, a "shaded bower" could be constructed to make members more comfortable on unbearably hot or sunny days.[151] The pool represented such a critical element of the nudist club that do-it-yourself articles appeared in *Sunshine and Health* explaining how to install heating and filtering equipment in swimming pools.[152] Providing a setting for relaxed conversation, providing a way to cool down after extended sunbathing sessions, and giving children another place to play, the swimming pool represented an essential attribute for any nudist park that did not have a natural lake or river.

The sporting facilities at nudist resorts constituted another forum for family fun and socializing. With health and fitness a central component of the nudist lifestyle, Sunshine Park provided a six-acre sports quadrangle illuminated by electrical fixtures. Constituting the heart of the club where members congregated, the sports quadrangle also represented the "ideal place to meet friends and influence people."[153] When not socializing, guests could play volleyball, shuffleboard, tennis, or badminton and engage in many other athletic activities well into the night.[154] While members liked to sample other sports and activities, the "national game of nudists everywhere" was volleyball.[155] The game grew in popularity among nudists for several reasons. In addition to being easily set up and lacking complicated rules, it allowed many players, both male and female, young and old, to participate simultaneously with relatively little opportunity for awkward running, jumping, or physical contact.[156] A game of volleyball also relieved the jitters of novice nudists by focusing the members' eyes away from each other and onto a ball and net. Providing a relaxed social atmosphere and the opportunity for exercise, fitness, and health, nudists appealed directly to postwar families in search of leisure.

When inclement weather descended on Sunshine Park, the huge forty-by-forty-six-foot clubhouse allowed members to continue to enjoy themselves with a variety of activities.[157] A record player and player piano played music for dancing and music aficionados. Meanwhile, the availability of chess, checkers, and books appealed to guests seeking relaxation. At night, the clubhouse often offered entertainment with shows that featured "professional—and not so professional talent."[158] In addition, a party held in the clubhouse usually commemorated every calendar holiday. From strenuous sporting activities in the hot sun to leisurely entertainment in the clubhouse, Sunshine Park provided a number of activities for its guests regardless of the weather.

To specifically appeal to mothers and to help men convince their wives to visit nudist camps, many camp managers put a great deal of effort and resources into children's play areas. Again assuming that women shouldered the responsibility for child care, one article in *Sunshine and Health* reiterated an unequal, gendered division of labor when it quoted a mother who appreciated having "some place where the kids [could] go" and she could "relax."[159] By "taking the trouble" to please the "short attention spans of children" through playgrounds, pool areas, and beaches, the camp avoided the problem of naked children "running around camp annoying all" and strengthened the "nudist cause of tomorrow by making a nudist childhood so very pleasant."[160] More importantly, attention to raising a child in a nudist camp embraced the postwar ideals of domesticity. Sunshine Park provided swings, seesaws, and sandboxes to "localize tornado damage."[161] Parks also supplied sporting equipment and games to entertain children, created a smooth surface area for wagons and tricycles, provided a shady grass area with picnic tables, erected a "playground apparatus," hung ropes for climbing, and constructed a kiddie pool with a small plastic slide.[162] With the children concentrated in one area, mothers sharing child-care responsibilities, and postwar gender norms secure, "the entire nudist family [could] enjoy their vacation to the utmost, and no one [felt] left out of the fun."[163]

Like postwar motels that increasingly began to offer a dining experience along with their sleeping accommodations, Sunshine Park presented several eating options for its guests. In a log structure fifty feet

Many managers of nudist camps put a great deal of effort and resources into children's play areas—another example of how nudism embraced postwar ideals of domesticity. (*Sunshine and Health*, August 1955, back cover; courtesy of the Sunshine and Health Publishing Company).

long and twenty-five feet wide, over 125 guests could eat breakfast for $0.75, lunch for $1.25, and dinner for $1.50.[164] Featuring a cook with thirty-one years of experience preparing meals such as roast beef, biscuits, and coffee, the park promised guests that they would not be disappointed with the quality of food. For members who wished to dine independently, the park also provided a "neat and spacious" picnic area for families to have a barbecue or eat the meals they prepared in their cabins or trailers.[165] In between meals, guests could also visit a snack bar that served sundaes, sandwiches, milk shakes, hoagies, and "what-have-you for those who don't care a hang about their figures."[166]

Similar to the promotion of Sunshine Park's redesigned entryway and its child-care options, the presentation of its dining facilities also reflected unequal gender arrangements. In an article written to a male audience, Lillian Wright boasted that undressed waitresses might add "extra piquancy" to the meal since they were "cuties who have as much eye appeal as the food."[167] Writing as an "older" person and taking time to discuss the children's playground, Wright's homemaker persona restrained her sexist and erotic statements while also reflecting the potential male voyeurism that prevailed at the resort. Although American nudism promoted its family-friendly facilities by denying the eroticism of social nakedness, some of its promotional literature revealed that many members continued to appreciate young, attractive, female bodies.

Not to be outdone by any local motels or hotels surrounding nearby Atlantic City, Sunshine Park provided several different accommodations for guests to choose from when planning their trip. Asserting that "you give up nothing in the way of comfort when you go back-to-nature at Sunshine Park," camp managers rented sleeping quarters by the week, month, or the "entire sunning season."[168] For members who made reservations well in advance, they could satisfy their "pioneering spirit" by staying in a "genuine log cabin." "Playing its ace," the management at Sunshine Park also provided two "immense dormitories" capable of housing sixty guests each.[169] The thirty rooms in each dormitory, designed to host individual families, opened into a screened hall that led to a lavatory center where guests would "find everything [they were] accustomed to at home."[170] Already available at a low rate, the dorms represented a particularly good deal with linen and bedding service provided for no charge.[171] While guests could still use their army-surplus tents as they had done in the past, many families chose to take advantage of the convenience and comfort of resort-style sleeping accommodations.

For members who had visited Sunshine Park for more than a year and desired more privacy, they could purchase a lot measuring twenty-five feet by one hundred feet within the camp grounds to construct a summer home. With lots close to the highway being the most affordable and river frontage being more expensive, the camp required that members sign a fifteen-year renewable lease, promise to follow a "minimum of management controls," and construct a home that would "further enhance the appearance of the community."[172] Preferring not to construct "palaces," members generally erected "neat cabins and homes that reflected the inclinations and status of their inhabitants."[173] With cabins to fit any budget, families could enjoy the comforts of home while still experiencing all the benefits and activities that Sunshine Park had to offer.

Unfortunately, the construction of cabins, more often than not, presented several problems for the manager of a nudist camp. The negotiations over the lease often led to hard feelings, the appearance of the final structure frequently did not live up to expectations, and maintenance of the permanent building proved costly and time consuming. Furthermore, many members did not want to invest in the construction of a cabin when they did not actually own the land where the structure would stand. While the intimacy and privacy of the summer cabin recreated the domestic environment of home, the potential financial disadvantages limited its popularity.

Trailers, placed in designated "parking areas," provided another popular form of accommodation at Sunshine Park and many other postwar nudist camps.[174] The nudist "trailer park" provided a convenient compromise for both the camp manager and members who desired more comfortable accommodations. Anticipating a "great upsurge in their appearances in nudist camps," many camp managers began constructing trailer parks across the United States.[175] In this "specifically planned area," the popular "vacation camp trailer" was parked in "somewhat more spacious individual parking spaces" next to a small patio with a water and electrical connection and a standardized pit to care for sink drainage water.[176] This area also included a "boundaried dirt or grass roadway" with a "convenient, non-hazardous entry and exit to the trailer parking plot."[177] Cheaper than building a cabin and involving considerably less financial risk while still providing the comfort of a summer home, camping trailers gave many nudists, who already visited the camp using their car, a fantastic way to frequent a nudist camp.

The rustic and secluded early nudist camps of the 1930s had come a long way by the 1950s. After an "uncertain beginning," when "singles and hesitant couples . . . making an unprecedented break in tradition" characterized most early visitors, nudists demanded "more and more of nudist parks." Over the decades, nudists transformed these once humble spaces into the "nudist resort" that had "come to be best represented by the family group."[178] With advertisements for Sunshine Park enticing "congenial couples and families" to "enjoy the benefits of sunbathing" and to partake in "sports, swimming, and boating" while staying in cabins and dormitory accommodations at "reasonable rates,"[179] it came as no surprise that the U.S. Internal Revenue Service in the summer of 1950 attempted to collect a 20 percent tax on the membership fees and dues of several California nudist camps. Previously, the nudist park had been considered a nonprofit organization, since "any social, athletic, or sporting features are merely incidental" to the main purpose of promoting nudism, which Norval Packwood defined broadly as an organization that fostered public health, fought against the "body taboo," and worked to reform obscenity laws.[180] However, in 1953 the IRS "changed its view" and decreed in the *Internal Revenue Bulletin* that a "club that 'promotes' nudism" should pay taxes like any other resort or club.[181] For better and for the worse, American nudism had emerged as an official form of recreation in the United States.

Michigan v. Hildabridle

The familial character promoted at nudist resorts and enforced through restrictive policies that excluded single men and people of color put the movement in a position to challenge local authorities who had previously raided camps and arbitrarily arrested members. Emblematic of many of the nudist clubs that emerged after the Second World War, Sunshine Gardens Health Resort, located near Battle Creek, Michigan, set the stage for one of the crucial legal battles in the history of American nudism. While nudist parks sprang up across the country in the 1950s, practicing nudism in the state of Michigan remained a risky proposition since the headline-grabbing *Ring* trial banned the lifestyle from the state in 1934. In the past, nudists had taken a nonconfrontational approach to early restrictive legal precedents and community outrage. In response to the hostile reaction of the residents of Chicago's Rogers Park (1931), the Ring decision (1934), and New York's McCall antinudist bill (1935), nudists chose to relocate to nearby areas that tolerated the practice. The headquarters of the ASA moved from New York City to New Jersey in the late 1930s, and Alois Knapp, a Chicago native, avoided controversy by establishing Zoro Nature Park in Roselawn, Indiana. In 1946, however, emboldened by the growth of resorts across the country and embracing the familial character of the movement, Elmer and Lucille Adams founded their nudist park nine miles outside Battle Creek, Michigan.

Like the naked man and woman who stood next to the gates of the ASA headquarters in New Jersey, Elmer and Lucille promoted their resort as husband and wife. The development of their camp resembled "more or less the same routine that most camps have undergone."[182] Satisfying their own personal interest in nudism, the couple acquired 140 sprawling acres with several ponds, numerous trees, and no buildings. Over the next ten years, they built a fence around the entire grounds, a recreational lodge measuring ninety-two feet long and thirty-two feet wide, a dormitory, a large pool, and an open area designated for volleyball, shuffleboard, and a variety of other athletic activities.[183] By the mid-1950s, the camp had added six more cabins and even an airstrip that allowed guests to travel to the isolated rural location by plane.[184] With the park quickly becoming a favorite spot of nudists around the country, Elmer and Lucille made sure that it projected the mom-and-pop character of American nudism by making it a rule that every man must be accompanied by his wife if he wished to visit or join the club.[185] Hosts to the Central Sunbathing Association Convention and the National Nudist Convention in 1953, Sunshine Gardens Health Resort rose to prominence with an appeal to married couples and families.

Despite the movement's best efforts to control the naked bodies at their camps and the growth of nudist resorts across the country, American nudism continued to attract critics. The Reverend Braxton Sawyer, an Arkansas radio evangelist, made it his personal mission to expose the evils of the movement. After hearing Rev. Sawyer "thundering" against nudism on his radio program, Norval Packwood invited the evangelical preacher to the ASA national convention being held in Battle Creek to "learn the real truth about nudism."[186] The preacher, "armed with a movie camera, color film, a tape recorder, and a public address system," drove his station wagon into the camp.[187] In so doing, he grabbed national headlines. Two male nudists and June Lange, the convention's press agent, asked the reverend to disrobe. When he refused, he attempted to force his way in, only to have his "burly bulk (5ft. 11 in., 225 lbs.) hit the dust."[188] Revived with a first-aid kit, a chair, and a sandwich, he again tried to enter the camp, only to fall "even harder."[189] Several national magazines, including *Time*, recorded the humorous event alongside a picture of Rev. Sawyer lying on his backside.[190] Although the media made the radio evangelist appear foolish and fanatical, the increased attention made the small community of Battle Creek take notice of its unusual neighbors.

On June 15, 1956, two police officers visited Sunshine Gardens. Seeing two or three people nude, they acquired their names and obtained warrants for their arrests. Two weeks later, accompanied by three other police cars, the same officers returned to Sunshine Gardens. Unable to find the people they had obtained warrants for, the police proceeded to raid the entire camp.[191] Seeing adults sunbathing among several children, the police charged Marvin Weissenborn, fifty-one; Earl Hildabridle, sixty-two; Harold Carter, forty-two; and Harold's wife, Ruth Carter, thirty-seven, with indecent exposure.[192] The four nudists were arrested using a statute based on the Ring decision, which read "any person who shall knowingly make any open or indecent exposure of his or her person or of the person of another shall be guilty of a misdemeanor," and the circuit court quickly found them guilty and sentenced them to thirty days in jail, two years probation, a fine of $250, and costs of $100 each.[193] For the judge and the jury, the defendants committed an obvious offense to public morals. As the case came to a close, the judge instructed the jury that a "common sense of morality which most people entertain is sufficient to apply the statute in this particular case."[194] Despite these nudists being middle-aged and white, despite their marital status, and despite the presence of their families, their public nakedness was found to be illicit and illegal.

Nudists immediately took steps to appeal what they felt constituted a grave miscarriage of justice.[195] Hildabridle argued that the Ring statute did not provide any "fixed standards of guilt upon which the penalty can be assessed," and as a result, it violated the equal protection clause of the Fourteenth Amendment.[196] The statute did not require the exposure to be lewd, to be in the presence of anyone or of someone of the opposite sex, to be in a public place, or to be motivated by any criminal intent. The definition of "open" and "indecent" also remained unclear. In a concealed enclosure, nudists only came in contact with the public when the police entered the camp grounds. If upheld, the decision would allow police officers to enter a home arbitrarily in order to observe suspected instances of public nudity. Enlisting the help of the ACLU, which considered the lack of a warrant a "civil liberties issue," and setting up a separate defense fund intended to raise $10,000, the ASA sought the reversal of what it considered an arbitrary statute.[197]

While Hildabridle appealed on the grounds that the Ring precedent denied his right to due process, the success of the case rested on the defense's ability to distinguish nudism from the violent male sexuality that had underscored the moral panics of the postwar period. According to Hildabridle, nudists had to overcome the public's inability to "separate indecency from nudity or immorality from exposure" and American society's "failure to realize that there is a distinction between the two," in order to demonstrate that nudists should not be equated with sex exhibitionists and voyeurs. He urged the court to "distinguish the nudist . . . from any and all persons who advocate the practice to satisfy erotic or immoral desires."[198] Rather than attempting to challenge all obscenity statutes outright, nudists tried to overturn the lower court's unfavorable verdict by distancing the movement from explicit forms of eroticism. They hoped to convince the Michigan Supreme Court that the exposure of the body among heterosexual, white families seeking health, relaxation, and recreation did not constitute a sexual act.

The controlled setting of the nudist resort as a vacationing experience and the moral character of its middle-class membership served as evidence that public nudity might not be inherently sexual. In an amicus curiae brief filed by the ASA, the organization portrayed the nudist lifestyle as a "form of recreation; a sport, much the same as bowling, skiing, golf, dancing, horseback riding, or a dozen others."[199] Aware that "it will not appeal to all," they saw "nude sunbathing as a form of relaxation" that a minority of people in the United States found enjoyable.[200] The ASA also sought to show that the organization did not condone sexual immorality. Referring to the "sex exhibitionist," the ASA lamented that this "type of exposure and impurity of motive is . . . reprehensible."[201] Noting that the organization put all applications through a rigorous screening process, it asserted that "every effort is made . . . to maintain high moral standards."[202] As a result, the ASA claimed that in its twenty-five-year history there had "not been one known or reported case of juvenile delinquency among children of nudist families."[203]

For the state, the presence of several families on the day of the raid exhibited the essential sordidness of public nudity. Naked adult bodies standing next to children's bodies within the gates of a nudist resort did not communicate innocent family fun to the local police and the prosecution. The explosion of young families after the war combined with the shifting boundaries of sexual liberalism to inspire widespread fears that children might be the victims of sexual predators.[204] Making repeated references to the presence of "four little girls of the respective ages of 8, 9, 11 and 12, and a 17 year old boy,"[205] the state accused nudists of an "impure motive" when they appeared naked in front of young children.[206] The state attorney focused his concern on the interaction of naked adult men with young girls. The shared experience of nudity between men and boys may not have been as threatening in the small town of Battle Creek, Michigan; as discussed in chapter 2, in rural areas, men of all ages and races frequently skinny-dipped in the local lake or river on a hot day. This experience, according to John Howard, remained so common that it doubled as a site for homosexual experimentation.[207] While the prosecutor may have been reluctant to upset the boundaries of sexual liberalism by publicly discussing the clandestine homosexual activity that occurred at rural lakes and streams, he did not hesitate to assert that the "exposure by mature men of their private parts to small girls would corrupt the morals of such children."[208] The fact that exposure occurred within the grounds of a nudist resort, according to the prosecuting attorney, had no relevance since the four young children "were not free agents . . . capable of embracing a belief" in nudism.[209] The state attorney declared it the "duty" of Michigan to "protect the children of this state."[210] The prosecution depicted the family-oriented nudist resort as a sign of moral decay, in the hope of holding the lower-court victory.

In addition, the state questioned the likelihood that the eroticism of naked bodies could be controlled at nudist resorts. The state attorney challenged the assumption that marriage sufficiently testified to the moral behavior of nudists. The defense had used the testimony of Lucille Adams and her husband, the owners of Sunshine Gardens, to introduce the way that a "high class nudist place" operated. The prosecution, however, took this opportunity to attack the rules of the nudist resort. After assuring the court that "married people were not allowed out there [Sunshine Gardens] without their spouses," the prosecution cross-examined Adams about an incident involving a married man and a single woman.[211] With Adams unable to identify this guest fully or explain why the police came to arrest the couple, the prosecuting attorney concluded his cross-examination of Adams by muttering under his breath, "We will have other witnesses."[212] Having listened to the prosecutor's "inferences and innuendoes" throughout the trial, Hildabridle's attorney then moved for a mistrial.[213] The prosecution's line of questioning and off-the-cuff statements, Hildabridle's attorney argued, deliberately tried to create a sense that "there is something behind the scenes here" since he had been unable to refute Adams's testimony about the "morality of the people together out there."[214] Although the judge instructed the jury to disregard any muttered inferences, he dismissed Hildabridle's motion for a mistrial and allowed the prosecutor to continue to inquire about the marital status of the visitors at Sunshine Gardens because the interaction of nude male and female bodies raised the possibility for illicit behavior as much as family recreation.

Several legal developments in the late 1950s favored the nudist movement's appeal of the lower court's unfavorable ruling. The legal legitimacy of the sexual-psychopath laws had been losing ground. Many experts considered the laws, passed over the course of the previous two decades, a failure brought on by politicians hoping to benefit politically from widespread public fear and anxiety.[215] The vague laws simply did not reduce crime or address the truly violent criminals. In this context, Justice John D. Voelker, presiding over the Michigan Supreme Court and *Michigan v. Hildabridle*, struck down the *Ring* precedent as another example of panic legislation. He asserted that the "Ring Case is less a legal opinion than an exercise in moral indignation." Suggesting that the lower-court judge was "aroused" by the details of the Ring trial, Justice Voelker dismissed the decision because it constituted a "platform from which to tell the world what *he* thinks about such queer newfangled shenanigans as nudism."[216] He thought that the lower-court judge was "so determined to smite nudism" that he "flatly assumed guilt" and completely ignored the "question of illegal search and arrest."[217] The issue of illegal search and seizure had also undergone dramatic changes in the postwar period. Several decisions issued by the U.S. Supreme Court in the 1950s and 1960s established that federal criminal procedures outlined in the Fourth Amendment of the Bill of Rights should also protect individuals from state-level authorities.[218] Empowered by these decisions, Justice Voelker argued that "moral indignation is a poor substitute for due process" and declared that the "embarrassing Ring Case" be "nominated for oblivion."[219]

Justice Voelker's long, detailed, and often colorfully written opinion contrasted starkly with the usually dry and objective tone of most legal decisions. The justice brought a unique approach to his legal writing. In 1958, he published *Anatomy of a Murder*, which critics still regard as "one of the classic courtroom novels of the time,"[220] and in 1960, he resigned from the bench to write courtroom dramatic fiction. Justice Voelker later based a chapter of his book *The Jealous Mistress* on the *Hildabridle* decision.[221] Using sarcasm, emotional phrases, and even indignation, legal scholars, almost fifty years later, recognized the literary style and tone from the *Hildabridle* decision not as a "paragon, but as a nonpareil."[222]

Despite Justice Voelker's colorfully written opinion, he still understood the need for caution in an earlier unpublished draft of his written decision that warned his fellow justices that concurring with his controversial defense of indecent exposure might be unpopular.[223] To maintain his own morality and the court's, he made it clear that his decision did not endorse the practice or merits of nudism. He prefaced his opinion by stating that he had never been a "disciple of the cult of nudism" and made it a point to say that the idea of going naked before others "revolts and horrifies" him.[224] Writing at a time when the majority of American society saw the naked body as private and intimate, Justice Voelker, despite his lengthy and animated defense of nudist rights, sought to maintain the impartiality of the court by distinguishing his moral values from those of individuals who subscribed to the ideals of American nudism.

Nevertheless, Justice Voelker did not shy away from asserting his position in a rapidly changing legal context. After a period of panic and fear that led to dramatic congressional persecutions, frequent violations of civil liberties, and unprecedented limits on free speech in the early Cold War years, enormous legal transformations began occurring by the close of the 1950s. From 1954 to 1964, the U.S. Supreme Court, influenced by organizations such as the ACLU and the National Association for the Advancement of Colored People (NAACP), issued a series of decisions that favored the advancement of civil liberties. The Court attacked racial segregation, ended religious exercises in the public schools, undermined censorship efforts, protected freedom of association, and introduced constitutional standards of due process.[225] Justice Voelker very much allied himself with this effort to expand civil liberties. Joining Justice John Talbot Smith and Justice Eugene Black as advocates of a "new philosophy" in the Michigan Supreme Court, Voelker and his two allies wrote numerous dissents that steadfastly "oppose[d] the forces of conservatism."[226] Furthermore, recognizing that the "world [is] locked in a death struggle between the David of democracy and the Goliath of giant totalitarianism," he argued in his *Hildabridle* decision that it was a bad time for the court to put its "stamp of approval on such a dubious departure from our traditional procedures and historic safeguards against invasion of our individual rights."[227]

Justice Voelker did not find the defendants sexually threatening. He asserted, "except for the fact that they were entirely unclothed, they might have been any group of people enjoying a rural weekend outing."[228] Feeling it "pertinent to further identify these defendants," the judge took notice of the "working class people" arrested at Sunshine Gardens. The police took custody of a sixty-two-year-old man who had worked at an automobile factory for "42 years continuously," a childless married woman who "worked in an Ohio supermarket," her forty-three-year-old husband, who had "worked 16 years as a machinist for the same employer," and a father of three children whose wife later died, who had "worked as an inspector in an automobile factory for 26 years."[229] With none of the defendants previously convicted for serious crimes, "sexual or otherwise," he saw the four defendants as hardworking citizens rather than sexual perverts.[230]

Recognizing the respectability of the defendants, Justice Voelker failed to see how the viewing of their naked bodies constituted a crime. Subscribing to the role the family played within the ideology of sexual liberalism in containing deviant sexuality, he did not assume that the mixing of naked adults and children in the space of the nudist resort represented or suggested an immoral sexual act. Rather, he implied that the state imposed this association on nudist activities. According to him, the presence of children at the camp, "far from accentuating any indecency, was itself additionally proof and insurance that no indecency or immorality was contemplated or intended by these defendants."[231] He found it "particularly monstrous to think" that the parents at the nudist camp intentionally and indecently exposed themselves to their own children.[232] This opinion reflected the accepted psychological approach toward nudity and childhood sexuality in the twentieth century. Inspired by Sigmund Freud's critique of Victorian culture and his contention that less shame and secrecy would lead to a more wholesome generation, popular psychologists such as Dr. Benjamin Spock wrote detailed articles in mainstream women's magazines such as the *Ladies' Home Journal* to assure parents that nudity within the family posed no intrinsic threat to the child.[233] While Dr. Spock fell far short of endorsing nudism, he advised readers to avoid overemphasizing the "'badness' of nudity," which produces "morbid shame and, sometimes, morbid curiosity," but also to practice nudity according to the parents' own modesty and comfort with their own naked bodies.[234] Echoing Dr. Spock, Justice Voelker concluded that the prosecution's claim that family nudity constituted a form of indecency was actually "gratuitously invest[ing] childhood with evil and erotic tendencies."[235]

By the late 1950s, it became possible to reexamine the intent behind public nudity. Justice Voelker asserted that where the "exposure is neither meant nor taken as indecent," it did not violate public decency.[236] He listed several hypothetical examples of public nakedness that did not intend to offend or shock the general public. Citing the case of a boy in a marching band whose penis pops out of his tight marching pants during a halftime performance, a naked sleepwalker who keeps bumping into people at night, and a scenario where the police use a ladder to look into a second-floor window of a private residence only to find an entire family naked in front of a sun lamp, he ruled that these examples of public exposure did not intend to shock the public. In this case, rather than parading "down the main street of Battle Creek," the defendants restricted their exposure to the grounds of Sunshine Gardens, far away from the public.[237]

Michigan v. Hildabridle represented both a practical and a symbolic achievement for American nudism. Declaring a "major victory" in the long battle to secure nudists' civil liberties, the ACLU praised Justice Voelker's opinion for explicitly detailing the logic and reasoning behind his dramatic ruling.[238] In addition, the ACLU's staff council declared Justice Voelker's opinion "so devastating" that it would ensure that "Michigan nudists [would] be left in peace for a while."[239] While Justice Voelker felt compelled by the issues of the case to write an impassioned opinion and while the decision represented a monumental victory for nudists around the country, the case received little attention from the national media or legal scholars.[240] Over a hundred camps had been operating successfully and largely without legal interference around the country for decades by the late 1950s. Overturning the outdated Ring case reflected larger legal trends, such as the expansion of federal protections against search and seizure at the state level. However, it did not represent a crucial turning point in the practice of nudism in the United States.[241] Rather, the verdict unceremoniously confirmed the acceptance of the postwar American nudist resort as a form of family recreation as opposed to a symbol of explicit eroticism.

Conclusion

The conservative ideology of domesticity during the early Cold War years provided an opening for American nudism to expand and prosper. The recreational character of nudist resorts fit seamlessly into a tourist boom fueled by the private family car, the availability of gas, and a booming economy. Here, with middle-aged men and women and their young children playing volleyball, sunbathing next to a lake or pool, or hiking through sprawling scenic grounds, the naked body's eroticism could be controlled and contained. Eliminating the possible uncontrolled eroticism of single men through exclusion and the recruitment of the heterosexual female body while also keeping the organization white by instituting a policy of segregation based on racist assumptions about the hypersexual racial other, nudism experienced enormous growth during a period otherwise known for its hostility to marginal lifestyles and ideas.

5

PORNOGRAPHY VERSUS NUDISM

The Contradictions of Twentieth-Century Sexual Liberalism

In March 1947, the U.S. Post Office seized *Sunshine and Health* (*S&H*) from the mails in Chicago, New York, Philadelphia, and several cities in Ohio. The coordinated actions by local post offices across the country signaled an unprecedented effort to remove the flagship nudist magazine from the mails. While officials had long tolerated nudist representations that resembled the young attractive Vargas Girls of *Esquire* or the nude female centerfolds in *Playboy*, they objected to the recent effort by the magazine to show the genitalia of naked men, women, and children as well as a range of body types not normally revealed in commercial publications. Officials asserted that permitting the magazine unrestricted access to American homes would be tantamount to accepting the "rights of all kinds of pornography" to use the "mails to destroy public morals."[1] Facing "complete financial ruin" but unwilling to censor the images, the editors of *S&H* declared the looming court battle a "challenge to every nudist, to every reader of this page, to every lover of freedom."[2] The legal debates that erupted around nudist magazines in 1947 and culminated in the U.S. Supreme Court's decision in 1958 to stop the Post Office's censorship of *S&H* redefined what constituted obscenity in the United States.

The ACLU saw the defense of *S&H* as an ideal way to expand civil liberties despite the anticommunist politics of the Cold War. The institution of the Federal Loyalty Program on March 21, 1947, along with the sensational trials of suspected Soviet spies and political radicals made the ACLU vulnerable to anticommunist attacks from organizations such as the American Legion. To avoid controversy and political persecution, ACLU leaders such as Roger Baldwin and Morris Ernst shifted the organization's focus away from the defense of political radicals to an agenda centered on civil rights, the separation of church and state, and the issue of censorship.[3] Yet the vocal resistance to public forms of sexuality in midcentury America also made the defense of *S&H* a risky endeavor. Several leaders within the organization feared that an extreme position in favor of sexual expression would produce adverse reactions from local community groups already hostile to the ACLU. As a result, the ACLU followed the path of respectability that many other organizations and individuals deployed to publicly address issues of sexuality in postwar America.[4] Although free speech advocates and nudists demanded that all forms of sexual display be protected under the First Amendment, the moderate leadership of the ACLU used the therapeutic principles that defined American nudism to avoid the issue of communism and to distance *S&H* from commercial sexual display. The attempts by the ACLU to distinguish good representations from bad representations of sex ultimately exposed the inability of the courts to maintain the contradictions of twentieth-century sexual liberalism.

In the years after the nudist movement's legal victories, the understated sensuality that had long played a role in defining nudism exploded in the United States. New magazines and films—all claiming to represent nudist ideals and principles—flooded newsstands and pornographic theaters. Magazine publishers and film producers, some with only slim ties to the movement, used the familial character and health-oriented principles of nudism to exhibit erotic images and content. The nudist movement's efforts to define public nudity as healthy, natural, and respectable made the display of the nude body and sex more widely available, and in the process, it undermined the heteronormative boundaries of sexual liberalism. Ultimately, the years of legal struggle linked nudism to the increasing commercialization of sex in the United States. The nudist movement's claims to respectability and propriety made the enormous expansion of the sex industry and the availability of sexually explicit materials in the 1960s and 1970s possible.

"It Is Easier to Sell Pictures of Naked Women"

The transformation of *S&H*'s content and appearance during and after the war caught the attention of the U.S. Post Office. In 1947, letter carriers began seizing the magazine at various points of delivery around the nation. Ilsley Boone immediately demanded a hearing to determine the mailability of *S&H*, and the Post Office appointed a trial examiner to evaluate the decency of the flagship nudist magazine. At these hearings, postal officials argued that the promotion of nudist principles in *S&H* concealed its commercial appeal to both heterosexual and homosexual readers. Calvin Hassell, who represented the Post Office, observed that with the "exception of an occasional volleyball game and people gathered around a swimming pool," the images showed "little activity—just naked people sitting or standing around." He concluded that "without the nude pictures the publication would have little if any sales appeal."[5]

The Post Office targeted *S&H* because its content appealed to the illicit desires of men. During the Cold War, antiobscenity activists shifted their attention from the "most vulnerable viewer," who was usually a child, to adult men due to a perceived "crisis in masculinity." According to many experts, moral reformers, and social commentators, men struggled to maintain a "soft" masculinity suitable for the home and a conformist society as well as a "hard" masculinity essential for defending the nation from foreign threats. The anxieties surrounding masculinity during the Cold War renewed campaigns against visual representations such as pornography and comic books because they eroticized male violence or implicitly encouraged homosexuality.[6] The many pictures of naked women displayed in nudist magazines raised similar concerns about male sexuality with postal officials. Hassell estimated the proportion of women to men displayed in *S&H* to be "four to one," which led him to assert that the "great bulk of subscribers are men" since "it is easier to sell pictures of naked women to men than it is to sell pictures to women who may not care for this sort of publication."[7] The relatively small nudist membership and the much-larger sales of *S&H* also implied that the magazine catered to a male consumer base. Boone testified that in 1948 he published forty thousand to ninety thousand copies of the magazine each month. Of these, six thousand to eight thousand went directly to mail subscribers, while newsstands distributed thirty thousand to sixty thousand issues each month.[8] For the Post Office, the large number of issues sold on newsstands signaled the availability of the magazine to a male audience that likely had very little interest in nudist principles. The Post Office voiced its concerns about the excess of sexualized males rather than the "vulnerable viewer" in order to justify the removal of nudist magazines from the U.S. mail system.

Hassell also targeted the subtle ways that homosexual men communicated with each other through the magazine's many classified advertisements. He believed the magazine acted as a "clearinghouse for obscene matter" because it provided readers "information directly and indirectly" about obtaining "obscene, lewd, lascivious and indecent matter" in "blind advertisements," "pen pal advertisements," and "photo lab advertisements."[9] Hassell singled out the wording of the photo-developing advertisements because he suspected that homosexuals used coded language to establish sexual contacts. He believed ads for "nude art photos" offering "confidential" service and promising readers that no pictures "would be altered or refused" revealed the "intentions of the advertisers" to exchange photos more graphic than those displayed in the magazine.[10] S&H posed a threat as a form of pornography that appealed to heterosexual excess as well as homosexual desire.

Postal inspectors also portrayed the sexual frankness promoted by nudists as evidence of the movement's effort to profit from erotica. Echoing liberal promoters of sex education in the twentieth century, many nudist leaders believed that sex represented a source of personal fulfillment and pleasure that was critical to establishing healthy relationships and a healthy family life. This view contradicted popular postwar sex-education policies that avoided controversy by deemphasizing open and honest instruction about sex and instead focused on preparing young adults for the practical challenges of family life.[11] Nudist leaders' unwillingness to be discreet when it came to sex education invited attacks from postal officials. Hassell cited an editorial that Boone wrote in the January 1947 issue of S&H in which he stated that the "sex urge" is the "most powerful urge to which mankind is subject" and that "sex always has been and always will be the ruler of life" as evidence of the longtime nudist leader's obsession with sex. Hassell then used Boone's admission that he exhibited "human sperm to the women at Sunshine Park and that one of the slides of sperm made was his own" to portray him as a pervert rather than a promoter of sex education.[12] The fact that he had sold numerous sex books in S&H, distributed pamphlets about sexual positions, and authored a review of Alfred Kinsey's *Sexual Behavior in the Human Male* provided additional evidence of Boone's unwavering interest in sex. Hassell went on to question why Boone sold a pamphlet titled *The Perfect Embrace: A Comparative Study of Coital*

Posture and advertised several sex books including *The Sex Life of the Unmarried Adult* and *Bust Culture* by Karl Peters. He concluded that the titles suggested "illicit sex relations" to consumers and pointed to "Boone's chief interest—sex."[13]

According to postal officials, the emphasis on sex in *S&H* encouraged and promoted aberrant sexual behaviors. The image of the sexual psychopath in postwar society haunted communities fearful that the era's domestic ideals could not contain male sexual desire. The Post Office exploited these anxieties when officials unearthed the "details of a controversy that raged within the nudist ranks about eight years ago."[14] The incident involved a young female nudist who charged "acts of intimacy—though not sexual relationship—on the part of Mr. Boone."[15] Just as many other nudists and club owners had done over the years, Rev. Boone had avoided legal troubles and public opprobrium by taking refuge in the public's unwillingness to confront intergenerational sex and the assumption within sexual liberalism that the family precluded illicit sexual contact. Seeking to break this silence, for seven days, the court heard testimony from the girl's father, mother, and husband regarding the incident. Hassell corroborated their testimony with a letter from Boone that "tacitly admits his immoral acts and both urges and threatens the [family] in an effort to prevent their testifying."[16] Hassell then lambasted Boone's attorney for "frantically" trying to keep the "evidence of the immorality of the chief originator and prophet of so-called 'nudism' in our fair land out of this record."[17] Boone's attorneys considered this testimony "legally irrelevant" but acknowledged that it constituted a "somewhat embarrassing" incident for Boone, and they felt that the "odor of herring is still unfortunate."[18] Like much of the legislation passed by politicians since the 1930s in response to a public panicked by the sexual psychopath, the accusations leveled against Boone by the Post Office aroused fear and suspicion just as much as they represented compelling evidence of the indecency of *S&H*.[19]

The alleged power of *S&H* to arouse violent male sexuality placed the long-running nudist publication outside the acceptable boundaries of sexual liberalism. Echoing the gendered arguments of postal officials, the hearing examiner asserted that the "displays of naked femininity" might not arouse the committed nudist, but they would surely "stir the sex impulses of and constitute sexual provocation to the average male person viewing them."[20] The hearing examiner focused on the excessive heterosexuality that *S&H* might provoke from what he assumed were heterosexual men who wanted to view images of naked women. Adding that adherents to the "cult of nudism . . . constitute an exceedingly small minority," the examiner stated that it required "little more than common sense" to conclude that the display of the naked body was "not acceptable to the aggregate community conscience and currently prevailing standards of morality in this country."[21]

"A Prudish Legal Strategy"

The ACLU understood *S&H* to be the official publication of a social movement and considered the Post Office's seizure of the magazine an attack on freedom of speech and the press. Roger Baldwin, a central figure involved in the founding of the ACLU and a moderate voice within the organization, saw the defense of nudist magazines as a way to avoid associations of the organization with communism during the Cold War. Rather than trumpet his own interest in going naked, Baldwin claimed that he did not "sponsor or endorse the beliefs of nudists." Not wanting to link the ACLU to radical ideologies or the politics of sexual liberation that had once been voiced in Greenwich Village, Baldwin limited his support of nudists to their "right to pursue their health ideas."[22] He devised a legal strategy that built on the nudist movement's contention that "commonplace nudity, far from stimulating immorality, . . . serves to diminish prurience" and approached the seizure of *S&H* as a "freedom of press issue . . . far different from that raised by a nude calendar or an entertainment magazine."[23] Baldwin believed that "a certain amount of prudishness" would remove the magazine from the "terms of the statutes and the court decisions and thus free it in the mails."[24]

To highlight the absence of commercial sexual display and the movement's commitment to health and sexual frankness, Baldwin solicited the opinion of several hundred expert witnesses including doctors, academics, publishers, and businessmen. He asked if they thought the images in *S&H* "incite the average person to lustfulness or thought of sexual impurity" and requested that the witnesses compare these representations to the "lurid photographs in tabloid newspapers, and suggestive advertisements and illustrations widely seen today."[25]

In this survey, Baldwin wanted to link the opinions of respected religious leaders, career professionals, and entrepreneurs to *S&H* while also highlighting the moral and aesthetic characteristics that separated the magazine from more provocative materials. Robert Searle, writing on behalf of the Protestant Council of the City of New York, found the issue of *S&H* to be "natural and without suggestive implication,"[26] Evans Clark, the director of the Twentieth Century Fund, did not see any "indication of lustful or impure intent,"[27] and according to Cecig Corwin of the Young Men's Christian Association (YMCA), the magazine presented the "convictions of nudists clearly and in a thoroughly wholesome manner."[28] Other respondents found the magazine's aesthetics unpleasant. James Truslow Adams, a leading historian, stated, "I have never seen such a collection of ugly women and they certainly do not excite me in the slightest";[29] Dorothy Kenyon, a liberal attorney active in the ACLU, thought most of the figures to be "definitely unattractive to put it charitably."[30] John Marquand, a prominent American novelist, added that the sight of these "ugly, ungainly people in the nude would cause the average person . . . to rush to the nearest clothing store."[31] According to these observers, *S&H*'s display of nudist principles stood apart from an emerging market of youth magazines that relied on sexual titillation to draw in their readers.

Legal absolutists within the ACLU along with nudist leaders took issue with Baldwin's strategy to distance nudism from sexually explicit material. Rev. Boone wanted a "definite gauge of obscenity as clear and distinct as a yard stick that would end the 'constant and unbearable litigation.'"[32] He believed that tolerating the censorship of certain indecent materials would leave nudists vulnerable to future censorship. Elmer Rice, a playwright and free speech activist in the ACLU, objected to Baldwin's strategy on different grounds. He feared that it set up standards of "propriety and impropriety" when the ACLU should be striving to defeat all standards of obscenity. He asserted that it was "completely out of line with ACLU policy" to tolerate the censorship of lustfulness. He did not like the "prudishness" of this strategy and urged Baldwin to approach the issue of freedom of speech and the press with the "same objectivity" that they did "all others."[33]

Boone employed a more confrontational approach that furthered the movement's commitment to sexual frankness and challenged the racial assumptions behind censorship. Although most Americans violently opposed the intimate interaction of blacks and whites, and many nudists voiced fears about admitting African Americans into nudist clubs, Boone used images of the indigenous nonwhite body to argue that the censorship policies of the Post Office discriminated against white nudist representations. When the Post Office seized the March 1947 issue of *S&H*, it announced a policy that "the breasts of white women but not the breasts of colored women" should be censored from the mails.[34] The assumed illicit sexuality of nonwhite bodies had long given license to discussions and depictions of sex. According to Catherine Lutz and Jane Collins, colonial racial assumptions combined with *National Geographic* magazine's scientific and literary prestige to make it one of the "few mass culture venues where Americans could see women's breasts."[35] In protest, Boone juxtaposed the images of a white topless woman next to a similarly naked African American woman and asserted that *National Geographic* had "published thousands of breasts of colored women without the slightest objection on the part of the post office."[36] Boone explained in the African American newspaper the *New York Amsterdam News* that he published the two photos to "force a showdown from the department" that would ultimately free his magazine from the obscenity statutes.[37] Boone's dramatic display of white and nonwhite bodies clashed with Baldwin's effort to distinguish nudist images from commercial sexual display.

Many other advocates of civil liberties supported Boone's use of racial liberalism to argue against the restrictions placed on what could and could not be seen in modern Western society. Anthropologists argued that incorporating the way other societies, cultures, and races viewed the body demonstrated the need to take into account relativity in American obscenity law. In trials dating back to the early 1930s, nudists had attempted to escape charges of public indecency or obscenity by gesturing toward indigenous forms of nudity. Attorneys regularly referenced the works of social Darwinists, such as William Graham Sumner's *Folkways*, to compare the different taboos toward nudity and to rationalize American nudism.[38] In 1955, Weston LaBarre, who received his Ph.D. in anthropology from Yale and taught at Duke University, echoed nudist arguments in an article titled "Obscenity: An Anthropological Appraisal."[39] He thought that American society at midcentury remained

In specifying the deletions of the nude which would meet with Post Office official approval, objection was registered against the full disclosure of the breasts of white women. This, it was explained, would fall under the ban as being a violation of the anti-obscenity statute

The ruling referred to on the opposite page has for many decades not been regarded as applicable to women of the colored race. The National Geographic Magazine has published thousands of breasts of colored women without the slightest objection on the part of the Post Office

When the Post Office seized the March 1947 issue of S&H, it announced a policy that "the breasts of white women but not the breasts of colored women" should be censored from the mails. In protest, Boone juxtaposed the image of a white topless woman next to the image of a similarly naked African American woman and asserted that *National Geographic* magazine had "published thousands of breasts of colored women without the slightest objection on the part of the post office." (*Sunshine and Health*, July 1947, 14–15; courtesy of the Sunshine and Health Publishing Company)

"ambivalent" toward the exposure of the naked body just like many other societies around the world. Referencing the practices of ancient Greeks and Peruvians as well as Muslim women in Africa, women in India, Samoans, Chinese, Eskimos, and Canary Islanders, he justified the need for relativity by describing a range of cultural approaches to regulating the body that varied from the draconian to the permissive. He found that the "ultimate obscenity has been the display of male genitals" and that the United States' prohibition of the breast appeared odd since the "total or partial nudity of the female body is quite . . . commonplace among people of the world."[40] Arguing that nakedness should be tolerated in American society by highlighting the subjective experience of nudity among different cultures and races, LaBarre called for a reevaluation of American attitudes toward nudism and implicitly demanded that the courts treat all people equally under the law.

"It Is Filthy, It Is Foul, It Is Obscene"

The ACLU's strategy to distance *S&H* from pornography initially proved successful for a time. Since 1947, the Post Office had seized issues of *S&H* at random points of delivery and relied on local hearings administered by its own trial examiners to avoid formal legal proceedings with Boone. The growth of the paperback industry and the mail-order trade in the postwar period heightened the anxieties of postal officials, who lamented the increasing amount "pornographic filth in the family mailbox."[41] In 1953, the local post office in Mays Landing, New Jersey, where Boone published and distributed *S&H*, hoped to reverse this trend by stopping the mailing of the magazine at the point of origin. This allowed Boone to seek an injunction against the Post Office in the D.C. federal district court. At trial, Boone and the ACLU argued that the pictures in *S&H* showed "people practicing nudism in a normal and healthy environment and in the happy enjoyment of thoroughly innocent activities" and were the "antithesis of anything suggestive or pornographic."[42] On June 23, 1953, the majority decision in the D.C. district court stated that the magazines "were not likely to promote lustful feelings or excite sexual passions" and granted a permanent injunction blocking the Post Office from seizing *S&H* from the mails.[43] The Post Office feared that this decision would limit the powers that Congress had granted it in order to censor materials under the 1873 Comstock act. It immediately appealed the decision, asserting that the lower court "incorrectly substituted its own opinion for the determination of the postmaster general."[44] Boone and the ACLU argued before the D.C. Circuit Court of Appeals that the Post Office's seizure of *S&H* constituted a "prior restraint upon the freedom of the press" and, as a result, violated the First and Fourth Amendments of the Constitution. On December 16, 1954, the majority of judges affirmed the lower court's injunction because the actions of the Post Office posed "grave constitutional questions."[45] The *New York Times* encapsulated the significance of the decision in its 1959 headline "Post Office Power as Censor Curbed."[46]

The Post Office reacted to the D.C. Circuit Court of Appeals decision by defying it immediately. On December 23, 1954, only a week after the decision, the postmaster at the Mays Landing Post Office seized four hundred copies of the February 1955 issue of *S&H*. Boone and the ACLU, confident that the courts would once again rule in their favor and bolster the legal status of *S&H*, filed a civil suit against the Post Office in the D.C. district court. Judge James Kirkland, who presided over the trial, saw the seizure of *S&H* as an issue of obscenity rather than a challenge to the First or Fourth Amendments. Kirkland intended to establish "what is art on the one hand, pornography on the other; what is decent on the one hand as against what is indecent on the other."[47] Kirkland's detailed written opinion provided the legal precedent that the U.S. Supreme Court used to clarify its ambiguous 1957 *Roth* decision and its intent to reshape modern American obscenity law.

Kirkland rejected Boone's argument that the nudist movement's commitment to sexual frankness legitimated the display of the naked body in *S&H*. He particularly objected to images that attempted to represent the "normal, natural person and reveals her as she was in fact." One "unusual picture," taken "within 12 feet of the camera," displayed two women in their "late twenties or early thirties," one of whom stood five foot seven and weighed "in the neighborhood of 250 pounds" and whom Kirkland described as "exceedingly obese" with "elephantine breasts that hang from her shoulder to her waist" and thighs that were also "very obese."[48] The effort to frankly show a range of body types in *S&H* challenged the increasingly dominant preference for the slender female body in the early twentieth century. The transition from the moral maternalism of the Victorian period to a modern conception of womanhood that emphasized sensuality and consumerism resulted, as the historian Peter Stearns has argued, in a "misogynist" emphasis on the thin female form, achieved through rigorous dieting regimens designed to constrain the indulgences of the new woman.[49] Reflecting these aesthetic assumptions and prejudices, Judge Kirkland considered nudist representations that did not conform to the idealized white, slim female body to be indecent.

The February 1955 cover, conversely, did not warrant censorship despite displaying a woman wearing heels with wind blowing in her hair, with a wide smile and chest propelled outward, and positioned against a rocky, gray background that made her soft, pale skin stand out. Al-

The effort to frankly show a range of body types in *S&H* challenged the increasingly dominant preference for the slender female body in the twentieth century. (*Sunshine and Health*, February 1955, 29; courtesy of the Sunshine and Health Publishing Company)

though the ACLU attempted to distinguish *S&H* from similar examples of commercial sexual display, Kirkland saw no reason to object to the photo because it did not show the "pubic area and there is no show of the genitalia by the angle at which the picture is shot." He acknowledged that the photographer used "shadowing on her chest" to create the effect of a "bosom larger by far than normal" and saw that it was "shot at such an angle as to elongate and make quite massive the breast as distinguished from the very small nipple," but he reasoned that the "plunging neckline has been accepted in the mores of the people" and that the "revealing of the breast would not in itself be obscene."[50] According to the historian Joan Jacobs Brumberg, the breasts represented a "particular preoccupation of Americans in the years after World War II"; movie stars known for their bust line, such as Jayne Mansfield, Jane Russell, and Marilyn Monroe, dominated the 1950s box office.[51] Similarly, naked female images in *S&H* that pleased the male heterosexual gaze posed little threat to public decency.

Judge Kirkland also did not object to the exposure of the nude nonwhite body. At trial, Boone again objected to obscenity laws that permitted the display of nonwhite naked bodies in publications such as *National Geographic* and wondered if the judicial system had "grown up enough" not to "draw a distinction because the picture happens to be of a white person rather than a Negro."[52] In response, the Post Office asserted, "we are a clothed people," and the practices of indigenous people in "Africa or some other foreign country in some other time is not the standard by which we should judge these pictures."[53] Judge Kirk-

Judge Kirkland reasoned that the "plunging neckline has been accepted in the mores of the people" and that the "revealing of the breast would not in itself be obscene." (*Sunshine and Health*, February 1955, cover; courtesy of the Sunshine and Health Publishing Company)

land agreed with the Post Office and rejected the nudists' attempts to make comparisons to a documentary film titled *La Tuka*. The nudists' attorneys argued that it should not make "any difference" that the film showed life in an African tribe rather than everyday Americans, only to have Judge Kirkland retort that "people . . . living on the tropical belts would not be relevant."[54] In his final written decision, Judge Kirkland made the racial politics of obscenity clear when he found nothing indecent about a "suggestive picture" of what appeared to be a "woman of Mexican birth, a very dark complexioned woman."[55] Entrenched racial stereotypes of nonwhite bodies as primitive, accessible, and hypersexual permitted the exhibition of the naked racial other. Since naked indigenous bodies likely aroused audiences just as much as those in S&H, the racial arguments made by nudist advocates did little to mute the magazine's eroticism.

Judge Kirkland, however, ruled unequivocally that any photos that showed the penis "obviously [have] no place even in illustrating the principles of nudism."[56] Kirkland likely considered the images of naked men to be directed toward gay male readers since many so-called beefcake photos in the postwar period masked their homoerotic content by embracing a rhetoric of health or bodybuilding that resembled the nudist movement's promotion of health and fitness.[57] In addition, the "representation of the male nude since the nineteenth century," according to Thomas Waugh, had become closely linked with the "homosexual artist" and homoeroticism.[58] In assessing one image, Kirkland described the "corona" of the penis in the photo as "clearly discernible," to the point that one could see that the "man is circumcised," and despite the very small size of the man in the photo, Kirkland strongly condemned the image, decrying, "it is filthy, it is foul, it is obscene, and the Court will hold such as a matter of fact."[59] Although small, captured from a distance, and not the main focus of the camera, the penis stood out as an exceptionally offensive image since it potentially signaled a source of homosexual desire.

Judge Kirkland, Rev. Boone, and the ACLU did reach a consensus regarding the decency of naked children's bodies. Kirkland ruled that children "photographed in a frontal view which reveals the diminutive and underdeveloped genitalia" should not be considered obscene "by virtue of their age of innocence." He supported this decision by stating that "such a view" represented the "common acceptance of the American people."[60] Evaluating an image of a young, naked girl sitting on a swing, with her "labia majora" clearly discernible, Kirkland asserted that one would have to be "prudish to hold that was an obscene picture."[61] Kirkland's permissive policy toward the display of children reflected an emerging effort by child psychologists to encourage a nonrepressive attitude toward the child's body. Many postwar parenting guides

Despite the very small size of the man in the photo, Judge Kirkland
strongly condemned images displaying the penis, decrying, "it is
filthy, it is foul, it is obscene, and the Court will hold such as a matter
of fact." (*Sunshine and Health*, February 1955, 9; courtesy of the
Sunshine and Health Publishing Company)

relied on Freudian psychoanalysis to recommend a permissive response
to childhood sexuality. In the "Facts of Life" section of the best-selling
The Common Sense Book of Baby and Child Care (1957), Dr. Benjamin
Spock addressed the topic of nudity in the home by recognizing that the
"excessive modesty" of the Victorian period had given way to "today's
casual attitude that is a lot healthier."[62] The effort to avoid psychological
maladjustment caused by the repression of childhood nudity influenced
Kirkland to allow the display of naked children.[63]

Although Judge Kirkland did not object to the display of attractive women, nonwhite bodies, or children's genitalia, he ultimately squashed the ACLU's attempt to distance S&H from commercial sexual display when he ruled that the inclusion of full-frontal male and female nudity constituted the main criterion for judging obscenity. He did not oppose artistic, medical, or scientific journals, books, magazines, and litera-ture that showed the "human form merely in the nude and beyond that not revealing the pubic area or the male or female genitalia." The fact that the nudist movement offered S&H "freely for sale to the general public who are not members of the nudist organization" while also ex-hibiting photographs "clearly revealing genitals, breasts and other por-tions of the body normally covered in public" revealed the magazine's commercial purpose and, according to Kirkland, made it obscene and nonmailable.[64]

Roth v. United States

The ACLU and Boone hoped to reverse the Kirkland decision when the U.S. Supreme Court took up the issue of obscenity in a case involv-ing a notorious smut dealer named Samuel Roth. For decades, the Supreme Court had avoided the issue of obscenity and deferred to lower state-court decisions that addressed postal censorship, question-able literature, or objectionable films. The most important of these decisions came in the early 1930s from the New York Supreme Court, which established that literature dealing with sexual themes and exhib-ited scholarly merit should not be considered obscene. Yet judges and juries across the country continued to struggle to reach a consensus on the issue of obscenity. For Chief Justice Earl Warren, the problem in the *Roth* case lay in the subjective nature of the laws regulating questionable materials. He observed that judges determined obscen-ity based "largely upon the effect that the materials have upon those who receive them," and as a result, the "line dividing the salacious or pornographic from literature or science is not straight and unwaver-ing" and "may have a different impact, varying according to the part of the community it reached."[65] The lack of a clear national obscenity standard compelled the justices of the U.S. Supreme Court to hear *Roth v. United States* in 1957.

Despite Roth's established pornography business, the ACLU followed the strategy it used to defend S&H, shying away from taking an absolutist position against Post Office censorship. The Post Office considered Samuel Roth "one of the biggest dealers in obscenity in the nation,"[66] and in 1956 federal prosecutors arrested him for advertising and selling a publication called *American Aphrodite*, which contained literary erotica and nude photography. The ACLU, as it had done in its defense of S&H, made arguments implying that certain forms of sexual expression warranted censorship. In its amicus brief, ACLU attorneys contended that the U.S. Supreme Court should not uphold Roth's arrest since the prosecutors failed to introduce evidence that his publications "will probably and immediately cause anti-social conduct."[67] This argument assumed that the introduction of evidence showing the danger of pornography justified postal censorship.

In a 6–3 decision, the U.S. Supreme Court upheld Roth's conviction and instituted a legal test of obscenity that distinguished acceptable representations of sex from "prurient" materials. Writing for the majority, Justice William Brennan stated that the First Amendment did not protect obscenity, which the courts have historically defined as material "utterly without redeeming social importance." Yet Justice Brennan also used *Roth* to protect forms of sexual expression that had "redeeming social importance." Declaring "sex and obscenity are not synonymous," Brennan echoed the moderate legal strategies used by the ACLU in *Roth* and its defense of S&H. He believed that the "portrayal of sex, e.g., in art, literature and scientific works is not itself sufficient reason to deny material the constitutional protection of freedom of speech and press." He asserted that it was "vital that the standards for judging obscenity safeguard the protection of speech and press for material which does not treat sex in a manner appealing to prurient interest."[68] In *Roth*, the justices of the Supreme Court intended to limit the types of materials considered obscene without granting full First Amendment protection.

Roth wrote the heteronormative boundaries of sexual liberalism into federal obscenity law by relying on community standards to be the arbiters of decency. Justice Brennan wrote that the courts should determine the obscenity of questionable materials by taking into account "the average person, applying contemporary community standards, the dominant theme of the material, taken as a whole, appeals to prurient interests."[69] By deferring to the shared values and morals of the community, the justices allowed the lower courts to suppress marginal sexualities even as they protected forms of sexual expression that appealed to heterosexual norms. The reliance on community standards to determine obscenity upset the justices on the Supreme Court who took a more absolutist position on free speech and the First Amendment. They feared that the law made it possible for the courts to exclude marginal voices and sexualities from public display, discussion, and debate. Justice William O. Douglas asserted in his dissent that the First Amendment should "allow protests even against the moral code that the standard of the day sets for the community."[70] Justice Douglas as well as fellow New Deal appointee Justice Hugo Black called for a strong First Amendment that protected even offensive forms of speech. Coming after the anticommunist purges of the early Cold War years, these justices recognized the risks of allowing the "majority" to dictate appropriate behaviors and beliefs. A stronger First Amendment would also remove the subjectivity that made federal obscenity law so difficult to apply uniformly across the nation. Even though the Supreme Court took up *Roth* to clarify federal obscenity law, the reluctance to grant First Amendment protections to illicit forms of speech left the decency or indecency of questionable materials—such as *Sunshine and Health*—open to interpretation.

The lower federal courts quickly used *Roth* to further restrict sexual expression. Boone and the ACLU argued in their appeal in the *S&H* case that Judge Kirkland violated the First Amendment when he declared many of the pictures in *S&H* to be obscene and nonmailable. Since Kirkland relied on "community standards" to judge the decency of the images in *Sunshine and Health*, the case offered an ideal opportunity to apply the test established in *Roth*. The D.C. Circuit Court of Appeals quickly asserted that the pictures "speak for themselves" and found Kirkland's "extensive, particularized descriptions of the offending and offensive material" to be "amply sustained." Pointing to Kirkland's effort to outline how each photo did or did not violate "community standards," the appellate judges ruled that *S&H* dealt with "sex in a manner appealing to prurient interest and hence is obscene, as *Roth* tells us."[71] Justifying the censorship of *S&H* by placing nudism firmly outside the heteronormative boundaries of sexual liberalism, the decision by the

D.C. Circuit Court of Appeals confirmed the fears of First Amendment advocates such as Justice Douglas and Rev. Boone.

Only through rulings after *Roth*—with cases such as *Sunshine Book Company v. Summerfield*—did the U.S. Supreme Court finally begin to clarify what constituted material with "redeeming social importance." The justices disapproved of several lower-court decisions that applied a narrow interpretation of what defined community standards and immediately took up a series of cases to clarify their intent. For the justices, the variety of content and images in *S&H* did not constitute obscenity under the test it established in *Roth*. Filing a writ of certiorari with the U.S. Supreme Court to review the recent decision issued by the D.C. Circuit Court of Appeals, Boone and the ACLU continued to argue that the display of naked men, women, and children in *S&H* constituted material with "redeeming social importance." Just as Boone had done in the Kirkland decision, he supplied the Court with copies of the February 1955 issue of *S&H*, and on January 13, 1958, in a unanimous decision, the Court granted a writ of certiorari and reversed the ruling of the D.C. Circuit Court of Appeals. Citing only *Roth v. United States* in its opinion, the Court ordered the lower court to take into account the therapeutic and recreational character of nudism when deciding on the decency of the pictures that the movement displayed in its magazine.[72] Chief Justice Warren reasoned in his concurring opinion in *Roth* that "it is not the book that is on trial; it is the person," and he asserted that the "conduct of the defendant is the central issue."[73] The materials sent through the mail by Samuel Roth, a known publisher of pornography, constituted obscenity. *S&H*, on the other hand, displayed similar images while also promoting the therapeutic benefits of going naked. The Court's intervention on behalf of *S&H* made it clear that it considered nudism to fall within the heteronormative boundaries of sexual liberalism. Yet *S&H* appealed to the nudist community as well as a variety of sexualities and erotic desires. Unintentionally, the *S&H* case opened the door to images and materials that exhibited little "socially redeeming" content and would likely clash with contemporary "community standards." In *Sunshine Book Company v. Summerfield*, the Supreme Court created a gray area in American obscenity law that undermined the heteronormative boundaries regulating sexual expression.

Garden of Eden

The distinction that the Supreme Court made in *Roth* between prurience and acceptable sexual expression also influenced the way state
courts ruled on nudist films. The 1954 release of *Garden of Eden* drew
large audiences across the country. Far from a typical small-scale production destined for adult-only theaters, the film had more than 958
play dates in thirty-six states and foreign countries and was seen by
over 1.6 million people.[74] Although the American Sunbathing Association lent its seal of approval, the production reaped in profits from
an audience that had little interest in the mental and physical benefits of going naked. A 1956 advertisement for the film did not speak
to nudists when it guaranteed the "complete and uncut version" that
stood apart from the "old, censor-cut Nudist Pictures!"[75] In Boston,
the movie "pulled lines of males" to a fourteen-hundred-seat theater
that made a "'wham of $15,000' in just the first week." In Los Ange-
les, despite an "adults-only policy," the film earned around $19,000 on
a single screen in its opening week.[76] The large male audiences that
packed the film's showings aroused the suspicions of the Board of
Regents of the University of the State of New York, which immediately
denied the film a license.

The actions of the Board of Regents of the University of the State
of New York against *Garden of Eden* came at a moment when the film
industry's policy of self-regulation began to crumble in response to legal
reforms, tough economic times, and changing consumer preferences in
the postwar period. In 1931, Hollywood studios adopted the Hays Production Code to avoid federal censorship by strictly regulating the production and content of their own films. Banning the depiction of sex,
including the display of nudity, this industry-wide standard went largely
unchallenged for decades. In 1948, the Supreme Court ruled in *United
States v. Paramount Pictures* that the vertical integration of the film industry, which allowed Hollywood studios to control the production,
distribution, and screening of their films, violated antitrust laws.[77] This
ruling resulted in a boom of independent theaters that did not have to
uphold the Hays Production Code. To make matters worse for the studio
system, the growing popularity of television severely curtailed theater
attendance. By the late 1950s, almost one-quarter of the nation's theaters

A 1956 advertisement for *Garden of Eden* did not speak to nudists when it guaranteed the "complete and uncut version" that stood apart from the "old, censor-cut Nudist Pictures!" (Courtesy of the American Civil Liberties Union Archive, 1950–1990, History and Philosophy Library, University of Illinois at Urbana-Champaign)

had closed, and film production decreased from 320 to 189 films a year.[78] Films that dealt with controversial content, displayed the body, or had sexual themes, however, continued to attract large audiences to many of the recently opened and unregulated independent theaters. In addition, soldiers who had just returned from war with "girlie magazines" and other literature banned in the United States were a particularly willing audience for controversial postwar films such as *A Streetcar Named De-*

sire (1951), *Baby Doll* (1956), *The Man with the Golden Arm* (1956), and foreign movies such as the Italian production *The Miracle* (1952).

The reliance on the exhibition of nudity in *Garden of Eden* to draw in audiences classified it with other nudist exploitation films that dated back to the 1930s. The exploitation films screened at independently owned art theaters between 1919 and 1959, according to Eric Schaefer, "relied on forbidden spectacle to differentiate themselves from classical Hollywood narrative films and conventional documentaries."[79] Small studios looking to eke out a profit despite subpar sets, inadequate film and sound equipment, and small budgets as well as inexperienced or untalented actors, writers, and directors turned to "titillating images" and "spectacle" to draw in audiences.[80] While the genre varied greatly in content and style, the narratives that drove exploitation films generally existed to highlight a shocking event, nude or scantily clad bodies, or the grotesque. In many ways, Walter Bibo's *Garden of Eden* resembled the other exploitation films that had come before it. Filmed at the Lake Como Club near Tampa Bay, Florida, starring an attractive actress, and featuring a romantic plotline, the film drew in audiences hoping to see naked bodies. Yet the relatively large investment made in producing the film, its careful display of the body, and the respectability of its main characters set *Garden of Eden* apart from other exploitation films. Like *S&H*, *Garden of Eden* blurred the boundaries between the illicit and the respectable and forced the New York State courts to redefine obscenity statutes that had stood for almost three decades.

The large investment that Excelsior Pictures producer Walter Bibo made in the production, casting, and filming of *Garden of Eden* gave the film legitimacy. Exploitation films generally had budgets that ranged from $10,000 to $60,000, were filmed in one or two weeks, and often spliced in scenes and sound to make a full-length feature film. Bibo, who had imported classic foreign films such as *The Golem*, *Barber of Seville*, and *Skipper Next to God*, expended over $300,000 to acquire the "finest cast and production staff" available for his nudist film.[81] Max Nosseck, who directed the film, had a "long list of superior Hollywood attractions" including action films such as *Dillinger* and *The Hoodlum* as well as family pictures such as *Black Beauty* and *The Return of Rin Tin Tin!*[82] The cameraman for *Garden of Eden*, Boris Kaufman, also came with a more-than-reputable résumé. In 1954, he won an Academy Award for his contributions to *On the Waterfront*.[83] Jamie O'Hara, the leading lady who played Susan Lattimore, acted in several roles on television, as did R. G. Armstrong, who played the film's grouchy father-in-law.

Furthermore, *Garden of Eden* distinguished itself by re-creating the domestic ideology featured in *S&H* through a family-oriented narrative that many critics considered dull and boring. In the 1930s, nudist films such as *Elysia* relied less heavily on narrative and exhibited far more nudity through a "discrete and integrated approach[] to . . . spectacle" that resembled a documentary film or news clip.[84] While *Elysia* followed a reporter named Mack through a nudist camp to research the recent interest in nudism, *Garden of Eden* focused on Susan Lattimore, a twenty-five-year-old war widow and mother of a six-year-old daughter hoping for a fresh start far away from her wealthy and overbearing father-in-law. Lattimore conveyed a moral, dignified, and domestic image. She also connoted middle-class status when she escaped her wealthy and domineering father-in-law.

Garden of Eden's intricate narrative, with its many scenes and characters, worked to "delay and foster anticipation of the spectacle of the camp scenes" while also positioning nudism within the boundaries of sexual liberalism as a protector of families.[85] Early in the film, Susan Lattimore's car stalls on her way to Miami, where she plans to begin a career in modeling. Fortuitously, a handsome man named Johnny comes to her aid and offers the mother and daughter room and board at the Garden of Eden. A bit of trepidation and skepticism follow Lattimore's discovery that she has taken refuge at a nudist camp, but her daughter's enthusiasm for going naked persuades her to try the lifestyle, participate in a club theater production, and become romantically involved with Johnny. Once her father-in-law discovers that she has been staying at a nudist club, he pursues legal action against the camp and attempts to have Susan declared an incompetent mother. When his lawyer informs him that the camp does not violate any local laws, he visits Garden of Eden, only to slowly accept the "absolute cleanly innocence of their [nudist] method of living."[86] By winning over Susan's father-in-law, nudism mends a broken family. Not only is Lattimore's daughter reunited with her grandfather, but after her mother's marriage to Johnny, she gains a new father.

The heartwarming conclusion of *Garden of Eden* did little to excite film critics. While newspapers rarely took notice of exploitation films,

Garden of Eden exhibited enough merit through its professional production and well-developed narrative to warrant review in several newspapers across the country. The *Tampa Daily News*, however, cautioned readers against expecting "something sensational" and suggested that they visit the "next exhibit of the Tampa Art Institute and save [their] money." The *New York Daily Mirror* added, "it runs 70 minutes but proves that anything can become boring." The *New York Times* described the film's plot as a "limp dramatic ritual with all the flair of a television commercial."[87] According to film critics, the nudist camp provided a remarkably uninteresting vehicle to exhibit the spectacle of nudity in *Garden of Eden*.

Walter Bibo attempted to minimize the spectacle of nudity by using the motions and gestures of nudism to desexualize nakedness. According to Linda Williams, hardcore pornography privileges close-ups of particular body parts, overlights easily obscured genitals, and employs sexual positions that favor maximum exposure.[88] In contrast to these pornographic conventions, the wide camera angles used in *Garden of Eden* to capture whole bodies engaging in numerous nonsexual activities relied on suggestion and subtlety to convey a feeling of nakedness. Keeping the genitalia of numerous naked male and female bodies of all ages on the screen hidden required precise and coordinated movements that followed timed patterns. The recreational activities of the nudist camp justified these often awkward and deliberate motions. A swing set, a small lawn, and an expansive lake served as the background for most of the scenes in the film that displayed naked bodies. Here, in synchronized patterns, children moved back and forth on swings, crossed in the foreground on tricycles along designated paths, tossed a large beach ball to one another, and ran toward the lake to dive into the water. Even the passive act of sunbathing could be infused with movement. One scene showed a woman lying in the sun only to turn away from the camera to watch several children splashing at the edge of the lake. Other naked adults walk in pairs away from the camera toward the water, only displaying their bodies from the rear. Although women walk with other women or with men, to avoid any hint of male homoeroticism, the film never shows two naked men walking together, interacting, or sunbathing. Not even motion could mute the eroticism of the naked male body, which had long been associated with homosexuality.[89] Rather than thrusting exposed breasts and genitalia onto the screen, *Garden of Eden* made audiences imagine nakedness by choreographing the movements of the nude body.

Other scenes provided the popular pornographic conventions expected in a nudist exploitation film. The popularity of volleyball among nudists provided an excuse to focus the camera's attention on topless women. As evidenced by Judge Kirkland's rulings permitting the display of topless women in *S&H*, the exposure of breasts in postwar society did not necessarily provoke the same moral condemnation aroused by the exhibition of genitalia. The emphasis placed on exposing the breasts in popular men's magazines such as *Playboy* and *Esquire* suggested that the prolonged display of the female breasts in *Garden of Eden* also held an erotic appeal for audiences. The eroticism of the volleyball match in *Garden of Eden* becomes apparent as a topless woman centers the shot directly in front of the camera, while the entire scene progresses through the voyeuristic gaze of Susan Lattimore's fully clothed father-in-law. Using a character in the film to watch naked figures or sexual acts constitutes one of the defining characteristics of hard-core pornography. In addition, the wearing of bright red pants by the game's participants turned the attention of the audience away from the whole body and toward the exposure of the breasts. The abandonment of specific movements and postures to hide the naked body resulted in a particularly titillating scene.

Despite *Garden of Eden*'s high production values, intricate family-oriented narrative, and highly choreographed scenes, the Board of Regents of the State of New York denied Bibo a license to show his film unless he removed all scenes that displayed naked bodies. Placed with the responsibility to protect the "educational interests of children and adults of the State,"[90] the Board of Regents felt that the film would almost certainly encourage juvenile delinquency. They asserted that it does "not take much imagination" to know what effect the "exhibition of young children, especially girls," would have on the "morons of all types, sex deviates, and even teenagers of little moral stamina . . . scattered in the audience."[91] Raising the specter of pedophilia and juvenile delinquency, they believed that "nothing is more likely to encourage these people to commit sex offenses than the exhibition of children."[92] The requirement that all nudity be removed from the film, however, undermined the main purpose of *Garden of Eden* and forced Bibo to appeal the Board of Regents' decision.

In the early 1950s, independent filmmakers, empowered by the deregulation of the studio system, challenged film censorship across the country. In New York, a number of cases put the Board of Regents on the defensive and forced the powerful censor to alter its legal arguments in the *Garden of Eden* case. In the past, the Board of Regents relied on the New York Appellate Division to automatically deny appeals from filmmakers who challenged its use of "prior restraint" to deny film licenses. Due to the size and influence of the New York market, the Board of Regents indirectly determined the content of films across the nation because it proved impractical to produce different versions of the film for individual states. In 1952, however, the U.S. Supreme Court undermined the authority of the states to censor films in its landmark *Miracle* decision (*Joseph Burstyn, Inc. v. Wilson*, 343 U.S. 495). Although it did not overturn all film censorship, the Court rejected the Board of Regents' use of "prior restraint" in films that the censorship board deemed "sacrilegious." After the Court's *Miracle* decision, state courts began to question the use of "prior restraint" in other obscenity cases involving a wide variety of content. By 1956, when the New York Appellate Division took up the *Garden of Eden* case, the Board of Regents felt compelled to supplement its arguments for "prior restraint" with the 1935 New York Penal Law 1140-b, which banned all nudist activities in the state. The Board of Regents argued that the film should be judged as if it were an actual nudist camp since there was little "difference between picture and reality."[93] This new legal strategy attempted to shift attention away from the issue of "prior restraint" and rearticulated the exhibition of naked bodies in the film as a violation of the penal code.

Bibo welcomed the opportunity to debate the legal merits of displaying the naked body. In his brief, he invoked the United States Court of Appeals' 1940 *Parmelee* decision when he asserted that "mere nudity, standing alone, is neither indecent nor obscene, and in this picture, besides nudity, there is nothing which could possibly corrupt the morals of its viewers or tend to do so, or could incite lascivious thoughts, or arouse lustful desires." He then claimed that almost every issue of *Life* magazine exhibited an image with more nudity than the scenes featuring naked bodies in the *Garden of Eden*.[94] Bibo also found it inconsistent that the

Board of Regents had licensed several motion pictures that contained scenes of "nude men, women, and children in such locales as the South Seas, Africa, and other parts of the world . . . dancing alone or together, and in other poses and postures far more intimate than any shown in this picture."[95] Bibo demanded that the courts provide his film "equal protection under the laws . . . without regard to the color of the skin of the players or the locale of the main action."[96] Bibo saw no reason that nudity should be treated as inherently indecent under state law, and he asserted that the Regents' attempt to use New York Penal Law 1140-b had no validity.

In 1956, the Appellate Division of the State Supreme Court of New York annulled the Board of Regents' decision to deny *Garden of Eden* a license, and the court signaled that the New York obscenity statutes were likely unconstitutional. Following similar rulings in other state courts across the country, the Appellate Division ruled that the film did "not reach a magnitude . . . that would warrant prior restraint" since there was "no full exposure of any adult nude body."[97] The court, however, stopped short of voiding the entire New York obscenity statute. While one judge recognized in his concurring opinion that the statute had been "voided or diluted in piecemeal fashion by the court so that practically no power remains," the judges all agreed that an "intermediate appellate level" court should not decide the constitutionality of the statute.[98] Despite this reluctance to overturn New York State's obscenity statute, the Appellate Division ignored the Regents' attempt to use New York Penal Law 1140-b to deny *Garden of Eden* a license, and in the process, it questioned the censor's legal authority.

Just as the Supreme Court's ruling in *Roth* forced the Post Office to stop censoring *S&H*, the 1957 decision enabled the New York State Court of Appeals to overturn the obscenity statutes that empowered the Board of Regents to deny *Garden of Eden* a license. In *Roth*, the Supreme Court protected sexual expression that exhibited "redeeming social importance" according to "contemporary community standards" and when judged in its entirety. The justices accepted, however, that prurient materials could still be ruled obscene. Taking up the *Garden of Eden* case immediately after the Supreme Court issued its *Roth* decision, the New York State Court of Appeals struggled to reach a consensus on the issue of obscenity. Writing for the majority, Judge Charles Desmond, who had written two procensorship law-review articles in 1953 and 1956, ruled that the scenes in *Garden of Eden* did not constitute indecency since they were "honestly relevant to the adequate expression of innocent ideas."[99] The majority accepted that the film depicted "wholesome" and "happy people in family groups practicing their sincere if misguided theory that clothing is deleterious to mental health."[100] Yet Judge Adrian P. Burke wrote an extensive dissent that contended that the film presented a "more alluring portrayal of those actions upon the screen" than one would see in a nudist camp.[101] He observed that the movie showed "protracted scenes of women in unwholesome, sexually alluring postures which are completely unnecessary to—and in fact a radical departure from—the activities of the nudist camp depicted." He specifically referred to a dream sequence in which Jamie O'Hare, "a comely young lady," disrobes "in a manner not unlike that generally utilized by professional ecdysiasts."[102] Burke believed the nudity featured in *Garden of Eden* served an illicit commercial purpose and should be considered obscene according to *Roth*. Ultimately, just as the Supreme Court had done with *S&H*, the majority decision pointed to the respectable characteristic of American nudism to argue that *Garden of Eden* did not constitute obscenity. By making it difficult to distinguish the illicit from the respectable, nudism played a significant role in the legal process that led the New York State Court of Appeals to reverse twenty-six years of precedent by declaring a term in its own statute unconstitutional, and according to the historian Laura Wittern-Keller, the *Garden of Eden* case established that the "state could no longer ban a film for indecency."[103]

"Gray Can Be a Very Drab and Dirty Color"

Politicians took notice when both federal and state courts consistently ruled that censors could no longer suppress nudist magazines and films. In 1961, the House Committee on Post Office and Civil Service held several hearings to reevaluate the issue of "obscene matter sent through the mail."[104] Representative Kathryn Granahan, a Democrat from Pennsylvania and chair of the committee, in her opening statement expressed concern about the new threat posed by "gray area products" such as nudist magazines.[105] In her interpretation, the recent Supreme Court decisions on obscenity benefited publications that "pussyfoot around

the edges but shrewdly stay just clear of subjecting themselves to prosecution."[106] Granahan considered magazines such as S&H to be "more
poisonous in their appeal to young boys and girls" since they "tend to
overcome home and church and civic guidance." She declared that "gray
can be a very drab and dirty color."[107]

Ironically, many longtime nudist leaders joined Granahan in expressing concern about the movement's legal victories. Although the nudist movement took advantage of the recent Supreme Court decision to
finally display the naked body without the shame communicated by
censorship, many leaders feared that the original ideals and principles
of nudism would be lost to an unregulated market of magazines and
films that linked nudity and nudism to the commercialization of sex.
For decades, nudist leaders and advocates had struggled to balance the
movement's therapeutic goals and its family-oriented recreational character with the erotic appeal of its magazines and camps. This struggle
ultimately contributed to the creation of a "gray area" in American obscenity law that allowed the marketing of sexual display.

The commercial potential of the naked body in the United States had
posed the greatest threat to the respectability of the American nudist
movement. The majority of Americans understood the naked body as
illicit and worthy of censorship when sold as an image in a magazine or
paraded onstage in front of mostly male audiences. Early attempts by
nudists to go naked in urban gymnasiums and on city beaches or parks
came under attack because police, moral reformers, and city officials
associated these gatherings with an illicit underworld. Censors also targeted nudist books, magazines, and films because their sales often far
exceeded the number of members claimed by the movement. Indeed,
the editors of nudist publications often deliberately chose images that
marketed the eroticism of the naked body to both heterosexual and homosexual men in order to financially support a national organization, to
fund the movement's many legal battles, and to help maintain a sprawling network of camps and clubs. At the same time, the nudist movement
maintained its respectability through a religious leadership that rejected
the shame and scorn attached to the naked body while celebrating the
therapeutic benefits of going naked with other men, women, and children. Furthermore, to avoid comparisons to risqué performances, many
nudists established camps in rural areas, where a culture of skinny-

dipping and camping muted the perceived eroticism that defined public nudity in the city. Through camps, magazines, and films, the nudist movement promoted the physical and mental benefits of going naked while also appealing to men and women of all sexualities.

Sundial

The legal victories won by the American nudist movement initially allowed *S&H* to celebrate the display of genitalia. Regular subscribers of the flagship nudist magazine had long complained that the censoring of genitalia from its images betrayed the principles of mental and physical health advocated by the nudist movement. After *Sunshine Book Company v. Summerfield* (1957), the editors began to openly display full-frontal male and female nudity. The November 1958 issue, for example, featured numerous images—large and small—showing solitary figures posing for the camera or several men and women engaged in nudist activities. The inside cover exhibited a large image of a solitary woman walking ankle deep in a shallow, tranquil lake surrounded by thick vegetation.[108] Past issues very likely would have been forced to airbrush a similar image or would have resorted to positioning her body deeper in the water or showing her backside.

Another full-page image in the middle of the issue symbolized the new liberated feeling of the long-censored magazine. The photo showed a standing, smiling woman holding a towel around her waist while a refreshing breeze uncovers her full-frontal naked body.[109] Unconcerned with censorship, the editors of *S&H* abandoned the props, awkward posing, and airbrushing that had long defined the flagship nudist magazine.

The display of genitalia in *S&H* likely pleased health enthusiasts as much as it appealed to men and women of all sexualities who had yearned for uncensored images of the naked male and female body. One picture exhibited a man and woman looking at a camera positioned just above their exposed genitalia.[110] In previous issues, the camera likely would have been used to block views of the genitalia in order to avoid conflict with censors who considered the appearance of both sexes in the same photo sexual and illicit. After the 1958 Supreme Court ruling, however, the picture used the placement of the camera to draw attention

After *Sunshine Book Company v. Summerfield* (1957), *Sunshine and Health*'s editors began to openly display full-frontal male and female nudity. (*Sunshine and Health*, November 1958, 9; courtesy of the Sunshine and Health Publishing Company)

to the midsections of the man and woman in the photo. By showing the man and woman deliberately glancing down at the camera—and at each other's genitalia—the image communicated to male and female readers that they too can look and suggested that members can use their own cameras to take similar pictures. *S&H* also did not hesitate to include images of male bodies that appealed to a gay male audience. One illustration featured a strong, athletic nude man holding a bow and arrow at the level of his genitalia.[111] It could easily have been included in one of the many physique magazines available to gay men in the early 1960s. Like the previous photograph's use of the camera, the bow and arrow serve to draw the reader's gaze to the penis while indirectly alluding to a more erotic image of a man firing an erect arrow. No longer restrained by the censors' guidelines, S&H included images once considered far too sexual for publication.

The new freedom that S&H enjoyed inspired other nudists to begin producing more daring magazines that did not turn away from explicitly promoting the sensuality of the naked body. Ed Lange, a former fashion photographer who had been part of organized nudism since 1938 and had contributed numerous photos to S&H, wanted to create a nudist magazine that would allow readers to "discover a way that would acknowledge the innate sensuality of all humans . . . without shame."[112] Carrying a reputation as a hedonist and rumored to be a swinger, Lange wanted to end what he considered to be nudist prudery. In 1962, he took advantage of the legal battles won by the nudist movement to begin publishing Sundial. In many ways, Sundial resembled S&H. Lange named the magazine after the club he frequented in Southern California and included information about other groups, upcoming events, and the philosophy of nudism. Yet Lange relied on Martin Luros, a publisher of girlie magazines such as Adam, Knight, and Cocktail, to produce and distribute his new magazine. Sundial, because it included content that represented nudist ideals and activities and used photos from nudist clubs, evaded the legal restraints that continued to prevent girlie magazines from displaying male and female genitalia, and it quickly became one of Luros's most profitable magazines. Hoping to build on this success, Luros gave Lange his own building and department to develop additional nudist titles. Although many nudists criticized Lange's sensual photos and worried that they would lead nudism away from its familial character and respectability, Lange's influence continued to grow in the nudist community. He later established the nudist resort Elysium Fields in Topanga Canyon, California, and eventually started his own press under the name Elysium Publishing Company. The partnership between Lange and Luros produced a market of nudist magazines that made it very difficult to disentangle the erotic from the respectable.

The attempts by Kathryn Granahan and her committee to expose the increasingly sexual character of magazines such as S&H and Sundial

A beautiful study of a perfect physique. Could the benefits of nudist living be more obvious?

Sunshine and Health also did not hesitate to include images of male bodies that appealed to a gay male audience. (*Sunshine and Health*, November 1958, 22; courtesy of the Sunshine and Health Publishing Company)

also brought to light the growing dissatisfaction of an older generation of nudist leaders who defended the therapeutic and nature-oriented principles of the movement. The images that appeared in *S&H*, and especially those on its covers, invited accusations from Granahan that the magazine sought to profit from men looking for female sexual display. Granahan accused the magazine of using paid models rather than actual nudists to illustrate its covers with attractive young women who posed seductively for the camera.[113] Testifying before the committee, the Reverend Henry Huntington, the first president of the National Nudist Council, responded to Rep. Granahan with equal disappointment. He regretted that S&H's "pictures, especially on the cover," promoted the "suggestion of the girly-girly magazine."[114] Huntington declared that the pictures made him "quite furious inside because really the movement is the essence of good health."[115] He believed that these images undermined the respectability of the nudist movement, and he concluded his testimony by maintaining that images displaying naked bodies without suggestive poses still should be considered "respectable and that actually it does have [a] purifying [effect]."[116] Aging leaders such as Rev. Huntington worried that the increasing eroticism displayed in nudist magazines threatened to undermine the movement's respectability.

The eroticism that existed next to the therapeutic ideals of the movement and that had subtly shaped the appearance and content of S&H for decades now exploded in dozens of magazines that used nudism to profit from the display of male and female genitalia. No longer fearing government censorship, nudist magazines began appearing with titles that emphasized nude display far more than an ideology of health, recreation, and family. Prior to the movement's legal victories, editors and nudist leaders relied on discreet titles such as Sunshine and Health to avoid direct references to nudity and potential legal troubles while also promoting the movement's health-oriented and recreational character. After 1958, publications employed titles such as International Nudist Sun (1965), Nude Image (1964), Nude Living (1961–1968), Nudism in Action (1963–1965), and Nude World (1962–1966) and graphically exhibited pubic hair, genitalia, and eroticism. In addition, many of these magazines, including Nude Image, Nude Living, and Nudism in Action, originated from Luros's publishing company based in North Hollywood, California.[117] According to the historian Robert Self, in the postwar era, urban decay caused by suburban flight led to the growth of sex-based businesses in the Hollywood region.[118] Sent from the increasingly well-known capital of mail-order pornography rather than a nudist club or organization, these magazines linked nudism to a growing postwar pornography industry centered in Southern California. By winning the approval of the Supreme Court, nudists unintentionally created a market of nudist magazines that promoted sexual display far more prominently than they promoted the movement's principles and ideals.

Nude on the Moon

The recreational and familial character of early postwar nudist films made pornographic films more widely available than ever before. The legal release of *Garden of Eden* in 1958 marked a significant turning point in the history of film. According to the film scholar Eric Schaefer, the *Garden of Eden* case effectively ended the "ban on nudity in motion pictures."[119] Winning the right to show nudity on the screen opened the door to a more explicit genre of nudist films. A new exploitation film genre known as "nudie cuties" emerged in the early 1960s. Films such as *Paradise Lost* (1959) and *Nude on the Moon* (1961) abandoned family-oriented plotlines in favor of light humor or parody and displayed mostly naked female bodies without relying on the setting of the nudist park.

The ridiculous plot, the absence of nudist rhetoric, and the voyeuristic exhibition of naked female bodies in *Nude on the Moon* classified the film as pornography. Whereas *Garden of Eden* revolved around the domestic problems of a widowed mother, *Nude on the Moon* featured two bachelor rocket scientists who attempt to build and launch a rocket ship to the moon.[120] Building on the sexual rhetoric and imagery of the Cold War rather than the health-oriented ideals of the nudist movement, the film uses the space race launched by President John F. Kennedy to develop a story line centered around a young, ambitious scientist who ignores the romantic interests of his attractive secretary because of his unwavering commitment to science. After a very low-budget launching sequence, the two scientists—dressed in red and green tights, cheap plastic helmets, and fire-extinguisher air tanks and equipped with a camera—step out of their ship to find lush vegetation, plenty of water, and large nuggets of gold lying on the ground. After wandering briefly, the two explorers stumble on a lunar nudist colony of women dressed only in G-strings and cheap wire Martian antennas. Not wanting dialogue to interfere with the display of naked female bodies, the women communicate with each other telepathically and do not directly "talk" with the two scientists. Still, the "Queen" of the group, played by the same actress who appeared earlier as the sexually frustrated secretary, immediately draws the attention and affections of the ambitious young scientist. As the younger scientist ogles his secretary's naked body, his partner documents the camp with his camera. Through the scientist's voyeuristic photography, the audience sees naked women reclining in the sun, bathing in ponds, and passing balls to one another. Like the photos now filling out the pages of nudist magazines, the film abandoned movements and poses once used to avoid the direct display of nudity. Instead, it exhibited activities that objectified the naked female body by focusing on the breasts and buttocks rather than the whole body. After returning the two scientists to Earth successfully, although without the camera to prove the spoils of their journey, the film concludes by flashing the naked body of the secretary using the imaginary gaze of the ambitious young scientist, who now seems far more interested in romance than scientific research. While still classified as a nudist film because it takes place in an imaginary space colony of naked women, *Nude on the Moon* made little attempt to justify the display of the female body through the presentation of nudist rhetoric or principles.

Films such as *Nude on the Moon* did not elude censors. The Board of Regents of the University of the State of New York, the same agency forced by the New York Supreme Court to allow the release of *Garden of Eden*, did not hesitate to deny *Nude on the Moon* a license. Yet the institution's approach to the film took into account the same "gray area" that concerned congressional representatives who worried about the mailing of obscene materials. Rather than assuming that any and all displays of nudity on the screen constituted indecency, the committee engaged in a "discussion of censorship problems" when they evaluated the film. To decide if the film should be denied a license, the board first had to determine "whether the sequences depicting life on the Moon were bona-fide nudist colony sequences or whether they should be classified as quasi burlesque." Although the board ruled the scenes "quasi burlesque at best" and recommended that the film be "rejected *in tote*," the acknowledgment of "bona-fide" nudist films suggested that other films that reflected more nudist-oriented plots and took place at actual nudist camps should receive official approval.[121]

The production of new films that claimed to display the naked body in the name of nudism, health, and recreation threatened to transform the public image of the nudist movement into an entirely erotic phenomenon. Ken Price, an assistant editor for *Sunshine and Health*, reviewed *Forbidden Paradise* (1958) as an example of the types of nudist films being released after the *Garden of Eden* decision. In his article, which he titled "So Far So Bad," Price critiqued films designed to sell "sex at the box office, with the nudist angle thrown in for good measure," because they threatened to promote an inaccurate image of the nudist movement.[122] Since "every film containing nude footage that can possibly bear the nudist tag has it pasted on," Price worried that these new films would distort the "true story of nudism."[123]

The location of the theater screening *Forbidden Paradise* confirmed the explicitly pornographic appeal of the film. Price attended a showing of the movie at the Paramount Theater in a part of downtown Los Angeles known as a gay pickup grounds. In the 1960s, according to the historian Whitney Strub, the Los Angeles Police Department targeted the theaters, bookstores, and newsstands around Main Street and Persian Square.[124] Located a block east of Main Street, the Paramount Theater represented another site where gay men could meet and engage in sexual behavior. A photo of the Paramount Theater that illustrated Price's article shows a dirty, run-down marquee advertising the nudist film in large, bold letters above a crowded street full of cars speeding past a dark, shadowy sidewalk. To remove any doubt as to what kind of movies were shown at the theater, a sign just below the admission prices announced the film as "adult fare." Exhibited in down-and-out theaters on the wrong side of town, nudist films entertained all male audiences looking for sexual display or a gathering place to engage in sexual acts.

Price resented the shoddy production of *Forbidden Paradise* because it linked nudism to cheap exploitation films and the commercialization of sex. Price assumed that the film, produced by Colorama Pictures and starring Ingeborg Schoner and Jan Hendriks, originated in Germany because the soundtrack carried German dialogue along with a "confusing overlay of English commentary." He then went on to critique the color of the film, which was "erratic and mostly green, blue, and brown shades." Price also expressed disappointment with the nudity displayed in the film. He objected to the fact that the main actors and actresses rarely appeared nude and that only "stock model shots" featured nudes who were "engaged in the most idiotic activities." He had hoped the film would

The location of the theaters screening nudist films after the *Garden of Eden* decision confirmed their explicitly pornographic appeal. (*Sunshine and Health*, November 1958, 25; courtesy of the Sunshine and Health Publishing Company)

exhibit the "inside of a nudist resort" in order to present a more accurate image of nudist life. Instead, the presentation "progressed by leaps and lurches—with careful shots of the nudes interspersed with a dull story, just enough to keep the audience in their seats and hoping for more and better views."[125] Nudist camps and principles occupied a marginal position in films such as *Forbidden Paradise* and *Nude on the Moon*, which explicitly sought to profit from sexual female display.

"Do You Ever Find Any Perversion among Your Nudists?"

The increasing sensuality of the nudist movement's magazines and films also made Kathryn Granahan's committee question the morality of the men and women who visited nudist camps. Berton Boone, the son of Ilsley Boone and then acting president of Sunshine Publishing Company, testified that almost all of the images used in *S&H* pictured nudists who regularly attended camps and participated in nudist activities. This shifted the committee's attention from visual materials to the nudist camps, their membership, and the screening processes of individual clubs. For the committee, the morality of practicing nudists proved as suspect as the content and images of the movement's magazines and films. To prove the moral character of nudists, Berton Boone testified that camps required all new members to conduct themselves "in a clean moral fashion," instituted trial visits where each applicant underwent a period of observation, and subjected men and women to character evaluations carried out by the national nudist organization.[126] This process, according to the committee, did little to assure the moral character of the members who visited nudist camps. Rep. Dominick V. Daniels, a Democrat from New Jersey, maintained that nudist clubs still had few procedures in place to prevent members with criminal backgrounds, such as a "woman [who] is a prostitute," from becoming a member of a resort or camp.[127] Rep. Granahan followed up this line of questioning by asking Boone, "Do you ever find any perversion among your nudists?"[128] Boone desperately sought to assure the committee that resorts strictly policed the sexual behavior of their members. He asserted, "when these things come to our attention, when we discover them, whether it be through an application blank or by someone reporting homosexuality, . . . these people are removed from the community."[129] Despite Boone's claims that individual clubs sought to enforce heterosexual memberships, the circulation of erotic nudist magazines and films put the moral character of the entire movement in doubt.

The growing public acceptance of the naked body at newsstands and in theaters meant that the movement's continuing promotion of health, nature, and family no longer seemed necessary or relevant to the general public. Nudist leaders nevertheless continued to cling to the image of respectability that had helped the movement defeat the censoring of its magazines and films. In response to the renewed opposition of the Granahan committee, for example, Ilsley Boone, his son Berton, and his daughter Margaret A. B. Pulis all testified about the respectable character of American nudism. Referring several times to Ilsley Boone as "Dad," Pulis answered questions about the images in *S&H* by invoking her status as a daughter, a mother, a grandmother, and a member of the PTA.[130] The three longtime nudist leaders wanted to maintain the family-oriented image of the movement. These efforts also continued to define the content of *S&H*. The emphasis placed on representing the movement's ideals and principles, however, appeared far too tame for many customers next to graphic nudist magazines that embraced and celebrated the sensuality of the naked body. Confirming Post Office suspicions that the majority of *S&H* sales resulted from readers who sought out pornography, the flagship nudist magazine went bankrupt in 1963. Committed to advancing the ideals of nudism, the nudist publication that began in 1933 and fought to defeat censorship laws across the country could no longer compete in a marketplace that offered even more explicit material uninterrupted by nudist principles and philosophy. By the early 1960s, Americans turned away from an understanding of nakedness as healthy and familial and embraced nudity in the form of commercialized sex.

FREE THE BEACH

Nudism and Naturism after the Sexual Revolution

By the late 1960s, the naked bodies that nudists had fought so hard to liberate from long-standing obscenity laws and social prejudices began appearing almost everywhere in American life and culture. At music concerts, in Broadway performances, on college campuses, in avant-garde art films—as well as in Hollywood blockbusters—and as part of protest marches, young adults across the country chose to remove their clothes for the entire world to see.[1] The baby boomers coming of age in the late 1960s brandished their naked bodies to challenge what they perceived to be the hypocritical values and social customs of mainstream American society. After John Lennon posed naked with Yoko Ono for the cover of their 1968 *Two Virgins* album, he spoke for many in his generation when he declared that "the main hangup in the world today is hypocrisy and insecurity" and that "being ourselves is what's important."[2] Going naked communicated the honest expression of one's self free of false pretenses and status symbols; it represented an effort to live closer to the natural environment, and it expressed a sexually liberated way of life. The "growing urge of more and more Americans to appear in public without any clothes on" inspired a lengthy October 1967 *Life* magazine article that explored the various reasons for the sudden acceptance of nudity among a "great many segments of society which would have rejected it two or three years ago."[3] The greater acceptance of public nudity in the late 1960s represented a dramatic change in a nation that had for so long disapproved of nudist activities, magazines, and films.

Several sociologists, psychologists, and sexologists looked to nudism to understand the public nudity phenomenon sweeping the United States, only to discover that most self-proclaimed nudists did not share the same liberated sexual attitudes and values espoused by the young men and women going naked in the late 1960s. Studies such as William Hartman, Marilyn Fithian, and Donald Johnson's *Nudist Society: An Authoritative, Complete Study of Nudism in America* (1970), Manfred F. DeMartino's *The New Female Sexuality: The Sexual Practices and Experiences of Social Nudists, "Potential" Nudists, and Lesbians* (1969), and Martin Weinberg's "The Nudist Management of Respectability" (1970) fit into an exploding market of sex manuals and studies in the 1970s written by academic experts and nontraditional writers who promised readers advice on how to "become less constrained by restrictions and inhibitions."[4] Yet the data these studies collected revealed a nudist membership dominated by middle-aged, predominantly middle-class married couples who clung to rules and restrictions designed to limit sexual expression and behavior.[5] After studying and interacting with nudists for over a decade, the prominent psychologist and sex researcher Albert Ellis found that nudist clubs upheld the "same kind of hypocritical, let's-never-squarely-face-the-issue view of sex that is prevalent in our general society, and that helps keep honest sexuality a secret, shameful thing."[6] He scoffed at rules that excluded single men, called for restricted diets, prohibited casual touching, and forced men to hide their erections. Although nudists played an important role in making it legal to go naked in public, in magazines, and on the screen, social commentators struggled to locate the origins of the sexual revolution in the values of the American nudist movement.

The "counterculture" that emerged in the late 1960s introduced an approach to sex that placed great value on authenticity, honesty, and trust. The New Left that centered early youth-culture activism in the 1960s continued to re-create unequal sexual relationships that privileged male pleasure and prioritized political reform and activism. As the youth culture shifted its interests toward "a counterculture more defined by its proclivities for sex, drugs, rock music, and rhetorical support for the revolution," they adopted a more experimental approach to sexuality.[7] Going naked at a commune, on the beach, or at a music concert furthered the counterculture's desire to remove the "barriers to full sensory experience."[8] Members of the counterculture, in contrast to the New Left and mainstream society, rejected a "double standard" that expected women to remain chaste while rewarding men for their sexual prowess. They openly engaged in casual sexual encounters, serial monogamy, and group sex and experimented with open marriage and explored homosexual relationships.[9] Sex represented a "thing of creativity and technique but also an arena of daily life wherein one might cultivate and share a deeper, truer, and more authentic sense of who one really was."[10] The secrecy, shame, and voluntary seclusion that defined organized nudism in the United States alienated the young men and women of the counterculture who sought an honest, open, authentic sexual experience.

The effort to maintain the respectable character of American nudism, even after its legal victories in the late 1950s, clashed with a new generation of activists who used public nudity to advocate for the politics of sexual liberation. The nudist movement that began in the 1930s promoting health, nature, and family transformed in the late 1960s and early 1970s into an assortment of organizations that challenged the heteronormative boundaries of sexual liberalism. The many young men and women drawn to nudist activities and groups no longer wanted to be confined in isolated rural clubs; they embraced sexual expression outside marriage and waged high-profile campaigns to change public attitudes about nudity. The widespread willingness of many Americans to reexamine the limits of acceptable sexual behavior influenced many nudists to reject the restrictive rules and exclusionary policies that had long defined American nudism. Nudists, adopting the European term *naturism*, created a more inclusive and sexually tolerant approach to nudism on sandy beaches, isolated river banks, and out-of-the-way parks. Naturists promoted a closer relationship with nature, advocated for nudity on public beaches and parks, and critiqued the intolerance of organized nudism. The progressive agenda of naturism brought together advocates of sexual freedom, feminists, people of color, gay men and women, and left-leaning activists.

With sexual liberalism under siege, the contradictions that once defined nudism—family oriented yet also a site of eroticism, a refuge for healthy conceptions of the body and a source of commercial pornography—fragmented the movement even as it made its growth possible. Feminist activists, in particular, rejected the assumption that good intentions and the family orientation of nudism/naturism guarded against illicit sexual behaviors. The debates raging over pornography in the 1980s influenced feminists to take a more critical view of naturist activities, its values of sexual liberation, and the representations featured in its magazines. Many feminists—frustrated by a fractured women's movement, the failure of the Equal Rights Amendment, and the lack of a progressive sexual-rights platform—shifted their focus from a broad critique of sexism and gender inequality to a campaign against pornography. Antipornography feminists alienated many civil libertarians and activists in the women's movement, especially lesbians, who opposed state censorship and the effort to impose a single conception of sexuality on society. Yet the critiques leveled against nudism and naturism by feminists resonated with a public seeking to reestablish limits on sexual expression. Throughout the 1980s, nudists and naturists confronted questions about the sexual exploitation of women, the problem of pedophilia, and the movement's relationship with pornography. The liberal sexual values that shaped naturism clashed with the politics of antipornography feminism and made it difficult for the two groups to work together toward a common goal. The conflict and division that erupted over pornography influenced naturism to increasingly define itself as a lifestyle that offered rest, relaxation, and nude recreation.

"A Situated Morality"

The late 1960s represented a transitional moment for the American nudist movement. Rev. Ilsley Boone, who worked tirelessly to establish nudism in the United States since the early 1930s, died in the fall of 1968.[11] Maurice Parmelee, whose *Nudism in Modern Life* helped establish the philosophy of nudism in the United States and became the subject of a congressional scandal during the Second World War, passed away in the spring of 1969.[12] That same year, Kurt Barthal, who organized the first nudist gatherings in New York City with fellow German immigrants, died at the age of eighty-five.[13] As many of the longtime leaders of nudism passed away, the number of nudist camps across the country grew to 130, and the membership of the American Sunbathing Association surged by 12 percent to fifty-six thousand members.[14] Paula Krammer, the owner and manager of Camp Goodland in Hackettstown, New Jersey, confirmed this growth at her club, which had grown to eleven hundred members by recently adding two hundred men and women. She explained that most of the new enlistees were "young adults who are interested in raising their children under the principles of health."[15] No longer the subject of constant police raids and still offering a number of resort-style facilities with lakes, swimming pools, cabins, and recreation halls as well as protected spaces for sunbathing, hiking, and a variety of other athletic activities, nudists clubs attracted a new generation of young men and women interested in experiencing the pleasures of social nudity in a rustic natural setting.

The participation of younger men and women in organized nudism remained small in comparison to a predominantly older, well-established, family-oriented membership. The increased interest in nudism from the mass-market sex-advice literature that emerged in the late 1960s produced extensive demographic data about the movement. The studies detailed the average age, education level, type of occupation, marital status, and church affiliation of American nudists. Surveying over two thousand nudists across the United States, William Hartman, Marilyn Fithian, and Donald Johnson's *Nudist Society* reported that nudist men averaged 40 years in age, 85 percent had graduated high school, and 20 percent had graduated from college. Almost 40 percent claimed a professional type of employment and boasted an income level 50 percent higher than the average Californian.[16] Nudist women averaged 38 years in age, and almost 50 percent reported their occupation as "housewife."[17] Similarly, Manfred DeMartino's *The New Female Sexuality* reported 34.7 years to be the average age of the 102 female nudists surveyed; 80 percent were married, 32 percent had graduated high school, 37 percent had received some college training, and the most frequently listed occupation was "housewife." In contrast, the 73 "potential nudists" DeMartino interviewed—women who were interested in nudist activities but who had never participated in organized nudism—had a much lower average age of 26.9 years.[18]

An older, family-oriented membership influenced most nudist clubs to maintain exclusionary policies and strict codes of conduct that limited sexual behavior. Since the 1950s, many nudist clubs in the United States excluded single males; prohibited drinking alcoholic beverages; discouraged unnecessary body contact, nude dancing, deliberate staring, and sexual jokes; and imposed strict rules regarding photography. In addition, individual members unofficially controlled the sexual behavior of other nudists by ostracizing men who had the misfortune of experiencing an erection, gossiping about women who regularly assumed provocative poses and postures, and whispering about guests who engaged in open displays of affection. Martin Weinberg, a sociologist at the Kinsey Institute who spent two summers as a participant-observer at a Chicago-area nudist club, argued that nudist clubs relied on numerous rules to construct a "situated morality" in response to the widely held perception that a close relationship existed between nudity and sexuality.[19] The restrictive atmosphere that prevailed at many nudist clubs began as a way to avoid police raids and to assure new members of the group's genuine commitment to the therapeutic principles of the movement.

The sexually liberated attitudes and values of many of the young people joining the movement, however, threatened to undermine the situated morality that prevailed at most nudist clubs. One nudist, for example, cited the less inhibited behaviors of "young people or carousers" as a reason to ban alcohol consumption at clubs, even though he regularly kept beer in his own refrigerator. He feared that drinking at camp might embolden "guys and girls" to "get fresh with someone else's girl." Nudists, according to him, had to "bend over backwards to keep people who are so inclined from going beyond the bounds of propriety."[20] At the ASA's 1967 annual convention at the Penn-Sylvan Health Society Camp, the organization rejected attempts to relax the ban against alcoholic beverages by voting down a motion that would have given individual clubs the right to make their own policies on the liquor question.[21] Well after the legal victories in the late 1950s, owners of nudist clubs continued to enforce policies that ensured the clubs appealed to respectable families rather than young singles and unmarried couples.

The exclusionary racial policies of many nudist clubs also discouraged the participation of many younger Americans who were sympathetic to the struggles of the civil rights movement. Although many university students volunteered in voter-registration campaigns and participated in protests against racial segregation in schools, on buses, and in local drugstores, an older nudist membership assumed that interracial sex remained deviant, and they feared that any association with the civil rights movement might further imperil the fragile respectability of American nudism. John Howard argues in his analysis of queer Mississippi that local residents who long ignored the queer incidents and behaviors around them began to consider the civil rights activism by white men and women from outside the state as an act of "perversion." This resulted in an increased awareness of queer behaviors by local Mississippi residents and a more "strident legal effort to ferret them out, punish them, and banish them."[22] The social and cultural prejudices against interracial sex did not remain confined to the South, as evidenced by a 1964 club newsletter written by the director and manager of the New York–based Stonehenge nudist group. The club manager responded to the recent passage of the antidiscrimination laws of Lyndon Johnson's Civil Rights Act by asserting that he was "not in favor of inviting a 'HUMAN SEA ASSAULT' of negroes upon our white parks" because it "would certainly result in a loss to both peoples." Although he did want to "accept those colored nudists that have honored us by wanting our companionship," he preferred to have "parks just about all of one color and others mixed and near enough so a nudist could choose the type of club that best suited the individual temperament."[23]

The racial prejudices of many nudists caused clubs to defy and resist antidiscrimination laws. In 1966, Sunshine Park in Mays Landing, New Jersey, which had been founded by Rev. Boone in 1937 and had served as the national headquarters of the movement for decades, refused to admit an African American woman, her female companion, and her two daughters.[24] After the woman wrote to her senator and attracted the attention of the Division of Civil Rights in the New Jersey Attorney General's Office, the owner of Sunshine Park apologized and claimed that the incident had been the result of a "misunderstanding."[25] The attempts to maintain an older, whites-only membership put the nudist movement at odds with many progressive and young Americans who supported the civil rights movement.

The anonymous social interactions that prevailed at nudist clubs and activities also betrayed calls for sexual liberation. High educational levels, professional occupations, and higher-than-average income levels meant that many nudists lived in communities and worked for companies that likely disapproved of nudism. Nudists often assumed that the majority of their neighbors, family, friends, and coworkers considered nudism a deviant behavior and associated the movement with sexual promiscuity and "nuts." Many anticipated severe social and economic sanctions if they revealed their interest in nudism. They feared that they would be labeled "odd," that their children would endure ridicule from their friends, and that their teenage daughters or wives would be considered "sexually available." Other nudists worried about losing their jobs or being passed over for promotion by their employers. According to Weinberg, only 10 percent of the nudists he interviewed for his study on nudism openly disclosed that they regularly visited a nudist club. Those who did share their interest in nudism generally chose to do so with friends or coworkers who they felt were likely to respond with a positive reaction. In their suburban homes, many nudists renovated floor plans and constructed higher backyard fences to ensure that their nude sunbathing would remain hidden from neighbors and visitors.[26] Even when visiting clubs, nudists worried about sharing their identities. One man described how he looked "behind to see if anyone [was] behind [him]" every time he entered a nudist club.[27] Nudists also protected their identities at clubs by rarely using last names and almost never discussing their place of employment. Even though nudists claimed to reject the shame attached to the naked body, many remained uncomfortable sharing their weekend activities and chose to live a double life.

As much as the reticent atmosphere of the nudist club attempted to preserve the respectable, white, family-oriented character of the movement, it also concealed a variety of extramarital sexual behaviors. The same sociological studies that detailed the demographic composition of the movement surveyed the sexual behaviors, preferences, and experiences of practicing nudists. Many of the respondents remained unwilling to discuss sex and refused to answer questions addressing sexual behavior. Yet through one-on-one interviews and in the data collected from willing respondents, the studies revealed that erections happened at clubs, that extramarital affairs did occur, that gay men and lesbians visited and joined nudist clubs, and that older, established married couples interested in the "swinging" phenomenon looked to nudism to meet other couples. The respectable atmosphere promoted at many nudist clubs protected men and women interested in exploring a variety of sexual behaviors.

The preference of many nudists to remain anonymous and the effort to maintain the movement's family-oriented character made nudism an ideal place to meet couples interested in discreetly exchanging sexual partners. "Wife swapping" or "swinging" grew in popularity in the mid-1960s as a largely suburban phenomenon in the United States. Mostly highly educated, professional men and women, dissatisfied with the routines of suburban life, experimented with the boundaries of monogamy at parties where several married couples came together, occasionally in the nude, engaged in small talk over drinks, and then transitioned to bedrooms with someone other than their spouse.[28] The nudist club provided a similar setting where couples felt comfortable openly propositioning fellow nudists to "swing." A thirty-seven-year-old nudist man and his wife who were "not interested in swinging" described being "approached by various nudists" to switch partners. Offended by the repeated unwanted advances, they changed their club membership. Another nudist woman, in her midthirties, endorsed swinging in the movement because it "filled an unacknowledged need for extramarital sex": "[It] enriched my marriage by demonstrating how much our mutual love meant to us."[29] The unstated acceptance of swinging in nudism provided opportunities for spontaneous sexual encounters between consenting couples. One woman described an incident in a "nudist group of two other people" besides her husband and herself in which they had sex as a group, while another woman recalled an incident involving "one man and five girls who were sitting around nude when it [group sex] started."[30] And yet the nudist movement's insistence that clubs keep extramarital behaviors hidden behind restrictive rules, exclusionary policies, and anonymous social interactions alienated many young people who saw public nudity as a way to liberate sex from repressive attitudes and beliefs.

The Sexual Freedom League

For Jefferson Poland, a young student activist attending San Francisco State University in the early 1960s, going naked on a beach, in a park, or on a public sidewalk represented a way to liberate sex from shame, guilt, and repression. After moving in with "two anarchist girls who practiced nudity and promiscuity" and meeting Leo F. Koch, a biologist who had been fired in 1960 by the University of Illinois because he endorsed premarital sex between advanced undergraduates, Poland began his campaign for sexual freedom by advocating "civil disobedience on a number of then-neglected domestic issues, including the rights of nudists."[31] After volunteering as a Congress of Racial Equality

(CORE) voter-registration worker in Plaquemine, Louisiana, in 1963, Poland moved to New York City, where he worked with Koch to form the New York City League for Sexual Freedom in 1964. The small organization enlisted an advisory committee that included the Beat poet Allen Ginsberg; Ginsberg's partner, Peter Orlovsky; the Living Theater directors Julian Beck and Judith Malina; the cofounder of the Washington, D.C., branch of the Mattachine Society, Franklin Kameny; and several other well-known Beat poets and authors active in Greenwich Village. Bringing together homosexuals, artists, and sex radicals and following the activist strategies of CORE, the League for Sexual Freedom set out to challenge the white, heteronormative boundaries of sexual liberalism that continued to influence the American nudist movement.

Poland's League for Sexual Freedom protested the limits placed on sexual expression in American society and defended marginal sexualities and practices. The belief that "sex without guilt and restriction is good, pleasurable, relaxing, and promotes a spirit of human closeness, compassion and good will" shaped the organization's efforts to change the way Americans thought about sex and eroticism.[32] It asserted that "marriage, engagement, or 'going steady'" was not necessary to "justify sexual relations," and it endorsed "wife and husband swapping, group sex, sex in public," as long as it was "mutually agreed upon between indulging parties."[33] It declared laws and restrictions that made sex between persons of different races to be unconstitutional, and it expressed support for repealing all laws that restricted a woman's "freedom of choice . . . in regard to having, not having children, birth control, and family planning."[34] It believed that films showing full-frontal male and female nudity should not be considered obscene and that sex engaged in by consenting parties for financial gain should be legal. In addition, it objected to the "fuss against children being exposed to sex or indulging in it" and asserted that a *sex organ in the hand of a child is more desirable than a toy machine gun.*"[35] The League for Sexual Freedom practiced a queer politics that celebrated marginal sexualities and campaigned to disrupt social and cultural assumptions that restrained sexual behaviors, maintained gender hierarchies, and imposed racial inequalities.

Poland identified with nudist ideals while also embracing the sensual pleasures of going naked among groups of men and women. Like nudists, he believed that the "body was naturally invigorated by sunshine, fresh air, and water," and he repeated nudists' arguments that the acceptance of nudity in everyday life would "break the vicious cycle which produces sexual criminals."[36] He also identified with the struggle to make nudism legal in the United States when he asserted that the "question of nudity is essentially the right to come and go without having one's own desires restricted by others who are unwilling to adopt the same desires."[37] Yet he also critiqued the sexual reticence of nudist clubs. He objected to the assumption that men who were "erotically stimulated" would be "inclined to impose themselves sexually on another." Instead, he believed that signs of "sexual excitement" were "normal and may be construed as a compliment if no coercion or force is involved."[38] Poland believed the eroticism of the naked body needed to be accepted rather than denied in order to remove the shame and guilt attached to sex.

Poland saw nudists as allies in his struggle for sexual freedom. In 1964, he sent an open letter to three hundred nudist clubs and groups introducing the New York City League for Sexual Freedom and soliciting support for a campaign to make "marked-off sections of public beaches" available to nudists.[39] He encouraged nudists across the country to make formal applications to their local and state governments to "use at least part of their tax-supported public beaches in the nude." Through this campaign, he hoped to attract newspaper and television attention and to create public discussion and debate. Inspired by his experiences working with CORE, he called on nudist organizations to "press for their rights by means of demonstrations" including the types of "nonviolent civil disobedience in the tradition of the negro freedom movement."[40] He suggested a "nude wade-in at a public beach similar to Negro wade-ins at white beaches," where clothed and unclothed demonstrators who were willing to "suffer arrest" demanded the right to sunbathe nude at public beaches.[41] Calling on nudists to advocate for nude sunbathing at public beaches, to participate in public demonstrations and campaigns, and to embrace the struggle for racial equality, Poland outlined a new vision for American nudism.

Poland's letters drew mixed responses from nudists. Many club directors worried that public demonstrations would ultimately undermine the respectable character of the movement. The director of the Sunny Sands Resort, "A Family Nudist Resort with the Accent on Comfort" located in Daytona Beach, Florida, expressed interest in Poland's "wade-ins," but he hesitated to "connect [the] club with anything as radical as a wade-in."[42] A member of the Christian Naturalist Society, located in Baltimore, Maryland, agreed with Poland that "all beaches, parks, or recreation areas should be available to nudists" but doubted that "'wade ins' would be effective in the same sense as 'sit-ins'" since a "roped off section" would just create a "morbid body consciousness among the non-nudists."[43] Other nudists expressed outright hostility to the activist goals of the League for Sexual Freedom. A member of the Shangri-La Guest Ranch in Phoenix, Arizona, asserted that nudists "would never go to a beach, and be in the nude, if non-nudists were allowed to attend." Casting aspersions on Poland's character, he wrote that it seemed unlikely that members of the League for Sexual Freedom had ever been to a nudist resort, and if they had, he speculated it "must have been a rotten one" since a good nudist resort is for "clean minded people." The letter writer made little effort to hide his disdain for young nudists interested in sexual liberation. He wrote that his club had "expelled 3 couples that should have made application to join [Poland's] sexual freedom league" and warned Poland, "keep your homos there as they could get their neck broke if they show up here."[44] With varying degrees of vitriol, the older, more established nudist membership rejected Poland's calls for activism on behalf of nude beaches.

Other responses to Poland's open letter revealed a substantial number of nudists, young and old, black and white, who supported a more vocal, sexually permissive, and racially tolerant nudist movement. The director of the Stonehenge nudist club in New York admired the "progressive courage" of the League for Sexual Freedom and chose to include Poland's letter in his newsletter along with a short summary of the group's goals. He believed that the group "may be an answer to our needs" to "bring our world out of its dark-age ignorant mentality."[45] Another letter, from an African American married nudist couple, asserted their commitment to "freedom in *all* of its phases." They felt "there was too much repression in regard to sex" and applauded Poland's efforts to create an "organized resistance to this."[46] Although most nudists chose to ignore Poland's calls for a more activist nudist movement, the support he did receive encouraged him to make public nudity one of the defining issues of his League for Sexual Freedom.

Despite the mixed support of organized nudism, on August 25, 1965, Jefferson Poland, wearing a flower in his hair and joined by two twenty-one-year-old women and a number of clothed picketers, carried out his nude "wade-in" at San Francisco's Aquatic Park.[47] The League for Sexual Freedom's first planned act of civil disobedience drew a number of reporters and a large crowd of spectators. The three nervous demonstrators made their way through the crowd to the water behind a placard that read, "WHY BE ASHAMED OF YOUR BODY?" After removing their clothes under the water, the three swam around the bay while reporters and the crowd urged them to return to shore. Not wanting to pass up the opportunity for publicity, Poland and his two fellow demonstrators came out of the water, holding hands, showing their naked bodies, and posing for the cameras. The police quickly arrived, covered the three with blankets, and arrested them for violating Section 115 of San Francisco's Municipal Code, which punished individuals for "swimming without proper attire." Although the event required Poland to spend five weekends in jail, it generated unprecedented interest in nude sunbathing at public beaches and recreational areas. At the very least, Poland felt confident that the "nudist message had reached San Francisco's large and growing 'hippy' minority through the mass media."[48] Encouraged by the success of his nude "wade-in," Poland continued his campaign for public nudity in Golden Gate Park, on the streets of Haight-Ashbury, and at several local Bay Area beaches.

After the nude "wade-in," student sexual freedom groups formed on college campuses around the country and advocated for students' access to birth control, called for an end to university policies that regulated sex on campus, and experimented with social nudity. The East Bay Sexual Freedom League, located near the University of California–Berkeley campus, sponsored a number of "nude parties" held at private residences where couples could attend, go naked if they chose to, and engage in sexual activity with willing partners.[49] In contrast to the secretive "swinging" activities at nudist clubs, the orgies held around the Berkeley campus in 1966 and 1967 were widely publicized and attracted single men and women, gay men and lesbians, African Americans, and respectable middle-aged married couples. Richard Thorne, a twenty-nine-year-old African American and the head of the East Bay Sexual Freedom League, explained that the parties helped attendees to free

On August 25, 1965, Jefferson Poland, wearing a flower in his hair and joined by two twenty-one-year-old women and a number of clothed picketers, carried out his nude "wade-in" at San Francisco's Aquatic Park. (Lee Baxandall, *World Guide to Nude Beaches and Recreation* [New York: Stonehill, 1980], 40)

themselves from the shame and guilt attached to sex. He declared, "man will only become free when he can overcome his own guilt and when society stops trying to manage his sex life for him." An article in *Time* magazine reported that the emergence of the nude parties continued an effort by students and nonstudents to "test limits of the permissible at Berkeley."[50] Through activist organizations, public demonstrations, and notorious sex parties, a new generation of young nudists rejected the heteronormative boundaries that had long defined American nudism and transformed the movement into a vehicle for sexual liberation.

The Free Beach Movement

After Jefferson Poland's nude "wade-in," groups of young men and women as well as members of local nudist clubs and dedicated beachgoers began looking for accessible beaches that provided enough privacy to go naked without offending other visitors or local residents. They searched for beaches surrounded by high cliffs, located far away from busy roads, and with few overlooking houses. A small, informal community quickly emerged and provided interested nude beachgoers information about safe, convenient locations and offered transportation to distant locales through ride sharing. This filled a void left by the reluctance of organized nudism to advocate for nude beach use. In the late 1950s, a weekend nudist event held at a beach near Santa Cruz, California, failed to persuade members to put aside their concerns about the social and financial risks of engaging in public activism.[51] By the mid-1960s, groups all along the California coast gathered at secluded beach sites with guitars, bongo drums, harmonicas, and flutes and enjoyed the sun, surf, and ocean air both with and without clothing. Sunbathing, socializing, holding heated discussions, dancing, drinking, using recreational drugs, and occasionally engaging in a variety of sexual behaviors, nude beachgoers encouraged a far more open and inclusive environment than the restrictive atmosphere enforced at most nudist clubs.

The growing informal interest in nude beaches led to the formation of an organization dedicated to identifying ideal nude beach sites and to making these locations permanent and legal. Darrell Tarver, a twenty-eight-year-old air force veteran from Texas and a graduate of San Francisco State University, established the Committee for Free Beaches in 1965. Like many members of the ASA, he found nude swimming and sunbathing "exhilarating, refreshing, and entirely wholesome." Tarver believed that people should be "permitted to use . . . beaches in this manner without suffering the harassments of indecent exposure laws." He applauded the many "free beaches" in Europe that legally permitted men and women to swim and sunbathe naked.[52] At these beaches, each individual chose "for himself what to wear, or not to wear." In contrast to nudist clubs, free beaches maintained a "free and open atmosphere" that lacked the rules and social pressures forcing people to remove their clothes.[53] Women, often a minority at nudist clubs and frequently pressured by husbands or boyfriends to join and participate in nudist activities, found the lack of coercion at free beaches especially appealing. The acceptance of clothing at the beach removed some of the discomfort and fear of undressing in front of the opposite sex and made free beaches far more welcoming for women who had a casual interest in nude swimming or sunbathing. Using European free beaches as a model, the Committee for Free Beaches began locating "areas suitable for nude bathing," sponsoring a "number of beach parties," and negotiating with property owners and public officials for the purpose of establishing a permanent free beach."[54]

Thirty miles south of San Francisco, the San Gregario State Beach provided the ideal setting for the parties and activities hosted by the Committee for Free Beaches. The committee identified a stretch of beach about a mile and a half long that ran just north of the state beach and south of several private residences. Hidden away by towering cliffs and a safe distance from the main highway, casual skinny-dippers had long frequented the site to swim and sunbathe in the nude without upsetting other beachgoers, attracting police attention, or disturbing neighbors living in the area. Tarver arranged for legal access to the site by negotiating an arrangement with a local landowner named Walter Bridge, who allowed visitors to use his road and park in exchange for a one-dollar fee per car. To avoid trouble with police and local residents, organizers also established a lookout system in which two volunteers, armed with field glasses and walkie-talkies, stood guard and quickly alerted nude bathers of approaching visitors or police. At first, news of the site spread by word-of-mouth, and small groups of thirty or forty people visited the site on weekends and arrived in carpools organized by the Committee for Free Beaches or the East Bay Sexual Freedom League. As word spread and underground newspapers such as the *Berkeley Barb* began advertising the location and its activities, crowds of five hundred or more began making the trek to San Gregorio Beach.[55]

The more open atmosphere and relaxed social setting of the San Gregorio Free Beach attracted many local nudists in addition to rebellious Bay Area university students. After visiting the site, Poland reported that the "most eager participants were several families from local nudist parks." The nudists visiting San Gregorio, according to Poland, disliked the "social cliques, racial barriers, and emotional blocks often found in nudist parks" and saw the free beach environment as a welcome alternative.[56] While many members of the ASA remained reluctant to advocate for nude sunbathing on public beaches, other nudists felt that the establishment of a "free beach" in the United States marked a new era of acceptance for nudism. Cec Cinder, a nudist active in the ASA since the mid-1950s and a frequent contributor to several nudist publications, felt compelled to visit San Gregorio in the summer of 1967 after hearing about the nude beach from fellow nudists. When he saw about eighty nudists and an equal number of clothed men and women gallivanting on the beach without any fighting or police harassment and only a limited number of voyeurs, Cinder declared that the "movement had entered a new phase": "We had broken out of our ghettoes. We had taken wing. Now our future was limitless." It made no difference to him that "this pioneering effort was the result of Bay Area students and hippies rather than the American Sunbathing Association."[57] The popularity of "free beaches" among nudists reflected a growing dissatisfaction with the restrictive policies of nudist clubs and their insular social environment as well as a greater willingness to openly practice nudism.

The sexually liberated atmosphere of the "free beach" especially appealed to many gay men and women, who saw the sites as an opportunity to relocate the naked social interactions they enjoyed in urban bathhouses to a more open and enjoyable setting. Since the beginning of the twentieth century, gay men had appropriated urban public bathhouses that Progressive Era reformers originally set up to provide bathing facilities for tenement dwellers. Hidden away from public view, bathhouses afforded privacy and protection for men looking to engage in sexual activity with other men.[58] The central place that the bathhouse occupied in the urban gay community for much of the twentieth century likely influenced homophile activists and organizations in the postwar period to embrace public nudity as a way of articulating homosexual liberation. Rudolf Gernreich, one of the cofounders of the Mattachine Society in the 1950s, openly identified himself as a nudist, and according to the historian David Allyn, he considered "freeing people from bodily shame . . . an important first step in preventing political repression."[59] The emergence of a more visible and vocal gay liberation movement after the Stonewall Riots in 1969 led to numerous instances of homosexual men and women publicly removing their clothes to advocate for sexual freedom and to communicate gay pride. In the spring of 1970, the Gay Liberation Front, a Marxist gay rights group, grabbed headlines when it participated in an antiwar rally in Washington, D.C., by wading naked in the reflecting pool in front of the Lincoln Memorial.[60] The opportunity to go naked with other men and women on a beach rather than in cramped, crowded, and dark bathhouses represented another way to advocate for gay liberation.

Gay men and lesbians interested in nude sunbathing found a place in the sun alongside student-led organizations such as the Sexual Freedom League and progressive nudist families. The influential role that Poland's Sexual Freedom League played in establishing free beaches in California reassured gay men and lesbians that they would be welcome at the beach. Poland identified himself as bisexual, and he vocally stressed the importance of gay rights. He even attempted to strip off his clothes at the first gay pride parade in Los Angeles, only to be stopped by the head of the gay rights organization ONE, Inc., who feared that this would lead to police harassment.[61] Beginning in the late 1960s, Baker Beach in San Francisco, Brooks Avenue Beach near Venice in Los Angeles, and Riis Beach in New York City developed reputations as popular places for gay men and women to sunbathe in the nude and to cruise for sexual companionship. Armistead Maupin captured the growing popularity of the free beach among San Francisco's vibrant gay and lesbian community in the 1970s in his iconic *Tales of the City*. He described a visit to "Devil's Slide beach" through the fictional character Michael, a homosexual, and his roommate and close friend, Mona, a lesbian. The "flowered hippie vans, city clunkers, organic pickups with shingled gypsy houses, and a dusty pack of Harley-Davidsons" that "jammed" the parking lot signaled to readers that Devil's Slide was a "free beach" that entertained the hippie community as much as gay men and women.[62] Maupin's description of Michael and Mona walking a great distance from the highway, paying a ticket taker a dollar for both of them to enter, climbing over rocks, and then settling down on a "sandy cove nestled amid the rocks" captured the free beach experience introduced at the San Gregorio Free Beach. Maupin also alluded to the potential for cruising and the opportunity to meet new sexual companions when Michael answers Mona's complaint that it must be "wall to wall flesh down there" with a leering "I hope so."[63]

The growing number of nude beachgoers in California and around the country did, however, draw the attention of local police. Isolated beaches where a legacy of informal skinny-dipping had developed over the years now began attracting hundreds of visitors looking to disrobe and enjoy the sun and surf. Crowds of clothed and unclothed beachgoers began visiting sites such as Black's Beach in La Jolla, Shark's Cove in Santa Barbara, and Pirate's Cove in Malibu.[64] In Massachusetts, several beaches in Cape Cod where vacationers had frequently enjoyed the pleasures of skinny-dipping saw hundreds of nude visitors. Residents who had long looked the other way when a couple or family decided to go au naturel at the beach began to grow increasingly irritated by the hundreds of mostly young people cavorting naked, drinking, littering, and illegally parking on the street.[65] In California, police responded to the complaints of local residents by regularly arresting nude sunbathers and charging them with indecent exposure, as defined by Section 314 of the California Penal Code, which stated, "Every person who willfully and lewdly, either exposes his person, or the private parts thereof, in any public place, or in any place where there are present other persons to be offended or annoyed thereby . . . is guilty of a misdemeanor."[66]

Unlike most members of the ASA, who wanted to avoid confronting public-indecency laws, the many young men and women participating in nude sunbathing at the beach chose to challenge prohibitions against public nudity. On the morning of August 7, 1970, Chad Smith and his male friend visited a beach in San Diego County where they disrobed, laid on their backs on a towel, and fell asleep. Although they walked far down the beach away from residents and other beachgoers, the police awoke them and proceeded to arrest Smith for indecent exposure.[67] Seeking to discourage others from going nude at the beach, the local court then found Smith guilty of violating Section 314 of the California Penal Code and gave him a suspended sentence and informal probation as long as he paid a $100 fine. The sentence, however, also required Smith to register as a sex offender.[68] This threatened to permanently stain his reputation and limited his future livelihood by subjecting him to a lifetime of police monitoring. The courts hoped that the threat of being labeled a sex offender would discourage nude sunbathing at public beaches.[69] The future of free beaches in the United States depended on the successful appeal of Smith's arrest.

The Chad Merrill Smith case revisited previous legal arguments presented by nudists who made it a point to distinguish nudity from illicit sexual activity. Like many other nudists arrested since the early 1930s in raids made on urban gymnasiums or on rurally situated clubs, Smith admitted that he "willfully" disrobed and sunbathed naked on the beach while also maintaining that no lewd behavior occurred as a result of his public nudity. The distinction between "willful" and "lewd" rested at the heart of Smith's defense since Section 314 of the California Penal Code stated that criminal indecent exposure occurred only when a person committed an act that was both "willful" and "lewd." In past cases, prosecutors had to show "something more than mere nudity," such as public masturbation or exposing oneself to minors, to convict a person under Section 314.[70] The police who arrested Smith stated that the "petitioner at no time had an erection or engaged in any activity directing attention to his genitals."[71] As a result, the judges presiding over the Supreme Court of California asserted that "mere nudity does not constitute a form of sexual activity" and ruled that the "necessary proof of sexual motivation was not and could not have been made in the case at bar."[72] The judges who threw out Smith's conviction gave individuals the right to sunbathe nude on an isolated California beach as long as they did not engage in sexual behavior.

After the favorable *Smith* decision, nude sunbathing seemed on the verge of gaining the mass acceptance that isolated nudist clubs struggled to achieve despite similar legal victories in the 1950s. In the summer of 1972, the *New York Times* noted "a trend to nudity" on the coast and assigned a reporter to profile Shark's Cove free beach in Santa Barbara.[73] The *Los Angeles Times* also documented the "nude impact" of the "summer of 1972" in an article that detailed the growing interest in nude sunbathing at Venice Beach.[74] In May 1974, the conservative San Diego city council made Black's Beach, a secluded location in La Jolla long popular with nude sunbathers, the first officially designated "swimsuit-optional" beach area in the United States.[75] A few months later, the Los Angeles city council's Police, Fire, and Civil Defense Committee voted unanimously to create "clothing optional zones" that would allow public nudity in certain parks and beaches while prohibiting nudity in all other areas.[76] Initially, council members received a great deal of letters expressing support for the ordinance. The *Los Angeles Times* even printed a number of letters to the editor that endorsed nude sunbathing, objected to police harassment on the beach, and affirmed the "beauty of the entire human body without arbitrarily excepting parts of it."[77]

Rebuffed by the Supreme Court of California, free beach opponents turned to local legislatures and city councils to turn back nude sunbathers. Free beaches frequently neighbored prosperous communities with powerful neighborhood associations that considered the large crowds of young naked beachgoers and the accompanying throngs of clothed voyeuristic onlookers a disruptive spectacle that would hurt property values. In December 1973, the Santa Barbara Board of Supervisors responded to upset residents by voting 3–2 to ban all nudity on public beaches including the very popular Shark's Cove free beach that had recently been profiled by the *New York Times*.[78] In Los Angeles, conservative groups expressed outrage that the city council had passed an ordinance that would allow "clothing optional zones" at public parks and beaches. The *Smith* decision meant little to local homeowners who considered nude beachgoers degenerate drug users and homosexuals who threatened to disrupt their exclusive neighborhoods.

Local police answered complaints from homeowners by using intimidation tactics meant to discourage nude sunbathing and by arresting more defiant nude bathers on charges that fell outside the purview of the *Smith* decision. Since the 1940s, police employed policies and tactics that used the threat of public exposure and prosecution to scare women seeking abortions.[79] On the California coast in the 1970s, police implemented similar tactics against nude sunbathers. They dressed in SWAT uniforms, mounted on horses, or screamed through bullhorns from helicopters to implore nude sunbathers to put on their clothes or face being arrested on indecent-exposure charges. While most sunbathers put on their clothes and fled from the beach immediately, officers used the sex-criminal classification that came with an indecent-exposure conviction to scare more committed individuals. The police knew, however, that the courts would dismiss indecent-exposure charges without proof that an illicit act had occurred on the beach. Once in custody, officers "offered" individuals a plea to a lesser charge of "disturbing the peace," which carried a twenty-five-dollar fine and did not require them to register as a sex offender.[80] The police anticipated that bringing nude sunbathers in contact with the criminal justice system would ultimately make individuals think twice about disrobing on public beaches.

The popularity of free beaches among gay men especially drew the ire of neighbors, police officers, and prosecutors. Gay rights groups saw the *Smith* decision as a boon. Sandy Blixton, a "left-wing organizer and member of the homosexual group Lavender People," anticipated that the summer would bring an "increase in activities" since the group could respond to any arrests with "a class action" suit against the police. Like generations of nudists before him, Blixton believed that "it's a healthy thing for people to express their freedom, to be able to feel the sun and get a tan."[81] Yet the police treated nude gay men at the beach much more harshly than they treated heterosexual nudists or even lesbian nude sunbathers. Blixton observed, "Our sisters have not been molested" by the police, or they received only light fines.[82] Heterosexual men arrested for going naked on public beaches usually escaped indecent-exposure charges by pleading to the lesser offense of disturbing the peace. The Los Angeles Police Department explained that most of the "Venice nudity" that resulted in the arrest of fifty men since the *Smith* decision involved "drinking and homosexuality" and included "sexual activity which would be considered lewd." In contrast to the lenient response to heterosexual nudists, the Los Angeles district attorney put gay male nudists on trial for indecent exposure, and in more than half the cases, the "evidence has been sufficient to convince the court of lewd intent."[83] The efforts of the police to prosecute gay men for indecent exposure curtailed the number of nude sunbathers on Venice Beach.

Religious groups, conservatives, and senior citizens, already unhappy with what they perceived to be an excessively permissive society, campaigned against the effort to make Venice Beach clothing optional. When the Reverend Timothy Manning, the archbishop of Los Angeles, publicly denounced the ordinance as "another instance of the permissiveness that is corroding our culture and victimizing our young people," hundreds of calls and letters from upset residents began to inundate the city council.[84] Councilmen Donald Lorenzen and Robert Wilkinson quickly introduced an antinudity amendment that prohibited all nudity at city parks and beaches. Wilkinson, who represented the more conservative West Valley district of Los Angeles, echoed the archbishop's opposition to the more permissive sexual climate by asserting, "it's enough we have pornography on the streets and all these nude bars without this [a clothing-optional beach]." He saw free beaches as a "cancer that could spread throughout the city."[85] Police chief Ed Davis also spoke out against the counterculture groups that promoted a message of sexual liberation at Venice Beach when he objected to "bongo drummers [who] encourage sexuality by sensuous dancing and simulated sex acts in rhythm." Noting that "crime and marijuana use is up 26% because of the nude bathers and the Peeping Toms it attracts," he urged the city

council to adopt the antinudity amendment, since the recent *Smith* decision made it difficult for police to make and prosecute individuals for
indecent exposure. The campaign against the Los Angeles city council's
clothing-optional ordinance reflected a conservative rejection of the
politics of sexual liberation advocated by many young students and activists in the late 1960s and early 1970s.

The absence of a strong, structured national organization made it difficult for free beach activists to respond to a well-organized and vocal
opposition. The respectable policies of organized nudism clashed with
the young activists, gay men and women, and sexually tolerant nudists
who frequented free beaches. The distrust, animosity, and dissatisfaction that free beach activists and organized nudists felt for one another
created a void of leadership and organization. Eugene Callen, a German
immigrant who maintained his interest in nudism after coming to the
United States in 1948, tried to bridge this void by establishing Beachfront
U.S.A. after he witnessed police harass nude bathers at Pirate's Cove
Beach in Malibu during the summer of 1972. The small organization
first proposed the clothing-optional zones to the Los Angeles city council as a way of avoiding future confrontations, protecting nude bathers from voyeurs, and securing more spacious sites.[86] While Beachfront
U.S.A. initially received strong support, the small group did not have the
resources or personnel to counter the enormous public resistance to the
measure. Despite the growing popularity of nude sunbathing on public
beaches, organized nudists chose not to support the "clothing optional"
ordinance before the Los Angeles city council.

Individual supporters of nude sunbathing took it upon themselves to
advocate for the free beach lifestyle. Robert Opel, a professional photographer who worked for the *Advocate*, a popular lesbian, gay, bisexual,
and transgender (LGBT) interest magazine founded in 1967, decided to
make a dramatic statement in support of the "clothing optional" ordinance. A few months earlier, Opel briefly gained fame when he streaked
across the stage at the forty-sixth Academy Awards. The incident infa-
mously prompted David Niven, who was introducing Elizabeth Taylor
at the time, to adlib, "Well, ladies and gentlemen, that was almost bound
to happen. . . . But isn't it fascinating to think that probably the only
laugh that man will ever get in his life is by stripping off and showing
his shortcomings?" On July 12, 1974, in front of an overflowing crowd of

four hundred supporters, the full Los Angeles city council, and police chief Ed Davis, Opel again unzipped his blue pants suit, jumped over a guard rail, and ran through the chamber naked, holding up his arms in a V shape and shouting, "Is this lewd?" He drew whistles and hoots and prompted one woman to jump out of the crowd, pointing her finger and screaming at the city council, "Is this what you want?"[87]

Opel spoke for many of the nude sunbathers who frequented Venice Beach. He was a professional photographer who later went on to operate the "Fey-way" art gallery in San Francisco, which showcased gay male erotic art and helped launch the careers of Robert Mapplethorpe and Tom of Finland. While the straggly haired gay activist and artist avoided arrest at the Academy Awards, police at the city council meeting immediately took Opel away and charged him with indecent exposure and disturbing the peace. At his trial, he explained that he wanted to "give the council an example of what a live nude person looked like, and to show them that there were no reasons to conclude that simply being nude was being lewd."[88] The jury agreed with Opel and convicted him of disturbing the peace rather than the more serious charge of indecent exposure. The jury spokesman stated that they "did not feel the defendant created a lewd act by approaching the council in the manner he did."[89] Opel's actions created a spectacle that promoted the ideas and principles of the free beach movement as well as the politics of sexual liberation.

The Los Angeles city council, despite the best efforts of Robert Opel and Beachfront U.S.A., declined to support the "clothing optional" ordinance and passed an antinudity measure that contradicted the state supreme court's decision regarding Chad Merrill Smith. The Los Angeles city council voted 12–1 to prohibit nudity at all city parks, playgrounds, and beaches and to punish transgressors with a $500 fine or six months in jail. The ACLU immediately filed a lawsuit against the ordinance, arguing that "state law regulates nude behavior and pre-empts all local laws on the subject."[90] The organization also asserted that prohibiting nude sunbathing violated the First Amendment because it constituted a form of expression. Beachfront U.S.A. filed its own lawsuit, arguing that the ordinance infringes on its right to freedom of religion and discriminates against women because it prohibits the exposure of the female breast but not the male breast. Los Angeles Superior Court Judge David N. Eagleson agreed that nude sunbathing did not constitute a sexual activity. He reasoned, however, that local laws had jurisdiction over whether men and women wore bathing suits in public precisely because it was not considered a sexual activity, which he asserted fell to the state government of California to regulate. By the beginning of August 1974, police began arresting the first nude sunbathers, who continued to protest that they were "not doing anything wrong."[91] The ongoing debates over the legality of nude sunbathing in the courtroom and on the beach threatened to endanger the future growth of the free beach movement in the United States.

The Naturlst Society

A similar dispute over the Truro Free Beach in the summer of 1974 in Cape Cod, Massachusetts, expanded the issue of nude sunbathing beyond the West Coast. A long tradition of skinny dipping prevailed at Truro Beach. Dating back to the 1920s, figures such as Dwight Macdonald, Max Eastman, Eugene O'Neil, John Reed, and Louise Bryant frequently took advantage of the private beaches in Cape Cod to skinny-dip, and the site developed a reputation as a nude beach. By the mid-1970s, hundreds of young students, activists, and committed nudists began flocking to the site to sunbathe and swim in the nude. The dramatic increase in traffic, noise, litter, and trespassing upset neighbors who had once been tolerant of discreet nude bathers on the local beaches. Responding to complaints in the summer of 1974, Lawrence Hadley, the Cape Cod National Seashore superintendent, wrote regulations into the *Federal Register* that prohibited nude bathing within the Cape Cod National Seashore. Free beach advocates immediately rallied to overturn the first federal policies against nude sunbathing at national parks.

The campaign to reclaim Truro Free Beach ultimately led to the formation of a national organization that gave voice to a new generation of nudists and redefined nudism as a lifestyle choice rather than a social movement. Lee Baxandall, a political activist, playwright, and publisher who had enjoyed nude sunbathing at the Truro Free Beach with his wife and child since 1968, responded to the federal prohibition of nudity by establishing the Free the Free Beach Committee. Unlike Eugene Callen and Beachfront U.S.A., Baxandall spoke for the many young students and activists interested in nude sunbathing, and he had the ability to co-ordinate large demonstrations to advocate for free beaches. After study-ing history, literature, and aesthetics at the University of Wisconsin at Madison and traveling abroad, where he developed an interest in the German playwright Berthold Brecht, Baxandall went on to write and direct his own off-Broadway plays and acted as an editor of the New Left periodical *Studies of the Left*. Skilled in theatrical drama, politics, and communication, Baxandall began coordinating a mass protest to reclaim Truro Free Beach. Baxandall, however, lacked the necessary per-mits to hold a formal demonstration on federal land. Instead, he reached out to the many young students and nude beachgoers in the area by promoting a "free beach party." While the ACLU of Massachusetts ap-pealed to the U.S. Court of Appeals, Baxandall advertised the event on posters that critiqued the new federal policy with an image of a bear in a park-ranger suit holding binoculars and a can of chemical mace and wearing a hat that read, "smutty." Underneath the image that mocked the intentions of the park rangers, the poster implored, "Come to the free beach party! Free the free beach! Dress optional."[92] In addition, Baxan-dall's friend Daniel Schecter, a Boston disc jockey, helped promote the "dress-optional celebration" on his popular radio show. On August 24, 1975, over two thousand men and women assembled on Truro's Brush Hollow free beach and removed their clothing. Far outnumbered, the local police and park rangers found it nearly impossible to enforce the recently enacted federal regulations. Local and national media reports that documented the huge crowds, the absence of arrests, and the lack of any serious problems suggested that the recently enacted regulations might be unnecessary. Free beach activists were frustrated by the am-biguous legal rulings that jeopardized nude beach sunbathing along the West Coast, but the successful experience in Cape Cod signaled to them that mass demonstrations represented an effective way to resist antinu-dity policies.

Baxandall recognized the need for an activist organization willing to promote social nudity outside the nudist club. The goals and ideals of the ASA, according to many free beach enthusiasts, represented the eco-nomic interests of "nudist park proprietors" rather than the interests of the average nudist. Free beach activists decried the "hidebound conser-vation of capital investment" that defined the ASA and led to the "tacky trailer parks that, willy nilly, now . . . symbolize the vision of a humanity free of clothes-compulsory ideology." Unhappy with the strict rules limiting sexual expression and the organization's isolationism, free beach activists rejected nudist clubs since they constituted "ghettos of free flesh behind walls of fig leaves and barbed wire." Baxandall, joining with other free beach activists across the United States, including Eugene Callen, the organizer of Beachfront U.S.A., envisioned an organization born out of the "youth rebellion of the 1960s" and dedicated to an "understanding of social nudity defined through the individual's relationship with nature."[93] Preferring the European concept of *naturism* over the "superficial term" *nudism*, Baxandall believed that social nudity played a vital role in the "restoration of nature's balances" and made it possible to "more completely 'humanize' our culture."[94] Public nudity, according to Baxandall, "permits us to heighten our awareness of how much we are like one another and as vulnerable as one another," and as result, "individuals grow in sensitivity and dispense with the trappings of difference and privilege and fear."[95] Baxandall outlined an organization built on egalitarian ideals and capable of bringing together the many different people, groups, and organizations that had long struggled in isolation to establish a strong, unified movement capable of responding to antinudity policies at the federal, state, and local levels.

The Naturist Society (TNS), established by Lee Baxandall and several other free beach activists in May 1980, promoted an activist approach to nudism through a decentralized organizational structure and a mission to increase public awareness of recreational social nudity. Baxandall's family printing business in Oshkosh, Wisconsin, served as the group's headquarters, where a few dedicated activists coordinated and scheduled events, distributed newsletters and magazines, collected information about sites friendly to nude sunbathing, and fielded calls from newspapers, television and radio stations, and magazines. Instead of promoting individual clubs, the organization held regular "gatherings" of members interested in social nudity. At gatherings, members assembled at hospitable sites in different regions of the country and discussed ways to promote recreational nude sunbathing, to confront legal challenges, and to reform nudist practices that they considered unnecessary or inappropriate.[96] To increase public awareness of the "free beach issue" and attract media attention, the organization also set up and sponsored events such as National Nude Beach Day. Held in mid-July or mid-August, the national spectacle sought to re-create the mass nude demonstration that occurred at Truro Free Beach in the summer of 1976. In 1983, TNS also commissioned the Gallup organization to survey American attitudes about nude sunbathing at designated beach sites. Based on a sample of 1,037 adults, the poll found that 71.6 percent of Americans believed people should be able to sunbathe nude at a "beach accepted for this purpose," and another 39.1 percent thought the government should set aside "special and secluded areas" for going naked.[97] The favorable poll numbers validated the mission of TNS and raised the organization's public profile.

The publication of Baxandall's *World Guide to Nude Beaches and Recreation* in 1980 dramatically increased awareness of naturism, free beaches, and social nudity. Baxandall and Jan Smith, who helped edit the project, wanted to make naturism accessible to "outdoors people" who already enjoyed to "backpack or canoe."[98] The self-described "life style book" shifted the free beach movement's focus from establishing designated, legal clothing-optional areas to enjoying already well-established locations popular with experienced naturists or nude sunbathers.[99] Smith explained that "naturists really aren't after designated nude beaches" since these attempts often "bring out the Moral Majority" and create an unfavorable impression of naturists.[100] She acknowledged that "there are laws on the books everywhere" prohibiting public nudity, but she saw room for leniency. The intent of most anti-nudity laws, according to Smith, was to "keep people from going naked down Main Street."[101] She believed that "if no one is offended, just let it happen" and that the authorities should be encouraged to adopt this approach.[102] Accordingly, the *World Guide to Nude Beaches and Recreation* included thousands of listings that described a particular location's natural features, provided a brief history, included detailed directions and parking information, and noted the presence or absence of hostile neighbors and/or local authorities. Many profiles also included large, attractive photos that advertised the specific charms and characteristics to be enjoyed at a particular site. The information provided by the guide made it possible for any individual, couple, or family to locate a spot to safely go naked almost anywhere in the United States or around the world.

Baxandall also saw the creation of TNS as an opportunity to confront the fractured sexual politics of the Left and to build a coalition among liberal activists, sex radicals, and feminists. During the late 1960s and 1970s, many women felt insulted, excluded, or exploited by the often sexist attitudes of the male-dominated anticapitalist New Left. In addition, although the counterculture encouraged women to explore their sexual desires, it often did so on male terms and for the benefit of male pleasure.[103] The rejection of the double standard and the endorsement of casual sex often only meant that men gained greater access to female bodies. Meanwhile, New Left political organizations continued to uphold traditional gender arrangements and relegated women to secretarial work or domestic responsibilities. The male leadership of the New Left responded to women who articulated a gendered critique of modern society with sexist heckles or feigned interest. The growth of a strong women's liberation movement directly confronted the sexism of mainstream society, the New Left, and the counterculture. Feminists demanded control over their bodies, critiqued sexist media representations, and campaigned for a platform of sexual rights that confronted rape, incest, and abortion.[104] Yet the women's movement also splintered as working-class women, women of color, and lesbians clashed with the interests of a leadership dominated by white, middle-class women. The confrontations and clashes that occurred over sex divided progressive politics and profoundly shaped the membership of TNS.

In the early 1980s, TNS brought together advocates of sexual freedom as well as feminists who critiqued the objectification of the female body. Jefferson Poland, who had previously been rebuffed by members of the ASA when he called for a more activist and sexually aware brand of nudism, found a place in TNS, where he assisted in providing information about nude sunbathing locations and frequently attended events. Ed Lange, the longtime nudist who maintained ties to the pornography industry and opened the sexually liberated Elysium resort in Tujunga Canyon in Los Angeles, also lent his support to TNS by hosting the organization's first "gathering" in 1980.[105] At the same time, Baxandall allied himself with feminist campaigns to condemn sexist, demeaning, and violent depictions of the female body in magazines, advertisements, Hollywood movies, and pornographic films. In his *World Guide to Nude Beaches and Recreation*, he critiqued the "tantalize-and-deliver sensationalism of our jaded consumer culture" that justified the "repression of healthy female nudity." He argued that women who undressed at free beaches were "shattering the invisible bonds of an inherited sex role" and denying "one of the chief means of mind and destiny control by the patriarchy."[106] He hoped that "mixed sex beaches" would bring "health to infants and elderly, straight and gay, male and female alike."[107]

Baxandall built alliances with feminist activists who made headlines across the country for going naked from the waist up in the name of "shirtfree equality." Nikki Craft, a committed feminist activist, street performer, and artist, founded the Cross Your Heart Network in 1981 after two police officers arrested her for sunbathing topless on a Santa Cruz beach.[108] Over the next fifteen years, the police arrested Craft more than seventeen times for removing her shirt in public in several different states, including Santa Cruz, California; Cape Cod, Massachusetts; Rochester, New York; and Oshkosh, Wisconsin. Craft organized the "shirtfree equality" movement to demonstrate that the "female body is not obscene, that women should have control over their bodies, and there is a difference between acceptance of human nudity and the exploitation and marketing of women's bodies in the pornography industry."[109] Craft asserted that laws denying women the right to go naked from the waist up—whether for sunbathing, for breastfeeding, or just for physical comfort—unfairly discriminated against women and enforced the sexist assumption that the female breast existed for male sexual pleasure. At demonstrations, Craft resisted the objectification of her body by dramatically standing with her arms raised, her unshaven armpits exposed, and her naked breasts in full view. Craft, who worked closely with Andrea Dworkin and several other prominent feminist activists, considered her campaign for "shirtfree equality" part of the larger struggle to eliminate pornographic depictions of women. Baxandall identified strongly with Craft's cause, and the two began working and living together at the Free Beach Documentation Center in Oshkosh, Wisconsin. Baxandall hoped to encourage more women to participate in naturism through the strong feminist perspective that Craft contributed to TNS publications, at organizational meetings, and at regional gatherings. A delicate alliance emerged between feminists and naturists through the close relationship that developed between Craft and Baxandall.

Baxandall also welcomed a growing interest in TNS among gay men and lesbians who saw naturism as an alternative to an urban gay identity defined by privilege, whiteness, and a depoliticized commercial culture. The ASA continued to characterize itself as being "pretty conservative" on the issue of homosexuality and reported that 64 percent of its members were married and that the organization was "geared to families and couples."[110] Baxandall, in contrast, encouraged interest from the gay and lesbian community through his *World Guide to Nude Beaches and Recreation*. In his entry for Lands End Beach in San Francisco's Golden Gate National Recreation Area, he noted a "totally nude and a very mixed scene by day; a gay crowd tends to take over after dusk." For New York City, he assured readers that "the 72nd Street Pier and Drydocks" was "by no means gays only," and he went on to document the "straight and gay subdivisions" at Jacob Riis Park. Another entry, on Cherry Grove and Fire Island Pines, informed readers that "gay is prevalent here," under a picture of two naked men holding each other and facing the camera, unashamed and revealing their genitalia.[111] The *World Guide* served as a valuable resource for gay men and lesbians across the United States looking for friendly destinations where they could safely and openly socialize while contributing to a tolerant community. TNS received numerous membership inquiries from gay men and lesbians across the country. Baxandall asked Murray Kaufman, a gay man from New York City who regularly participated in naturist activities, to take an active role in organizing a special interest group dedicated to gays and lesbians. In 1983, Kaufman set up Gay and Lesbian Naturists (GLN) and formed the group Males Au Naturel (MAN) in the New York City area. Over the next several years, GLN enlisted 395 members and oversaw the formation of thirty-three other independent groups across the United States.

The rural orientation of naturist activities appealed to many gay men and women, who did not identify with the bicoastal orientation of urban gay life and, instead, sought out communities that practiced what Scott Herring has termed "critical rusticity." The emergence in the 1970s of trendy "gay urban ghettos" in New York City, Los Angeles, and San Francisco along with national gay publications such as the *Advocate* that promoted a middle-class, cosmopolitan image of gay urban communities betrayed the "intersectional Gay Liberation Front

Lee Baxandall's *World Guide to Nude Beaches and Recreation*
helped gay men and lesbians across the United States locate
friendly destinations where they could safely and openly
socialize while contributing to a tolerant nudist community.
(Lee Baxandall, *World Guide to Nude Beaches and Recreation*
[New York: Stonehill, 1980], 88)

politics that engaged with concurrent critiques of racial, imperial and
capitalist norms" and alienated many activists, people of color, and
nonurban gay men and women. In response, according to Herring,
"critical rusticity" emerged in a number of publications that exhibited
a rural orientation and a desire to create an "intersectional opportunity
to geographically, corporeally, and aesthetically inhabit non-normative
sexuality that offers new possibilities for the sexually marginalized out-

side the metropolis as well as inside it."[112] Gay naturist activities often occurred outside the "bar scene" on beaches or at rustic campgrounds far away from the metropolis. In 1985, Kaufman held one of the first weekend "gatherings" for GLN at the naturist campground Summit Lodge in Ohio, and beginning in 1986, the group held the annual GLN "gathering" in eastern Pennsylvania in the Pocono Mountains. In the early 1990s, *OutWeek* magazine, an activist gay and lesbian publication that featured articles on politics, AIDS, the arts, and popular culture, profiled the intersectional politics of gay naturism in an article titled "Grin and Bare It." The article introduced naturism as a "delightfully subversive act" in the "gay male community, fettered as it is by classism, sexism, and body-image oppression."[113] The article explained the increasing need for gay naturists to "politicize their existence" in the face of a "dual suppression" that saw "their own gay community" view them with "suspicion," while they were "still not readily welcome in the nudist milieu."[114] The act of disrobing in a rustic setting or on a beach as a gay man or lesbian represented a rejection of the heterosexism of organized nudism as well as a rejection of the cosmopolitan consumerism that dominated representations of gay urban life in the late twentieth century.

Gay naturism also played a role in challenging the racism of the gay urban lifestyle. "Grin and Bare It" focused on Liddell Jackson, "an activist, a Black gay man and a nudist" who appeared naked on *The Phil Donahue Show* in 1990 with his white partner, Bill Schilling. With images of the two naked men holding each other illustrating the article, the couple discussed the challenges that faced gay people of color who were interested in naturism. Jackson believed that racial anxieties prevented more people of color from participating in naturism. He asserted, "Nudity reflects a sense of privilege. People of color don't have a sense of privilege to do what the mainstream does. We have trouble embracing any concept that is not in the mainstream." The pressure that people of color felt to conform to white mainstream society made it difficult to reject the widespread acceptance of clothing. Kaufman also stated, "Nudism plus gayness is a double whammy for [people of color]." Nevertheless, Jackson maintained that "there is less bigotry in gay nude circles," and another black gay naturist felt "less racism here [naturism] than in the bar scene."[115] For many people of color, participating in naturism represented a way to encourage experimental behaviors and to challenge the racism of the urban gay lifestyle.

The political battles over pornography threatened to undo the fragile coalition that had formed under TNS. Andrea Dworkin, Catharine MacKinnon, and Susan Brownmiller led an effort to equate all forms of pornography with rape and sexual violence and called on the women's movement to advocate for the suppression of these materials.[116] Similarly, Nikki Craft found it increasingly difficult to reconcile the way naturists advocated body acceptance with their use of "sexualized photos . . . to promote sales of naturist publications."[117] After Craft began attending naturist conferences in 1982, she quickly observed that the movement "had yet to be touched by feminism," and she took it upon herself to reform the way naturists treated women and represented the bodies of women and children in their publications.[118] She believed that "pornographers had long exploited nudists," since the leadership of the nudist movement had made "little or no attempt to separate themselves and their values from those of pornographers." Craft set out to "confront the lie repeated by nudists and naturist leaders that 'nudity has nothing to do with sex.'"[119]

As the family faded away as a viable moral constraint within the boundaries of sexual liberalism, a growing concern about child pornography emerged in the late 1970s and informed Craft's critiques of naturism/nudism. In the past, nudists responded to concerns about the involvement of naked children at nudist clubs and their display in the movement's magazines by covering up instances of abuse, excluding single men from clubs, and arguing that the enjoyment of children reflected the natural pleasures of going naked. By the mid-1970s, however, moral reformers, child-welfare advocates, and conservative politicians made child pornography a national issue. In the 1960s and 1970s, civil libertarians argued that adult men and women willingly consented to making and consuming pornography and that government suppression violated their right to privacy. Unable to challenge this argument as the heteronormative boundaries of sexual liberalism crumbled and led to a dramatic expansion in pornography, activists and child-welfare advocates argued that children did not have the ability to consent, and any picture featuring a naked child should be considered obscene, capable of influencing adults to commit sexual abuse, and inherently damaging to the child in the photo. The new concern about child pornography led to widespread public support for legal intervention, with few civil libertarians offering opposition. In 1977, New York police closed down many of the bookstores and movie theaters that offered child pornography in Times Square, and the news media, including magazines such as *Redbook, Parents, Newsweek, U.S. News & World Report, Ms.*, and *Time*, as well as the television show *60 Minutes*, sensationalized the issue of child pornography. A number of books presenting research and analysis on the issue of child pornography and sexual abuse also began to appear between 1978 and 1981. The increased public awareness of child pornography led several states, including Arizona, Connecticut, Delaware, Illinois, Missouri, New Hampshire, Ohio, and Wisconsin, to pass laws against making and distributing images of naked children or minors engaged in sexual acts. In addition, in Washington, D.C., several congressional hearings addressed the issue of child pornography, and in the spring of 1977, the House passed the Kildee-Murphy Bill, which prohibited the manufacture, distribution, and possession of child pornography, by a vote of 401–0.

As part of the feminist campaign against rape, activists also spoke out against the sexual abuse of children, and when Craft witnessed "apparent child molesters . . . apprehended" or removed from naturist events she attended, she grew suspicious of the "claims of wholesome nudity . . . when applied to justify photographs that are intended to appeal to those who sexualized children."[120] Disturbed by what she considered a disproportionate number of child predators active in the nudist movement, she joined with Michele Handler, a lifelong nudist and a fellow feminist activist, to put together a slide show that would "bring the reality of the sexual molestation of children into the public, and particularly into the naturist, view."[121] The growing public concern over child pornography in the late 1970s and the participation of feminists in TNS brought new attention to the sexual abuses that had long been avoided, ignored, or covered up by the naturist and nudist movements.

Baxandall supported Craft's "campaign to rid nudism/naturism of its covert appeals to infantillistic pornography seekers and to outright pedophiles."[122] Baxandall dedicated a special issue of *Clothed with the Sun* (*CwS*), the official publication of TNS, to feminist critiques of pornography and child sexual abuse after the release of the final report of the Attorney General's Commission on Pornography (called the Meese commission, after the U.S. attorney general Edwin Meese). The 1986 Meese commission, the Reagan administration's answer to the permissive 1970 Presidential Commission on Pornography, used a series of public hearings and the testimony of feminists such as Andrea Dworkin to condemn various forms of pornographic magazines, films, pictures, and phone services. The summer issue of *CwS* prominently featured Craft's critiques of *Playboy*, *Penthouse*, and the ACLU and exhibited her various demonstrations for "shirtfree equality" and her participation in a women's music festival.[123] Although Baxandall objected to an approach that considered "mere nudity . . . inherently suspect," he credited the Reagan administration's Meese commission for addressing "a real concern for the degradation of women, as financed, produced, and distributed by a heartless pornography industry."[124]

In addition to giving feminists a voice in *CwS*, Baxandall personally wrote to naturist and nudist leaders imploring them to stop their questionable marketing strategies, to remove inappropriate advertisements, and to take steps to avoid attracting child predators. In one letter to Ed Lange, he objected to the way several of his titles used the label "for adults 21 and above only" to attract buyers interested in pornography. Baxandall asked Lange to stop distributing a foreign title called *Jeunes et Naturelles* along with his own publication, *Young and Natural*, because he found the images in the magazines particularly offensive. He described one issue that contained "336 frontal images of nude juveniles," which the photographers shot "at their shorter-than-adult subjects from the level of these small breasts, vaginas and penises." He believed these titles appealed "directly to pedophiles and encourages them to feel welcome in nudist naturist circles."[125] In another letter to the ASA, Baxandall objected to the organization's reliance on the revenues it received from the magazine *Health and Efficiency*. He disapproved of the magazine because of its "crass appeal to the 'men's magazine' market" and because it led readers to *Jeunes et Naturelles*.[126] He then threatened to publicize the ASA's relationship with the magazine if it did not revoke all its previous agreements with questionable publications.

Craft, nevertheless, encountered the same sexist attitudes and disregard for feminist issues in TNS that made other feminists reluctant to support progressive political organizations. Lange dismissed Craft's efforts as "moralistic" and accused her of "beating a dead horse." Several other naturists voiced their displeasure with the issue of CwS dedicated to feminist critiques of pornography. One naturist demanded "no more issues devoted to Nikki Craft and her ravings" and asserted, "it is wrong of the naturists to provide this ongoing forum." He thought the focus on feminism detracted from the "peacefulness and sense of well-being that comes from the nude lifestyle."[127] Another naturist felt "betrayed" by the magazine. He recalled that the "Naturist philosophy originally defined did not include support of Radical Feminist Activists, nor did it support active direct suppression of Pornography." He resented the "prejudicial hate that these feminists have for men" and asserted that it did not "fit well into Naturism."[128] Despite naturism's liberal sexual values, feminist critiques of pornography, child sexual abuse, and sexual violence provoked sexist responses from many naturist leaders and members.

A controversy over a nude picture that Baxandall selected for a photo spread in CwS ultimately poisoned the fragile coalition that formed between feminists and naturists. Craft and several other feminist naturists objected to the spring 1987 issue of CwS because it featured a color center spread that displayed an "eighteen-year-old woman with partially shaved pubic hair coyly playing to the camera."[129] Craft asserted that the photos represented an effort by Baxandall to placate subscribers upset by the issue he dedicated to feminism the previous summer by showing that "they could still depend on CwS to 'deliver.'"[130] Michele Handler considered the images "an insult to women and feminists values, and a betrayal of feminist naturists." Handler, one of TNS's most effective organizers, resigned in protest from several committees and stopped participating in naturist events and causes. Melinda Vadas, a feminist unaffiliated with naturism, thought the photos displayed the woman in "demeaning, sexualized poses, fetishized and fuckable," and she declared Baxandall a "pornographer."[131]

In addition, the conflicting legal strategies and objectives of feminists and naturists came to the forefront in a class-action suit brought by Craft and ten other women against the Cape Cod National Seashore. TNS offered its full support in 1986 when the police arrested the women for removing their shirts and violating the antinudity regulations first established in the mid-1970s. Craft wanted to use the case to advance the cause of gender equality. She argued that the antinudity regulations violated the women's Fourth Amendment rights because they treated "women differently than men" by requiring women to keep their "chests covered" due to "male-defined mores and a sexist definition of 'nudity.'" Baxandall, on the other hand, had no interest in "changing public opinion on whether the chests of women are nude." He saw an opportunity to "relieve all government regulations of what body parts may be exposed."[132] When the attorney hired by Baxandall chose to argue the case on First Amendment grounds, Craft and several other women in the group voiced their strong objections to a legal strategy that they felt ignored their feminist principles and agenda. In December 1988, Craft along with five other plaintiffs withdrew their support just as the U.S. district court in Boston prepared to issue its ruling. The action infuriated Baxandall, who had invested more than $36,000 in the case. He believed that Craft engineered the withdrawal in retaliation for being fired from TNS because of her "radical feminist" agenda and then evicted from the apartment they shared after the two clashed over the centerfold spread in *CwS*. The alliance that formed between naturism and feminism fell apart due to personal disagreements and conflicting political agendas.

After Craft broke with TNS, she continued to raise concerns about how the organization's commitment to sexual freedom and expression provided a sanctuary for pornographers and child molesters. For Craft, Jefferson Poland's ongoing participation in TNS events and gatherings and his regular contributions to naturist literature stood out as a disturbing example of the way naturism ignored the sexual abuses occurring within the movement. Poland, who played a key role in sparking interest in the free beach movement and in advocating for sexual freedom in the 1960s, molested a young girl on Black's Beach in San Diego, California, in the early 1980s. When the police issued a warrant for his arrest in 1983, Poland fled the country and evaded capture until 1988, despite being on San Diego's "most wanted" list. Once arrested, Poland admitted that he had "fondled the girl's vulva and occasionally performed cunnilingus on her," and he received a one-year sentence in county jail and five years probation.[133] In prison, Poland maintained ties with naturist publications by contributing reviews of nude beaches he had visited while on the run in Asia and Australia.

Craft wanted to use naturism's ongoing relationship with Poland to raise public awareness about the way naturists ignored the problem of pedophilia. Craft wrote a letter of protest to the editors of *Nude and Natural* (formerly *Clothed with the Sun*) regarding Poland's column, and she demanded the magazine instead make the convicted child molester explain the way he "used the naturist/nudist movement to get kids. And make him name the names of men he worked with and tell who are the pedophiles."[134] Poland, desperate to resume a role in the naturist press, began corresponding with Baxandall and published an article in *Nude and Natural* titled "Pedophile Confession."[135] Rather than expose the problem of pedophilia, Poland attempted to garner sympathy from readers by reporting his attempts to castrate himself in prison and his willingness, as part of his probation, to receive injections of medroxyprogesterone every two weeks to depress his libido. He also blamed the victim and her parents for his actions. He described how he met the child's parents through "swinging" activities and that they had asked him to regularly babysit while they "attended or hosted adults only orgies."[136] He then regretted the "extreme changeability of kids" and the way "nudist children tend to become more prudish as they grow older."[137]

The involvement of feminist activists within naturism and the greater willingness to address the issue of intergenerational sex made it difficult for nudist leaders to cover up, rationalize, or dismiss illicit incidents involving children at nudist/naturist events and activities. While Poland's "confession" disturbed Craft, Baxandall's accompanying "editor's note" proved far more alarming since it highlighted the way naturists avoided the problem of pedophilia. Baxandall referred to Poland's case as "unique," he maintained that "the negligence described here is rare in nudist or naturist contexts," and he asserted, "accusations based on a 'profile' alone should be strictly avoided!"[138] Baxandall also defended Poland's attempt to hold the parents responsible for the abuse by writing that it "goes without saying that neglect of the children's best interests was the tragic blind spot of the parents no less than the abuser."[139] Craft accused Baxandall of "coddling a child molester" in order to benefit "the magazine publishers, the nudist/naturist photographers (i.e. the business interest of the movement)."[140] The failure on the part of Baxandall to confront the issue of pedophilia in naturism and nudism and his acrimonious split with Craft and several other feminist naturists signaled that TNS remained far more committed to upholding the ideals of sexual liberation as well as the business of nude recreation than to incorporating feminist critiques and ensuring the safety of nudist children.

Conclusion

With the heteronormative boundaries of sexual liberalism under siege, the nudist movement fragmented as student activists, civil libertarians, feminists, and an older generation of nudists clashed over the politics of sexual liberation. A new generation of youthful activists interested in going naked on public beaches and parks challenged a nudist organization that maintained an older, "respectable" membership, clung to exclusionary racial policies, and remained hostile to sexual experimentation and alternative sexualities. The growing acceptance of gay men and lesbians, people of color, and casual eroticism within nudism/naturism signaled a dramatic turn away from the heteronormative values that had defined nudism during an era of sexual liberalism. This transformation also drew attention to the sexual abuses and ideological conflicts that had long been hidden by nudists' efforts to maintain the organization's respectability. Feminists raised concerns about the sexual exploitation and objectification of nudist/naturist women and the sexual dangers facing nudist children. The lack of any definitive boundaries regulating sexual expression and behavior created enormous division and acrimony among nudists and naturists.

Fractured by the politics of pornography, TNS reevaluated its strained relationship with the ASA, and the two organizations worked together over the next two decades to transform nudism and naturism into a premier tourist activity. The activist philosophy of TNS and its focus on public lands and beaches put it at odds with the ASA, which prioritized the financial interests of club owners and an aging membership that had little interest in disrupting the status quo. After years advocating for legal nude sunbathing on public lands, TNS remained limited to promoting only a few officially sanctioned clothing-optional beaches or parks scattered across the United States. While San Diego's Black's Beach, Austin's Hippie Hollow, and Santa Cruz's Bonny Doon Beach continued to attract large groups of nude sunbathers, *CwS* featured numerous advertisements from ASA-sponsored nudist clubs, and TNS held many of its "gatherings" at ASA-affiliated clubs. The need to reverse a declining and aging membership also caused many ASA nudist-club owners to welcome the naturists and free beach advocates whom they had once considered "riffraff." In the late 1980s and early 1990s, several influential members of the ASA and TNS attempted to join forces through formal collaborative networks in which the two organizations could share resources, labor, and knowledge in order to better respond to the legal obstacles and challenges that impeded the growth of nude recreation at clubs as well as on public lands. While a lack of funding made it difficult to sustain this effort, the recognition that the two organizations shared many of the same goals, ideals, and interests laid the foundation for a partnership that dramatically expanded the place of nude recreation in the United States.

EPILOGUE

Nudism in the New Millennium

🌿

In the 1990s, recreation, commercialism, and profits replaced the progressive sexual politics that had divided nudists and naturists since the late 1960s. As the American economy began to surge on the profits of Internet companies, financial speculation allowed by the deregulation of the banking industry, and the beginnings of a volatile real estate bubble, nudism and naturism experienced an enormous period of growth. The number of nudist clubs and resorts affiliated with the American Sunbathing Association jumped from 189 in 1983 to more than 260 by 2002. Membership also climbed 20 percent, increasing to fifty thousand dues-paying members, almost 80 percent of whom were more than thirty-five years old. Nudism and naturism appealed to aging baby boomers who had disposable income and who were nostalgic for the rebellious culture of their youth. Just as iconic 1960s musicians such as Simon and Garfunkel, the Rolling Stones, and the Beatles put together reunion tours, special concerts, or signed lucrative licensing agreements to take advantage of baby boomers yearning to viscerally relive their youth, nudism/naturism's association with the Summer of Love made it an attractive destination for the thirty-five-and-older crowd.[1] Yet few of the nudist clubs, resorts, time-shares, cruises, and beaches that sprung up to cater to this niche tourist market embraced the nude sex parties and beach orgies that Jefferson Poland's Sexual Freedom League promoted, nor did they attempt to re-create the organic atmosphere of the free beach. Instead, they offered luxurious accommodations, spa services, elegant dining, and well-maintained grounds with multiple swimming pools, hot tubs, tennis courts, and jet skiing. With some nude resorts charging $300 to $400 a night, the profits generated by nude recreation soared from $120 million in 1992 to more than $400 million in 2003. An ABC News report officially announced, "Nude recreation has gone mainstream."[2]

Middle-aged men and women going naked at a nudist resort or a clothing-optional beach no longer seemed as shocking in a society where the limits placed on commercial sexuality had largely disappeared— giving rise to a multibillion-dollar pornography industry, sex clubs, titillating Hollywood films, suggestive advertisements, and any number of fetish industries, phone sex operations, sex toy manufacturers, and escort services. Despite the findings of the Meese commission and the protestations from the Christian Right, the courts rejected most efforts to censor depictions of sex involving adults and struck down attempts by Congress to regulate pornography on the Internet. As the pornography industry generated profits in the billions with an assortment of magazines and films that appealed to a variety of sexualities and fetishes, and blockbuster hits such as *Fatal Attraction* (1987) and *Basic Instinct* (1992) entertained mass audiences with less graphic depictions of sex, nudity, and violence, nude sunbathing and volleyball appeared harmless, if not comical. In a 2001 *New York Times* profile of nude recreation, the sociologist Jeremy Levin asserted that going naked was not a "political statement anymore," and the article observed that the "power of the unclothed body to shock is waning" thanks to the "proliferation of frank imagery in film and advertising and an increase in Internet sites like the all-nude Webcast nakednews.com, or such cable television shows as 'Sex and the City' or 'Oz', where nakedness is common enough to seem nearly compulsory."[3]

In 1994, the ASA recognized the growing acceptance of nudity in American society and culture by adopting the name American Association for Nude Recreation (AANR). Using the language of gay liberation, the president of the AANR, George Volak, announced the name change by declaring, "It's time we finally came out of the closet."[4] The announcement signaled a more tolerant stance toward homosexuality and a more public approach to promoting nude recreation. The new moniker removed the shame attached to the euphemism *sunbathing*, a term adopted in the 1930s to distance the organization from commercial pornographers who used the term *nudist* to market their magazines, films, and theater performances. It also signaled to individuals casually interested in visiting a resort that they did not have to be a committed "nudist," nor were they required to participate in a movement. The acceptance of nudity in American society made it possible for major corporations to partner with the AANR. Travel companies such as Hertz, Alamo, Enterprise, and Budget as well as 1-800-Flowers, Vermont Teddy Bear, and the hat company Tilley all offered special discounts to nudists and naturists. Even Apple Computers, which maintains a strict policy prohibiting any sexual images or content from its app store, approved the 2011 AANR app for the iPhone.[5]

With the nudist movement once seen as a threat to the respectability of communities such as Rogers Park in Chicago or small towns such as Allegan, Michigan, many mayors and city officials welcomed the high-priced nudist resorts popping up across the country as valuable sources of tax revenue and as a way to increase property values. The opening of the Desert Shadows resort in 1992 in the struggling uptown section of Palm Springs received support from local officials who relaxed building restrictions, provided a liquor license despite a local law meant to deny the same privilege to strip clubs, and contributed city funds to assist major expansions and additions made to the resort. The resort was built on the site of Doris Day's Chandler Inn and Errol Flynn's Lone Palm Inn, an old haunt of Frank Sinatra. Steve Payne, who previously worked for Marriott and Hilton, oversaw several multimillion-dollar expansions to the resort that added several swimming pools, tennis courts, restaurants, an indoor and outdoor spa, and three waterfalls. In the late 1990s, Payne added thirty-eight two-story luxury condominiums across the street, prompting the construction of a 140-foot bridge that allowed guests to visit the resort while remaining nude. The resort now occupied an entire city block where prostitutes and drug dealers had once scared tourists away. Palm Springs Mayor Will Kleindienst reflected on the $185,000 the city had contributed to the "Nude Bridge" by boasting, "We're very proud of what they've done for that part of the community."[6] Charging up to $300 to $400 a night, raising property values, and attracting wealthy tourists to once-blighted areas, luxury nudist resorts such as Desert Shadows made headlines in newspapers such as the *Wall Street Journal* as major contributors to urban-renewal efforts and as valuable sources of tax revenue.[7]

The rustic and secluded camps that had shaped nudism in the United States for decades struggled to compete with the luxurious amenities and well-maintained grounds of the new resorts emerging across the country. For much of the twentieth century, the rural, out-of-the-way nudist camps that dotted the American countryside offered refuge to urban dwellers who wanted to go naked into nature and avoid local police, neighbors, and politicians determined to put a stop to nudist activities. Nudists, naturists, and casual nude sunbathers, however, no longer saw seclusion as an asset, and the simple, no-frills outdoor settings of many older camps failed to appeal to guests seeking recreation and luxurious amenities. Elysia, originally founded by Hobart Glassey in the early 1930s in the San Bernardino Mountains and the former backdrop for *Elysia* (1933) and *The Unashamed* (1938), closed in 2007. Flora "Flo" Nelson, who owned and managed the camp since 1954, when she and her husband purchased the grounds and renamed it McConville after the previous owner, blamed the camp's demise on "newer members [who] wanted to change it into a country club-type setting" more amenable to "lazy people who want to be waited on."[8] Although her camp had a pool, tennis courts, and several rustic cabins, it lacked electricity and required a long, winding drive through the mountains. While other early nudist camps, such as Lake O' Woods in Valparaiso, Indiana, updated their grounds and continued to attract guests, the closure of camps unable or unwilling to invest in expensive renovations reflected the decreasing need for seclusion and organized nudism's emerging status as a high-end tourist activity.

The emergence of nudism and naturism as a profitable niche in the tourist industry drew the attention of politicians eager to reestablish limits on sexual expression through the issue of child pornography and pedophilia. The increased attention given to protecting children from sexual predators by journalists, child-welfare advocates, feminist activists, and legal authorities led to an enormous increase in arrests, the passage of strict state laws that required the disclosure of the identities of convicted sex offenders to community members after their release from prison, and a number of sensational news-media programs and television movies on particularly heinous child rapists and murders. By the mid-1990s, the availability of what seemed like an infinite variety of illicit content on the Internet streaming into homes, accessible to children, and largely unregulated by the government exacerbated already heightened fears about child sexual abuse. Parents as well as politicians feared that the exchange of child pornography on the Internet encouraged and emboldened child predators and that chat rooms on providers such as America Online and CompuServe provided an opportunity for pedophiles to lure children away from the safety of their homes. For many Americans, sexual predators seemed to be just a click away, and they looked to the government to restore order.

The "culture wars" of the 1990s put the issue of child sexual abuse and the Internet at the forefront of American politics. The election of President Bill Clinton in 1992 angered many social conservatives who disapproved of Hillary Clinton's feminist background and considered the president's extramarital affairs an insult to the traditional family. After Bill Clinton failed to resolve the status of gays and lesbians serving in the armed forces, the historian Philip Jenkins argues that the president responded to attacks made by advocates of traditional morality and family by "defending the interests of children."[9] The president mentioned the Polly Klaus incident in his 1994 State of the Union Address, he campaigned in 1996 for a national registry of sex offenders, and he supported legislation that offered to severely restrict the content available on the Internet.[10] In 1995, President Clinton signed into law a bill amending the Communications Decency Act so that anyone who made offensive material available online to children less than eighteen years old would be subject to fines and prison terms. If upheld, the law had the potential to severely limit what could be seen, expressed, and consumed on websites. In 1997, however, the U.S. Supreme Court unanimously struck down the law, affirming that constitutional protections extended to the Internet and ruling that the government cannot deny the constitutional rights of adults to protect the moral sensibilities of children. Nevertheless, the strong social, political, and cultural consensus that government needed to protect children on the Internet from sexual predators signaled the resurgent influence that age began to have in defining and regulating the boundaries of sexual expression in the United States at the end of the twentieth century.

The focus on protecting children from sexual predators put nudist and naturist activities under renewed scrutiny. After Representative Mark Foley of Florida's Sixteenth Congressional District was elected in 1994, he made a name for himself as one of the most outspoken opponents of child pornography. In June 2003, he wrote letters to the governor and attorney general of Florida asking them to review the legality of a program for teenagers at the Lake Como nudist resort in Land O'Lakes, Florida. Foley brought additional public attention to the issue of child sex and nudism when he appeared on CNN for a segment titled "What's Wrong with Nude Camps for Teens?" and asserted, "You put 11 and 18-year-olds together in a camp where they're nude, I think it is a recipe for disaster. It is like putting a match next to a gasoline can. You'll have disasters sooner or later."[11] In 2006, however, Rep. Foley came under scrutiny as a suspected pedophile when reports surfaced that he sent salacious texts from his phone to underage male pages. Foley's effort to bring attention to nudist activities may have originated from his own experiences as a teenager at the Sacred Heart Catholic School, where a priest "took him biking and skinny-dipping and massaged him in the nude, often bringing him to saunas for fondling."[12] The importance placed on protecting children from sexual predators proved so powerful that it led to the exposure of the influential politician leading the effort to limit child pornography. The heightened anxieties surrounding children's sexuality at the beginning of the twenty-first century made it very difficult for nudist leaders to quickly cover up instances of sexual abuse or to explain away the threat of pedophilia by invoking the familial character of the movement.

In addition to conservative politicians, the antipornography activist Nikki Craft continued her campaign to expose the sexual abuses that occurred at nudist camps. In 1992, she clashed with the longtime nudist leader Ed Lange on the *Jenny Jones Show*, a national television talk show that courted confrontation and controversy by surprising guests with jilted ex-lovers, hated rivals, and ideological opponents. Talk shows such as the *Jenny Jones Show* reflected a larger shift in the news media toward sensationalist coverage and helped popularize the professional and activist literatures on rape, child sexual abuse, and pornography.[13] In 1995, Craft also set up the Nudist/Naturist Hall of Shame website to document the prevalence of pedophilia in nudism/naturism with links to news reports, personal testimonials, and nudist correspondence attempting to cover up the issue of pedophilia at nudist clubs, beaches, and events. The website did not go unnoticed by the public. By 2001, according to the Institute of Global Communications, a web-hosting site for nonprofit organizations, the Hall of Shame website had received 7,403,971 visits from 761,270 unique users.[14] Craft reached out to the many visitors to her site by asking for additional information from individuals who lived near nudist resorts, who grew up in nudist families, or who served in nudist organizations. She provocatively asked, "Are you tired of pedophiles, sex predators, nudist apathy and the practices and policies that cause it all to proliferate?"[15] With cable news shows seeking out controversy and scandal to generate ratings, and the Internet providing a forum for individual activists to speak out against the nonconfrontational policies of nudism/naturism, the issue of intergenerational sex could not be ignored, dismissed, or rationalized by nudist/naturist leaders.

The familial character of nudism no longer communicated natural innocence, respectability, and wholesomeness; it aroused suspicion and threatened to undermine the profits of heavily invested nudist resorts. The days when hostile judges passed over images of nudist children, proclaiming them decent, or when nudist leaders easily covered up an incident of pedophilia before it became a national controversy came to an end at the turn of the twentieth century. In October 2011 a forty-nine-year-old Texas man who had taken videos of himself molesting children at a central Texas nudist resort and at his home was sentenced to fifty years in prison. In Ottawa, a treasurer of a nudist club received a five-year sentence for possessing child pornography, and a British couple that set up a nudist/naturist site to lure children into engaging in a number of illicit activities was convicted of numerous charges including sexual assault on a child.[16] While the AANR remained steadfast that it had "promoted nudist family values at its resorts and clubs since 1931," and it continued to promise that "clubs foster a wholesome, nurturing environment for members and their families," a culture of suspicion began to pervade nudist resorts and free beaches.[17] Numerous resorts across the country chose to ban cell phones to prevent images of naked children from appearing on the Internet, and Nicky Hoffman, a co-owner of TNS and the publisher/editor of *Nude and Natural*, asserted that if naturists see "someone taking photographs, that camera might end up in the water."[18] Other guests at resorts commented on nudist blogs that events such as the McMartin trial, a high-profile case in the 1980s involving a Manhattan Beach preschool where a number of children falsely accused the owner and her son of sexual abuse and ritual torture, made them think twice about being alone with small children while naked. Others worried that child predators might take advantage of the trusting culture at nudist resorts and began to find the friendly interactions of adults with little girls or boys suspect.[19] The greater attention given to child sexual abuse in the later part of the twentieth century and the revelation that a number of incidents involving pedophilia had occurred at nudist resorts and free beaches made many nudists and naturists question the AANR's assertion that social nudism fosters a "wholesome, nurturing environment for members and their families."[20]

One well-known resort caused controversy when it ignored the official family-friendly nudist policy of the AANR and refused to admit children entirely. In February 2011, the new owners of Desert Shadows Resort, renamed Desert Sun Resort following another expensive remodeling project, made the decision to deny entry to all children. Not long after John and Elizabeth Young purchased the well-known Palm Springs nudist resort, the FBI visited them to warn them about the "size and scope of the Internet's child porn industry." One FBI agent described nudist resorts as a "candy store" for sexual predators. Unlike nudist clubs that enjoyed visits from regular members and families, luxury nudist resorts such as Desert Sun saw more first-time guests, many of whom had never participated in nudism or naturism and were strangers to regular visitors.[21] When an incident occurred involving a child at Desert Sun, the Youngs worried about admitting other child predators, and for their own protection, they decided to prohibit children from entering the resort. Many nudists considered the banning of children a signal that a club or resort catered to individuals seeking sexual activity, swinging, or group sex and spoke out against the well-known resort for undermining the familial character of the movement. One nudist hired an attorney to threaten a lawsuit under California's Unruh Civil Rights Act, which prohibited restaurants, hotels, and other businesses from discriminating against anyone on the basis of "sex, race, color, religion, ancestry, national origin, disability, medical condition, genetic information, marital status, or sexual orientation."[22] Fearful of prosecution, the Youngs consulted a judge and wrote in a brief to the court that it had been "common practice among pedophiles in recent years to attend 'family nudism' resorts" and that it was very difficult to determine "whether any particular individual harbors—or worse, will act on—some improper or wrongful desire toward children."[23] The recent efforts by journalists, politicians, and law enforcement to reestablish the boundaries regulating sexual expression and behavior through the threat that sexual predators posed to children caused many nudists to question the familial character that had long defined the movement in the United States.

At the dawn of the new millennium, the perceived vulnerability of children—more than the sexual dangers posed by single men, people of color, radical sexual politics, or even commercial sex—threatened to undermine the credibility of American nudism as a legitimate social movement. For much of the twentieth century, the erotic appeal that nudism held for men and women of all sexualities posed the greatest threat to the movement's respectability. Only rarely did the presence of children at nudist clubs, nude beaches, and in nudist magazines and films raise the concerns of politicians, judges, and censors. In the 1930s, local police, moral reformers, and politicians associated nudism with an urban underworld of commercial sexuality. During the Second World War, the uncensored genitalia of adult men and women caused postal officials to begin seizing nudist magazines from the mail. The pictures of naked children, however, failed to arouse the ire of even the most disapproving judges. At the same time, an emerging network of rural nudist camps promoted an ideology of domesticity that excluded single men and people of color while celebrating family, nature, and recreation. Club owners and nudist leaders quickly covered up any incidents of pedophilia. The faith placed in the family to contain illicit sexuality protected nudism from further suspicion and scrutiny.

Only as the heteronormative boundaries of sexual liberalism came under attack did the safety of nudist children begin to emerge as a serious concern. The legal victories achieved by the nudist movement in the late 1950s led to a dramatic increase in commercial sexual display and made it possible for the many baby boomers coming of age in the late 1960s to experiment with public nudity at beaches, parks, music concerts, and political protests. The emergence of a more tolerant and inclusive approach to nudism that welcomed liberal activists, advocates of sexual freedom, gay men and lesbians, people of color, and feminists produced contentious debates over the politics of pornography and the threat of child sexual abuse, not to mention the ideological character of naturism and nudism. The struggle to sever nudism/naturism's relationship with the pornography industry and nudism/naturism's unwillingness to confront the problem of child sexual abuse at nudist resorts and nude beaches led to the disillusionment of many feminists. The fractured and contentious sexual politics that divided naturists in the 1980s reflected the decreasing confidence in the family to contain and restrict illicit sexuality and behavior.

The familial character that had long defined nudism in the United States came under increased scrutiny as the boundaries limiting sexual expression shifted to protect children from sexual predators. The need to stop the sexual abuse of children replaced the proscriptions against interracial intimacy, homoeroticism, and commercial sexuality. The accusations that Michael Jackson molested children at his famous Neverland Ranch, the revelations that Catholic priests sexually abused generations of young boys, and the child sexual abuse scandal that rocked the venerable Penn State University football program in 2012 represent only the more sensational instances that have fueled fears of pedophilia. Numerous other reports—detailing incidents of children being molested at school or day camp, being kidnapped, raped, and murdered, or being lured across the country by adults they met online or of adolescents being seduced by their high school teachers—signaled that the media, the courts, and politicians considered child sexual abuse unacceptable and an abhorrent behavior that demanded action and prosecution. It demonstrated that age once again served as the defining limit on sexual behavior and expression. In the nineteenth century, moral reformers worried that illicit materials corrupted the moral character of America's youth, and they banned books, magazines, and artistic reproductions that they considered questionable or potentially illicit. At the beginning of the twenty-first century, parents, politicians, and journalists once again cited the need to protect children as a reason to regulate sexual expression. The fears and anxieties surrounding children's bodies redefined the interaction of naked men, women, and children at nudist resorts and beaches as illicit, risky behavior. As the media reported more and more instances of nudists caught molesting children or collecting and distributing child pornography, a culture of suspicion began to pervade nudist resorts, and prosperous resort owners sought to protect their investments by prohibiting young children. The debates, discussions, and anxieties surrounding the child's body within the nudist movement and in American culture and society revealed that the family lacked the ability to protect its most vulnerable members from eroticism and sexual danger at the beginning of the twenty-first century. Once again nudists will have to negotiate the shifting boundaries of sexual expression in the United States.

NOTES

Introduction

1. Kurt Barthal, "America's Oldest Nudist Group," *Nudist*, May 1933, 20.
2. Brigitte Koenig, "Law and Disorder at Home: Free Love, Free Speech, and the Search for an Anarchist Utopia," *Labor History* 45, no. 2 (May 2004): 199–223; John C. Spurlock, *Free Love: Marriage and Middle-Class Radicalism in America, 1825–1860* (New York: NYU Press, 1990).
3. Barthal, "America's Oldest Nudist Group," 20.
4. George L. Mosse, *Nationalism and Sexuality: Middle-Class Morality and Sexual Norms in Modern Europe* (Madison: University of Wisconsin Press, 1985); Brandon Taylor and Wilfried van der Will, eds., *The Nazification of Art: Art, Design, Music, Architecture and Film in the Third Reich* (Winchester, UK: Winchester Press / Winchester School of Art, 1990); John Williams, *Turning to Nature in Germany: Hiking, Nudism, and Conservation, 1900–1940* (Stanford: Stanford University Press, 2007); Chad Ross, *Naked Germany: Health, Race and the Nation* (Oxford, UK: Berg, 2005); Dagmar Herzog, *Sex after Fascism: Memory and Morality in Twentieth-Century Germany* (Princeton: Princeton University Press, 2005); Michael Hau, *The Cult of Health and Beauty in Germany: A Social History, 1890–1930* (Chicago: University of Chicago Press, 2003); Karl Eric Toepfer, *Empire of Ecstasy: Nudity and Movement in German Body Culture, 1910–1935* (Berkeley: University of California Press, 1997).
5. Maurice Parmelee, *Nudism in Modern Life: The New Gymnosophy* (New York: Knopf, 1931); Frances Merrill and Mason Merrill, *Among the Nudists* (New York: Knopf, 1931); Francis Merrill and Mason Merrill, *Nudism Comes to America* (New York: Knopf, 1932); Jan Gay, *On Going Naked* (Garden City, NY: Garden City, 1932).
6. "Principles and Standards," *Nudist*, May 1933, 3.
7. Susan E. Cayleff, *Wash and Be Healed: The Water-Cure Movement and Women's Health* (Philadelphia: Temple University Press, 1987), 53, 66, 74; James C. Whorton, *Nature Cures: The History of Alternative Medicine in America* (Oxford: Oxford University Press, 2002), 81–85; Jane B. Donegan, *"Hydropathic Highway to Health": Women and Water-Cure in Antebellum America* (Westport, CT: Greenwood, 1986).
8. For women's discomfort with breast and gynecological exams, see Leslie J. Reagan, "Projecting Breast Cancer: Self-Examination Films and the Making of a New Cultural Practice," in *Medicine's Moving Pictures: Medicine, Health, and Bodies in*

American Film and Television, ed. Leslie J. Reagan, Nancy Tomes, and Paula A. Treichler (Rochester, NY: University of Rochester Press, 2007), 163–195; Carolyn Herbst Lewis, "Waking Sleeping Beauty: The Premarital Pelvic Exam and Heterosexuality during the Cold War," *Journal of Women's History* 17, no. 4 (2005): 86–110; Barron H. Lerner, *The Breast Cancer Wars: Hope, Fear, and the Pursuit of a Cure in Twentieth-Century America* (New York: Oxford University Press, 2001), 41–68; Terri Kapsalis, *Public Privates: Performing Gynecology from Both Ends of the Speculum* (Durham: Duke University Press, 1997). For alternative cancer healers who appealed to women, see Eric S. Juhnke, *Quacks and Crusaders: The Fabulous Careers of John Brinkley, Norman Baker, and Harry Hoxsey* (Lawrence: University Press of Kansas, 2001), 109; and Barbara Clow, *Negotiating Disease: Power and Cancer Care, 1900–1950* (Montreal: McGill-Queen's University Press, 2001).

9. John D'Emilio and Estelle Freedman, *Intimate Matters: A History of Sexuality in America*, 2nd ed. (Chicago: University of Chicago Press, 1997), 241.

10. Beth L. Bailey, *From Front Porch to Back Seat: Courtship in Twentieth-Century America* (Baltimore: Johns Hopkins University Press, 1988).

11. Randy D. McBee, *Dance Hall Days: Intimacy and Leisure among Working-Class Immigrants in the United States* (New York: NYU Press, 2000); Kathy Peiss, *Cheap Amusements: Working Women and Leisure in Turn-of-the-Century New York* (Philadelphia: Temple University Press, 1986); Joanne J. Meyerowitz, *Women Adrift: Independent Wage Earners in Chicago, 1880–1930* (Chicago: University of Chicago Press, 1988).

12. Leigh Ann Wheeler, *Against Obscenity: Reform and the Politics of Womanhood in America, 1873–1935* (Baltimore: Johns Hopkins University Press, 2004); Helen Lefkowitz Horowitz, *Rereading Sex: Battles over Sexual Knowledge and Suppression in Nineteenth-Century America* (New York: Knopf, 2002); Molly McGarry, "Spectral Sexualities: Nineteenth-Century Spiritualism, Moral Panics, and the Making of U.S. Obscenity Law," *Journal of Women's History* 12 (2000): 8–29; Nicola Beisel, *Imperiled Innocents: Anthony Comstock and Family Reproduction in Victorian America* (Princeton: Princeton University Press, 1997); Linda Gordon, *Woman's Body, Woman's Right: A Social History of Birth Control in America* (New York: Grossman, 1976).

13. Marc Stein, "*Boutilier* and the U.S. Supreme Court's Sexual Revolution," *Law and History Review* 23, no. 3 (Fall 2005): 491–536; Andrea Friedman, *Prurient Interests: Gender, Democracy, and Obscenity in New York City, 1909–1945* (New York: Columbia University Press, 2000); Leslie J. Reagan, *When Abortion Was a Crime: Women, Medicine, and Law in the United States, 1867–1973* (Berkeley: University of California Press, 1997); George Chauncey, *Gay New York: Gender, Urban Culture, and the Making of the Gay Male World, 1890–1940* (New York: Basic Books, 1994); Whitney Strub, "Black and White and Banned All Over: Race, Censorship and Obscenity in Post-war Memphis," *Journal of Social History* 40, no. 3 (2007): 685–715; Leigh Gilmore, "Obscenity, Modernity, Identity: Legalizing *The*

Well of Loneliness and *Nightwood*," *Journal of the History of Sexuality* 4, no. 4 (1994): 603–624.

14. Peggy Pascoe, *What Comes Naturally: Miscegenation Law and the Making of Race in America* (Oxford: Oxford University Press, 2009); Elise Lemire, *"Miscegenation": Making Race in America* (Philadelphia: University of Pennsylvania Press, 2002); Alex Lupin, *Romance and Rights: The Politics of Interracial Intimacy, 1945–1954* (Jackson: University Press of Mississippi, 2003); Rachel F. Moran, *Interracial Intimacy: The Regulation of Race and Romance* (Chicago: University of Chicago Press, 2001); Martha Hodes, ed., *Sex, Love, Race: Crossing Boundaries in North American History* (New York: NYU Press, 1999); Toni Morrison, *Playing in the Dark: Whiteness and the Literary Imagination* (Cambridge: Harvard University Press, 1992).

15. James Gilbert, *A Cycle of Outrage: America's Reaction to the Juvenile Delinquent in the 1950s* (New York: Oxford University Press, 1986); Estelle B. Freedman, "'Uncontrolled Desires': The Response to the Sexual Psychopath, 1920–1960," *Journal of American History* 74, no. 1 (1987): 83–106.

16. Margot Canaday, *The Straight State: Sexuality and Citizenship in Twentieth-Century America* (Princeton: Princeton University Press, 2009); David K. Johnson, *The Lavender Scare: The Cold War Persecution of Gays and Lesbians in the Federal Government* (Chicago: University of Chicago Press, 2006); Andrea Friedman, "The Smearing of Joe McCarthy: The Lavender Scare, Gossip, and Cold War Politics," *American Quarterly* 57, no. 4 (2005): 1105–1129; Allan Bérubé, *Coming Out under Fire: The History of Gay Men and Women in World War Two* (New York: Free Press, 1990); John D'Emilio, *Sexual Politics, Sexual Communities: The Making of a Homosexual Minority in the United States, 1940–1970*, 2nd ed. (Chicago: University of Chicago Press, 1998); Leisa D. Meyer, *Creating GI Jane: Sexuality and Power in the Women's Army Corps during World War II* (New York: Columbia University Press, 1996); Donna Penn, "The Sexualized Woman: The Lesbian, the Prostitute, and the Containment of Female Sexuality in Postwar America," in *Not June Cleaver: Women and Gender in Postwar America, 1945–1960*, ed. Joanne Meyerowitz (Philadelphia: Temple University Press, 1994), 358–381; Jennifer Terry, *An American Obsession: Science, Medicine, and Homosexuality in Modern Society* (Chicago: University of Chicago Press, 1999); John D'Emilio, "The Homosexual Menace: The Politics of Sexuality in Cold War America," in *Passion and Power: Sexuality in History*, ed. Kathy Peiss and Christina Simmons, with Robert A. Padgug (Philadelphia: Temple University Press, 1989), 226–240.

17. Peter Gardella, *Innocent Ecstasy: How Christianity Gave America an Ethic of Sexual Pleasure* (New York: Oxford University Press, 1985).

18. Samuel Walker, *In Defense of American Liberties: A History of the ACLU* (Carbondale: Southern Illinois University Press, 1999), 99.

19. Ibid., 38.

20. Chad Heap, *Slumming: Sexual and Racial Encounters in American Nightlife, 1885–1940* (Chicago: University of Chicago Press, 2009); Lillian Faderman and Stuart Timmons, *Gay L.A.: A History of Sexual Outlaws, Power Politics, and Lipstick Lesbians* (New York: Basic Books, 2006); Lewis A. Erenberg, *Steppin' Out: New York Nightlife and the Transformation of American Culture, 1890–1930* (Westport, CT: Greenwood, 1981); Chauncey, *Gay New York*; Timothy Gilfoyle, *City of Eros: New York City, Prostitution, and the Commercialization of Sex, 1790–1920* (New York: Norton, 1992).

21. Michael B. Smith, "'The Ego Ideal of the Good Camper' and the Nature of Summer Camp," *Environmental History* 11, no. 1 (2006): 70–101; Leslie Paris, "The Adventures of Peanut and Bo: Summer Camps and Early-Twentieth-Century American Girlhood," *Journal of Women's History* 12, no. 4 (2001): 47–76; Susan A. Miller, *Growing Girls: The Natural Origins of Girls' Organizations in America* (New Brunswick: Rutgers University Press, 2007).

22. Smith, "Ego Ideal of the Good Camper," 71; Paris, "Adventures of Peanut and Bo," 53.

23. John Howard, *Men Like That: A Southern Queer History* (Chicago: University of Chicago Press, 1999), 47.

24. Ibid.; Beth Bailey, *Sex in the Heartland* (Cambridge: Harvard University Press, 1999).

25. John A. Jakle, *The Tourist: Travel in Twentieth-Century North America* (Lincoln: University of Nebraska Press, 1985), 185–198; Kathleen Franz, *Tinkering: Consumers Reinvent the Early Automobile* (Philadelphia: University of Pennsylvania Press, 2005).

26. Marguerite S. Shaffer, *See America First: Tourism and National Identity, 1880–1940* (Washington, DC: Smithsonian Institution Press, 2001), 93–168; Daniel M. Wrobel and Patrick T. Long, eds., *Seeing and Being Seen: Tourism in the American West* (Lawrence: Center of the American West, University of Colorado at Boulder / University of Kansas Press, 2001); Hal K. Rothman, *Devil's Bargains: Tourism in the Twentieth-Century American West* (Lawrence: University of Kansas Press, 1998), 143–167; Jakle, *Tourist*; Susan Sessions Rugh, "Branding Utah: Industrial Tourism in the Postwar American West," *Western Historical Quarterly* 37 (Winter 2006): 445–472; Clark Davis, "From Oasis to Metropolis: Southern California and the Changing Context of American Leisure," *Pacific Historical Review* 61, no. 3 (1992): 357–386; Susan G. Davis, "Landscapes of Imagination: Tourism in Southern California," *Pacific Historical Review* 68, no. 2 (1999): 173–191.

27. Cindy S. Aron, *Working at Play: A History of Vacations in the United States* (New York: Oxford University Press, 1999), 3.

28. Karen Christel Krahulik, *Provincetown: From Pilgrim Landing to Gay Resort* (New York: NYU Press, 2005); Esther Newton, *Cherry Grove, Fire Island: Sixty Years in America's First Gay and Lesbian Town* (Boston: Beacon, 1993); Paul Pattullo, *Last Resorts: The Cost of Tourism in the Caribbean* (London: Cassell, 1996); Jevin

Meethan, "Place, Image and Power: Brighton as a Resort," in *The Tourist Image: Myths and Myth Making in Tourism*, ed. Tom Selwyn (Chichester, UK: Wiley, 1996), 179–196.

29. Martin S. Pernick, *The Black Stork: Eugenics and the Death of "Defective" Babies in American Medicine and Motion Pictures since 1915* (New York: Oxford University Press, 1995); Lisa Cartwright, *Screening the Body: Tracing Medicine's Visual Culture* (Minneapolis: University of Minnesota Press, 1995); Reagan, Tomes, and Treichler, *Medicine's Moving Pictures*.

30. Reagan, Tomes, and Treichler, *Medicine's Moving Pictures*, 6.

31. Susan E. Lederer, "Repellent Subjects: Hollywood Censorship and Surgical Images in the 1930s," *Literature and Medicine* 17 (1998): 91–113.

32. Hodes, *Sex, Love, Race*; Morrison, *Playing in the Dark*.

33. Sam Brinkley, *Getting Loose: Lifestyle Consumption in the 1970s* (Durham: Duke University Press, 2007), 165.

Chapter 1: Indecent Exposure

1. "24 Seized in Raid on Nudist Cult Here," *New York Times*, December 8, 1931, 3.

2. "Frees 19 Nudists in Gymnasium Raid," *New York Times*, December 15, 1931, 16.

3. "24 Seized in Raid on Nudist Cult Here," 3.

4. Sarah Banet-Weiser, *The Most Beautiful Girl in the World: Beauty Pageants and National Identity* (Berkeley: University of California Press, 1999); Elwood Watson and Darcy Martin, eds., *"There She Is, Miss America": The Politics of Sex, Beauty, and Race in America's Most Famous Pageant* (New York: Palgrave Macmillan, 2004); Lois W. Banner, *American Beauty* (Chicago: University of Chicago Press, 1984); Jeff Wiltse, *Contested Waters: A Social History of Swimming Pools in America* (Chapel Hill: University of North Carolina Press, 2007); Angela J. Latham, "Packaging Woman: The Concurrent Rise of Beauty Pageants, Public Bathing, and Other Performances of Female 'Nudity,'" *Journal of Popular Culture* 29, no. 3 (1995): 149–167.

5. Leigh Ann Wheeler, *Against Obscenity: Reform and the Politics of Womanhood in America, 1873–1935* (Baltimore: Johns Hopkins University Press, 2004); Andrea Friedman, "'The Habitats of Sex-Craved Perverts': Campaigns against Burlesque in Depression-Era New York City," *Journal of the History of Sexuality* 7, no. 2 (1996): 203–238; Robert Clyde Allen, *Horrible Prettiness: Burlesque and American Culture* (Chapel Hill: University of North Carolina Press, 1991).

6. Arne L. Suominen, "Observing the German Methods," *Official Naturopath and Herald of Health: Official Journal of the American Naturopathic Association and the American School of Naturopathy*, February 1937, 40. The *American Medical Directory*, published by the American Medical Association, did not list Suominen as a recognized physician in the state of Illinois. In his article, he abbreviated his credentials as "D.N.," or Doctor of Naprapathy, indicating that he most likely did not attend a formal medical school endorsed by the American Medical Association.

7. "Rogers Pk. vs. Sun Bathers! To a Decision," *Chicago Daily Tribune*, March 20, 1932, 1.

8. James C. Whorton, *Nature Cures: The History of Alternative Medicine in America* (Oxford: Oxford University Press, 2002), 223.

9. Ibid.

10. Bernarr Macfadden, *The Power and Beauty of Superb Womanhood* (New York, 1901), 63; James C. Whorton, *Crusaders for Fitness: The History of American Health Reformers* (Princeton: Princeton University Press, 1982), 296–303.

11. Marilyn Thornton Williams, *Washing "the Great Unwashed": Public Baths in Urban America, 1840–1920* (Columbus: Ohio State University Press, 1991), 84–85.

12. Ibid., 95.

13. Ibid.

14. Wiltse, *Contested Waters*, 89.

15. Ibid., 89–90.

16. "Council Asked to Approve Plan of Sun Bathers," *Chicago Daily Tribune*, March 10, 1932, 1.

17. Latham, "Packaging Woman"; Wiltse, *Contested Waters*; "Council Asked to Approve Plan of Sun Bathers," 1.

18. Kathleen D. McCarthy, "Nickel Vice and Virtue: Movie Censorship in Chicago, 1907–1915," *Journal of Popular Film* 5, no. 1 (1976): 38.

19. Robert Sklar, *Movie-Made America: A Cultural History of Movies* (New York: Vintage Books, 1975), 126.

20. Alison M. Parker, *Purifying America: Women, Cultural Reform, and Pro-censorship Activism, 1873–1933* (Urbana: University of Illinois Press, 1997), 30; Wheeler, *Against Obscenity*, 12; Nicola Beisal, *Imperiled Innocents: Anthony Comstock and Family Reproduction in Victorian America* (Princeton: Princeton University Press, 1997), 151–155; Paul S. Boyer, *Purity in Print: Book Censorship in America from the Gilded Age to the Computer Age*, 2nd ed. (Madison: University of Wisconsin Press, 2002), 12; Andrea Friedman, *Prurient Interests: Gender, Democracy, and Obscenity in New York City, 1909–1945* (New York: Columbia University Press, 2000), 126–127.

21. "Rogers Pk. Calls on Her Sons to Fight Sun Baths," *Chicago Daily Tribune*, March 21, 1932, 1.

22. Parker, *Purifying America*, 30.

23. "Rogers Pk. vs. Sun Bathers! To a Decision," 1.

24. "Protest Sent Mayor on Plan for Sun Bathing," *Chicago Daily Tribune*, March 19, 1932, 1; "Rogers Pk. vs. Sun Bathers! To a Decision," 1.

25. Gail Danks Welter, *The Rogers Park Community: A Study of Social Change, Community Groups, and Neighborhood Reputation* (Chicago: Center for Urban Policy, Loyola University of Chicago, 1982), 5–6.

26. "Rogers Pk. vs. Sun Bathers! To a Decision," 1.

27. "Protest Sent Mayor on Plan for Sun Bathing," 1.

28. "Rogers Pk. vs. Sun Bathers! To a Decision," 1.

29. "Rogers Pk. Calls on Her Sons to Fight Sun Baths," 1.

30. Robert G. Spinney, *City of Big Shoulders: A History of Chicago* (DeKalb: Northern Illinois University Press, 2000), 188–191.

31. "It's a Dark Day for Sun Bathing; Mayor Says 'No,'" *Chicago Daily Tribune*, March 22, 1932, 1.

32. Ibid.

33. Ibid.

34. Ibid.

35. Ibid.

36. "Official Brings Back Tidings of the Nude Cults," *Chicago Daily Tribune*, September 9, 1932, 1.

37. Ibid.

38. Ibid.

39. Ibid.

40. "10,000 Sign Plea for Nude Sun Bathing," *Chicago Daily Tribune*, June 9, 1933, 1.

41. Ibid.

42. Ibid.

43. On February 15, 1933, an Italian gunman attempted to assassinate president-elect Franklin D. Roosevelt at a rally being held in Miami, Florida, and instead fatally wounded Mayor Cermak, who died on March 6, 1933.

44. "Deny Sun Bath Pen; Knotless Lumber Costly," *Chicago Daily Tribune*, June 10, 1933, 1.

45. Ibid.

46. Ibid.

47. Ibid.

48. Friedman, *Prurient Interests*, 4, 5.

49. Jill Fields, *An Intimate Affair: Women, Lingerie, and Sexuality* (Berkeley: University of California Press, 2007), 79–113.

50. Latham, "Packaging Woman," 151.

51. Display ad, *New York Times*, June 26, 1934, 7.

52. Banner, *American Beauty*, 265–270.

53. Ibid., 269.

54. Clifford Putney, *Muscular Christianity: Manhood and Sports in Protestant America, 1880–1920* (Cambridge: Harvard University Press, 2001); Michael S. Goldstein, *The Health Movement: Promoting Fitness in America* (New York: Twayne, 1992); Jan Todd, "Bernarr Macfadden: Reformer of Feminine Form," *Journal of Sports History* 14, no. 1 (Spring 1987): 61–75; Whorton, *Crusaders for Fitness.*

55. Whorton, *Crusaders for Fitness*, 286.

56. Frances Merrill and Mason Merrill, *Among the Nudists* (New York: Knopf, 1933); Frances Merrill and Mason Merrill, *Nudism Comes to America* (New York: Knopf, 1932); Maurice Parmelee, *Nudism in Modern Life: The New Gymnosophy* (New York: Knopf, 1931); Jan Gay, *On Going Naked* (Garden City, NY: Garden City, 1932).

57. Latham, "Packaging Woman," 165.
58. Allen, *Horrible Prettiness*; Friedman, "Habitats of Sex-Crazed Perverts."
59. George Chauncey, *Gay New York: Gender, Urban Culture, and the Making of the Gay Male World, 1890–1940* (New York: Basic Books, 1994), 214.
60. "24 Seized in Raid on Nudist Cult Here," 3.
61. Ibid.
62. Chauncey, *Gay New York*, 214.
63. Friedman, "Habitats of Sex-Crazed Perverts."
64. The Goldstein case became an important precedent for future trials resulting from police raids on nudist gymnasiums. In *New York v. Burke* (1934), the nudists' attorneys introduced whole sections of the early trial's testimony and the written judgment into the record as part of their defense. As a result, the earlier trial's testimony and judgment were preserved in *New York v. Burke* (1934), excerpts from *People ex rel. Walter Bloomer v. Thomas McCabe, et al.*, in Brief of Appellants, 18, Records of Higher State Courts, New York State Archives, Albany, New York.
65. Ibid.
66. Ibid., 18.
67. Ibid., 21.
68. Ibid., 21.
69. Ibid., 20.
70. Ibid.
71. Ibid.
72. "Nudism as Educational and Social Force," *Literary Digest*, October 1933, 16.
73. Ibid.
74. Ibid.
75. "3 Held in Nudist Raid," *New York Times*, April 14, 1934, 7.
76. Chauncey, *Gay New York*, 354.
77. Friedman, "Habitats of Sex-Crazed Perverts," 222.
78. Philip Jenkins, *Moral Panic: Changing Concepts of the Child Molester in Modern America* (New Haven: Yale University Press, 1998), 49–93.
79. Friedman, "Habitats of Sex-Crazed Perverts," 222.
80. *New York v. Burke*, "Record on Appeal," 6.
81. Ibid.
82. Ibid.
83. Ibid.
84. Ibid.
85. Ibid.
86. Ibid.
87. Ibid.
88. Ibid.
89. Ibid.
90. *New York v. Burke*, "Respondent's Brief," 26.

91. *New York v. Burke*, "Record on Appeal," 24.
92. Ibid.
93. Ibid.
94. Allen, *Horrible Prettiness*, 250.
95. *New York v. Burke*, "Record on Appeal," 41.
96. Ibid.
97. Ibid.
98. Ibid.
99. Ibid.
100. Leigh Ann Wheeler, *How Sex Became a Civil Liberty* (New York: Oxford University Press, 2012), 44.
101. *New York v. Burke*, "Record on Appeal," 40.
102. *New York v. Burke*, Brief of Appellants, 7.
103. Ibid., 6.
104. Ibid., 7.
105. Ibid., 23.
106. Ibid.
107. Ibid.
108. *People v. Burke*, 243 App. Div. 83, 276 N.Y.S. 402 (1934).
109. *People v. Burke*, 276 N.Y.S at 404.
110. Al Smith to Honorable Herbert Lehman, December 27, 1934, 13682 Central Subject and Correspondence Files, 1919–1954, 1959–1983, Governor Office Records, New York State Archives, Albany, New York.
111. Ibid.
112. Robert A. Slayton, *Empire Statesman: The Rise and Redemption of Al Smith* (New York: Free Press, 2001).
113. Friedman, *Prurient Interests*, 139–140.
114. "Catholics Begin Fight on Nudism," *New York Times*, January 3, 1935, 25.
115. Ibid.
116. Ibid.
117. Ibid.
118. Ibid.
119. Ibid.
120. Ibid.
121. Ibid.
122. "Nudists See Smith 'Inconsistent' Foe," *New York Times*, January 4, 1935, 26.
123. "Catholics Deny Wide Reform Aim," *New York Times*, January 15, 1935, 23.
124. "Anti-Nudist Bill Obtains No Backing," *New York Times*, February 6, 1935, 5.
125. Ibid.
126. Ibid.
127. "Oppose Anti-Nudist Bill," *New York Times*, February 3, 1935, 28; signers of the protest included the Reverend Dr. Charles Francis Potter of the First Humanist Society; the Reverend Dr. Guy Emory Shipler, editor of the *Churchman*, an

Episcopal publication; Professor Arthur L. Swift of the Union Theological Seminary; the Reverend John Howard Melish, rector of the Church of the Holy Trinity; the Reverend Roswell D. Barnes of the Washington Heights Presbyterian Church; Rabbi Jonah B. Wise of the Central Synagogue; the Reverend Allan Knight Chalmers of the Broadway Congregational Tabernacle; and Professor Ellsworth Huntington of Yale University.

128. Ibid.
129. Ibid.
130. Ibid.
131. Ibid.
132. "Nudist Bill Reported," *New York Times*, March 14, 1935, 2.
133. "Albany Votes Bill Outlawing Nudism; Leaders Wrangle," *New York Times*, April 16, 1935, 1.
134. "Compensation Law Revised at Albany," *New York Times*, March 20, 1935, 10.
135. "Albany Votes Bill Outlawing Nudism," 1.
136. Ibid.
137. Ibid.
138. Ibid.
139. Ibid.
140. Ibid.
141. "Anti-Nudist Bill Voted," *New York Times*, April 9, 1935, 12.
142. "Albany Votes Bill Outlawing Nudism," 1.
143. The *New York World-Telegram* resulted from the 1931 merger of the *New York World*, owned by the heirs of Joseph Pulitzer, with the *Evening Telegram*, owned by Scripps Howard. The continuing influence of Pulitzer's *World* gave the newspaper a liberal reputation, but over the next two decades, the ownership of Scripps Howard resulted in an increasingly conservative perspective.
144. "Letters to Lehman," *Nudist*, July 1935, 24.
145. Ibid.
146. Henry Huntington, "The Seething Pot," *Nudist*, July 1935, 13.
147. Ibid.
148. "Nudists Win Case in Appeals Court," *New York Times*, May 1, 1935, 6.
149. "Anti-Nudism Bill Signed by Lehman," *New York Times*, May 14, 1935, 2.
150. Ibid.
151. Ibid.
152. "La Guardia Champions Cleaner Shows," *New York Times*, June 6, 1939, 15.
153. Ibid.

Chapter 2: Out in the Open
1. Alois Knapp, "Chicago's Zoro Nature Park," *Nudist*, October 1933, 12.
2. "Lorena Knapp, July 4, 1886–August 24, 1950," *Sunshine and Health*, November 1950, 20–21.
3. "Chicago's Zoro Nature Park," 12.

4. Kathy Peiss, *Cheap Amusements: Working Women and Leisure in Turn-of-the-Century New York City* (Philadelphia: Temple University Press, 1986); John D'Emilio, *Sexual Politics, Sexual Communities: The Making of a Homosexual Minority in the United States, 1940–1970*, 2nd ed. (Chicago: University of Chicago, 1998); George Chauncey, *Gay New York: Gender, Urban Culture, and the Making of the Gay Male World, 1890–1940* (New York: Basic Books, 1994); Joanne J. Meyerowitz, *Women Adrift: Independent Wage Earners in Chicago, 1880–1930* (Chicago: University of Chicago Press, 1988); Kevin Mumford, *Interzones: Black/White Sex Districts in Chicago and New York in the Early Twentieth Century* (New York: Columbia University Press, 1997); John Kasson, *Houdini, Tarzan, and the Perfect Man: The White Male Body and the Challenge of Modernity in America* (New York: Hill and Wang, 2001).

5. John Howard, *Men Like That: A Southern Queer History* (Chicago: University of Chicago Press, 1999), 35.

6. Ibid.

7. Michael L. Lewis, ed., *American Wilderness: A New History* (Oxford: Oxford University Press, 2007).

8. Susan A. Miller, *Growing Girls: The Natural Origins of Girls' Organizations in America* (New Brunswick: Rutgers University Press, 2007); Michael B. Smith, "'The Ego Ideal of the Good Camper' and the Nature of Summer Camp," *Environmental History* 11, no. 1 (2006): 70–101; Leslie Paris, "The Adventures of Peanut and Bo: Summer Camps and Early-Twentieth-Century American Girlhood," *Journal of Women's History* 12, no. 4 (2001): 47–76.

9. Kasson, *Houdini, Tarzan, and the Perfect Man*, 157–218.

10. Jim Motavalli, *Naked in the Woods: Joseph Knowles and the Legacy of Frontier Fakery* (Cambridge, MA: Da Capo, 2007).

11. Samuel Scoville, Jr., *Boy Scouts in the Wilderness* (New York: Century, 1919).

12. Smith, "Ego Ideal of the Good Camper," 71; Paris, "Adventures of Peanut and Bo," 53.

13. Howard, *Men Like That*, 47.

14. Rev. Ilsley Boone, "Selecting a Nudist Camp," *Nudist*, April 1934, 12.

15. John A. Jakle, *The Tourist: Travel in Twentieth-Century North America* (Lincoln: University of Nebraska Press, 1985).

16. "Chicago's Zoro Nature Park," 12.

17. Boone, "Selecting a Nudist Camp," 12.

18. Jeff Wiltse, *Contested Waters: A Social History of Swimming Pools in America* (Chapel Hill: University of North Carolina Press, 2007), 87–120.

19. "Chicago's Zoro Nature Park," 12.

20. Ibid.

21. Ibid.

22. Ibid.

23. Sam Weller, "Solving Financial Problems of the Local Group," *Nudist*, November 1936, 19–20.

24. Ibid.
25. Ibid.
26. Elton Raymond Shaw, *The Body Taboo* (Binghamton, NY: Vail-Ballou, 1937), 191.
27. Ibid.
28. J.Q.F., of the United States Senate, "Legal Nudism in Maryland," *Nudist*, April 1934, 15.
29. "Nudists Call on America to Take Off Its Clothes," *Chicago Daily Tribune*, August 26, 1936, 3.
30. The indecency statutes in the state of Indiana did not change until 1976. See Richard A. Posner and Katherine B. Silbaugh, *A Guide to America's Sex Laws* (Chicago: University of Chicago Press, 1996), 88–89.
31. "Chicago's Zoro Nature Park," 12.
32. Sidney R. Thompson, "Why Not Enjoy Your Camera?," *Nudist*, January 14, 1938, 14.
33. Ibid.
34. "Chicago's Zoro Nature Park," 12.
35. Ibid.
36. "Elysia at Elsinore," *Nudist*, March 1934, 15.
37. Ibid.
38. Ibid.
39. *Michigan v. Ring* (1934), Record, 3, State Law Library, Library of Michigan, Lansing, Michigan.
40. Ibid.
41. Ibid., 4.
42. Virginia Gardner, "Nudist Cult Leaders to Face Hearing in Michigan Today," *Chicago Daily Tribune*, September 21, 1933, 3.
43. *Michigan v. Ring* (1934), Record, 7.
44. Ibid., 31.
45. Ibid.
46. Ibid., 7.
47. Ibid.
48. Ibid., 19–20.
49. Judith R. Walkowitz, *City of Dreadful Delight: Narratives of Sexual Danger in Late-Victorian London* (Chicago: University of Chicago Press, 1992), 121–135; Leslie J. Reagan, *When Abortion Was a Crime: Women, Medicine, and Law in the United States, 1867–1973* (Berkeley: University of California Press, 1997), 160–193; Lisa Duggan, *Sapphic Slashers: Sex, Violence, and American Modernity* (Durham: Duke University Press, 2000), 32–60.
50. "Nudist Colony Heads in Court," *Los Angeles Times*, September 22, 1933, 3; "Court Battle in Nudist Camp Case Promised," *Washington Post*, September 22, 1933, 3.
51. Duggan, *Sapphic Slashers*, 40.
52. Virginia Gardner, "Nudist Cult Leaders to Face Hearing in Michigan Today," *Chicago Daily Tribune*, September 21, 1933, 3.

53. Alyssa Picard, "'To Popularize the Nude in Art': Comstockery Reconsidered," *Journal of the Gilded Age and Progressive Era* 1, no. 3 (2002): 195–224; Molly McGarry, "Spectral Sexualities: Nineteenth-Century Spiritualism, Moral Panics, and the Making of U.S. Obscenity Law," *Journal of Women's History* 12, no. 2 (2000): 8–29.

54. Virginia Gardner, "Nudist Leader Is Found Guilty of Indecencies," *Chicago Daily Tribune*, October 25, 1933, 3.

55. Shaw, *Body Taboo*, 158. Ophelia Ring's trial was later postponed until after the outcome of her husband's trial. This may have been to ensure that their two children would not be abandoned should the couple both be convicted and sentenced to jail.

56. Gardner, "Nudist Leader Is Found Guilty of Indecencies," 3.

57. *Michigan v. Ring* (1934), Brief for Appellant, 1–2, State Law Library, Library of Michigan, Lansing, Michigan.

58. Linda Gordon, *Woman's Body, Woman's Right: A Social History of Birth Control in America* (New York: Grossman, 1976); Chauncey, *Gay New York*; Reagan, *When Abortion Was a Crime*.

59. Reagan, *When Abortion Was a Crime*, 237; David J. Garrow, *Liberty and Sexuality: The Right to Privacy and the Making of "Roe v. Wade"* (New York: Macmillan, 1994).

60. *Michigan v. Ring* (1934), Brief for Appellant, 22, 32.

61. Ibid., 10.

62. Ibid., 11.

63. Ibid., 52.

64. Ibid., 51.

65. Ibid., 54.

66. Ibid.

67. Ibid., 57.

68. *Michigan v. Ring* (1934), Record, 24.

69. Ibid.

70. Ibid.

71. Ibid.

72. Ibid., 17.

73. Ibid., 24.

74. Ibid., 17.

75. Virginia Gardner, "Allegan Nudist Trial Opens to Capacity House," *Chicago Daily Tribune*, October 24, 1933, 3.

76. Ibid.

77. Ibid.

78. Ibid.

79. *Michigan v. Ring* (1934), Brief for Respondent, 22, State Law Library, Library of Michigan, Lansing, Michigan.

80. Ibid.

81. Ibid.
82. "Michigan Nudist Leader Is Given 60 Days in Jail," *Chicago Daily Tribune*, November 19, 1933, 20.
83. "Wife of Nudist Pleads Guilty; On Probation; Mate, Fred C. Ring, Is Now in Jail," *Chicago Daily Tribune*, June 21, 1934, 15.
84. Frederick Arthur Geib, "The Sociology of a Social Movement" (master's thesis, Brown University, 1956), 24.
85. Ibid.
86. Ibid.
87. "I.N.C.," *Nudist*, May 1933, 2.
88. Ibid.
89. Ibid.
90. Ibid.
91. Ibid.
92. Kathleen McLaughlin, "Doctors Call Nudism Loony," *Chicago Daily Tribune*, October 29, 1933.
93. Ibid.
94. Gretta Palmer, "I'll Be Seeing More of You," *Commentator* 1, no. 4 (May 1937): 95–99.
95. Anthony Turano, "Nudism Denuded," *American Mercury* 38, no. 150 (1936): 161–166.
96. James Whorton, *Nature Cures: The History of Alternative Medicine in America* (New York: Oxford University Press, 2002), 95.
97. Ibid., 195.
98. Gordon, *Woman's Body, Woman's Right*, 249–300.
99. Nancy Tomes, *The Gospel of Germs: Men, Women, and the Microbe in American Life* (Cambridge: Harvard University Press, 1998), 58; also see Daniel Freund, *American Sunshine: Diseases of Darkness and the Quest for Natural Light* (Chicago: University of Chicago Press, 2012).
100. "Cures by Sun's Rays to Be Studied," *New York Times*, August 12, 1928, 6.
101. William Goldsmith, "Sunshine and Health," *Nudist*, January 1935, 18.
102. Ibid.
103. Maurice Parmelee, *Nudism in Modern Life: The New Gymnosophy* (New York: Knopf, 1931), 109.
104. J. Henry Hallberg, "How the Sun Builds Health and Beauty," *Nudist*, September 1933, 23.
105. Ibid.
106. Ibid.
107. Martin S. Pernick, *The Black Stork: Eugenics and the Death of "Defective" Babies in American Medicine and Motion Pictures since 1915* (New York: Oxford University Press, 1995); Lisa Cartwright, *Screening the Body: Tracing Medicine's Visual Culture* (Minneapolis: University of Minnesota Press, 1995); Leslie J. Reagan, Nancy Tomes, and Paula A. Treichler, eds., *Medicine's Moving Pictures: Medicine, Health,*

and Bodies in American Film and Television (Rochester, NY: University of Rochester Press, 2007).

108. Eric Schaefer, *"Bold! Daring! Shocking! True!": A History of Exploitation Films, 1919–1959* (Durham: Duke University Press, 1999), 41.

109. "Chi Censors Pink 2 Pix; Others Nix 'Elysia,' Nudie," *Variety*, January 1934, 4; "Boring but Banned," *Variety*, November 21, 1933, 31; "Ban Nudie Pic," *Variety*, December 1933, 14.

110. Schaefer, *"Bold! Daring! Shocking! True!,"* 271.

111. *Elysia*, directed by Bryan Foy (1933; Something Weird Video, 2009).

112. Ibid.

113. Gail Bederman, *Manliness and Civilization: A Cultural History of Gender and Race in the United States, 1880–1917* (Chicago: University of Chicago Press, 1995).

114. *Elysia*.

115. Ibid.

116. Augustus Rollier, *Heliotherapy* (London: Oxford Medical Publications, 1923), 23.

117. Samuel Watson, "Heliotherapy in Tuberculosis," *Southwestern Medicine* 9, no. 1 (1925): 8.

118. Plato Schwartz, "Heliotherapy," *Boston Medical and Surgical Journal* 191, no. 4 (1924): 243.

119. Arnaldo Cortesi, "Pope Denounces Nudism as Pagan," *New York Times*, March 6, 1935, 3.

120. Ibid. For historical studies of German nudism, see John Williams, *Turning to Nature in Germany: Hiking, Nudism, and Conservation, 1900–1940* (Stanford: Stanford University Press, 2007); Brandon Taylor and Wilfried van der Will, eds., *The Nazification of Art: Art, Design, Music, Architecture and Film in the Third Reich* (Winchester, UK: Winchester Press / Winchester School of Art, 1990); Josie McLellan, "State Socialist Bodies: East German Nudism from Ban to Boom," *Journal of Modern History* 79, no. 1 (2007): 48–79; Chad Ross, *Naked Germany: Health, Race and the Nation* (Oxford, UK: Berg, 2005); Karl Eric Toepfer, *Empire of Ecstasy: Nudity and Movement in German Body Culture, 1910–1935* (Berkeley: University of California Press, 1997).

121. Cortesi, "Pope Denounces Nudism as Pagan," 3.

122. Ibid.

123. Ilsley Boone, *Joys of Nudism* (Binghamton, NY: Greenburg, 1934), 102.

124. Henry Strong Huntington, "Nudism and Religion," *Nudist*, October 1933, 14.

125. Boone, *Joys of Nudism*, 102.

126. Methodist Minister, "Nudism at First Hand," *Nudist*, May 1933, 4; "Nudism and Sex," *Nudist*, June 1933, 22; A Congregational Minister, "Slowing Down Life's Tempo," *Nudist*, June 1933, 25; An English Minister, "Sunshine, Clothes, and the Body," *Nudist*, June 1933, 25; Henry Strong Huntington, "Nudism and Religion," *Nudist*, October 1933, 14; Episcopalian Minister, "The Passing of False Shame," *Nudist*, April 1934, 23; Congregational Minister, "The Verdict," *Nudist*, August 1934, 23; Alexander Frederick, "Yet Another Heaven," *Nudist*, December 1934, 19;

Henry Strong Huntington, "The Ecclesiastics and Nudism," *Nudist*, May 1935, 8; Rev. David Cole, "Why I Am a Nudist Believer," *Nudist*, September 1937, 9; Donald Craigie, "Three Score Years Ago—and Now," *Nudist*, February 1939, 7; Carl Easton Williams, "He Still Creates Us 'Naked and Unashamed,'" *Nudist*, September 1940, 9.

127. Boone, *Joys of Nudism*, 102.

128. Ibid., 103.

129. Ibid.

130. Ibid., 114.

131. Ibid., 113.

132. "Founder of Cult Defends Nudism at Faith Session: Minimizes Sex Interest," *Chicago Tribune*, September 13, 1933, 3.

133. A Congregational Minister, "Slowing Down Life's Tempo," 25.

134. "Founder of Cult Defends Nudism at Faith Session," 3; A Congregational Minister, "Slowing Down Life's Tempo," 25.

135. A Congregational Minister, "Slowing Down Life's Tempo," 25.

136. Francis Merrill and Mason Merrill, *Nudism Comes to America* (New York: Knopf, 1932). The authors explained that they focused on founding members of camps or people who were interested in nudism prior to visiting a camp. They left out "converts" and those who came into the movement through friends. This selection process was determined by available information.

137. Ibid., 86.

138. Ibid., 101. In addition to their own survey, Francis and Mason Merrill also listed the religious statistics of the American League for Physical Culture. The 111 applications seemed to corroborate their own findings. "The religious classifications are as follows: 38 no religion; 27 Protestant (no sect indicated); 14 Roman Catholic; 12 Lutheran; 8 Episcopalian; 6 Hebrew; 2 Unitarian; 2 Theosophist (man and wife); 1 ex-Baptist; 1 Hindu (an East Indian)."

139. Margaret Sanger, *Woman and the New Race* (Elmsfield, NY: Maxwell, 1969), 180.

140. Peter Gardella, *Innocent Ecstasy: How Christianity Gave America an Ethic of Sexual Pleasure* (New York: Oxford University Press, 1985), 130–141.

141. "Founder of Cult Defends Nudism at Faith Session," 3.

142. Ibid.

143. Ibid.

144. Howard C. Warren, "Social Nudism and the Body Taboo," *Psychological Review* 40 (1933): 160–182.

145. Ibid., 177–178.

146. Ibid., 181.

147. Maurice Parmelee, "Adventure in Many Lands," 14, folder 8, Maurice Parmelee Papers, Manuscripts and Archives, Yale University Library, New Haven, Connecticut.

148. Ibid., 373.

149. Ibid., 389.

150. Ibid.

151. Parmelee, *Nudism in Modern Life*, 175.

152. Havelock Ellis, foreword to ibid., 1–2.

153. Maurice Parmelee, *Personality and Conduct* (New York: Moffat, Yard, 1918), 267.

154. Ibid.

155. Jennifer Terry, *An American Obsession: Science, Medicine, and Homosexuality in Modern Society* (Chicago: University of Chicago Press, 1999), 183–184.

156. Jan Gay, *On Going Naked* (Garden City, NY: Garden City, 1932), 55.

157. Ibid., 26.

158. Maurice Parmelee, "Play Function of Sex," 83, folder 48, Maurice Parmelee Papers, Manuscripts and Archives, Yale University Library, New Haven, Connecticut.

159. Ibid., 51.

160. Ibid., 85.

161. Henry Huntington to Maurice Parmelee, May 1963, folder 10, Maurice Parmelee Papers, Manuscripts and Archives, Yale University Library, New Haven, Connecticut; Maurice Parmelee to Henry Huntington, May 8, 1963, "Henry Huntington, 1963–64," ibid.

162. Maurice Parmelee to Wallace Keynes Walker, September 6, 1959, folder 7, ibid. Parmelee demanded that Rev. Boone pay him royalties for the fifty thousand copies of *Nudism in Modern Life* that Boone claimed to have sold through the *Nudist*. The dispute created a major rift in their relationship and served as an early example of Boone's dubious management of the nudist movement's finances.

163. "Fifth Annual Meeting of the International Nudist Conference (Newly Named the American Sunbathing Association)," *Nudist*, November 1936, 7. The title "Fifth Annual Meeting of the International Nudist Conference" was likely chosen to associate the fledgling American nudist movement with the more established *Nacktkultur* groups in Germany. Very few, if any, of the guests at the conference traveled from international locales.

164. Ibid.; these states included California, Colorado, Florida, Illinois, Indiana, New Jersey, New York, and Pennsylvania.

165. Ibid.

166. Ibid.

167. "Nudists' Rigid Cliques and Creed Told," *Chicago Daily Tribune*, August 24, 1936, 1.

168. "Nudists' Rigid Social Cliques and Creed Told," 1; "Nudists Report Ranks Grow," *New York Times*, August 23, 1936, N8; "Nudists Elect New Officers," *Los Angeles Times*, August 25, 1936, 11; "Nudism Strips Mind of 'Decay,' Says Its Editor," *Washington Post*, August 24, 1936, X4; "International Nudists Elect New President," *Hartford Courant*, August 25, 1936, 9.

169. "Nudists' Rigid Social Cliques and Creed Told," 1.

170. Ibid.

171. Ibid.

172. Ibid.

173. Ibid.
174. Ibid.
175. Ibid.
176. "Nudists Call on America to Take Off Its Clothes," 3.
177. "Fifth Annual Meeting," 9.
178. Ibid.

Chapter 3: Between the Covers

1. Paul S. Boyer, *Purity in Print: Book Censorship in America from the Gilded Age to the Computer Age*, 2nd ed. (Madison: University of Wisconsin Press, 2002), 208–211; Marjorie Heins, *Not in Front of the Children: "Indecency," Censorship, and the Innocence of Youth* (New York: Hill and Wang, 2001), 25.
2. Margot Canaday, "Building a Straight State: Sexuality and Social Citizenship under the 1944 G.I. Bill," *Journal of American History* 90, no. 3 (December 2003): 935–957; John D'Emilio, *Lost Prophet: The Life and Times of Bayard Rustin* (New York: Free Press, 2003); David K. Johnson, *The Lavender Scare: The Cold War Persecution of Gays and Lesbians in the Federal Government* (Chicago: University of Chicago Press, 2006); Andrea Friedman, "The Smearing of Joe McCarthy: The Lavender Scare, Gossip, and Cold War Politics," *American Quarterly* 57, no. 4 (2005): 1105–1129; Leslie J. Reagan, *When Abortion Was a Crime: Women, Medicine, and Law in the United States, 1867–1973* (Berkeley: University of California Press, 1997), 162–164.
3. Henry Huntington to Maurice Parmelee, May 4, 1963, "Henry Huntington, 1963–64," Maurice Parmelee Papers; Maurice Parmelee to Henry Huntington, May 8, 1963, ibid.
4. Maurice Parmelee, "Adventures in Many Lands: An Autobiographical Memoir," 2, unpublished ms., MS 1744, Box 3, folder 7, Maurice Parmelee Papers, Manuscripts and Archives, Yale University, New Haven, Connecticut.
5. Ibid., 4.
6. Ibid., 5.
7. Ibid.
8. Ibid.
9. Parmelee, "Adventures in Many Lands," 6.
10. Edward De Grazia, *Censorship Landmarks* (New York: Bowker, 1969), xi.
11. Molly McGarry, "Spectral Sexualities: Nineteenth-Century Spiritualism, Moral Panics, and the Making of U.S. Obscenity Law," *Journal of Women's History* 12, no. 2 (2000): 8–29; Leigh Ann Wheeler, "Rescuing Sex from Prudery and Prurience: American Women's Use of Sex Education as an Antidote to Obscenity, 1926–1932," *Journal of Women's History* 12, no. 3 (2000): 173–195; Andrea Friedman, *Prurient Interests: Gender, Democracy, and Obscenity in New York City, 1909–1945* (New York: Columbia University Press, 2000); Heins, *Not in Front of the Children*; Leigh Ann Wheeler, *Against Obscenity: Reform and the Politics of Womanhood in America, 1873–1935* (Baltimore: Johns Hopkins University Press, 2004).

12. Arthur Cauldwell, "Maurice Parmelee, a Nudist Pioneer," 6, unpublished ms., American Nudist Research Library, Cypress Cove Nudist Resort, Kissimmee, Florida.

13. *Parmelee v. United States*, 113 F. 2d 729, 730 (1940).

14. Ibid. at 730.

15. Kenneth Clark, *The Nude: A Study in Ideal Form* (New York: Fantheon, 1956), 3.

16. Marguerite S. Shaffer, "Marguerite S. Shaffer on the Environmental Nude," *Environmental History* 13, no. 1 (2008): 126–139; Lynda Nead, *The Female Nude: Art, Obscenity, and Sexuality* (London: Routledge, 1992); Helen McDonald, *Erotic Ambiguities: The Female Nude in Art* (London: Routledge, 2001); Clark, *Nude*; Anne Hollander, *Seeing through Clothes* (New York: Viking, 1975).

17. Parmelee, "Adventures in Many Lands," 7.

18. Samuel Walker, *In Defense of American Liberties: A History of the ACLU* (Carbondale: Southern Illinois University Press, 1999), 83–84.

19. *Parmelee*, 113 F. 2d at 731.

20. Ibid. at 731, 732.

21. *Parmelee v. United States*, Brief on Behalf of Appellant, 4, Ni. 7332, 1939, National Archives and Records Administration, College Park, Maryland.

22. Ibid., 5.

23. Ibid.

24. Ibid.

25. Ibid., 6–7.

26. *Parmelee*, 113 F. 2d at 736.

27. Ibid. at 737.

28. Ibid.

29. Ibid. at 732.

30. Ibid. at 735, 736.

31. Ibid. at 735.

32. "Nudity in Art Upheld as Proper By Court," *New York Times*, May 15, 1940, 14; "Court Reverses Ruling against Nudist Book," *Washington Post*, May 15, 1940, 19.

33. Frank Waldrop, "Case of Mr. Parmelee," *Washington Times-Herald*, February 25, 1942, 10.

34. Parmelee, "Adventures in Many Lands," chap. 28, pp. 3–4.

35. "Dies Hits 35 U.S. Officials as Reds: Finds a Nudist Is Planner for Post-war Era," *Chicago Daily Tribune*, March 30, 1942, 1.

36. Congressman Edward E. Cox of Georgia, speaking in regard to Maurice Parmelee, on March 30, 1942, House of Representatives, 77th Cong., 2d sess., 88 Cong. Rec. 3204–3205.

37. Ibid.

38. Parmelee, "Adventures in Many Lands," 1–2.

39. Ibid., 3.

40. Walker, *In Defense of American Liberties*, 120–121.

41. Congressman Cox, speaking in regard to Maurice Parmelee.

42. Ibid.
43. Maurice Parmelee, *The Principles of Anthropology and Sociology in Their Relations to Criminal Procedure* (New York: Macmillan, 1908); Maurice Parmelee, *Inebriety in Boston* (New York: Eagle, 1909); Maurice Parmelee, *Science of Human Behavior, Biological and Psychological Foundations* (New York: Macmillan, 1913); Maurice Parmelee, *Poverty and Social Progress* (New York: Macmillan, 1916); Maurice Parmelee, *Criminology* (New York: Macmillan, 1918); Maurice Parmelee, · *Personality and Conduct* (New York: Moffat, Yard, 1918); Maurice Parmelee, *Oriental and Occidental Culture* (New York: Macmillan, 1928); Maurice Parmelee, *Bolshevism, Fascism, and the Liberal Democratic State* (New York: Wiley, 1934); Maurice Parmelee, *In the Fields and Methods of Sociology* (New York: Ray Long and Richard R. Smith, 1934); Maurice Parmelee, *Farewell to Poverty* (New York: Wiley, 1935).
44. Congressman Cox, speaking in regard to Maurice Parmelee.
45. Ibid.
46. Ibid.
47. Ibid.
48. Ibid.
49. "An Appropriate Haven," *Chicago Daily Tribune*, March 31, 1942, 10.
50. "Wallace Lashes Out at Dies for Digging Up Facts," *Chicago Tribune*, March 30, 1942, 2; "Wallace Hits Dies as Aiding the Axis," *New York Times*, March 30 1942, 1; "Dies' Attack on Economic War Aides Irks Wallace," *Washington Post*, March 30, 1942, 1; "Wallace-Dies Row Flares," *Los Angeles Times*, March 30, 1942, 1; "New Charges of Dies Hit by Wallace," *Hartford Courant*, March 30, 1942, 1.
51. "Wallace Lashes Out at Dies for Digging Up Facts," 2.
52. Ibid.
53. Ibid.
54. Ibid.
55. Ibid.
56. Ibid.
57. Ibid.
58. Ibid.
59. Congressman James F. O'Connor of Montana, speaking in regard to Mr. Dies and his Committee on Un-American Activities, on March 31, 1942, 77th Cong., 2d sess., 88 Cong. Rec. A1282.
60. Ibid.
61. Ibid.
62. Ibid.
63. "Dies in the Spring," *Nation*, April 1, 1942, 385–386.
64. Ibid., 386.
65. Ibid.
66 Ibid.
67. "Dies versus Parmelee," *Sunshine and Health*, June 1942, 9–10.

68. Ibid.

69. Ibid.

70. Ibid.

71. Ibid.

72. "Wallace Lashes Out at Dies for Digging Up Facts," 2; "Wallace Hits Dies as Aiding the Axis," 1; "Dies' Attack on Economic War Aides Irks Wallace," 1; "Wallace-Dies Row Flares," 1; "New Charges of Dies Hit by Wallace," 1.

73. "Dies Nudist Find Brings Protests of 'Crackpotism,'" *Chicago Daily Tribune*, April 1, 1942, 13.

74. "Dies' Attack on Economic War Aides Irks Wallace," 1.

75. Congressman Cox, speaking in regard to Maurice Parmelee.

76. Ibid.

77. Congressman Noah M. Mason of Illinois, speaking in regard to Maurice Parmelee and his *Nudism in Modern Life*, on March 30, 1942, House of Representatives, 77th Cong., 2d sess., 88 Cong. Rec. 3204–3205.

78. "Delights of Life Sans Clothing Read into Congressional Record," *Washington Post*, March 31, 1942, 1.

79. Ibid.

80. Parmelee, "Adventures in Many Lands," 12.

81. Congressman John J. Cochran of New York, speaking in regard to the Dies committee on April 28, 1942, 77th Cong., 2d sess., 88 Cong. Rec. 3754.

82. Congressman James F. O'Connor of Montana, speaking in regard to the Dies committee on April 28, 1942, 77th Cong., 2d sess., 88 Cong. Rec. 3754.

83. Ibid.

84. Ibid.

85. Ibid.

86. "Dies Wins House Committee O.K. on 110,000 Fund," *Chicago Daily Tribune*, April 23, 1942, 11. There were 291 yeas and 64 nays, with 1 voting "present" and 75 not voting. Congressman O'Connor, speaking in regard to the Dies committee, 3757.

87. "The Five Year Plan and the Annual Meeting," *Sunshine and Health*, August 1942, 22.

88. Ibid

89. Ibid.

90. "The Five Year Plan Moves On," *Sunshine and Health*, March 1943, 6.

91. Ibid.

92. Ibid.

93. Ibid.

94. Ibid.

95. Ibid.

96. Ibid.

97. Ibid.

98. Ibid.

99. Ibid.
100. Ibid.
101. Ibid.
102. Paul Hadley, "War Restrictions on Photography," *Sunshine and Health*, March 1943, 30.
103. Ibid.
104. "The Publisher's Desk," *Sunshine and Health*, October 1943, 1.
105. "The Publisher's Desk," *Sunshine and Health*, May 1943, 1.
106. Ibid.
107. "Editorial Comment—The War First—Then a New World," *Sunshine and Health*, January 1943, 7.
108. For example, see "Yes Sir! We Did It!!!," *Sunshine and Health*, October 1944, 27.
109. "Publisher's Desk," *Sunshine and Health*, August 1942, 1.
110. "Editorial Comment—The War First—Then a New World," 7.
111. Ibid.
112. *Sunshine and Health*, February 1943, 16.
113. "We, the War and the Present Emergency," *Sunshine and Health*, May 1942, 12.
114. "The Benefits of Graduated Sun Bathing on a Troopship," *Journal of the American Medical Association* 124, no. 1 (1944): 51.
115. Ibid.
116. Ibid.
117. Ibid.
118. Ibid.
119. "Publisher's Desk," *Sunshine and Health*, August 1944, 1.
120. "Nude Culture," *Sunshine and Health*, February 1943, 2.
121. "Nude Culture," *Sunshine and Health*, December 1943, 25.
122. Ibid.
123. Ibid.
124. "President's Message," *Sunshine and Health*, July 1943, 26.
125. Ibid.
126. Ibid.
127. Ibid.
128. Ibid.
129. "Publisher's Desk," *Sunshine and Health*, April 1942, 1.
130. Ibid.
131. "Publisher's Desk," *Sunshine and Health*, August 1944, 1.
132. "From a Brother in Khaki," *Sunshine and Health*, June 1942, 2; "With the British Empire Forces," *Sunshine and Health*, April 1942, 3; "With Our Armed Forces," *Sunshine and Health*, April 1942, 3.
133. "Photography Guide for S&H," *Sunshine and Health*, October 1944, 30.
134. Ibid.
135. Herbert Webb, "A Nudist Photographer Talks," *Sunshine and Health*, January 1942, 13.

136. "Photography Guide for S&H," 30.

137. Ibid.

138. Ilsley Boone, "On the Obscenity of Nudist Pictures," *Sunshine and Health*, October 1942, 28.

139. Webb, "Nudist Photographer Talks," 13.

140. Ibid.

141. Ibid.

142. Ibid.

143. Sally Stein, "The President's Two Bodies: Stagings and Restagings of FDR and the New Deal Body Politic," *American Art* 18, no. 1 (2004): 32–57; Geoffrey C. Ward, *A First-Class Temperament: The Emergence of Franklin Roosevelt* (New York: Harper and Row, 1989), 732–794; Hugh Gregory Gallagher, *FDR's Splendid Deception* (New York: Dodd, Mead, 1985); Robert S. McElvaine, *The Great Depression: America, 1929–1941* (New York: Times Books, 1984), 97, 106.

144. Webb, "Nudist Photographer Talks," 13.

145. Jeaxd M. Carrier, "How and Why We Take Pictures at Elysian League," *Sunshine and Health*, May 1943, 15.

146. Ibid.

147. Ibid.

148. Ibid.

149. Ibid.

150. "Editorial Comment," *Sunshine and Health*, September 1944, 9.

151. "Nude Culture," *Sunshine and Health*, April 1942, 2; "Nude Culture," *Sunshine and Health*, February, 1943, 2; "Letters from Men Afield," *Sunshine and Health*, January 1944, 4.

152. "Editorial Comment," *Sunshine and Health*, September 1944, 9.

153. Allan M. Brandt, *No Magic Bullet: A Social History of Venereal Disease in the United States since 1880* (New York: Oxford University Press, 1987), 31–37; Mark Thomas Connelly, *The Response to Prostitution in the Progressive Era* (Chapel Hill: North Carolina University Press, 1980); Ruth Rosen, *The Lost Sisterhood: Prostitution in America, 1900–1918* (Baltimore: John Hopkins University Press, 1982).

154. Marilyn Hegarty, *Victory Girls, Khaki-Wackies, and Patriotutes: The Regulation of Female Sexuality during World War II* (New York: NYU Press, 2007), 85.

155. Debs Myers, "Pfc. Alois Knapp, Nudist," *Yank* 4, no. 1 (June 22, 1945): 7.

156. Ibid.

157. Despina Kakoudake, "Pinup: The American Secret Weapon in World War II," in *Porn Studies*, ed. Linda Williams (Durham: Duke University Press, 2004), 362; see also Joanne Meyerowitz, "Women, Cheesecake, and Borderline Material: Responses to Girlie Pictures in the Mid-Twentieth-Century U.S.," *Journal of Women's History* 8, no. 3 (1996): 9–35; Robert Westbrook, "'I Want a Girl, Just Like the Girl that Married Harry James': American Women and the Problem of Political Obligation in World War II," *American Quarterly* 42, no. 4 (1990): 587–614.

158. Kakoudake, "Pinup," 362.
159. "Nude Culture," *Sunshine and Health*, February 1943, 2.
160. "Nude Culture," *Sunshine and Health*, December 1943, 25.
161. "Letters from Men Afield," *Sunshine and Health*, January 1944, 4.
162. Ibid.
163. "Nude Culture," *Sunshine and Health*, April 1943, 3.
164. Ibid.
165. Ibid.
166. Ibid.
167. "The Adventures of Hughie," *Sunshine and Health*, February 1945, 6.
168. Ibid.; Robert Dean, *Imperial Brotherhood: Gender and the Making of the Cold War* (Amherst: University of Massachusetts Press, 2001); K. A. Cuordileone, "Politics in an Age of Anxiety: Cold War Political Culture and the Crisis of American Masculinity, 1949–1960," *Journal of American History* 87, no. 2 (2000): 515–545; Frank Costigliola, "'Unceasing Pressure for Penetration': Gender, Pathology, and Emotion in George Kennan's Formation of the Cold War," *Journal of American History* 83, no. 2 (1997): 1309–1339.
169. "Adventures of Hughie," 6.
170. John D'Emilio, *Sexual Politics, Sexual Communities: The Making of a Homosexual Minority in the United States, 1940–1970*, 2nd ed. (Chicago: University of Chicago Press, 1998); Leisa D. Meyer, *Creating GI Jane: Sexuality and Power in the Women's Army Corps during World War II* (New York: Columbia University Press, 1996).
171. David K. Johnson, "Physique Pioneers: The Politics of 1960s Gay Consumer Culture," *Journal of Social History* 43, no. 4 (2010): 867–892.
172. Bruce of L.A. Photographs, ca. 1950–1966, CN 7665, Human Sexuality Collection, Cornell University, Ithaca, New York.
173. Allan Bérubé, *Coming Out under Fire: The History of Gay Men and Women in World War Two* (New York: Free Press, 1990), 16.
174. Ibid.
175. Ibid.
176. "Letters from Men Far Afield," *Sunshine and Health*, August 1944, 6.
177. "A Nude Night in Normandy," *Sunshine and Health*, March 1945, 6.
178. Ibid.
179. Ibid.
180. Martin Meeker, *Contacts Desired: Gay and Lesbian Communications and Community, 1940s–1970s* (Chicago: University of Chicago Press, 2006), 26.
181. Whitney Strub, "The Clearly Obscene and the Queerly Obscene: Heteronormativity and Obscenity in Cold War Los Angeles," *American Quarterly* 60, no. 2 (2008): 386.
182. Myers, "Pfc. Alois Knapp, Nudist," 7.
183. Richard Meyer, *Outlaw Representation: Censorship and Homosexuality in Twentieth-Century American Art* (Oxford: Oxford University Press, 2002), 171–174.

184. Myers, "Pfc. Alois Knapp, Nudist," 7.
185. Ibid.; Bérubé, *Coming Out under Fire*, 125–126.
186. Myers, "Pfc. Alois Knapp, Nudist," 7.
187. I arrived at this number by systematically counting the images in *Sunshine and Health* from 1933 to 1963.
188. "Publisher's Desk," *Sunshine and Health*, January 1947, 1.
189. Ibid.
190. Ibid.
191. Ibid.
192. Ibid.

Chapter 4: Naked in Suburbia

1. "Reader's Forum: Gather Ye Singles While Ye May," *Sunshine and Health*, August 1946, 3.
2. Ibid.
3. Ibid.
4. Cindy S. Aron, *Working at Play: A History of Vacations in the United States* (New York: Oxford University Press, 1999), 3.
5. Karen Christel Krahulik, *Provincetown: From Pilgrim Landing to Gay Resort* (New York: NYU Press, 2005); Esther Newton, *Cherry Grove, Fire Island: Sixty Years in America's First Gay and Lesbian Town* (Boston: Beacon, 1993); Paul Pattullo, *Last Resorts: The Cost of Tourism in the Caribbean* (London: Cassell, 1996); Jevin Meethan, "Place, Image and Power: Brighton as a Resort," in *The Tourist Image: Myths and Myth Making in Tourism*, ed. Tom Selwyn (Chichester, UK: Wiley, 1996), 179–196.
6. Ellen Furlough, "Packaging Pleasures: Club Méditerranée and French Consumer Culture, 1950–1968," *French Historical Studies* 18, no. 1 (1993): 65–81.
7. Karen Dubinsky, *The Second Greatest Disappointment: Honeymooning and Tourism at Niagara Falls* (New Brunswick: Rutgers University Press, 1999), 13.
8. Frederick Arthur Geib, "The Sociology of a Social Movement" (master's thesis, Brown University, 1956), 24.
9. "A Symposium on Singles," *Sunshine and Health*, June 1950, 9.
10. Ibid.
11. "Letter to the Editor: Discrimination against Single Nudists," *Sunshine and Health*, March 1947, 5.
12. "Reader's Forum: What about It Singles?," *Sunshine and Health*, July 1947, 4.
13. Linda Gordon, *Heroes of Their Own Lives: The Politics and History of Family Violence, 1880–1960* (New York: Viking, 1988), 204–249.
14. Fred Burnett to Norval Packwood, January 5, 1957, American Nudist Research Library, Cypress Cove Nudist Resort, Kissimmee, Florida.
15. Fred Barnett to Mr. Heider, January 16, 1957, American Nudist Research Library.
16. Fred Burnett to Norval Packwood, January 5, 1957, American Nudist Research Library.

17. Ibid.; Fred Burnett to Norval Packwood, January 9, 1957, American Nudist Research Library; Les Bowser (Northwest Sunbathing Association President) to Dear Friends, American Nudist Research Library.
18. Fred Barnett to Mr. Heider, January 16, 1957, American Nudist Research Library.
19. Norval Packwood to Fred Burnett, January 7, 1957, American Nudist Research Library.
20. Ibid.
21. Donald Johnson, "Organizing and Directing a Nudist Club," *Sunshine and Health*, August 1951, 10.
22. "Ideas on the Single Man Problem," *Sunshine and Health*, October 1946, 10.
23. "Single Man Problem Solved?," *Sunshine and Health*, June 1948, 21.
24. Evelyn Rawlings, "Women's Page," *Sunshine and Health*, June 1947, 28.
25. John C. Salmon, "One Answer to the Singleton," *Sunshine and Health*, June 1949, 20. For this wide-ranging sentiment, also see "Editorial Comment: The Single Man Problem," *Sunshine and Health*, November 1954, 9.
26. "Ideas on the Single Man Problem," 10.
27. "Zoro Nature Park," *Sunshine and Health*, April 1958, 6.
28. "Letter to the Editor: Discrimination against Single Nudists," *Sunshine and Health*, March 1947, 5.
29. Ken Price, "Dear Mr. Anonymous," *Sunshine and Health*, March 1962, 4.
30. David Allyn, *Make Love, Not War: The Sexual Revolution, an Unfettered History* (New York: Little, Brown, 2000), 28.
31. Kermit Josephs, "The Homosexual Nudist," *One* 7, no. 4 (1959): 26–27.
32. Ibid., 27.
33. Ibid., 26.
34. Ibid.
35. Ibid.
36. Ibid., 27.
37. "Reader's Forum: Single Joins Group," *Sunshine and Health*, September 1947, 3.
38. "Reader's Forum: Excluded, but Supporting," *Sunshine and Health*, July 1949, 4.
39. "Reader's Forum: No Superfluity of Males," *Sunshine and Health*, November 1949, 5.
40. Ibid.
41. Ibid.
42. Ibid.
43. "Symposium on Singles," 9.
44. Ibid.
45. Ibid.
46. "Reader's Forum: Nudism Needs Youth," *Sunshine and Health*, June 1947, 6.
47. Ibid.
48. "Reader's Forum: Discusses the Single Man Problem," *Sunshine and Health*, September 1947, 3.

49. "Letters to the Editor: Discrimination against Single Nudists," *Sunshine and Health*, March 1947, 5.
50. "Reader's Forum: What's All This about Singles?," *Sunshine and Health*, October 1947, 3.
51. "Reader's Forum: A Single Tells His Story," *Sunshine and Health*, October 1947, 3.
52. "Reader's Forum: Wanted Singletons near Gary," *Sunshine and Health*, June 1948, 4.
53. Ibid.
54. "Reader's Forum: What's All This about Singles?," 3.
55. Ibid.
56. "How Can He Best Tell Her about Nudism?," *Sunshine and Health*, January 1949, 6.
57. Ibid.
58. Evelyn Rawlings, "Women's Page," *Sunshine and Health*, June 1947, 28.
59. Evelyn Zimmerman, "Women's Page," *Sunshine and Health*, July 1947, 22.
60. Ibid.
61. Ibid.
62. Mary Columbus, "Why We Women Went to Camp," *Sunshine and Health*, April 1952, 15–16.
63. Ibid., 15.
64. Ibid., 16.
65. Zimmerman, "Women's Page," 22.
66. For example, see Dwight King, "Just Elsie and I," *Sunshine and Health*, September 1947, 7; Mrs. H. A. Brich, "I'm Glad I Learned," *Sunshine and Health*, June 1948, 7; Ireene Bringle, "Why All the Excitement," *Sunshine and Health*, August 1948, 11; Edgar Allamon, "In Spite of Herself," *Sunshine and Health*, December 1948, 7; Bonnie and Norm, "Our First Experience as Nudists," *Sunshine and Health*, December 1949, 7; Ben and Esther, "How a Peace Officer and His Family Became Nudists," *Sunshine and Health*, February 1950, 14; Eleanor, "I Discover a New World," *Sunshine and Health*, May 1950, 11; Captain Alan Rogers, "How My Family Became Nudists," *Sunshine and Health*, June 1950, 14; Ken Price, "A Vacation for Mother," *Sunshine and Health*, April 1955, 7.
67. "For Women Only—A Childhood Vow," *Sunshine and Health*, March 1949, 21.
68. Sylvia Ward, "Women's Page: Does Your Child Crave Sex Information?," *Sunshine and Health*, October 1947, 21.
69. "Our Women's Own Page—Your Obstetrician May Be Too Impersonal," *Sunshine and Health*, April 1948, 19.
70. Margaret A. B. Pulis, "Eat Healthy and Like It," *Sunshine and Health*, April 1948, 21.
71. "Marge's Mail Mart," *Sunshine and Health*, September 1956, 22.
72. Dick Falcon, "Trim & Firm Those Hips and Thighs," *Sunshine and Health*, July 1959, 10.

73. John Garrison, "Some Nudist Women I Have Known," *Sunshine and Health*, June 1948, 7.

74. Geib, "Sociology of a Social Movement," 22. Donald Johnson, an official of the American Sunbathing Association and of the Eastern Sunbathing Association, offered Geib "photostats of canceled checks, court orders and judgments, notarized testimonies, and similar evidence" to corroborate these accusations (ibid.).

75. Margaret A. B. Pulis, "President's Message," *Sunshine and Health*, December 1948, 25.

76. Ibid.

77. Margaret A. B. Pulis, "One Mother to Another," *Sunshine and Health*, December 1947, 6.

78. Geib, "Sociology of a Social Movement," 43. Although Geib does not disclose the actual name of the camp at which he did his fieldwork, one can deduce from the location he describes that this is more than likely Sunshine Park, the national headquarters of the American Sunbathing Association.

79. Ibid.

80. Ibid., 52.

81. Ibid., 50.

82. Ibid., 52.

83. Kevin Mumford, *Interzones: Black/White Sex Districts in Chicago and New York in the Early Twentieth Century* (New York: Columbia University Press, 1997); Eileen Boris, "'You Wouldn't Want One of 'Em Dancing with Your Wife': Racialized Bodies on the Job in World War II," *American Quarterly* 50, no. 1 (1998): 77–108; Philip Jenkins, *Moral Panic: Changing Concepts of the Child Molester in Modern America* (New Haven: Yale University Press, 1998), 95–98.

84. "Editorial Comment: Is There a Color Line in Nudism?," *Sunshine and Health*, June 1943, 9.

85. "Reader's Forum: For Racial Segregation," *Sunshine and Health*, January 1946, 3.

86. Ibid.

87. Herbert Nipson, "Nudism and Negroes," *Ebony*, March 1951, 94.

88. Ibid.

89. Ibid.

90. Linus Hogenmiller, "Speaking of Nudism," *Sunshine and Health*, August 1937, 22; E. J. Samuel, "On Negro Nudism," *Sunshine and Health*, August 1945, 21.

91. Glenn Vernam, "Man's Oldest Enemy," *Sunshine and Health*, May 1944, 19.

92. Ibid.

93. Ibid

94. Ibid.

95. For other work that examines the naturalized "savage," see Jennifer L. Morgan, "'Some Could Suckle over Their Shoulder': Male Travelers, Female Bodies, and the Gendering of Racial Ideology, 1550–1770," *William and Mary Quarterly*, 3rd ser., 54, no. 1 (1997): 167–192; Londa Schiebinger, *Nature's Body: Gender in the*

Making of Modern Science (Boston: Beacon, 1993); Sander L. Gilman, "Black Bodies, White Bodies: Toward and Iconography of Female Sexuality in Late Nineteenth-Century Art, Medicine, and Literature," *Critical Inquiry* 12, no. 1 (1985): 204–242; Catherine A. Lutz and Jane L. Collins, *Reading National Geographic* (Chicago: University of Chicago Press, 1993), 172–179.

96. Linus Hogenmiller, "Speaking of Nudism," *Sunshine and Health*, August 1937, 22.

97. Alois Knapp, "President's Message," *Sunshine and Health*, June 1943, 25.

98. Ibid.

99. Ibid.

100. Beth L. Bailey and David Farber, "The 'Double V' Campaign in World War II Hawaii: African Americans, Racial Ideology, and Federal Power," *Journal of Social History* 26, no. 4 (1993): 817.

101. Lewis Harding White, "Western Secretary: The Scopes and Aims of Modern Nude Culture," *Sunshine and Health*, September 1944, 25–26.

102. E. J. Samuels, "Light Out of Darkness," *Sunshine and Health*, November 1944, 19.

103. Ibid.

104. Ibid.

105. Nipson, "Nudism and Negroes," 93.

106. Ibid.

107. Ibid.

108. "Editorial Comment: Is There a Color Line in Nudism?," 9.

109. Steve Brenton, "A Plan for Colored Nudists," *Sunshine and Health*, June 1945, 7.

110. Ibid.

111. "Editorial Comment: Is There a Color Line in Nudism?," 9.

112. E. J. Samuels, "On Negro Nudism," *Sunshine and Health*, August 1945, 21.

113. Ibid.

114. Ibid.

115. Ibid.

116. Ibid.

117. "Letter to the Editor: Opposes Segregation," *Sunshine and Health*, October 1945, 3.

118. Ibid.

119. Ibid.

120. Ibid.

121. Ibid.

122. John Jakle, *The Tourist: Travel in Twentieth-Century North America* (Lincoln: University of Nebraska Press, 1985), 185–198; Kathleen Franz, *Tinkering: Consumers Reinvent the Early Automobile* (Philadelphia: University of Pennsylvania Press, 2005).

123. Marguerite S. Shaffer, *See America First: Tourism and National Identity, 1880–1940* (Washington, DC: Smithsonian Institution Press, 2001), 93–168; Daniel M. Wrobel and Patrick T. Long, eds., *Seeing and Being Seen: Tourism in the American West* (Lawrence: Center of the American West, University of Colorado at Boulder / University of Kansas Press, 2001); Hal K. Rothman, *Devil's Bargains:*

Tourism in the Twentieth-Century American West (Lawrence: University of Kansas Press, 1998), 143–167; Jakle, *Tourist*; Susan Sessions Rugh, "Branding Utah: Industrial Tourism in the Postwar American West," *Western Historical Quarterly* 37 (Winter 2006): 445–472; Clark Davis, "From Oasis to Metropolis: Southern California and the Changing Context of American Leisure," *Pacific Historical Review* 61, no. 3 (1992): 357–386; Susan G. Davis, "Landscapes of Imagination: Tourism in Southern California," *Pacific Historical Review* 68, no. 2 (1999): 173–191.

124. Michael B. Smith, "'The Ego Ideal of the Good Camper' and the Nature of Summer Camp," *Environmental History* 11, no. 1 (2006): 70–101; Leslie Paris, "The Adventures of Peanut and Bo: Summer Camps and Early-Twentieth-Century American Girlhood," *Journal of Women's History* 12, no. 4 (2001): 53.

125. On auto-camping, see Jakle, *Tourist*, 152–168.

126. Kenneth Webb saw nudity as the "fifth freedom" in an Eden-like setting that would also be free of fear, want, hunger, and religious persecution; see Smith, "Ego Ideal of the Good Camper," 71; Paris, "Adventures of Peanut and Bo," 53.

127. U.S. Bureau of the Census, *U.S. Census of Population: 1950, Vol. II, Characteristics of the Population, Part 1, U.S. Summer* (Washington, DC: U.S. Government Printing Office, 1953).

128. Ibid.

129. Ibid.

130. Ibid.

131. Ibid.; Alice Kessler-Harris, *A Woman's Wage: Historical Meanings and Social Consequences* (Lexington: University Press of Kentucky, 1990), 81–112.

132. Geib, "Sociology of a Social Movement," 59.

133. Precisely accounting for the number of active nudist camps constitutes a difficult task due to their preference for anonymity and the tendency of the ASA to list dummy clubs in order to boost its numbers and standing. Ibid., 24.

134. Norval Packwood, "A Ruling by the Commissioner of Internal Revenue," *Sunshine and Health*, March 1951, 16.

135. According to Frederick Geib's "Sociology of a Social Movement," the public relations director of the American Sunbathing Association reported that the organization issued seventy-five hundred memberships. Since many of these represented family memberships, allowing two, three, or four individuals to attend different camps across the country, the public relations director estimated that the organization had around twenty thousand active members. Obviously, this number does not include unaffiliated clubs, members of rival organizations, or casual visitors who refrained from officially joining out of fear of exposure. A more accurate number may actually be much larger.

136. Richard White, *"It's Your Misfortune and None of My Own": A History of the American West* (Norman: University of Oklahoma Press, 1991); Donald Worster, *Rivers of Empire: Water, Aridity, and the Growth of the American West* (New York: Pantheon Books, 1985).

137. Geib, "Sociology of a Social Movement," 24.

138. Ibid.

139. See Harold Lawson, "Managing the Camp," *Sunshine and Health*, July 1947, 10; Donald Johnson, "Organizing and Directing a Nudist Camp," *Sunshine and Health*, August 1951, 10; Ilsley Boone, "How to Select a Camp Site," *Sunshine and Health*, February 1949, 19; "So You Want to Build a Camp," *Sunshine and Health*, October 1954, 3.

140. Rev. Boone, after the passage of the 1934 antinudist bill in New York, established Sunshine Park as the national headquarters of the American Sunbathing Association in 1937.

141. Dana, "Sunshine Park: A Nudist Mecca," *Sunshine and Health*, June 1954, 14.

142. "Sunshine Opens," *Sunshine and Health*, August 1946, 12–13.

143. Ibid.

144. Dana, "Sunshine Park: A Nudist Mecca," 14.

145. Ken Price, "Sunshine Park—1957," *Sunshine and Health*, August 1957, 6.

146. Ibid.

147. Ibid.

148. Ibid.

149. Jakle, *Tourist*, 195–198.

150. "So You Want to Build a Camp," 3.

151. Ibid.

152. Harold Palmer, "Heating and Filtering Swimming Pools," *Sunshine and Health*, June 1951, 7.

153. Dana, "Sunshine Park: A Nudist Mecca," 14.

154. "Sunshine Park—1957," 6.

155. Ed Lange, "The Nudist National Game," *Sunshine and Health*, July 1951, 19.

156. Ibid.

157. "Sunshine Park—1957," 6.

158. Ibid.

159. Christopher Bernard, "Play Areas Need Planning Too," *Sunshine and Health*, August 1955, 9.

160. Ibid.

161. "Sunshine Park—1957," 6.

162. Bernard, "Play Areas Need Planning Too," 9.

163. "Sunshine Park—1957," 6.

164. Ibid.

165. Ibid.

166. Lillian Wright, "The New Look at Sunshine Park," *Sunshine and Health*, August 1961, 2.

167. Ibid., 2.

168. "Sunshine Park—1957," 6.

169. Ibid.

170. Ibid.

171. Ibid.

172. Ibid.

173. Ibid.

174. Christopher Bernard, "The Trailer Park Alternative to Cabins," *Sunshine and Health*, September 1954, 12.

175. Ibid.

176. Ibid.

177. Ibid.

178. "Sunshine Park—1957," 6.

179. For one example of these frequent advertisements, see "Plan Now for a Visit to SUNSHINE PARK," *Sunshine and Health*, July 1950, 26.

180. Packwood, "Ruling by the Commissioner of Internal Revenue," 16.

181. Phillip Warren, "Here's Switch: Make Taxpayer Out of a Nudist: U.S. Rules Exposure Is a Social Activity," *Chicago Tribune*, November 11, 1953, B1.

182. Elmer Adams and Lucille Adams, "The Sunshine Gardens Health Resort," *Sunshine and Health*, July 1951, 2.

183. Ibid.

184. Lucille Adams and Elmer Adams, "Sunshine Gardens Report," *Sunshine and Health*, July 1953, 4.

185. Ibid.

186. "The Preacher and the Nudists," *Time* 64 (August 16, 1954): 46.

187. Ibid.

188. Ibid.

189. Ibid.

190. "Loaded for Bare, Nudists Toss Prying Preacher Out of Eden," *Battle Creek Enquirer*, August 1954; "Nudist Parents Do Not Know Best, Preacher Says," *New York Daily News*, January 16, 1955, 36; "Latest News about the Battle Creek Case," *Bulletin* 5, no. 12 (December 1956): 1.

191. *Michigan v. Hildabridle* (1956), Appellant Brief, 6, State Law Library, Library of Michigan, Lansing, Michigan.

192. "4 Seized in Nudist Raid Are Bound Over for Trial," *Battle Creek Enquirer*, July 11, 1956; "Clio Nudist among Four Free on Bond," *Flint Journal*, September 16, 1956.

193. *Michigan v. Hildabridle*, Appellant Brief, 7.

194. Ibid., 10.

195. "Board of Trustees Act on Important Motions," *Bulletin* 5, no. 11 (November 1956): 1.

196. *Michigan v. Hildabridle*, Appellant Brief, 9; Jenkins, *Moral Panic*, 91–93.

197. Alan Reitman, memorandum to the files, September 27, 1956, Box 777, folder 3, *Michigan v. Hildabridle*, 1958, American Civil Liberties Union Archives 1950–1990, History and Philosophy Library, University of Illinois at Urbana-Champaign (hereafter cited as ACLU/UIUC); "Some More Figures on Battle Creek Drive," *Bulletin* 5, no. 12 (December 1956): 4; Norval Packwood to Patrick Murphy Malin, September 1956, Box 777, folder 3, *Michigan v. Hildabridle*, 1958, ACLU/UIUC;

Alan Reitman to Arthur Donelson, September 25, 1956, Box 777, folder 3, *Michigan v. Hildabridle* 1958, ACLU/UIUC.

198. *Michigan v. Hildabridle*, Appellant Brief, 33.

199. *Hildabridle v. Michigan* (1956), Amicus Curiae Brief of the American Sunbathing Association, Inc., 11, State Law Library, Library of Michigan, Lansing, Michigan.

200. Ibid., 11.

201. Ibid., 35.

202. Ibid., 36.

203. Ibid., 40.

204. Jenkins, *Moral Panic*, 72.

205. See *Michigan v. Hildabridle* (1956), Brief of the People of the State of Michigan, 9, 15, 16, 18, 20, 21, State Law Library, Library of Michigan, Lansing, Michigan.

206. Ibid., 20.

207. John Howard, *Men Like That: A Southern Queer History* (Chicago: University of Chicago Press, 1999), 35.

208. *Michigan v. Hildabridle*, Brief of the People of the State of Michigan, 18–19.

209. Ibid., 15.

210. Ibid.

211. Ibid., 9.

212. *Michigan v. Hildabridle* (1956), Appendix, 7a, State Law Library, Library of Michigan, Lansing, Michigan.

213. Ibid.

214. Ibid., 8a.

215. Jenkins, *Moral Panic*, 93.

216. *Michigan v. Hildabridle*, 353 Mich. 562, 587 (1958).

217. Ibid., 583.

218. Leslie J. Reagan, *When Abortion Was a Crime: Women, Medicine, and Law in the United States, 1867–1973* (Berkeley: University of California Press, 1997), 166; Lawrence M. Friedman, *Crime and Punishment in American History* (New York: Basic Books, 1993), 303.

219. *Michigan v. Hildabridle*, 353 Mich. at 587.

220. Jon L. Breen, *Novel Verdicts: A Guide to Courtroom Fiction*, 2nd ed. (Lanham, MD: Scarecrow, 1999), 212; Robert Traver [John D. Voelker], *Anatomy of a Murder* (New York: St. Martin's, 1958).

221. Eileen Kavanagh, "Robert Traver as Justice Voelker—The Novelist as Judge," *Scribes Journal of Legal Writing* 10, no. 91 (2005): 92; Robert Traver [John D. Voelker], *The Jealous Mistress* (Boston: Little, Brown, 1968), 79–93.

222. Kavanagh, "Robert Traver as Justice Voelker," 93.

223. Ibid., 123.

224. *Michigan v. Hildabridle*, 353 Mich. at 578.

225. Samuel Walker, *In Defense of American Liberties: A History of the ACLU* (Carbondale: Southern Illinois University Press, 1999), 117–157; G. Theodore Mitau, *Decade of Decision: The Supreme Court and the Constitutional Revolution,*

1954–1964 (New York: Scribner, 1967); Richard H. Sayler, Barry B. Boyer, and Robert E. Gooding, eds., *The Warren Court: A Critical Analysis* (New York: Chelsea House, 1980).

226. Kavanagh, "Robert Traver as Justice Voelker," 97.

227. *Michigan v. Hildabridle*, 353 Mich. at 592–593.

228. Ibid., 567.

229. Ibid.

230. Ibid.

231. Ibid., 582.

232. Ibid.

233. Benjamin Spock, "Dr. Spock Talks with Mothers," *Ladies' Home Journal,* September 1955, 26–38. Also See Dr. Spock's discussion of "parental nudity" in the home in his *The Common Sense Book of Baby and Child Care* (New York: Duell, Sloan, and Pearce, 1957), 379–380.

234. Spock, "Dr. Spock Talks with Mothers," 34.

235. *Michigan v. Hildabridle*, 353 Mich. at 591.

236. Ibid.

237. Ibid., 584.

238. "Feature Press Service, Weekly Bulletin # 1971," November 17, 1958, Box 777, folder 3, *Michigan v. Hildabridle*, 1958, ACLU/UIUC.

239. Ibid.

240. No articles covering the *Hildabridle* decision appeared in the *Detroit Free Press*, the *Chicago Tribune*, the *New York Times*, the *Washington Post*, the *Los Angeles Times*, or the *Hartford Courier* in the days after the Michigan Supreme Court reached its decision on September 9, 1958.

241. Kavanagh, "Robert Traver as Justice Voelker," 92.

Chapter 5: Pornography versus Nudism

1. William O'Brien, in "Official Transcript of Proceedings before the Post Office Department," 93, U.S. District Court for DC, Civil Action No. 74-55, *Sunshine Book Co. v. Summerfield*, Box 1578, tabbed, 16W3/17/32/02, RG 21, National Archives and Records Administration, College Park, Maryland.

2. "Publisher's Desk—In Temporary Mourning," *Sunshine and Health*, May 1947, 1.

3. The American Civil Liberties Union formed in response to the Red Scare of 1919 in order to oppose antiunion government policies and to defend the civil liberties of political radicals. Samuel Walker, *In Defense of American Liberties: A History of the ACLU* (Carbondale: Southern Illinois University Press, 1999), 11–45; Judy Kutulas, *The American Civil Liberties Union and the Making of Modern Liberalism, 1930–1960* (Chapel Hill: University of North Carolina Press, 2006), 1–15.

4. Joanne J. Meyerowitz, *How Sex Changed: A History of Transsexuality in the United States* (Cambridge: Harvard University Press, 2002); Martin Meeker, *Contacts Desired: Gay and Lesbian Communications and Community, 1940s–1970s* (Chicago: University of Chicago Press, 2006).

5. Calvin W. Hassell, "In the Matter of the Mailability of the May and July 1948 Issues of 'Sunshine and Health' under the Provisions of 18 U.S. Code 334," Box 759, folder 2, *Sunshine and Health* 1947–50, American Civil Liberties Union Archives 1950–1990, History and Philosophy Library, University of Illinois at Urbana-Champaign (hereafter cited as ACLU/UIUC).

6. Andrea Friedman, "Sadists and Sissies: Anti-pornography Campaigns in Cold War America," *Gender & History* 15, no. 2 (August 2003): 201–227.

7. O'Brien, in "Official Transcript of Proceedings before the Post Office Department," 79–80.

8. Hassell, "In the Matter of the Mailability," 7.

9. Ibid.

10. Ibid.

11. Jeffrey P. Moran, *Teaching Sex: The Shaping of Adolescence in the 20th Century* (Cambridge: Harvard University Press, 2000), 118–155; Susan K. Freeman, *Sex Goes to School: Girls and Sex Education before the 1960s* (Urbana: University of Illinois Press, 2008).

12. Hassell, "In the Matter of the Mailability," 6.

13. Ibid.

14. Harold Lenenthal to Cliff Forester, Official Correspondence, 1948, Box 759, folder 2, *Sunshine and Health* 1947–50, ACLU/UIUC.

15. Ibid.

16. Hassell, "In the Matter of the Mailability," 18.

17. Ibid.

18. Lenenthal to Forester.

19. Philip Jenkins, *Moral Panic: Changing Concepts of the Child Molester in Modern America* (New Haven: Yale University Press, 1998), 90–93.

20. "Initial Decision and Recommendations of Hearing Examiner," U.S. District Court for DC, Civil Action No. 74-55, *Sunshine Book Co. v. Summerfield*, Box 1578, tabbed, 16W3/17/32/02, RG 21, National Archives and Records Administration, College Park, Maryland, 6.

21. Ibid., 5.

22. Roger Baldwin, "Affidavit: In the Matter of Sunshine and Health, May 1948 Issue," June 1948, annex A, Box 759, folder 3, *Sunshine and Health* Cont., ACLU/UIUC.

23. Ibid.

24. Roger Baldwin to Elmer Rice, January 7, 1948, Box 759, folder 2, *Sunshine and Health* 1947–50, ACLU/UIUC.

25. Baldwin, "Affidavit," annex A.

26. Robert Searle to Roger Baldwin, June 1948, annex A, Box 759, folder 3, *Sunshine and Health* Cont., ACLU/UIUC.

27. Evans Clark to Roger Baldwin, June 1948, annex A, ibid.

28. Cecig B. Corwin to Roger Baldwin, June 1948, annex A, ibid.

29. James Truslow Adams to Roger Baldwin, June 1948, annex A, ibid.

30. Dorothy Kenyon to Roger Baldwin, June 1948, annex A, ibid.

31. John Marquand to Roger Baldwin, June 1948, annex A, ibid.
32. Ilsley Boone to Roger Baldwin, October 14, 1947, Box 759, folder 2, *Sunshine and Health*, 1947–50, ACLU/UIUC.
33. Elmer Rice to Roger Baldwin, January 2, 1948, ibid.
34. *Sunshine and Health*, July 1947, 14–15.
35. Catherine A. Lutz and Jane L. Collins, *Reading "National Geographic"* (Chicago: University of Chicago Press, 1993), 172–178.
36. *Sunshine and Health*, February 1955, 14.
37. "Nude Bodies Pose Problem," *New York Amsterdam News*, June 28, 1947.
38. William Graham Sumner, *Folkways: A Study of the Sociological Importance of Usages, Manners, Customs, Mores, and Morals* (New York: Dover, 1906), 446.
39. Weston LaBarre, "Obscenity: An Anthropological Appraisal," *Law & Contemporary Problems* 20 (1955): 533.
40. Ibid.
41. Quoted in Friedman, "Sadists and Sissies," 216.
42. *Summerfield v. Sunshine Book Company*, 221 F. 2d 42 (D.C. Cir. 1954).
43. Ibid.
44. Ibid.
45. Ibid
46. Luther Huston, "Post Office Power as Censor Curbed," *New York Times*, December 17, 1954, 22.
47. *Sunshine Book Company v. Summerfield*, 128 F. Supp. 564, 567 (1955).
48. Ibid., 571–572.
49. Peter Stearns, *Fat History: Bodies and Beauty in the Modern West* (New York: NYU Press, 1997), 71– 88.
50. *Sunshine Book Company v. Summerfield*, 128 F. Supp. at 570–571.
51. Joan Jacobs Brumberg, *The Body Project: An Intimate History of American Girls* (New York: Vintage Books, 1997), 108–109; Marilyn Yalom, *A History of the Breast* (New York: Knopf, 1997), 191–202.
52. John Rogge, in "Official Transcript of Proceedings before the Post Office Department," 58–59.
53. O'Brien, in ibid., 46–47.
54. Ibid., 29–30.
55. *Sunshine Book Company v. Summerfield*, 128 F. Supp. at 573.
56. Ibid., 571.
57. David K. Johnson, "Physique Pioneers: The Politics of 1960s Gay Consumer Culture," *Journal of Social History* 43, no. 4 (2010): 867–892; Maria Wyke, "Herculean Muscle! The Classicizing Rhetoric of Body-building," *Arion* 4 (1997): 59–60.
58. Thomas Waugh, *Hard to Imagine: Gay Male Eroticism in Photography and Film from Their Beginnings to Stonewall* (New York: Columbia University Press, 1996), 9.
59. *Sunshine Book Company v. Summerfield*, 128 F. Supp. at 571.

60. Ibid., 570.
61. Ibid., 571.
62. Benjamin Spock, *The Common Sense Book of Baby and Child Care* (New York: Duell, Sloan, and Pearce, 1957), 379.
63. Henry Jenkins, "The Sensuous Child: Benjamin Spock and the Sexual Revolution," in *The Children's Culture Reader*, ed. Henry Jenkins (New York: NYU Press, 1998), 209–230.
64. *Sunshine Book Company v. Summerfield*, 128 F. Supp. at 570, 573.
65. *Roth v. United States*, 354 U.S. 476, 495 (1957).
66. "Dealer in Obscenity Gets a 5-Year Term," *New York Times*, February 8, 1956, 26.
67. Walker, *In Defense of American Liberties*, 234.
68. *Roth v. United States*, 354 U.S. at 484, 487, 488 (1957).
69. Ibid., 489.
70. Ibid., 513.
71. *Sunshine Book Company v. Summerfield*, 101 U.S. App D.C. 358 (1957).
72. On the same basis, the Court also ruled in favor of nudist magazines in *Mounce v. United States*, 355 U.S. 180 (1957), a companion case that involved the seizure of imported magazines.
73. *Roth v. United States*, 354 U.S. at 495.
74. *Excelsior Pictures Corp. v. Regents of the University of the State of New York*, 165 N.Y.S. 2d 42, Record on Appeal, April 4, 1957, 3, Records of Higher State Courts, New York State Archives, Albany, New York.
75. "Garden of Eden," Box 776, folder 24, *Garden of Eden*, ACLU/UIUC.
76. "Best L.A. Labor Day Biz in 5 Yrs.; Dragnet Hooking Sock $56,400, 3 Sites; Egyptian Big 40G, Eden 19G," *Variety*, September 8, 1954, 8.
77. Barbara Wilinsky, "'A Thinly Disguised Art Veneer Covering a Filthy Sex Picture': Discourses on Art Houses in the 1950s," *Film History* 8, no. 2 (1996): 143–158.
78. Edward De Grazia, *Banned Films: Movies, Censors, and the First Amendment* (New York: Bowker, 1982), 97; Frank Walsh, *Sin and Censorship: The Catholic Church and the Motion Picture Industry* (New Haven: Yale University Press, 1996), 241–328; Gregory D. Black, *Hollywood Censored: Morality Codes, Catholics and the Movies* (Cambridge: Cambridge University Press, 1994).
79. Eric Schaefer, *"Bold! Daring! Shocking! True!": A History of Exploitation Films, 1919–1959* (Durham: Duke University Press, 1999), 95.
80. Ibid.
81. *Excelsior Pictures Corp v. Regents of the University of the State of New York*, Record on Appeal, 3.
82. Ibid.
83. Ibid.
84. Schaefer, *"Bold! Daring! Shocking! True!,"* 83.
85. "Garden of Eden: The First Motion Picture to Bear the Seal of Approval of the Great American Sunbathing Association," *American Nudist Leader* 35 (1954): 6–9.
86. Ibid.

87. *New York World-Telegram and Sun*, December 18, 1957; *Tampa Daily News*, January 27, 1955; *New York Daily Mirror*, December 18, 1957; *New York Times*, December 18, 1957.

88. Linda Williams, *Hard Core: Power, Pleasure, and the "Frenzy of the Visible"* (Berkeley: University of California Press, 1989), 80.

89. Waugh, *Hard to Imagine*.

90. *Excelsior Pictures Corp v. Regents of the University of the State of New York*, 165 N.Y.S. 2d 42, Brief of Petitioner, April 4, 1957, 4, Records of Higher State Courts, New York State Archives, Albany, New York.

91. Ibid., 5.

92. Ibid.

93. Ibid.

94. Ibid., Brief of Petitioner-Respondent, May 3, 1957, 10.

95. Ibid., 11.

96. Ibid.

97. *Excelsior Pictures Corp. v. Regents of the University of the State of New York*, 165 N.Y.S. 2d 42 (1957).

98. Ibid.

99. Ibid.

100. Ibid.

101. Ibid.

102. Ibid.

103. Laura Wittern-Keller, *Freedom of the Screen: Legal Challenges to State Film Censorship, 1915–1981* (Lexington: University Press of Kentucky, 2008), 194.

104. House Committee on Post Office and Civil Service, *Obscene Matter Sent through the Mail: Hearings before the Subcommittee on Postal Operations*, 87th Cong., 1st sess. (1961).

105. Ibid., 2.

106. Ibid.

107. Ibid.

108. *Sunshine and Health*, November 1958, inside cover.

109. Ibid., 9.

110. Ibid., 3.

111. Ibid., 23.

112. Dian Hanson, *Naked as a Jaybird* (Berlin: Taschen, 2003), 26.

113. House Committee on Post Office and Civil Service, *Obscene Matter Sent through the Mail*, 104.

114. Ibid., 106.

115. Ibid.

116. Ibid.

117. See the annotated bibliography of nudist publication in the appendix of William E. Hartman, Marilyn Fithian, and Donald Johnson, eds., *Nudist Society: An*

Authoritative, Complete Study of Nudism in America (New York: Crown, 1970), 407–419.

118. Robert Self, "Sex in the City: The Politics of Sexual Liberation in Los Angeles, 1963–79," *Gender & History* 20, no. 2 (2008): 288–311.

119. Schaefer, *"Bold! Daring! Shocking! True!,"* 300.

120. *Nude on the Moon*, directed by Doris Wishman (1961; Something Weird Video, 2009).

121. "Memorandum from Maurice V. Tofani to Mr. Sidney Bernstein," License Application Case Files, 1921–1965—Nude on the Moon, Film Censorship Records, New York State Archives, Albany, New York.

122. Ken Price, "So Far So Bad," *Sunshine and Health*, October 1960, 25.

123. Ibid.

124. Whitney Strub, "The Clearly Obscene and the Queerly Obscene: Heteronormativity and Obscenity in Cold War Los Angeles," *American Quarterly* 60 no. 2 (2008): 386–389.

125. Price, "So Far So Bad," 25.

126. House Committee on Post Office and Civil Service, *Obscene Matter Sent through the Mail*, 289.

127. Ibid.

128. Ibid., 299.

129. Ibid., 300.

130. Ibid., 311–313.

Chapter 6: Free the Beach

1. David Allyn, *Make Love, Not War: The Sexual Revolution, an Unfettered History* (New York: Little, Brown, 2000), 41, 80–81, 132–133; Martin Esslin, "Nudity: Barely the Beginning?," *New York Times*, December 15, 1968, D18.

2. Quoted in Jean Teeters, "Lennon and Nudity," AbsoluteEslewhere.net, http://articles.absoluteelsewhere.net/Articles/lennon_nudity.html (accessed May 16, 2012).

3. Paul O'Neil, "Nudity: Being a Somewhat Scandalized Report on the Growing Urge of More and More Americans to Appear in Public without Any Clothes On," *Life*, October 13, 1967, 107–116.

4. Sam Brinkley, *Getting Loose: Lifestyle Consumption in the 1970s* (Durham: Duke University Press, 2007), 172.

5. William E. Hartman, Marilyn Fithian, and Donald Johnson, eds., *Nudist Society: An Authoritative, Complete Study of Nudism in America* (New York: Crown, 1970); Manfred F. DeMartino, *The New Female Sexuality: The Sexual Practices and Experiences of Social Nudists, "Potential" Nudists, and Lesbians* (New York: Julian, 1969); Martin Weinberg, "The Nudist Management of Respectability" (1970), Kinsey Institute Library, Indiana University, Bloomington, Indiana; Fred Ilfred, Jr., and Roger Lauer, *Social Nudism in*

America (New Haven, CT: College and University Press, 1964); Lawrence Casler, "Some Sociopsychological Observations in a Nudist Camp: A Preliminary Study," *Journal of Social Psychology* 64, no. 2 (1964): 307–323; Leonard Blank and Robert H. Roth, "Voyeurism and Exhibitionism," *Perceptual and Motor Skills* 24 (1967): 391–400.

6. Albert Ellis, *If This Be Sexual Heresy* (New York: Lyle Stuart, 1963), 66.

7. Whitney Strub, *Perversion for Profit: The Politics of Pornography and the Rise of the New Right* (New York: Columbia University Press, 2011), 146.

8. Gretchen Lemke-Santangelo, *Daughters of Aquarius: Women of the Sixties Counterculture* (Lawrence: University Press of Kansas, 2009), 66.

9. Ibid., 71.

10. Brinkley, *Getting Loose*, 177.

11. "Dr. Ilsley Boone, Nudist, 89, Dead: A Founder of Movement in U.S. Was a Baptist Pastor," *New York Times*, December 12, 1968, 47.

12. "Maurice Parmelee, Economist Ousted for Nudism Stand, Dies," *New York Times*, March 28, 1969, 50.

13. Cec Cinder, *The Nudist Idea* (Riverside, CA: Ultraviolet, 1998), 577.

14. Judy Klemesrud, "Don't Forget to Pack Your Birthday Suit," *New York Times*, August 29, 1971, XX1.

15. Ibid.

16. Hartman, Fithian, and Johnson, *Nudist Society*, 79–82.

17. Ibid., 85.

18. DeMartino, *New Female Sexuality*, 12.

19. Weinberg, "Nudist Management of Respectability," 6.

20. Ibid.

21. "Nudists Reject Liquor," *New York Times*, August 11, 1967, 38; Elliot Carlson, "'Should Nudes Drink': A Dispute Is Bared at Nudist Colonies," *New York Times*, October 21, 1968.

22. John Howard, *Men Like That: A Southern Queer History* (Chicago: University of Chicago Press, 1999), 172–173.

23. Clayton Freese, "Stonehenge News," September 14, 1964, 5, in "New York City Nudism," 1964, Carton 1, folder 33, Sexual Freedom League Records, 1962–1983, BANC MSS 83/181 c, Bancroft Library, University of California–Berkeley (hereafter cited as SFL Records).

24. "Jersey Nudist Park Accused of Refusing to Admit a Negro," *New York Times*, June 16, 1966, 49.

25. "Jersey Nudist Camp Owner Apologizes to Negro Woman," *New York Times*, June 22, 1966, 14.

26. Sarah Schrank, "Naked Houses: The Architecture of Nudism and the Rethinking of the American Suburb," *Journal of Urban History* 38, no. 4 (2012): 635–661.

27. Weinberg, "Nudist Management of Respectability," 6.

28. Allyn, *Make Love, Not War*, 207.

29. Hartman, Fithian, and Johnson, *Nudist Society*, 110–111.

30. DeMartino, *New Female Sexuality*, 130.

31. Jefferson Poland, "Picketing for Sex," in *Sex Marchers*, ed. Jefferson Poland and Sam Sloan (New York: Ishi, 1962), 11.

32. "Sexual Freedom League Handbook," 1968, 1, Carton 1, folder 11, SFL Records.

33. Ibid.

34. Ibid., 4.

35. Ibid., 3.

36. Ibid., 2.

37. Ibid.

38. Ibid.

39. Freese, "Stonehenge News," 6.

40. Ibid.

41. Ibid.

42. A. R. Blazing to Jefferson Poland, August 25, 1964, Carton 1, folder 33, SFL Records.

43. Marlin Ballard to Jefferson Poland, May 27, 1964, Carton 1, folder 33, SFL Records.

44. Jerry Shaw to Jefferson Poland, August 26, 1964, Carton 1, folder 33, SFL Records.

45. Freese, "Stonehenge News," 6.

46. Mac and Ellie Collins to Jefferson Poland, September 18, 1964, Carton 1, folder 33, SFL Records.

47. Poland, "Picketing for Sex," 18–22.

48. "San Francisco Nude-Ins by Jefferson Poland," April 1968, Carton 1, folder 33, SFL Records.

49. Sam Sloan, "Making the League Sexual," in Poland and Sloan, *Sex Marchers*, 87–107.

50. "Free-Sex Movement," *Time*, March 11, 1966, 66.

51. In 1958, Stan Sohler, president of the American Sunbathing Association, organized a gathering of almost one hundred nudists at Davenport Landing, twelve miles north of Santa Cruz, California. Sohler cleared the event, known as "XB-58," with local police, barred alcohol, and denied entry to single men and women. He wanted to demonstrate that public beaches constituted a trouble-free site for nudist activities. Despite an uneventful afternoon of activities, the nudist-club owners who played an influential role in shaping ASA policies found little reason to support nudist activities on public beaches. Cinder, *Nudist Idea*, 587–589.

52. Jefferson Poland, "Committee for Free Beaches," in Poland and Sloan, *Sex Marchers*, 82. The popularity of nude beaches in Europe is discussed in Dagmar Herzog, *Sex after Fascism: Memory and Morality in Twentieth-Century Germany* (Princeton: Princeton University Press, 2005), 203–204.

53. Poland, "Committee for Free Beaches," 82.

54. "Unusable Background on SG," April 1966, Carton 5, folder 19, SFL Records.

55. Poland, "Committee for Free Beaches," 84–85.

56. Ibid., 80.

57. Cinder, *Nudist Idea*, 594.
58. George Chauncey, *Gay New York: Gender, Urban Culture, and the Making of the Gay Male World, 1890–1940* (New York: Basic Books, 1994).
59. Allyn, *Make Love, Not War*, 24–25.
60. Ibid., 157.
61. Ibid., 162.
62. Armistead Maupin, *Tales of the City* (1978; repr., New York: Harper Perennial, 2007), 99.
63. Ibid., 99.
64. Kristi Witker, "The Seaweed Bikini, or, My Day at a California Nudist Beach," *New York Times*, August 29, 1971, XX11; Judith Kinnard, "On Coast, a Trend to Nudity," *New York Times*, June 29, 1972, 44; Doug Smith, "Summer '72: Nude Impact at Beaches," *Los Angeles Times*, October 1, 1972, WS1; "'Dress Optional' for Naked Protest," *Chicago Tribune*, August 18, 1975, 8.
65. Jane Weisman Stein, "Black's Beach: A Gawk in the Sun," *Los Angeles Times*, August 5, 1975, E1.
66. Cal. Pen. Code, § 314, subd. 1.
67. *Chad Merrill Smith v. California*, 7 Cal. 3d 362 (1972).
68. "But at a Secluded Beach: Court OKs Nude Sunbathing," *Los Angeles Times*, June 14 , 1972, A3.
69. Smith, "Summer of '72," WS1.
70. *Chad Merrill Smith v. California*, 7 Cal. 3d 362 (1972).
71. Ibid.
72. Ibid.
73. Judith Kinnard, "On Coast, a Trend to Nudity," *New York Times*, June 29, 1972, 44.
74. Smith, "Summer of '72," WS1.
75. Jane Weisman Stein, "Black's Beach: A Gawk in the Sun: Lawsuit Pending over Swimsuit Optional Zone," *Los Angeles Times*, August 5, 1975, E1.
76. "'Nude Zone' Plan Wins Approval of City Council Unit," *Los Angeles Times*, June 28, 1974, D1.
77. Monica Gray, Michael Waller, and John C. Schaffer, "Nude Sunbathing at Venice Beach," *Los Angeles Times*, June 30, 1974, 12.
78. Cinder, *Nudist Idea*, 607.
79. Leslie J. Reagan, *When Abortion Was a Crime: Women, Medicine, and Law in the United States, 1867–1973* (Berkeley: University of California Press, 1997), 161.
80. Smith, "Summer '72," WS1.
81. Doug Smith, "Nude Bathers Plan Battle for Beach in Venice," *Los Angeles Times*, March 9, 1972, WS1.
82. Ibid.
83. Smith, "Summer '72," WS1.
84. Irv Burleigh, "Letters, Calls Deplore Nudity on City Beaches," *Los Angeles Times*, July 11, 1974, SF1.
85. Ibid.

86. Cinder, *Nudist Idea*, 608–609.

87. Erwin Baker, "'Stroller' Strips, Council Follows with Nudity Ban," *Los Angeles Times*, July 12, 1974, A1.

88. William Farr, "Nude Not Lewd—Only Disruptive," *Los Angeles Times*, October 4, 1947, B1.

89. Ibid.

90. Myrna Oliver, "Judge Upholds Ban on Nudity: Police Make 1st Arrest," *Los Angeles Times*, August 3, 1974, 1.

91. Ibid.

92. "Nude Bathers Move to Reclaim Cape Cod Beach," *New York Times*, August 18, 1975, 23.

93. Lee Baxandall, *World Guide to Nude Beaches and Recreation*, ed. Jan Smith (New York: Stonehill, 1980), 18, 9.

94. Ibid., 9.

95. Ibid.

96. Mark Storey, "The History of the Naturist Society," *Nude & Natural* 28, no. 3 (2009): 24.

97. Ibid., 28.

98. Richard P. Jones, "A Liberating Experience: Skinny-Dippers Get Organized," *Los Angeles Times*, September 9, 1981, F11.

99. Baxandall, *World Guide*, 9.

100. Jones, "Liberating Experience," F11.

101. Ibid.

102. Ibid.

103. Lemke-Santangelo, *Daughters of Aquarius*, 64–65.

104. Sandra Morgan, *Into Our Hands: The Women's Health Movement in the United States* (New Brunswick: Rutgers University Press, 2002).

105. Storey, "History of the Naturist Society," 24.

106. Baxandall, *World Guide*, 12.

107. Ibid., 18.

108. Nikki Craft, "The Nikki Wiki: All About Nikki Craft," November 2008, http://www.nikkicraft.com (accessed October 10, 2011).

109. Nikki Craft, "Liberty Summer," *Clothed with the Sun* 6, no. 2 (1986): 56.

110. Jay Blotcher, "Grin and Bare It: The World of Gay Nudists," *OutWeek*, June 19, 1990, 35.

111. Baxandall, *World Guide*, 38, 87–88.

112. Scott Herring, *Another Country: Queer Anti-Urbanism* (New York: NYU Press, 2010), 68.

113. Blotcher, "Grin and Bare It," 35.

114. Ibid.

115. Ibid.

116. See Andrea Dworkin, *Pornography: Men Possessing Women* (New York: Plume, 1979); Andrea Dworkin and Catharine MacKinnon, *Pornography and Civil Rights:*

A New Day for Women's Equality (Minneapolis, MN: Organizing Against Pornography, 1988).

117. Nikki Craft, "Busting Mr. Short-Eyes," *On the Issues: The Progressive Woman's Quarterly* 4 (Winter 1995): 20.

118. Nikki Craft, "Nudism, 'Naturism,' & Naturism: A Tainted Heritage," *Clothed with the Sun* 6, no. 2 (1986): 76.

119. Ibid., 76.

120. Ibid., 77, 78.

121. Ibid, 78.

122. Lee Baxandall to Ed Lange, December 10, 1987, available online at Nikki Craft's No Status Quo, http://www.nostatusquo.com/ACLU/NudistHallofShame/lange/BaxLange.html (accessed October 10, 2011).

123. See "*Playboy* and Naturism," "Who Pleads for Porn?," and "Citizen Action against Porn," in *Clothed with the Sun* 6, no. 2 (1986): 41–51.

124. Lee Baxandall, "Naturists & The Meese Commission Report," *Clothed with the Sun* 6, no. 2 (1986): 37.

125. Baxandall to Lange, December 10, 1987.

126. Lee Baxandall to Arne Erikson, March 23, 1988, available online at Nikki Craft's No Status Quo, http://www.nostatusquo.com/ACLU/NudistHallofShame/BaxASA.html (accessed October 10, 2011).

127. "Ravings," *Clothed with the Sun* 7, no. 1 (1987): 11.

128. "Joining the Fundamentalists," *Clothed with the Sun* 7, no. 1 (1987): 12.

129. Nikki Craft, "Feminist Plaintiffs Withdraw from Cape Cod Nudity Case," Nudist/Naturist Hall of Shame, http://nudisthallofshame.info/Shirtfree3.html (accessed December 21, 2011).

130. Ibid.

131. Ibid.

132. Lisbeth Lipari, "Dissention Rips Nudists, Feminists," *Provincetown Advocate*, December 22, 1988.

133. Jefferson Poland, "Pedophile Confession," *Nude and Natural* 10, no. 1 (1990): 78.

134. Nikki Craft, "Jefferson Clitlick Freedom Poland: Convicted Naturist Pedophile," Nudist/Naturist Hall of Shame, http://nudisthallofshame.info/Clitlick.html (accessed December 12, 2011).

135. Poland, "Pedophile Confession," 78.

136. Ibid.

137. Ibid.

138. Ibid.

139. Ibid.

140. Craft, "Jefferson Clitlick Freedom Poland."

Epilogue

1. Katie Hafner, "The Boys in the Band Are in AARP: It's a Life of Married Sex, Cholesterol Drugs and Rock 'n' Roll," *New York Times*, June 17, 2007; Jon Pareles,

"Simon and Garfunkel, Together Again, but Worn by Time," *New York Times*, December 3, 2003.

2. Buck Wolf, "Nude Resorts on a Winning Streak," ABC News Online, July 11, 2006, http://abcnews.go.com/Entertainment/WolfFiles/story?id=2206613.

3. Guy Trebay, "All Undressed and So Many Places to Go," *New York Times*, September 2, 2001.

4. John Sikes, Jr., "ASA Becomes American Association for Nude Recreation," *Bulletin* 43, no. 8 (1994): A1.

5. AANR, "There's an (AANR) App for That," February 2, 2011, http://www.aanr.com/downloads/press/?file=958.

6. Deborah Sullivan Brennan, "The State: Pedestrian Bridge Users Can Be Barefoot—or Bare-Bottomed; A Palm Springs Span Lets Nudist Resort Guests Pass Unseen over Busy Indian Canyon Drive," *Los Angeles Times*, February 23, 2003.

7. Evan Perez, "Tourism Expose—Clothing-Optional Resorts Are Taking Off, Targeting Affluent, Au Naturel Crowd," *Wall Street Journal*, January 17, 2003.

8. Cecilia Rasmussen, "It's a Wrap for a Rustic, Remote Nudist Refuge," *Los Angeles Times*, March 4, 2007, 2.

9. Philip Jenkins, *Moral Panic: Changing Conceptions of the Child Molester in Modern America* (New Haven: Yale University Press, 1998), 198.

10. The kidnapping and murder of Polly Klaas from her Petaluma, California, home in 1993 gained national media attention as police and volunteers searched for her body for over two months. The case helped galvanize support for California's three-strikes law since her killer was on parole at the time of the murder. At the federal level, it also helped the passage of legislation such as Megan's Law (Sexual Offender Act of 1994), which required persons convicted of sex crimes against children to notify local law enforcement of any changes in their address or employment after release from prison or a psychiatric facility. President Clinton used these incidents to present himself as an advocate for child safety and to guard against attacks on his own moral character.

11. "Transcripts: What's Wrong with Nude Camps for Teens," aired June 20, 2003, CNN Online, http://edition.cnn.com/TRANSCRIPTS/0306/20/se.18.html (accessed June 4, 2012).

12. Gail Sheehy and Judy Bachrach, "Don't Ask . . . Don't E-mail," *Vanity Fair*, January 2007.

13. Jenkins, *Moral Panic*, 138.

14. Institute of Global Communications, http://www.igc.org.

15. Nudist/Naturist Hall of Shame home page, http://nudisthallofshame.info.

16. Associated Press, "Child Pornographer at Nudist Camp Sentenced," ABC News Online, October 24, 2011, http://abclocal.go.com/story?section=news/state&id=8403013; "Child Porn Nets Prison Term," *Windsor Star*, January 27, 2012, http://www2.canada.com/windsorstar/news/story.html?id=938255c5-31ab-49f9-a8a2-b1bf3fe04d33; "Couple Set Up Nudist Forum Website as Cover for

Paedophile Ring, Court Hears," *Mirror Online*, September 28, 2011, http://www.mirror.co.uk/news/uk-news/couple-set-up-nudist-forum-273632.

17. AANR, "About the American Association for Nude Recreation: Feel the Freedom," http://www.aanr.com/about-aanr (accessed July 24, 2012).

18. Nicky Hoffman, quoted in Ashley Powers, "Nudist Resort's Banning of Children Riles Naturist Community," *Los Angeles Times*, March 30, 2012.

19. Julius, "My Meeting with Desert Sun Resort Owner John Young," nothingtodread.com, http://nothingtodread.com/desert-sun-resort-banning-kids-is-prudent/ (accessed July 24, 2012).

20. AANR, "About the American Association for Nude Recreation."

21. Rebecca Walsh, "Nudist Resort's No Kids Rule the Focus of Lawsuit," *Desert Sun*, March 28, 2012; "Banning Children from a Nudist Resort Is Prudent," *Desert Sun*, April 11, 2012.

22. California Civil Code sec. 51(b), available online at http://leginfo.legislature.ca.gov/faces/codes_displaySection.xhtml?lawCode=CIV&sectionNum=51.

23. Rebecca Walsh "Nudist Resort's No Kids Rule the Focus of Lawsuit," *Desert Sun*, March 28, 2012; "Banning Children from a Nudist Resort Is Prudent," *Desert Sun*, April 11, 2012; Ashley Powers, "Nudist Resort's Banning of Children Riles Naturist Community," *Los Angeles Times*, March 30, 2012.

BIBLIOGRAPHY

Archival Collections

American Civil Liberties Union Archives 1950–1990, History and Philosophy Library, University of Illinois at Urbana-Champaign
    Box 759, folder 2, *Sunshine and Health* 1947–50
    Box 759, folder 3, *Sunshine and Health* Cont.
    Box 776, folder 24, *Garden of Eden*
    Box 777, folder 3, *Michigan v. Hildabridle*, 1958
American Nudist Research Library, Cypress Cove Nudist Resort, Kissimmee, Florida
    American Nudist Leader
    The Bulletin
    Clothed with the Sun
    Legal Records, Correspondence, Personal Papers and News Clippings
    Nude and Natural
    The Nudist (1933–1940)
    Sunshine and Health (1940–1963)
Bancroft Library, University of California–Berkeley
    Sexual Freedom League Records, 1962–1982, BANC MSS 83/181 c
Human Sexuality Collection, Cornell University, Ithaca, New York
    Bruce of L.A. Photographs, ca. 1950–1966, CN 7665
Kinsey Institute Library, Indiana University, Bloomington, Indiana
    Martin Weinberg, "The Nudist Management of Respectability" (1970)
Manuscripts and Archives, Yale University Library, New Haven, Connecticut
    Maurice Parmelee Papers
National Archives and Records Administration, College Park, Maryland
    Parmelee v. United States, Brief on Behalf of Appellant, Ni. 7332, 1939
    Sunshine Book Co. v. Summerfield, Box 1578, tabbed, 16W3/17/32/02, RG 21
New York State Archives, Albany, New York
    Film Censorship Records
    Governor Office Records
    Records of Higher State Courts
State Law Library, Library of Michigan, Lansing, Michigan
    Michigan v. Ring (1934)
        Brief for Appellant
        Brief for Respondent
        Record

Michigan v. Hildabridle (1956)
Amicus Curiae Brief of the American Sunbathing Association, Inc.
Appellant Brief
Appendix
Brief of the People of the State of Michigan

Legal Decisions
Chad Merrill Smith v. California, 7 Cal. 3d 362 (1972)
Excelsior Pictures Corp. v. Regents of the University of the State of New York, 165
    N.Y.S. 2d 42 (1957)
Joseph Burstyn, Inc. v. Wilson, 343 U.S. 495 (1952)
Michigan v. Hildabridle, 353 Mich. 562. (1958)
Michigan v. Ring, 267 Mich. 657 (1934)
Mounce v. United States 355 U.S. 180 (1957)
Parmelee v. United States, 113 F. 2d 729 (1940)
People v. Burke et al., 243 App. Div. 83, 276 N.Y.S. 402 (1934)
Roth v. United States, 354 U.S. 476 (1957)
Summerfield v. Sunshine Book Company, 221 F. 2d 42 (D.C. Cir. 1954)
Sunshine Book Company v. Summerfield, 128 F. Supp. 564 (1955), 101 U.S. App. D.C.
    358 (1957)
United States v. Paramount Pictures, 334 U.S. 131 (1948)

Films
Elysia. Directed by Bryan Foy. 1933. Something Weird Video, 2009.
Forbidden Paradise. Directed by Maximilian Meyer. 1958.
Garden of Eden. Directed by Max Nosseck. 1954. Something Weird Video, 2009.
Nude on the Moon. Directed by Doris Wishman. 1961. Something Weird Video, 2009.
This Nude World. Directed by Michael Mindlin. 1933. Something Weird Video, 2009.
The Unashamed. Directed by Peter McConville. 1938.

Newspapers
Battle Creek Enquirer
Chicago Tribune
Detroit Free Press
Hartford Courant
Los Angeles Times
New York Amsterdam News
New York Daily Mirror
New York Daily News
New York Times
New York World-Telegram
Provincetown Advocate

Tampa Daily News
Washington Post

Congressional Records

Congressman John J. Cochran of New York, speaking in regard to the Dies committee, on April 28, 1942, 77th Cong., 2d sess., 88 Cong. Rec. 3754.

Congressman Edward E. Cox of Georgia, speaking in regard to Maurice Parmelee, on March 30, 1942, House of Representatives, 77th Cong., 2d sess., 88 Cong. Rec. 3204–3205.

Congressman Noah M. Mason of Illinois, speaking in regard to Maurice Parmelee and his *Nudism in Modern Life*, on March 30, 1942, House of Representatives, 77th Cong., 2d sess., 88 Cong. Rec. 3204–3205.

Congressman James F. O'Connor of Montana, speaking in regard to Mr. Dies and his Committee on Un-American Activities, on March 31, 1942, and April 28, 1942, 77th Cong., 2d sess., 88 Cong. Rec. A1282, 3754.

House Committee on Post Office and Civil Service, *Obscene Matter Sent through the Mail: Hearings before the Subcommittee on Postal Operations*, 87th Cong., 1st sess. (1961).

Books and Articles

Allen, Robert Clyde. *Horrible Prettiness: Burlesque and American Culture*. Chapel Hill: University of North Carolina Press, 1991.

Allyn, David. *Make Love, Not War: The Sexual Revolution, an Unfettered History*. Boston: Little, Brown, 2000.

Aron, Cindy S. *Working at Play: A History of Vacations in the United States*. New York: Oxford University Press, 1999.

Bailey, Beth L. *From Front Porch to Back Seat: Courtship in Twentieth-Century America*. Baltimore: Johns Hopkins University Press, 1988.

———. *Sex in the Heartland*. Cambridge: Harvard University Press, 1999.

Bailey, Beth L., and David Farber. "The 'Double-V' Campaign in World War II Hawaii: African Americans, Racial Ideology, and Federal Power." *Journal of Social History* 26, no. 4 (1993): 817–843.

Banet-Weiser, Sarah. *The Most Beautiful Girl in the World: Beauty Pageants and National Identity*. Berkeley: University of California Press, 1999.

Banner, Lois W. *American Beauty*. Chicago: University of Chicago Press, 1984.

"Ban Nudie Pic." *Variety*, December 1933, 14.

Baxandall, Lee. *World Guide to Nude Beaches and Recreation*. Edited by Jan Smith. New York: Stonehill, 1980.

Bederman, Gail. *Manliness and Civilization: A Cultural History of Gender and Race in the United States, 1880–1917*. Chicago: University of Chicago Press, 1995.

Beisel, Nicola. *Imperiled Innocents: Anthony Comstock and Family Reproduction in Victorian America*. Princeton: Princeton University Press, 1997.

———. "Morals versus Art: Censorship, the Politics of Interpretation, and the Victorian Nude." *American Sociological Review* 58, no. 2 (1993): 145–162.

"Benefits of Graduated Sun Bathing on a Troopship, The." *Journal of the American Medical Association* 124, no. 1 (1944): 51.

Bérubé, Allan. *Coming Out under Fire: The History of Gay Men and Women in World War Two*. New York: Free Press, 1990.

"Best L.A. Labor Day Biz in 5 Yrs.: Dragnet Hooking Sock $56,400, 3 Sites; Egyptian Big 40G, Eden 19G." *Variety*, September 8, 1954, 8.

Black, Gregory D. *Hollywood Censored: Morality Codes, Catholics and the Movies*. Cambridge: Cambridge University Press, 1994.

Blank, Leonard, and Robert H. Roth. "Voyeurism and Exhibitionism." *Perceptual and Motor Skills* 24 (1967): 391–400.

Blotcher, Jay. "Grin and Bare It: The World of Gay Nudists." *Outweek*, June 19, 1990, 35.

Boone, Ilsley. *Joys of Nudism*. Binghamton, NY: Greenburg, 1934.

"Boring but Banned." *Variety*, November 21, 1933, 31.

Boris, Eileen. "'You Wouldn't Want One of 'Em Dancing with Your Wife': Racialized Bodies on the Job in World War II." *American Quarterly* 50, no. 1 (1998): 77–108.

Boyer, Paul S. *Purity in Print: Book Censorship in America from the Gilded Age to the Computer Age*. 2nd ed. Madison: University of Wisconsin Press, 2002.

Brandt, Allan M. *No Magic Bullet: A Social History of Venereal Disease in the United States since 1880*. New York: Oxford University Press, 1987.

Breen, Jon L. *Novel Verdicts: A Guide to Courtroom Fiction*. 2nd ed. Lanham, MD: Scarecrow, 1999.

Brinkley, Sam. *Getting Loose: Lifestyle Consumption in the 1970s*. Durham: Duke University Press, 2007.

Brumberg, Joan Jacobs. *The Body Project: An Intimate History of American Girls*. New York: Vintage Books, 1997.

Canaday, Margot. "Building a Straight State: Sexuality and Social Citizenship under the 1944 G.I. Bill." *Journal of American History* 90, no. 3 (December 2003): 935–957.

———. *The Straight State: Sexuality and Citizenship in Twentieth-Century America*. Princeton: Princeton University Press, 2009.

Cartwright, Lisa. *Screening the Body: Tracing Medicine's Visual Culture*. Minneapolis: University of Minnesota Press, 1995.

Casler, Lawrence. "Some Sociopsychological Observations in a Nudist Camp: A Preliminary Study." *Journal of Social Psychology* 64, no. 2 (1964): 307–323.

Cayleff, Susan E. *Wash and Be Healed: The Water-Cure Movement and Women's Health*. Philadelphia: Temple University Press, 1987.

Chauncey, George. *Gay New York: Gender, Urban Culture, and the Making of the Gay Male World, 1890–1940*. New York: Basic Books, 1994.

"Chi Censors Pink 2 Pix; Others Nix 'Elysia,' Nudie." *Variety*, January 1934, 4.

Cinder, Cec. *The Nudist Idea*. Riverside, CA: Ultraviolet, 1998.

Clark, Kenneth. *The Nude: A Study in Ideal Form*. New York: Fantheon, 1956.

Clow, Barbara Natalie. *Negotiating Disease: Power and Cancer Care, 1900–1950*. Montreal: McGill-Queen's University Press, 2001.

Connelly, Mark Thomas. *The Response to Prostitution in the Progressive Era*. Chapel Hill: North Carolina University Press, 1980.

Costigliola, Frank. "'Unceasing Pressure for Penetration': Gender, Pathology, and Emotion in George Kennan's Formation of the Cold War." *Journal of American History* 83, no. 2 (1997): 1309–1339.

Craft, Nikki. "Busting Mr. Short-Eyes." *On the Issues: The Progressive Woman's Quarterly* 4 (Winter 1995): 20.

Cuordileone, K. A. "'Politics in an Age of Anxiety': Cold War Political Culture and the Crisis in American Masculinity, 1949–1960." *Journal of American History* 87, no. 2 (2000): 515–545.

Davis, Clark. "From Oasis to Metropolis: Southern California and the Changing Context of American Leisure." *Pacific Historical Review* 61, no. 3 (1992): 357–386.

Davis, Susan G. "Landscapes of Imagination: Tourism in Southern California." *Pacific Historical Review* 68, no. 2 (1999): 173–191.

Dean, Robert D. *Imperial Brotherhood: Gender and the Making of Cold War Foreign Policy*. Amherst: University of Massachusetts Press, 2001.

De Grazia, Edward. *Banned Films: Movies, Censors, and the First Amendment*. New York: Bowker, 1982.

———. *Censorship Landmarks*. New York: Bowker, 1969.

DeMartino, Manfred F. *The New Female Sexuality: The Sexual Practices and Experiences of Social Nudists, "Potential" Nudists, and Lesbians*. New York: Julian, 1969.

D'Emilio, John. "The Homosexual Menace: The Politics of Sexuality in Cold War America." In *Passion and Power: Sexuality in History*, edited by Kathy Peiss and Christina Simmons, with Robert A. Padgug, 226–240. Philadelphia: Temple University Press, 1989.

———. *Lost Prophet: The Life and Times of Bayard Rustin*. New York: Free Press, 2003.

———. *Sexual Politics, Sexual Communities: The Making of a Homosexual Minority in the United States, 1940–1970*. 2nd ed. Chicago: University of Chicago Press, 1998.

D'Emilio, John, and Estelle Freedman. *Intimate Matters: A History of Sexuality in America*. 2nd ed. Chicago: University of Chicago Press, 1997.

"Dies in the Spring." *Nation*, April 1, 1942, 385–386.

Donegan, Jane B. *"Hydropathic Highway to Health": Women and Water-Cure in Antebellum America*. Westport, CT: Greenwood, 1986.

Dubinsky, Karen. *The Second Greatest Disappointment: Honeymooning and Tourism at Niagara Falls*. New Brunswick: Rutgers University Press, 1999.

Duggan, Lisa. *Sapphic Slashers: Sex, Violence, and American Modernity*. Durham: Duke University Press, 2000.

Dworkin, Andrea. *Pornography: Men Possessing Women*. New York: Plume, 1979.

Dworkin, Andrea, and Catharine MacKinnon. *Pornography and Civil Rights: A New Day for Women's Equality*. Minneapolis, MN: Organizing Against Pornography, 1988.

Ellis, Albert. *If This Be Sexual Heresy*. New York: Lyle Stuart, 1963.

Erenberg, Lewis A. *Steppin' Out: New York Nightlife and the Transformation of American Culture, 1890–1930*. Westport, CT: Greenwood, 1981.

Faderman, Lillian, and Stuart Timmons. *Gay L.A.: A History of Sexual Outlaws, Power Politics, and Lipstick Lesbians*. New York: Basic Books, 2006.

Fields, Jill. *An Intimate Affair: Women, Lingerie, and Sexuality*. Berkeley: University of California Press, 2007.

Franz, Kathleen. *Tinkering: Consumers Reinvent the Early Automobile*. Philadelphia: University of Pennsylvania Press, 2005.

Freedman, Estelle B. "'Uncontrolled Desires': The Response to the Sexual Psychopath, 1920–1960." *Journal of American History* 74, no. 1 (1987): 83–106.

Freeman, Susan K. *Sex Goes to School: Girls and Sex Education before the 1960s*. Urbana: University of Illinois Press, 2008.

"Free-Sex Movement." *Time*, March 11, 1966, 66.

Freud, Sigmund. *Inhibitions, Symptoms and Anxiety*. London: L. and Virginia Woolf at the Hogarth Press and the Institute of Psycho-analysis, 1936.

Freund, Daniel. *American Sunshine: Diseases of Darkness and the Quest for Natural Light*. Chicago: University of Chicago Press, 2012.

Friedman, Andrea. "'The Habitats of Sex-Craved Perverts': Campaigns against Burlesque in Depression-Era New York City." *Journal of the History of Sexuality* 7, no. 2 (1996): 203–238.

———. *Prurient Interests: Gender, Democracy, and Obscenity in New York City, 1909–1945*. New York: Columbia University Press, 2000.

———. "Sadists and Sissies: Anti-pornography Campaigns in Cold War America." *Gender & History* 15, no. 2 (2003): 201–227.

———. "The Smearing of Joe McCarthy: The Lavender Scare, Gossip, and Cold War Politics." *American Quarterly* 57, no. 4 (2005): 1105–1129.

Friedman, Lawrence M. *Crime and Punishment in American History*. New York: Basic Books, 1993.

Furlough, Ellen. "Packaging Pleasures: Club Méditerranée and French Consumer Culture, 1950–1968." *French Historical Studies* 18, no. 1 (1993): 65–81.

Gallagher, Hugh Gregory. *FDR's Splendid Deception*. New York: Dodd, Mead, 1985.

Gardella, Peter. *Innocent Ecstasy: How Christianity Gave America an Ethic of Sexual Pleasure*. New York: Oxford University Press, 1985.

Garrow, David J. *Liberty and Sexuality: The Right to Privacy and the Making of "Roe v. Wade."* New York: Macmillan, 1994.

Gay, Jan. *On Going Naked*. Garden City, NY: Garden City, 1932.

Geib, Frederick Arthur. "The Sociology of a Social Movement." Master's thesis, Brown University, 1956.

Gilbert, James. *A Cycle of Outrage: America's Reaction to the Juvenile Delinquent in the 1950s*. New York: Oxford University Press, 1986.

Gilfoyle, Timothy J. *City of Eros: New York City, Prostitution, and the Commercialization of Sex, 1790–1920*. New York: Norton, 1992.

Gilman, Sander L. "Black Bodies, White Bodies: Toward an Iconography of Female Sexuality in Late Nineteenth-Century Art, Medicine, and Literature." *Critical Inquiry* 12, no. 1 (1985): 204–242.

Gilmore, Leigh. "Obscenity, Modernity, Identity: Legalizing *The Well of Loneliness* and *Nightwood*." *Journal of the History of Sexuality* 4, no. 4 (1994): 603–624.

Goldstein, Michael S. *The Health Movement: Promoting Fitness in America*. New York: Twayne, 1992.

Gordon, Linda. *Heroes of Their Own Lives: The Politics and History of Family Violence, 1880–1960*. New York: Viking, 1988.

———. *Woman's Body, Woman's Right: A Social History of Birth Control in America*. New York: Grossman, 1976.

Hall, G. Stanley. *Adolescence: Its Psychology and Its Relations to Physiology, Anthropology, Sociology, Sex, Crime, Religion and Education*. New York: D. Appleton, 1905.

Hanson, Dian. *Naked as a Jaybird*. Berlin: Taschen, 2002.

Hartman, William E., Marilyn Fithian, and Donald Johnson, eds. *Nudist Society: An Authoritative, Complete Study of Nudism in America*. New York: Crown, 1970.

Hau, Michael. *The Cult of Health and Beauty in Germany: A Social History, 1890–1930*. Chicago: University of Chicago Press, 2003.

Heap, Chad. *Slumming: Sexual and Racial Encounters in American Nightlife, 1885–1940*. Chicago: University of Chicago Press, 2009.

Hegarty, Marilyn. *Victory Girls, Khaki-Wackies, and Patriotutes: The Regulation of Female Sexuality during World War II*. New York: NYU Press, 2007.

Heins, Marjorie. *Not in Front of the Children: "Indecency," Censorship, and the Innocence of Youth*. New York: Hill and Wang, 2001.

Herring, Scott. *Another Country: Queer Anti-Urbanism*. New York: NYU Press, 2010.

Herzog, Dagmar. *Sex after Fascism: Memory and Morality in Twentieth-Century Germany*. Princeton: Princeton University Press, 2005.

Hodes, Martha, ed. *Sex, Love, Race: Crossing Boundaries in North American History*. New York: NYU Press, 1999.

Hollander, Anne. *Seeing through Clothes*. New York: Viking, 1975.

Horowitz, Helen Lefkowitz. *Rereading Sex: Battles over Sexual Knowledge and Suppression in Nineteenth-Century America*. New York: Knopf, 2002.

Howard, John. *Men Like That: A Southern Queer History*. Chicago: University of Chicago Press, 1999.

Ilfred, Fred, Jr., and Roger Lauer. *Social Nudism in America*. New Haven, CT: College and University Press, 1964.

Jakle, John A. *The Tourist: Travel in Twentieth-Century North America*. Lincoln: University of Nebraska Press, 1985.

Jenkins, Henry. "The Sensuous Child: Benjamin Spock and the Sexual Revolution." In *The Children's Culture Reader*, edited by Henry Jenkins, 209–230. New York: NYU Press, 1998.

Jenkins, Philip. *Moral Panic: Changing Concepts of the Child Molester in Modern America*. New Haven: Yale University Press, 1998.

Johnson, David K. *The Lavender Scare: The Cold War Persecution of Gays and Lesbians in the Federal Government.* Chicago: University of Chicago Press, 2006.

———. "Physique Pioneers: The Politics of 1960s Gay Consumer Culture." *Journal of Social History* 43, no. 4 (2010): 867–892.

Josephs, Kermit. "The Homosexual Nudist." *One* 7, no. 4 (1959): 26–27.

Juhnke, Eric S. *Quacks and Crusaders: The Fabulous Careers of John Brinkley, Norman Baker, and Harry Hoxsey.* Lawrence: University Press of Kansas, 2002.

Kakoudake, Despina. "Pinup: The American Secret Weapon in World War II." In *Porn Studies,* edited by Linda Williams, 335–369. Durham: Duke University Press, 2004.

Kapsalis, Terri. *Public Privates: Performing Gynecology from Both Ends of the Speculum.* Durham: Duke University Press, 1997.

Kasson, John F. *Houdini, Tarzan, and the Perfect Man: The White Male Body and the Challenge of Modernity in America.* New York: Hill and Wang, 2001.

Kavanagh, Eileen. "Robert Traver as Justice Voelker—The Novelist as Judge." *Scribes Journal of Legal Writing* 10, no. 91 (2005): 91–128.

Kessler-Harris, Alice. *A Woman's Wage: Historical Meanings and Social Consequences.* Lexington: University Press of Kentucky, 1990.

Kinsey, Alfred C. *Sexual Behavior in the Human Female.* Philadelphia: Saunders, 1953.

Koenig, Brigitte. "Law and Disorder at Home: Free Love, Free Speech, and the Search for an Anarchist Utopia." *Labor History* 45, no. 2 (May 2004) 199–223.

Krahulik, Karen Christel. *Provincetown: From Pilgrim Landing to Gay Resort.* New York: NYU Press, 2005.

Kutulas, Judy. *The American Civil Liberties Union and the Making of Modern Liberalism, 1930–1960.* Chapel Hill: University of North Carolina Press, 2006.

LaBarre, Weston. "Obscenity: An Anthropological Appraisal." *Law & Contemporary Problems* 20 (1955): 533–543.

Latham, Angela J. "Packaging Woman: The Concurrent Rise of Beauty Pageants, Public Bathing, and Other Performances of Female 'Nudity.'" *Journal of Popular Culture* 29, no. 3 (1995): 149–167.

Lederer, Susan E. "Repellent Subjects: Hollywood Censorship and Surgical Images in the 1930s." *Literature and Medicine* 17 (1998): 91–113.

Lemire, Elise. *"Miscegenation": Making Race in America.* Philadelphia: University of Pennsylvania Press, 2002.

Lemke-Santangelo, Gretchen. *Daughters of Aquarius: Women of the Sixties Counterculture.* Lawrence: University Press of Kansas, 2009.

Lerner, Barron H. *The Breast Cancer Wars: Hope, Fear, and the Pursuit of a Cure in Twentieth-Century America.* New York: Oxford University Press, 2001.

Lewis, Carolyn Herbst. "Waking Sleeping Beauty: The Premarital Pelvic Exam and Heterosexuality during the Cold War." *Journal of Women's History* 17, no. 4 (2005): 86–110.

Lewis, Michael, ed. *American Wilderness: A New History.* Oxford: Oxford University Press, 2007.

Lipari, Lisbeth. "Dissention Rips Nudists, Feminists." *Provincetown Advocate*, December 22, 1988.

Lupin, Alex. *Romance and Rights: The Politics of Interracial Intimacy, 1945–1954*. Jackson: University Press of Mississippi, 2003.

Lutz, Catherine, and Jane L. Collins. *Reading "National Geographic."* Chicago: University of Chicago Press, 1993.

Macfadden, Bernarr. *The Power and Beauty of Superb Womanhood*. New York, 1901.

Maupin, Armistead. *Tales of the City*. 1978. Reprint, New York: Harper Perennial, 2007.

McBee, Randy D. *Dance Hall Days: Intimacy and Leisure among Working Class Immigrants in the United States*. New York: NYU Press, 2000.

McCarthy, Kathleen D. "Nickel Vice and Virtue: Movie Censorship in Chicago, 1907–1915." *Journal of Popular Film* 5, no. 1 (1976): 38.

McDonald, Helen. *Erotic Ambiguities: The Female Nude in Art*. London: Routledge, 2001.

McElvaine, Robert S. *The Great Depression: America, 1929–1941*. New York: Times Books, 1984.

McGarry, Molly. "Spectral Sexualities: Nineteenth-Century Spiritualism, Moral Panics, and the Making of U.S. Obscenity Law." *Journal of Women's History* 12, no. 2 (2000): 8–29.

McLellan, Josie. "State Socialist Bodies: East German Nudism from Ban to Boom." *Journal of Modern History* 79, no. 1 (March 2007): 48–79.

Meeker, Martin. *Contacts Desired: Gay and Lesbian Communications and Community, 1940s–1970s*. Chicago: University of Chicago Press, 2006.

Meethan, Jevin. "Place, Image and Power: Brighton as a Resort." In *The Tourist Image: Myths and Myth Making in Tourism*, edited by Tom Selwyn, 179–196. Chichester, UK: Wiley, 1996.

Merrill, Frances, and Mason Merrill. *Among the Nudists*. New York: Knopf, 1931.

———. *Nudism Comes to America*. New York: Knopf, 1932.

Meyer, Leisa D. *Creating GI Jane: Sexuality and Power in the Women's Army Corps during World War II*. New York: Columbia University Press, 1996.

Meyer, Richard. *Outlaw Representation: Censorship and Homosexuality in Twentieth-Century American Art*. Oxford: Oxford University Press, 2002.

Meyerowitz, Joanne J. *How Sex Changed: A History of Transsexuality in the United States*. Cambridge: Harvard University Press, 2002.

———, ed. *Not June Cleaver: Women and Gender in Postwar America, 1945–1960*. Philadelphia: Temple University Press, 1994.

———. *Women Adrift: Independent Wage Earners in Chicago, 1880–1930*. Chicago: University of Chicago Press, 1988.

———. "Women, Cheesecake, and Borderline Material: Responses to Girlie Pictures in the Mid-Twentieth-Century U.S." *Journal of Women's History* 8, no. 3 (1996): 9–35.

Miller, Susan A. *Growing Girls: The Natural Origins of Girls' Organizations in America*. New Brunswick: Rutgers University Press, 2007.

Mitau, G. Theodore. *Decade of Decision: The Supreme Court and the Constitutional Revolution, 1954–1964*. New York: Scribner, 1967.

Moran, Jeffrey P. *Teaching Sex: The Shaping of Adolescence in the 20th Century*. Cambridge: Harvard University Press, 2000.

Moran, Rachel F. *Interracial Intimacy: The Regulation of Race and Romance*. Chicago: University of Chicago Press, 2001.

Morgan, Jennifer L. "'Some Could Suckle over Their Shoulder': Male Travelers, Female Bodies, and the Gendering of Racial Ideology, 1500–1770." *William and Mary Quarterly*, 3rd ser., 54, no. 1 (1997): 167–192.

Morgan, Sandra. *Into Our Hands: The Women's Health Movement in the United States*. New Brunswick: Rutgers University Press, 2002.

Morrison, Toni. *Playing in the Dark: Whiteness and the Literary Imagination*. Cambridge: Harvard University Press, 1992.

Mosse, George L. *Nationalism and Sexuality: Middle-Class Morality and Sexual Norms in Modern Europe*. Madison: University of Wisconsin Press, 1985.

Motavalli, Jim. *Naked in the Woods: Joseph Knowles and the Legacy of Frontier Fakery*. Cambridge, MA: Da Capo, 2007.

Mumford, Kevin J. *Interzones: Black/White Sex Districts in Chicago and New York in the Early Twentieth Century*. New York: Columbia University Press, 1997.

Myers, Debs. "Pfc. Alois Knapp, Nudist." *Yank* 4, no. 1 (June 22, 1945): 7.

Nead, Lynda. *The Female Nude: Art, Obscenity, and Sexuality*. London: Routledge, 1992.

Newton, Esther. *Cherry Grove, Fire Island: Sixty Years in America's First Gay and Lesbian Town*. Boston: Beacon, 1993.

Nipson, Herbert. "Nudism and Negroes." *Ebony*, March 1951, 93–111.

"Nudism as Educational and Social Force." *Literary Digest*, October 1933, 16.

O'Neil, Paul. "Nudity: Being a Somewhat Scandalized Report on the Growing Urge of More and More Americans to Appear in Public without Any Clothes On." *Life*, October 13, 1967, 107–116.

Palmer, Gretta. "I'll Be Seeing More of You." *Commentator* 1, no. 4 (May 1937): 95–99.

Paris, Leslie. "The Adventures of Peanut and Bo: Summer Camps and Early-Twentieth-Century American Girlhood." *Journal of Women's History* 12, no. 4 (2001): 47–76.

Parker, Alison M. *Purifying America: Women, Cultural Reform, and Pro-censorship Activism, 1873–1933*. Urbana: University of Illinois Press, 1997.

Parmelee, Maurice. *Bolshevism, Fascism, and the Liberal Democratic State*. New York: Wiley, 1934.

———. *Criminology*. New York: Macmillan, 1918.

———. *Farewell to Poverty*. New York: Wiley, 1935.

———. *Inebriety in Boston*. New York: Eagle, 1909.

———. *In the Fields and Methods of Sociology*. New York: Ray Long and Richard R. Smith, 1934.

———. *Nudism in Modern Life: The New Gymnosophy*. New York: Knopf, 1931.

———. *Oriental and Occidental Culture*. New York: Macmillan, 1928.

———. *Personality and Conduct.* New York: Moffat, Yard, 1918.

———. *Poverty and Social Progress.* New York: Macmillan, 1916.

———. *The Principles of Anthropology and Sociology in Their Relations to Criminal Procedure.* New York: Macmillan, 1908.

———. *Science of Human Behavior, Biological and Psychological Foundations.* New York: Macmillan, 1913.

Pascoe, Peggy. *What Comes Naturally: Miscegenation Law and the Making of Race in America.* Oxford: Oxford University Press, 2009.

Pattullo, Paul. *Last Resorts: The Cost of Tourism in the Caribbean.* London: Cassell, 1996.

Peiss, Kathy. *Cheap Amusements: Working Women and Leisure in Turn-of-the-Century New York City.* Philadelphia: Temple University Press, 1986.

Peiss, Kathy, and Christina Simmons, with Robert Padgug, eds. *Passion and Power: Sexuality in History.* Philadelphia: Temple University Press, 1989.

Penn, Donna. "The Sexualized Woman: The Lesbian, the Prostitute, and the Containment of Female Sexuality in Postwar America." In *Not June Cleaver: Women and Gender in Postwar America, 1945–1960,* edited by Joanne Meyerowitz, 358–381. Philadelphia: Temple University Press, 1994.

Pernick, Martin S. *The Black Stork: Eugenics and the Death of "Defective" Babies in American Medicine and Motion Pictures since 1915.* New York: Oxford University Press, 1995.

Picard, Alyssa. "'To Popularize the Nude in Art': Comstockery Reconsidered." *Journal of the Gilded Age and Progressive Era* 1, no. 3 (2002): 195–224.

Poland, Jefferson, and Sam Sloan, eds. *Sex Marchers.* New York: Ishi, 1962.

Posner, Richard A., and Katherine B. Silbaugh. *A Guide to America's Sex Laws.* Chicago: University of Chicago Press, 1996.

"Preacher and the Nudists, The." *Time* 64 (August 16, 1954): 46.

Putney, Clifford. *Muscular Christianity: Manhood and Sports in Protestant America, 1880–1920.* Cambridge: Harvard University Press, 2001.

Reagan, Leslie J. "Projecting Breast Cancer: Self-Examination Films and the Making of a New Cultural Practice." In *Medicine's Moving Pictures: Medicine, Health, and Bodies in American Film and Television,* edited by Leslie J. Reagan, Nancy Tomes, and Paula A. Treichler, 163–195. Rochester, NY: University of Rochester Press, 2007.

———. *When Abortion Was a Crime: Women, Medicine, and Law in the United States, 1867–1973.* Berkeley: University of California Press, 1997.

Reagan, Leslie J., Nancy Tomes, and Paula A. Treichler, eds. *Medicine's Moving Pictures: Medicine, Health, and Bodies in American Film and Television.* Rochester, NY: University of Rochester Press, 2007.

Rollier, Augustus. *Heliotherapy.* London: Oxford Medical Publications, 1923.

Rosen, Ruth. *The Lost Sisterhood: Prostitution in America, 1900–1918.* Baltimore: John Hopkins University Press, 1982.

Ross, Chad. *Naked Germany: Health, Race and the Nation.* Oxford, UK: Berg, 2005.

Rothman, Hal. *Devil's Bargains: Tourism in the Twentieth-Century American West.* Lawrence: University Press of Kansas, 1998.

Rugh, Susan Sessions. "Branding Utah: Industrial Tourism in the Postwar American West." *Western Historical Quarterly* 37 (Winter 2006): 445–472.

Sanger, Margaret. *Woman and the New Race.* Elmsfield, NY: Maxwell, 1969.

Sayler, Richard H., Barry B. Boyer, and Robert E. Gooding, eds. *The Warren Court: A Critical Analysis.* New York: Chelsea House, 1980.

Schaefer, Eric. *"Bold! Daring! Shocking! True!": A History of Exploitation Films, 1919–1959.* Durham: Duke University Press, 1999.

Schiebinger, Londa. *Nature's Body: Gender in the Making of Modern Science.* Boston: Beacon, 1993.

Schrank, Sarah, "Naked Houses: The Architecture of Nudism and the Rethinking of the American Suburbs." *Journal of Urban History* 38, no. 4 (2012): 635–661.

Schwartz, Plato. "Heliotherapy." *Boston Medical and Surgical Journal* 191, no. 4 (1924): 243.

Scoville, Samuel, Jr. *Boy Scouts in the Wilderness.* New York: Century, 1919.

Self, Robert O. "Sex in the City: The Politics of Sexual Liberalism in Los Angeles, 1963–79." *Gender & History* 20, no. 2 (2008): 288–311.

Selwyn, Tom, ed. *The Tourist Image: Myths and Myth Making in Tourism.* Chichester, UK: Wiley, 1996.

Shaffer, Marguerite S. "Marguerite S. Shaffer on the Environmental Nude." *Environmental History* 13, no. 1 (2008): 126–139.

———. *See America First: Tourism and National Identity, 1880–1940.* Washington, DC: Smithsonian Institution Press, 2001.

Shaw, Elton Raymond. *The Body Taboo.* Binghamton, NY: Vail-Ballou, 1937.

Sklar, Robert. *Movie-Made America: A Cultural History of Movies.* New York: Vintage Books, 1975.

Slayton, Robert A. *Empire Statesman: The Rise and Redemption of Al Smith.* New York: Free Press, 2001.

Smith, Michael B. "'The Ego Ideal of the Good Camper' and the Nature of Summer Camp." *Environmental History* 11, no. 1 (2006): 70–101.

Spinney, Robert G. *City of Big Shoulders: A History of Chicago.* DeKalb: Northern Illinois University Press, 2000.

Spock, Benjamin. *The Common Sense Book of Baby and Child Care.* New York: Duell, Sloan, and Pearce, 1957.

———. "Dr. Spock Talks with Mothers." *Ladies' Home Journal*, September 1955, 26–38.

Spurlock, John C. *Free Love: Marriage and Middle-Class Radicalism in America, 1825–1860.* New York: NYU Press, 1990.

Stearns, Peter N. *Fat History: Bodies and Beauty in the Modern West.* New York: NYU Press, 1997.

Stein, Marc. "*Boutilier* and the U.S. Supreme Court's Sexual Revolution." *Law and History Review* 23, no. 3 (2005): 491–536.

Stein, Sally. "The President's Two Bodies: Stagings and Restagings of FDR and the New Deal Body Politic." *American Art* 18, no. 1 (2004): 32–57.

Strub, Whitney. "Black and White and Banned All Over: Race, Censorship and Obscenity in Post-war Memphis." *Journal of Social History* 40, no. 3 (2007): 685–715.

———. "The Clearly Obscene and the Queerly Obscene: Heteronormativity and Obscenity in Cold War Los Angeles." *American Quarterly* 60, no. 2 (2008): 373–398.

———. *Perversion for Profit: The Politics of Pornography and the Rise of the New Right* New York: Columbia University Press, 2011.

Sumner, William Graham. *Folkways: A Study of the Sociological Importance of Usages, Manners, Customs, Mores, and Morals.* New York: Dover, 1906.

Suominen, Arne L. "Observing the German Methods." *Official Naturopath and Herald of Health: Official Journal of the American Naturopathic Association and the American School of Naturopathy*, February 1937, 40.

Taylor, Brandon, and Wilfried van der Will, eds. *The Nazification of Art: Art, Design, Music, Architecture and Film in the Third Reich.* Winchester, UK: Winchester Press / Winchester School of Art, 1990.

Terry, Jennifer. *An American Obsession: Science, Medicine, and Homosexuality in Modern Society.* Chicago: University of Chicago Press, 1999.

Todd, Jan. "Bernarr Macfadden: Reformer of Feminine Form." *Journal of Sports History* 14, no. 1 (Spring 1987): 61–75.

Toepfer, Karl Eric. *Empire of Ecstasy: Nudity and Movement in German Body Culture, 1910–1935.* Berkeley: University of California Press, 1997.

Tomes, Nancy. *The Gospel of Germs: Men, Women, and the Microbe in American Life.* Cambridge: Harvard University Press, 1998.

Traver, Robert [John D. Voelker]. *Anatomy of a Murder.* New York: St. Martin's, 1958.

———. *The Jealous Mistress.* Boston: Little, Brown, 1968.

Turano, Anthony. "Nudism Denuded." *American Mercury* 38, no. 150 (1936): 161–166.

U.S. Bureau of the Census. *U.S. Census of Population: 1950, Vol. II, Characteristics of the Population, Part 1, U.S. Summer.* Washington, DC: U.S. Government Printing Office, 1953.

Walker, Samuel. *In Defense of American Liberties: A History of the ACLU.* Carbondale: Southern Illinois University Press, 1999.

Walkowitz, Judith R. *City of Dreadful Delight: Narratives of Sexual Danger in Late-Victorian London.* Chicago: University of Chicago Press, 1992.

Walsh, Frank. *Sin and Censorship: The Catholic Church and the Motion Picture Industry.* New Haven: Yale University Press, 1996.

Ward, Geoffrey C. *A First-Class Temperament: The Emergence of Franklin Roosevelt.* New York: Harper and Row, 1989.

Warren, Howard C. "Social Nudism and the Body Taboo." *Psychological Review* 40 (1933): 160–182.

Watson, Elwood, and Darcy Martin, eds. *"There She Is, Miss America": The Politics of Sex, Beauty, and Race in America's Most Famous Pageant.* New York: Palgrave Macmillan, 2004.

Watson, Samuel. "Heliotherapy in Tuberculosis." *Southwestern Medicine* 9 no. 1 (1925): 8.

Waugh, Thomas. *Hard to Imagine: Gay Male Eroticism in Photography and Film from Their Beginnings to Stonewall*. New York: Columbia University Press, 1996.

Welter, Gail Danks. *The Rogers Park Community: A Study of Social Change, Community Groups, and Neighborhood Reputation*. Chicago: Center for Urban Policy, Loyola University of Chicago, 1982.

Westbrook, Robert B. "'I Want a Girl, Just Like the Girl That Married Harry James': American Women and the Problem of Political Obligation in World War II." *American Quarterly* 42, no. 4 (1990): 587–614.

Wheeler, Leigh Ann. *Against Obscenity: Reform and the Politics of Womanhood in America, 1873–1935*. Baltimore: Johns Hopkins University Press, 2004.

———. *How Sex Became a Civil Liberty*. New York: Oxford University Press, 2012.

———. "Rescuing Sex from Prudery and Prurience: American Women's Use of Sex Education as an Antidote to Obscenity, 1926–1932." *Journal of Women's History* 12, no. 3 (2000): 173–195.

White, Richard. *"It's Your Misfortune and None of My Own": A History of the American West*. Norman: University of Oklahoma Press, 1991.

Whorton, James C. *Crusaders for Fitness: The History of American Health Reformers*. Princeton: Princeton University Press, 1982.

———. *Nature Cures: The History of Alternative Medicine in America*. Oxford: Oxford University Press, 2002.

Wilinsky, Barbara. "'A Thinly Disguised Art Veneer Covering a Filthy Sex Picture': Discourses on Art Houses in the 1950s." *Film History* 8, no. 2 (1996): 143–158.

Williams, John. *Turning to Nature in Germany: Hiking, Nudism, and Conservation, 1900–1940*. Stanford: Stanford University Press, 2007.

Williams, Linda. *Hard Core: Power, Pleasure, and the "Frenzy of the Visible."* Berkeley: University of California Press, 1989.

Williams, Marilyn Thornton. *Washing "the Great Unwashed": Public Baths in Urban America, 1840–1920*. Columbus: Ohio State University Press, 1991.

Wiltse, Jeff. *Contested Waters: A Social History of Swimming Pools in America*. Chapel Hill: University of North Carolina Press, 2007.

Wittern-Keller, Laura. *Freedom of the Screen: Legal Challenges to State Film Censorship, 1915–1981*. Lexington: University Press of Kentucky, 2008.

Worster, Donald. *Rivers of Empire: Water, Aridity, and the Growth of the American West*. New York: Pantheon Books, 1985.

Wrobel, David W., and Patrick Long, eds. *Seeing and Being Seen: Tourism in the American West*. Lawrence: Center of the American West, University of Colorado at Boulder / University Press of Kansas, 2001.

Wyke, Maria. "Herculean Muscle! The Classicizing Rhetoric of Body-building." *Arion* 4 (1997): 59–60.

Yalom, Marilyn. *A History of the Breast*. New York: Knopf, 1997.

INDEX

ABOUT THE AUTHOR

Brian Hoffman received his Ph.D. in history from the University of Illinois at Urbana-Champaign. He has taught the history of medicine at the University of California–San Francisco and American studies at Wesleyan University. He lives in Guilford, Connecticut.

3 1901 04865 5080